I0020436

VMware vSphere 5.5 Cookbook

A task-oriented guide with over 150 practical recipes to install, configure, and manage VMware vSphere components

Abhilash G B

BIRMINGHAM - MUMBAI

VMware vSphere 5.5 Cookbook

Copyright © 2015 Packt Publishing

All rights reserved. No part of this book may be reproduced, stored in a retrieval system, or transmitted in any form or by any means, without the prior written permission of the publisher, except in the case of brief quotations embedded in critical articles or reviews.

Every effort has been made in the preparation of this book to ensure the accuracy of the information presented. However, the information contained in this book is sold without warranty, either express or implied. Neither the author, nor Packt Publishing, and its dealers and distributors will be held liable for any damages caused or alleged to be caused directly or indirectly by this book.

Packt Publishing has endeavored to provide trademark information about all of the companies and products mentioned in this book by the appropriate use of capitals. However, Packt Publishing cannot guarantee the accuracy of this information.

First published: July 2013

Second edition: February 2015

Production reference: 1210215

Published by Packt Publishing Ltd.
Livery Place
35 Livery Street
Birmingham B3 2PB, UK.

ISBN 978-1-78217-285-7

www.packtpub.com

Credits

Author

Abhilash G B

Reviewers

Kenneth van Ditmarsch

Andy Grant

Daniel Langenhan

Commissioning Editor

Usha Iyer

Acquisition Editors

Saleem Ahmed

Harsha Bharwani

Content Development Editor

Athira Laji

Technical Editors

Mrunmayee Patil

Shruti Rawool

Copy Editors

Neha Karnani

Shambhavi Pai

Adithi Shetty

Project Coordinator

Harshal Ved

Proofreaders

Simran Bhogal

Stephen Copestake

Maria Gould

Paul Hindle

Indexer

Rekha Nair

Production Coordinator

Nilesh R. Mohite

Cover Work

Nilesh R. Mohite

About the Author

Abhilash G B (@abhilashgb) is a virtualization specialist, author, designer, and a VMware vExpert (2014 and 2015) who specializes in the areas of data center virtualization and cloud computing.

He is a VMware Certified Advanced Professional in Data Center Administration (VCAP4-DCA and VCAP5-DCA). He also holds other VMware certifications, including VCP3, VCP4, VCP5-DCV, and VCP-Cloud. He has been in the IT industry for more than a decade and has been working on VMware products and technologies since the start of 2007.

Abhilash is also the author of two other well selling books: *VMware vSphere 5.1 Cookbook* and *Disaster Recovery Using VMware vSphere Replication and vCenter Site Recovery Manager*, both by Packt Publishing.

He is a passionate author willing to contribute more titles to the VMware community and an aspiring engineer keen to indulge in designing and creating great solutions.

I would like to dedicate this book to my family. Without their patience and support, this book would not have been possible.

Thanks to Kenneth van Ditmarsch, Andy Grant, and Daniel Langenhan, the technical reviewers of this book, for their valuable input.

Special thanks to Harsha Bharwani (acquisition editor), Karthik Vedam (project coordinator), Athira Laji (content development editor), and Mrunmayee Patil and Shruti Rawool (technical editors) for their support during the course of writing this book.

About the Reviewers

Kenneth van Ditmarsch is a very experienced freelance virtualization consultant. As one of the few VMware Certified Design Experts (VCDX), he has a clear added value in virtualization infrastructure projects. His knowledge and extensive project experience has greatly improved over the last few years he has spent at VMware and as a result of several specialized consulting engagements he has worked on.

Kenneth agreed to review this book based on his extensive VMware product experience. Also, you can visit his personal blog on virtualization at `http://www.virtualkenneth.com`.

Andy Grant is a technical consultant for HP Enterprise Services. His primary focus is data center infrastructure and virtualization projects across a number of industries, including government, healthcare, forestry, financial, gas and oil, and international contracting. He currently holds a number of technical certifications, including VCAP4/5-DCA/DCD, VCP4/5, MCITP:EA, MCSE, CCNA, Security+, A+, and HP ASE BladeSystem.

Outside of work, Andy enjoys hiking, action pistol sports, and spending time adventuring with his son.

Daniel Langenhan is a virtualization expert with formidable skills in architecture, design, and implementation for large multitier systems. His experience and knowledge of process management, enterprise-level storage, and Linux and Windows operating systems has made him and his business a highly sought after international consultancy in the Asia Pacific and European regions for multinational clientele in the areas of finance, communication, education, and government. He has been working with VMware products since 2002 and has been directly associated with VMware since 2008. He has a proven track record of successful integrations of virtualization into different business areas while minimizing cost and maximizing reliability and effectiveness of the solution for his clients.

Daniel's expertise and practical approach to VMware has resulted in the publication of the following books:

- *Instant VMware vCloud Starter, Packt Publishing*
- *VMware View Security Essentials, Packt Publishing*
- *VMware vCloud Director Cookbook, Packt Publishing*
- *VMware vRealize Orchestrator Cookbook, Packt Publishing*

He has also lent his expertise to many other publishing projects as a technical reviewer.

www.PacktPub.com

Support files, eBooks, discount offers, and more

For support files and downloads related to your book, please visit www.PacktPub.com.

Did you know that Packt offers eBook versions of every book published, with PDF and ePub files available? You can upgrade to the eBook version at www.PacktPub.com and as a print book customer, you are entitled to a discount on the eBook copy. Get in touch with us at service@packtpub.com for more details.

At www.PacktPub.com, you can also read a collection of free technical articles, sign up for a range of free newsletters and receive exclusive discounts and offers on Packt books and eBooks.

https://www2.packtpub.com/books/subscription/packtlib

Do you need instant solutions to your IT questions? PacktLib is Packt's online digital book library. Here, you can search, access, and read Packt's entire library of books.

Why subscribe?

- ▶ Fully searchable across every book published by Packt
- ▶ Copy and paste, print, and bookmark content
- ▶ On demand and accessible via a web browser

Free access for Packt account holders

If you have an account with Packt at www.PacktPub.com, you can use this to access PacktLib today and view 9 entirely free books. Simply use your login credentials for immediate access.

Instant updates on new Packt books

Get notified! Find out when new books are published by following @PacktEnterprise on Twitter or the *Packt Enterprise* Facebook page.

Table of Contents

Preface

With more and more data centers being virtualized using its technologies, VMware is still the undisputed leader in providing virtualization solutions ranging from server virtualization to storage and network virtualization. Despite the efforts from Citrix and Microsoft, VMware's vSphere product line is still the most feature-rich and futuristic in the virtualization industry. Knowing how to install and configure the latest vSphere components is important to give yourself a head start towards virtualization using VMware. This book covers the installation and upgrade of the vSphere environment and also the administration tasks that one would commonly need to handle when managing a VMware infrastructure.

VMware vSphere 5.5 Cookbook is a task-oriented, fast-paced, practical guide to installing and configuring vSphere 5.5 components. It will take you through all of the steps required to accomplish various configuration tasks with less reading. Most of the tasks are accompanied with relevant screenshots and flowcharts with the intention to provide visual guidance as well. The book concentrates more on the actual task rather than the theory around it, making it easier to understand what is really needed to achieve the task. However, most of the concepts have been well described to help you understand the background and working.

The main highlight of this book is the use of the vSphere 5.5 Web Client to accomplish most tasks. Although a few tasks cannot be accomplished using the new Web Client with the current vSphere version, VMware will be integrating them into the Web Client in its future product releases. The other highlights include chapters covering vSphere Host Profiles, vSphere Auto Deploy, ESXi Image Builder, and VMware Update Manager. This book also covers command-line methods for important tasks.

What this book covers

Chapter 1, Upgrading to vSphere 5.5, discusses the procedures involved in upgrading an existing vSphere infrastructure to vSphere 5.5. It covers upgrading the vCenter Server, the ESXi host, and the virtual machine tools and virtual machine hardware.

Chapter 2, Performing a New Installation of vSphere 5.5, walks you through the procedures involved in deploying a new vSphere 5.5 infrastructure. It covers the installation of ESXi, vCenter Server, and the deployment of the vCenter Server virtual appliance.

Chapter 3, Using vSphere Host Profiles, covers the use of Host Profiles to create, manage, and use ESXi host configuration templates.

Chapter 4, Using ESXi Image Builder, walks you through the process of creating, managing, and applying image profiles to ESXi hosts.

Chapter 5, Using vSphere Auto Deploy, covers the procedures involved in forming an Auto Deploy infrastructure to enable faster provisioning of stateless or stateful ESXi hosts.

Chapter 6, Configuring vSphere Networking, explains how to set up and configure vSphere networking using vSphere Standard Switches and vSphere Distributed Switches. It covers advanced network configurations such as port mirroring, NetFlow, and the use of PVLANs.

Chapter 7, Creating and Managing VMFS Datastores, walks you through the process of creating and managing VMFS datastores. It also covers the use of datastore clusters and storage DRS.

Chapter 8, Managing iSCSI and NFS Datastores, covers the procedures involved in configuring and managing iSCSI and NSA storage on ESXi hosts.

Chapter 9, vSphere Storage Policies and Storage I/O Control, covers the use of storage policies to ensure that the VMs are placed in datastores categorized into different tiers and how to use storage I/O control to manage the I/O bandwidth between VMs running on them.

Chapter 10, Creating and Managing Virtual Machines, covers the procedures involved in creating and managing virtual machines in a vSphere infrastructure.

Chapter 11, Configuring vSphere HA, covers the configuration of high availability on ESXi clusters.

Chapter 12, Configuring vSphere DRS, DPM, and VMware EVC, covers the configuration of vSphere Distributed Resource Scheduler, Distributed Power Management, and VMware Enhanced vMotion Compatibility on an ESXi cluster.

Chapter 13, Upgrading and Patching Using vSphere Update Manager, covers the installation and configuration of vSphere Update Manager and the Update Manager Download Service (UMDS) to manage patching and upgrading of ESXi hosts.

Chapter 14, Using vSphere Management Assistant, covers the deployment and configuration of vMA 5.5 to run commands/scripts remotely on ESXi.

Chapter 15, Monitoring the Performance of a vSphere Environment, covers different methods to monitor the performance of ESXi and virtual machines in a vSphere infrastructure.

What you need for this book

You will learn about the software requirements for every vSphere component covered in this book in their respective chapters, but to start with a basic lab setup, you will need at least two ESXi hosts, a vCenter Server, a Domain Controller, a DHCP server, a DNS server, and a TFTP Server. For learning purposes, you don't really need to run ESXi on physical machines. You can use VMware Workstation to set up a hosted lab on your desktop PC or laptop, provided the machine has adequate compute and storage resources. For shared storage, you can use any of the free virtual storage appliances listed as follows:

- Celerra UBER 3.2 can be downloaded at `http://nickapedia.com/2010/10/04/play-it-again-sam-celerra-uber-v3-2/`
- OpenFiler can be downloaded at `https://www.openfiler.com`
- HP StoreVirtual Storage can be downloaded at `http://www8.hp.com/in/en/products/data-storage/storevirtual.html`

Who this book is for

This book is for anyone who wants to learn how to install and configure VMware vSphere components. It is an excellent handbook for administrators or for anyone looking for a head start in learning how to upgrade, install, and configure vSphere 5.5 components. It is also a good task-oriented reference guide for consultants who design and deploy vSphere.

Sections

In this book, you will find several headings that appear frequently (Getting ready, How to do it..., How it works..., There's more..., and See also).

To give clear instructions on how to complete a recipe, we use these sections as follows:

Getting ready

This section tells you what to expect in the recipe, and describes how to set up any software or any preliminary settings required for the recipe.

How to do it...

This section contains the steps required to follow the recipe.

How it works...

This section usually consists of a detailed explanation of what happened in the previous section.

There's more...

This section consists of additional information about the recipe in order to make the reader more knowledgeable about the recipe.

See also

This section provides helpful links to other useful information for the recipe.

Conventions

In this book, you will find a number of text styles that distinguish between different kinds of information. Here are some examples of these styles and an explanation of their meaning.

Code words in text, database table names, folder names, filenames, file extensions, pathnames, dummy URLs, user input, and Twitter handles are shown as follows: "The `esxcfg-mpath` command available at ESXi's command-line interface can be used to view the multipathing information corresponding to the LUN."

A block of code is set as follows:

```
https://<IP Address or FQDN>:9443/vsphere-client
```

Any command-line input or output is written as follows:

```
esxcli storage filesystem list
```

New terms and **important words** are shown in bold. Words that you see on the screen, for example, in menus or dialog boxes, appear in the text like this: "Navigate to **Home | Hosts and Clusters**. Click on the **Cluster** option and then click on **Hosts**."

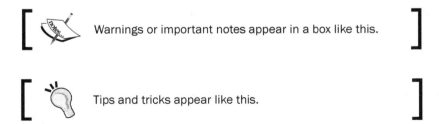

Warnings or important notes appear in a box like this.

Tips and tricks appear like this.

Reader feedback

Feedback from our readers is always welcome. Let us know what you think about this book—what you liked or disliked. Reader feedback is important for us as it helps us develop titles that you will really get the most out of.

To send us general feedback, simply e-mail `feedback@packtpub.com`, and mention the book's title in the subject of your message.

If there is a topic that you have expertise in and you are interested in either writing or contributing to a book, see our author guide at `www.packtpub.com/authors`.

Customer support

Now that you are the proud owner of a Packt book, we have a number of things to help you to get the most from your purchase.

Downloading the color images of this book

We also provide you with a PDF file that has color images of the screenshots/diagrams used in this book. The color images will help you better understand the changes in the output. You can download this file from `https://www.packtpub.com/sites/default/files/downloads/B03256_Coloredimages.pdf`.

Errata

Although we have taken every care to ensure the accuracy of our content, mistakes do happen. If you find a mistake in one of our books—maybe a mistake in the text or the code—we would be grateful if you could report this to us. By doing so, you can save other readers from frustration and help us improve subsequent versions of this book. If you find any errata, please report them by visiting `http://www.packtpub.com/submit-errata`, selecting your book, clicking on the **Errata Submission Form** link, and entering the details of your errata. Once your errata are verified, your submission will be accepted and the errata will be uploaded to our website or added to any list of existing errata under the Errata section of that title.

To view the previously submitted errata, go to `https://www.packtpub.com/books/content/support` and enter the name of the book in the search field. The required information will appear under the **Errata** section.

Piracy

Piracy of copyrighted material on the Internet is an ongoing problem across all media. At Packt, we take the protection of our copyright and licenses very seriously. If you come across any illegal copies of our works in any form on the Internet, please provide us with the location address or website name immediately so that we can pursue a remedy.

Please contact us at `copyright@packtpub.com` with a link to the suspected pirated material.

We appreciate your help in protecting our authors and our ability to bring you valuable content.

Questions

If you have a problem with any aspect of this book, you can contact us at `questions@packtpub.com`, and we will do our best to address the problem.

1
Upgrading to vSphere 5.5

In this chapter, we will cover the following recipes:

- ▸ Downloading vCenter 5.5
- ▸ Carrying out pre-upgrade checks
- ▸ Upgrading the Single Sign-On (SSO) component
- ▸ Upgrading the vSphere Web Client
- ▸ Upgrading the vCenter Inventory Service
- ▸ Performing an upgrade of vCenter Server
- ▸ Upgrading ESXi to Version 5.5
- ▸ Upgrading vCenter Server Appliance (VCSA) to Version 5.5
- ▸ Upgrading VMware Tools
- ▸ Upgrading the virtual machine hardware
- ▸ Scheduling the virtual machine hardware upgrade

Introduction

At the time of writing this book, VMware vSphere 5.5 was the current major version of the core vSphere suite of products from VMware. The previous version was vSphere 5.1. The improvements and enhancements included in vSphere 5.5 make an upgrade worth it. The goal of this chapter is to help you understand and execute the process of upgrading your core vSphere infrastructure. The core includes your ESXi hypervisor, vCenter Server, and vCenter Server's components. The upgrade of the third-layer products that leverage the core vSphere infrastructure, such as vCloud Director and VMware View, are not covered in this chapter as they are beyond the scope
and purpose of this book.

Before we begin, let me introduce you to the core infrastructure components that will be upgraded:

- ► **VMware vCenter Server**: The possibility of an upgrade or the need for a new build will depend on the current version of vCenter and the supported upgrade path

- ► **vCenter Single Sign-On**: This will be upgraded if the current version is 5.1; if not, it will be a new installation of this component

- ► **vCenter Inventory Service**: This will be upgraded if the current version is 5.1; if not, it will be a new installation of this component

- ► **vSphere Web Client**: This will be upgraded if the current version is 5.1; if not, it will be a new installation of this component

- ► **vSphere Update Manager**: This should be upgraded before the ESXi hosts, if you intend to use it to upgrade the hosts

- ► **vSphere Auto Deploy**: This is a requirement to upgrade vSphere Auto Deploy to the same version as vCenter Server

- ► **VMware ESXi**: This can either be upgraded by booting the server using the ISO image, by using vSphere Update Manager, or by updating the image profile if the existing servers are auto-deployed

VMware vCenter Server

vCenter Server is management software that helps manage and configure your virtual environment. It comes in two flavors, one being a standard Windows installation and the other in the form of a Linux-based virtual appliance. While the Windows-based installation of vCenter helps you segregate the components according to your needs, the Linux-based installation packages all the components into a single deployment package. While most large virtual environments use the Windows-based installation of vCenter, the vCenter Server Virtual Appliance finds its place in comparatively smaller environments. However, it is important to note that it now supports up to 100 ESXi hosts and 3000 virtual machines.

VMware vCenter Server Virtual Appliance

The VMware vCenter Appliance is a Linux appliance with all necessary modules and a built-in database. This appliance comes in handy when you want to deploy a vCenter instance without having to go through the installation procedure. As it is a Linux VM, you don't have to install a compatible Windows OS (VM / physical machine) and license it.

vCenter Single Sign-On

vCenter Single Sign-On (SSO) will be the first component to be upgraded or installed. It is an authentication service released with vSphere 5.1. With Version 5.5, it has been re-architected from the ground up to be simple to plan and deploy, and easier to manage.

It is an authentication gateway that takes authentication requests from various registered components and validates the credential pair against the identity sources added to the SSO server. All the other vSphere components are registered to the SSO server during their installation. At the time of writing this book, the following are the components that could register and leverage SSO 5.5's ability:

- VMware vCenter Server 5.5
- VMware vCenter Inventory Service 2.0
- VMware vCenter Orchestrator 5.1 and 5.5
- VMware vShield Manager 5.5
- VMware vCloud Director
- VMware vSphere Web Client 5.5
- VMware vSphere Data Protection
- VMware Log Browser
- vCAC 6.0

SSO supports authentication against the following identity sources:

- Active Directory
- Active Directory as an LDAP server
- Open LDAP
- Local OS
- Its local authentication domain: `vsphere.local`

Once authenticated, the SSO client is provided with a token for further exchanges. The advantage here is that the user or the administrator of the client service is not prompted for a credential pair (username/password) every time it needs to authenticate.

VMware has recoded SSO from scratch. It no longer uses an external database. It now has a single deployment mode. SSO 5.1 had three deployment modes, namely: Basic, High Availability, and Multisite. For the HA and Multisite modes, there was the concept of a primary node; only one primary node could exist in a particular SSO environment. You always had to plan and decide on the deployment mode before installing SSO, because, once deployed in a particular mode, changing to a different mode wasn't an easy job. This is however not the case with SSO 5.5, where we now have a single deployment mode and three placement methods:

▶ **First SSO server**: This is used when deploying the first SSO server at the site. This can either be done during the simple installation or by running the SSO installer separately on a different machine.

▶ **Additional SSO server**: This is used to spawn an additional SSO server at the same site. This additional instance will not be involved in any failover or load balancing with the first SSO server by default, but a third-party load balancer can be used achieve this.

▶ **Additional SSO server at a new site**: This is used to spawn an additional SSO server at a different (remote) site. The additional SSO servers deployed at the remote sites cannot be involved in a failover:

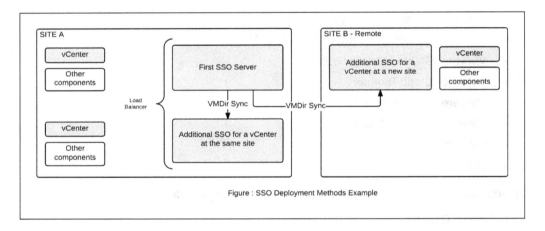

Figure : SSO Deployment Methods Example

 Here, **VMDir** (short for VM Directory) is SSO's LDAP-based internal directory used to store identity sources, SSO users, and policies. It is the source of truth for the `vsphere.local` domain.

vCenter Inventory Service

The vCenter inventory service is a read cache for use with the vSphere Web Client. It stores information pertaining to the vSphere Web Client inventory, thereby reducing the number of reads that need to hit the vCenter Server's database. It takes away some of the load handled by the vCenter Service (vpxd).

vSphere Web Client

Starting with vSphere 5.0, VMware introduced a web client component that can be used to manage vSphere environments. vSphere Web Client is an independent server component that is installed and then accessed via a web browser. It is independent because, unlike the older web client or the vSphere Client based on C#, you no longer have to connect the client to vCenter Server. It connects to its own server and this server component will let you add multiple vCenter Servers to its web-based GUI:

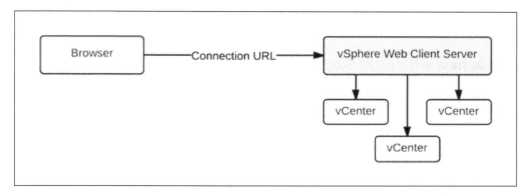

With vSphere 5.5, there are a few improvements with the web client in terms of performance, tagging, and so on.

For more information, refer to the release notes at `http://www.vmware.com/files/pdf/vsphere/VMware-vSphere-Platform-Whats-New.pdf`.

Although I will be using vSphere Web Client for most of the tasks in the chapters, you could still use the vSphere Client to perform some of the same tasks. However, there are certain tasks that can only be done using the vSphere Client. For example, not all aspects of the VMware Update Manager plugin are available for use with the vSphere Web Client. Having said that, VMware will be moving all of the vSphere management GUIs to the web client in future versions of vSphere. So, it would be good to get accustomed to the vSphere Web Client interface now.

 Keep in mind, vSphere Web Client requires Flash to be installed for the GUI to work.

vSphere Update Manager

vSphere Update Manager automates the process of patching or upgrading ESXi hosts in an environment. It can also be used to upgrade the virtual machine hardware and VMware tools of the virtual machines. Update Manager does not have a standalone user interface. You will be required to download and install its plugin on the machine where you have vSphere Client installed. Even with the release of vSphere 5.5, not all of its functionalities are available via the vSphere Web Client. After a vCenter Server upgrade, the next component to upgrade will be Update Manager. This is done to facilitate upgrading the ESXi hosts. Read *Chapter 13, Upgrading and Patching Using vSphere Update Manager*, to understand the installation, configuration, and the use of the solution.

What is new with ESXi 5.5?

ESXi hypervisor is an abstraction layer that enables running of different virtual machines sharing the same physical hardware.

The vSphere 5.5 release is more scalable than before. The ESXi hypervisor now supports up to 4 TB of memory and 320 logical CPUs (pCPUs). It adds support for up to 16 NUMA nodes. The total supported vCPU count is now 4096.

Here is a table comparing scalability offered by vSphere 5.1 and 5.5:

Feature	vSphere 5.1	vSphere 5.5
Logical processors (pCPUs)	160	320
Memory	2 TB	4 TB
NUMA nodes	8	16
vCPUs	2048	4098

For more information on product maximums, compare the vSphere 5.1 and 5.5 Configuration Maximums guides at `http://www.vmware.com/pdf/vsphere5/r51/vsphere-51-configuration-maximums.pdf` (vSphere 5.1) and `http://www.vmware.com/pdf/vsphere5/r55/vsphere-55-configuration-maximums.pdf` (vSphere 5.5).

More details on what is new with vSphere 5.5 is included in *What's New in the VMware vSphere® 6.0 Platform* at `http://www.vmware.com/files/pdf/vsphere/VMware-vSphere-Platform-Whats-New.pdf`.

As the whitepaper introduces the components pretty neatly, we will not be doing the same in this book. This book will introduce you to the new changes in the respective chapters for vSphere 5.1 and 5.5.

The vSphere 5.5 upgrade path

Before you proceed with the upgrade, you need to understand the order in which the components should be upgraded. The rule-of-thumb is to upgrade vCenter Server prior to upgrading the ESXi server or any other solutions.

Here is the order of upgrade:

1. Verify all other solutions are compatible with the new vSphere version and also check HCL.

2. Upgrade the vCenter Server components to Version 5.5.

3. Upgrade Update Manager to Version 5.5.

4. Upgrade the ESXi host to Version 5.5.

5. Apply the vSphere licenses.

6. Upgrade VMware Tools.

7. Upgrade the virtual machine hardware.

8. Upgrade the other solutions (such as Update Manager and Site Recovery Manager) to versions compatible with vSphere 5.5.

Downloading vCenter 5.5

The vCenter 5.5 installation bundle can be downloaded from the VMware downloads page for vSphere.

How to do it...

We can use the following steps to download vCenter 5.5:

1. Go to the downloads page using the URL `https://my.vmware.com/web/vmware/downloads`.

2. Click on the **Download Product** hyperlink corresponding to **VMware vSphere**.

3. On the **Download VMware vSphere** webpage, locate **VMware vCenter** under needed license.

4. Click on the **Go to Downloads** URL corresponding to the vCenter entry to reach the web page titled **Download VMware vCenter Server**.

5. Download the vCenter Server ISO image.

Carrying out pre-upgrade checks

vCenter Server 5.5 is a 64-bit software and requires a 64-bit Windows operating system to be installed. It also requires a 64-bit ODBC DSN to be created in order to connect to the database. Note that, with this new release of vCenter, VMware has removed support for Windows 2003 operating systems.

Here is a list of supported operating systems vCenter 5.5 can be hosted on:

- Windows Server 2008 x64 Service Pack 2
- Windows Server 2008 x64 R2 Service Pack 1
- Windows Server 2008 x64 R2 Service Pack 2
- Windows Server 2012 x64

If your current vCenter Server is hosted on a Windows version not supported by vCenter 5.5, then the upgrade is not possible. You will have to perform a fresh install and point it to the existing database for a DB upgrade.

It is recommended that you check the *VMware Compatibility Guide* web page for changes in the supportability of your current software or hardware. The hardware components might sometimes need a firmware upgrade to work as expected when used with a newer release of vSphere. The *VMware Compatibility Guide* web page is available at www.vmware.com/go/hcl.

Running the installer to perform the upgrade is a pretty straightforward procedure. However, there are a few pre-upgrade checks that have to be performed to make sure that the upgrade can be done without any hassles.

How to do it...

The following are the pre-upgrade checks (details for each check are mentioned later):

1. Verify the software requirements for vCenter Server.
2. Check ESXi host compatibility with vCenter.
3. Run the vCenter Host Agent Pre-Upgrade Checker.
4. Check database compatibility.
5. Get a backup for the SSL certificates.

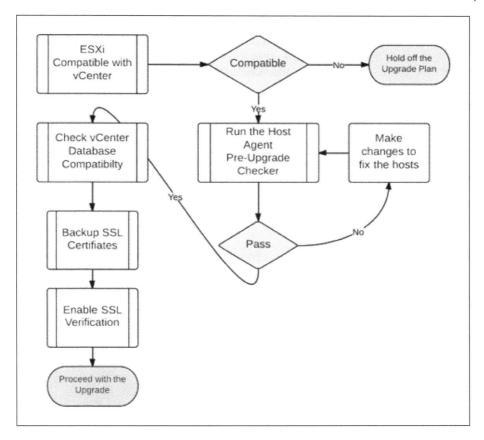

In the diagram, you see that the vCenter upgrade plan needs to be held off if the running version of ESXi will not be compatible with vCenter 5.5 after the vCenter upgrade. If the upgrade is performed disregarding this fact, then you will end up with an environment that is not compatible with vCenter. At this stage, you would need to validate different approaches to form a new vSphere 5.5 environment. One of them could be to upgrade both, the running vCenter and ESXi to a version that would make them supported candidates for an upgrade to vSphere 5.5. Another approach is to plan on forming a new vSphere 5.5 infrastructure by performing a fresh installation of all the components, though this would require virtual machine downtime.

Checking ESXi host compatibility with vCenter

This is the most important check prior to initiating a vCenter upgrade. The rationale behind this check is to make sure that the ESXi hosts that you currently use to host your virtual machines can be managed by the new version of the vCenter that we are planning to upgrade to.

 vCenter Server 5.5 can be used to manage ESX/ESXi 4.x, ESXi 5.0.x, ESXi 5.1.x, and ESX 5.5.

VMware maintains a VMware Product Interoperability Matrixes web portal that can be used to determine when the new version of vCenter can manage the existing hosts.

The URL for the web portal is `http://www.vmware.com/resources/compatibility/sim/interop_matrix.php`.

Running the VMware vCenter Host Agent Pre-Upgrade Checker

The VMware vCenter Host Agent Pre-Upgrade Checker feature is run to generate a report showing issues detected on the ESX servers that would prevent a successful upgrade of the vCenter Host Agent software on the ESXi hosts:

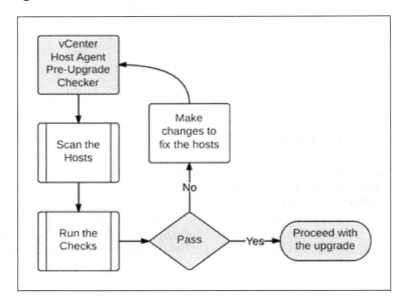

Host Agent Upgrade Checker is installed as a separate tool. The installer can be initiated from the **Welcome screen** of the vCenter 5.5 Installation image (ISO) using the following steps:

1. Bring up the vCenter 5.5 Installation DVD's welcome screen.

2. Click on the item **Host Agent Pre-Upgrade Checker** and click on **Install**.

3. Supply the fully-qualified domain name (FQDN) of the vCenter Server machine and the login credentials.

4. You will be presented with two scan options: **Standard Mode** and **Custom Mode**. Standard mode will scan all the ESXi hosts managed by the vCenter, whereas Custom mode will let you select the host to perform the scan on.

5. Run the pre-check by clicking on **Run Pre-check**, and click on **Next** once the check is complete.

6. On the next screen, check the reports generated.

Checking database compatibility

VMware supports the use of an Oracle or Microsoft SQL database server to host vCenter Server's database. During the installation of vCenter Server, the existing database is upgraded for use with the new version. For this to work, the database server should be compatible with the version of vCenter Server being installed—in this case, vCenter 5.5.

To check if the current database server is compatible with vCenter 5.5, you should use the Solution/database interoperability option at the VMware Product Interoperability Matrices web portal (http://partnerweb.vmware.com/comp_guide2/sim/interop_matrix.php).

Backing up SSL certificates

It is recommended you back up the existing certificates issued for vCenter Server. The certificate files are stored in the SSL directory. The site of the SSL directory varies, based on the Windows operating system the current vCenter is running on:

Operating system	vCenter SSL folder path
Windows 2003	%ALLUSERSPROFILE%\Application Data\ VMware\VMware VirtualCenter\SSL
Windows 2008	%ALLUSERSPROFILE%\VMWare\VMware VirtualCenter\SSL
Windows 2012	%ALLUSERSPROFILE%\VMWare\VMware VirtualCenter\SSL

The following screenshot shows the contents of the SSL folder:

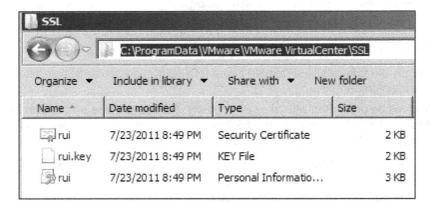

Enabling SSL certificate verification

By enabling SSL certificate verification, vCenter Server will verify the validity of the SSL certificates of the ESX servers when establishing SSL connections with them. This step is required if you are upgrading form vCenter 4.1.x.

This can be enabled on the vCenter Server, by navigating to **Administration** | **vCenter Server Settings** | **SSL Settings** and selecting the **vCenter requires verified host SSL certificates** checkbox:

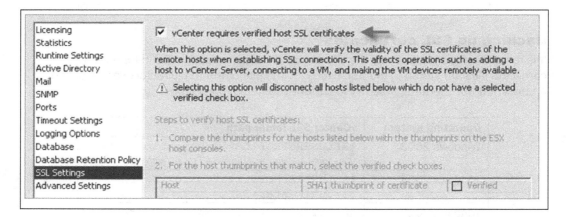

Upgrading the Single Sign-On component

To perform an upgrade of the **Single Sign-On** (**SSO**) server component, you will need the vCenter Installation DVD's ISO image mounted to the Windows virtual machine hosting the SSO server.

 This section of the chapter only applies if you have an existing vCenter 5.1 environment, and the SSO server is segregated onto a different machine.

How to do it...

The following procedure will guide you through the steps required in upgrading the SSO server from Version 5.1 to 5.5:

1. When the vCenter installation DVD's welcome screen appears, select **vCenter Single Sign-On** under the **Custom Install** category and click on **Install** to start the setup:

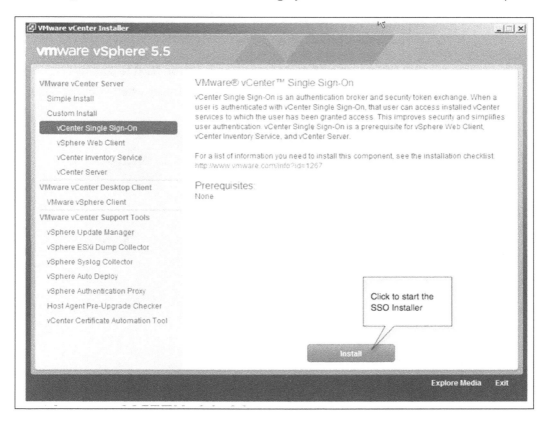

2. The first screen of the installation wizard workflow will indicate that it has detected an earlier version of SSO. Click on **Next** to continue:

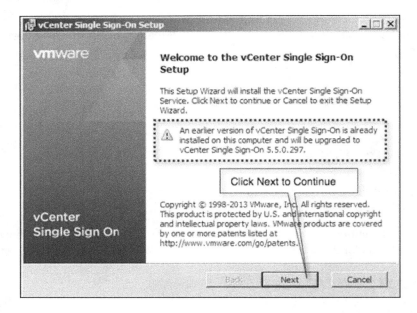

3. Accept the **END USER LICENSE AGREEMENT** and click on **Next** to continue.

4. The installer will run a check on the prerequisites and display whether or not it has passed. Click on **Next** to continue:

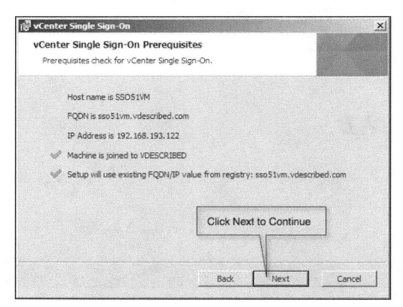

5. The next screen will inform you that the installer will migrate the existing SSO data to the new version. It is just informational, click on **Next** to continue:

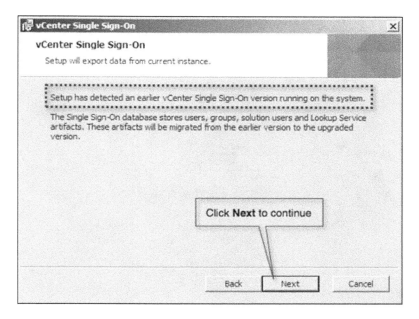

6. Select an upgrade mode. In this case, we have selected the option **First existing vCenter Single Sign-On Server**. Click on **Next** to continue:

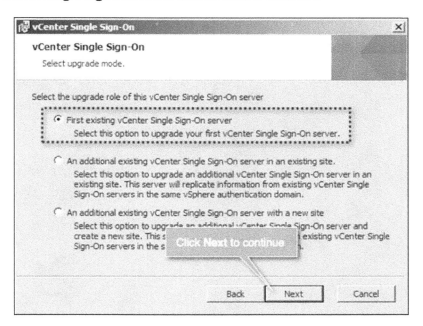

7. Set a password for the administrator of the default SSO domain `vsphere.local` and click on **Next** to continue:

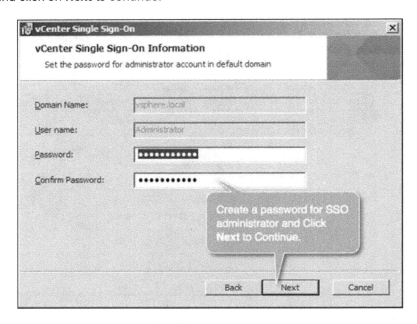

8. Specify the **Site name** and click on **Next** to continue. It is this part of the installation/ upgrade that makes the SSO instance site-aware:

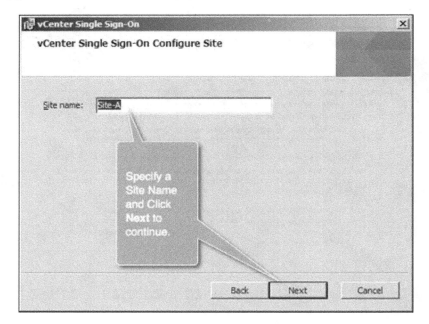

9. Change the destination install folder if necessary. In this case, we leave it unmodified. Click on **Next** to continue:

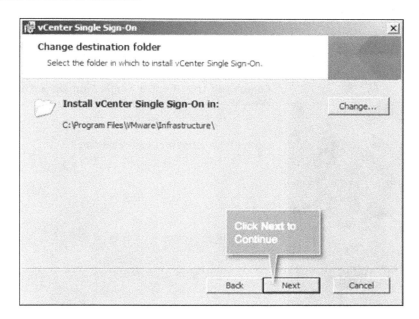

10. Review the summarized installation options and click on **Install** to initiate the installation process:

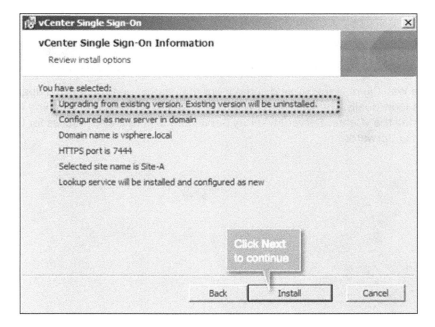

11. Once the installation is completed successfully, you will be presented with a wizard screen indicating that the installation has been completed. Click on **Finish** to exit the wizard workflow:

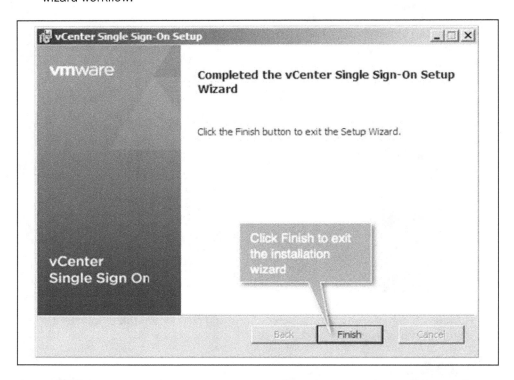

Upgrading the vSphere Web Client

The vSphere Web Client is the second component that should upgraded when upgrading components individually. The Web Client is ideally installed on the same machine that you intend to install the vCenter Server Inventory Service on. The upgrade process for the Web Client is straightforward.

How to do it...

The following procedure will guide you through the steps required to upgrade the vSphere Web Client Server component:

1. Launch the installer for the vSphere Web Client from the vCenter Installation DVD:

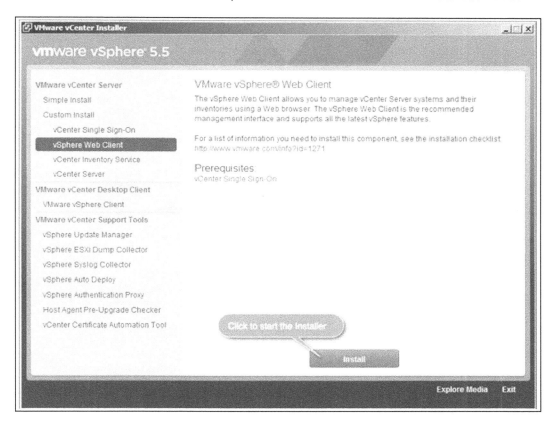

2. Choose the language the installer should be presented with and click on **OK**.

3. The first screen of the installer wizard will indicate that it has detected the presence of an earlier version of the vSphere Web Client. Click on **Next** to continue:

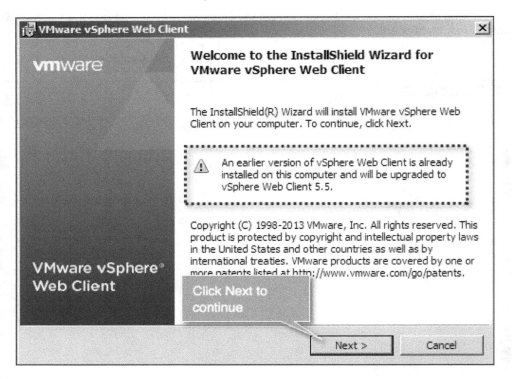

4. Accept the **VMWARE END USER LICENSE AGREEMENT** and click on **Next** to continue.

5. Modify the default ports *only* if necessary. In this case, we are using the default setting. Click on **Next** to continue:

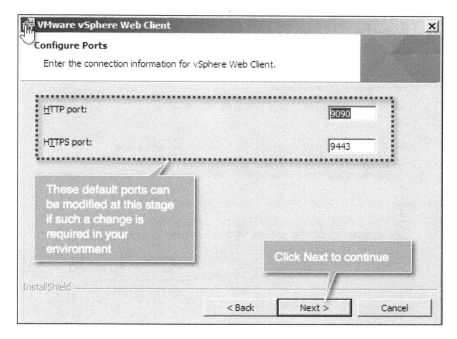

6. Supply the SSO administrator password so that the Web Client component can be registered as a client to the SSO server:

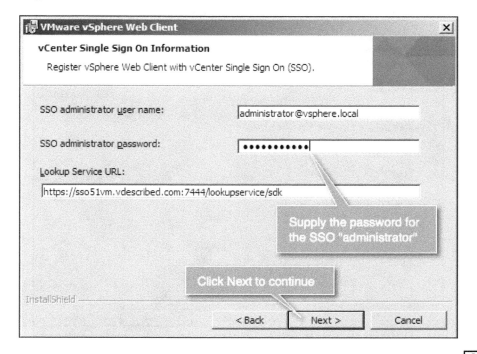

7. You might be prompted to accept the SSO Lookup Service SSL certificate. Click on **Yes** to continue:

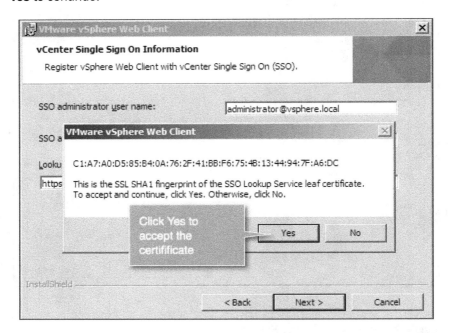

8. On the **Ready to Install** screen, click on **Install** to start the installation:

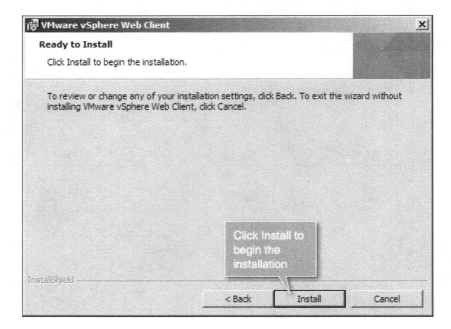

9. Once the installation is complete, click on **Finish** to exit the wizard. There will be an informational message suggesting that you wait for a few minutes before trying to access the Web Client for the first time. Click on **OK**:

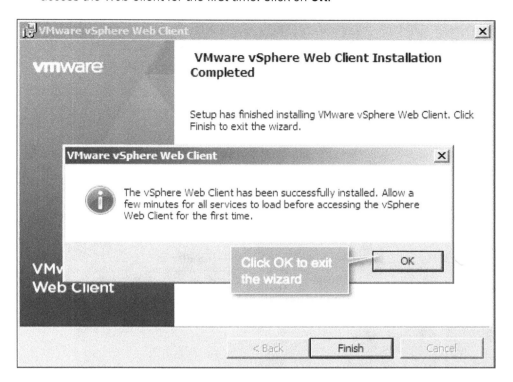

There's more...

The following syntax and URL will help you to connect to the vSphere Web Client server:

- ▶ **Syntax**: https://<IP address or FQDN of the server where vSphere Web Client is installed>/vsphere-client

- ▶ **Example**: https://192.168.193.50:9443/vsphere-client/

Upgrading the vCenter Inventory Service

The vCenter Inventory Service is the third and last component that should be upgraded before upgrading vCenter Server. Upgrading this component is performed using its installer for Version 5.5.

How to do it...

The following procedure will guide you through the steps required to upgrade the vCenter Inventory Service component:

1. Launch the installer for vCenter Inventory Service from the vCenter Installation DVD's welcome screen by selecting it and clicking on Install:

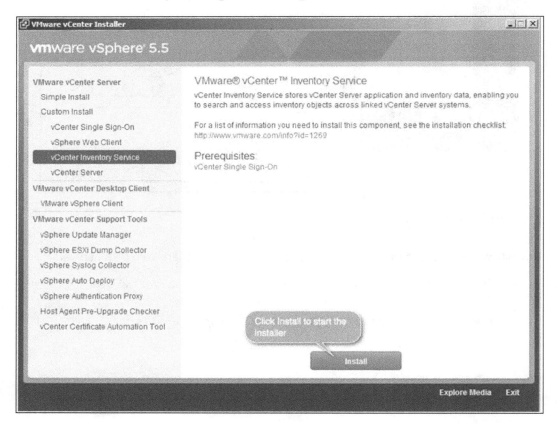

2. Choose the language the installer should be presented with and click on **OK**.

3. The first screen of the installer wizard will indicate the presence of an earlier version of vCenter Inventory Service. Click on **Next** to continue:

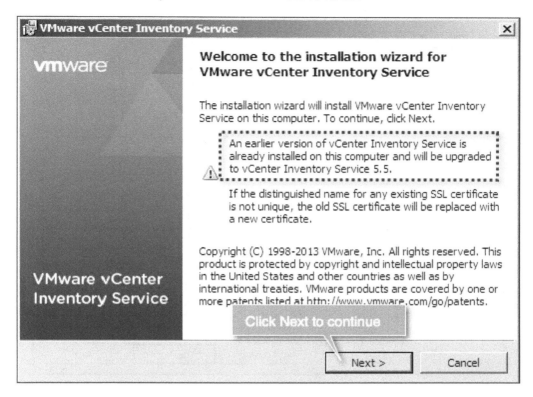

4. Accept the **VMWARE END USER LICENSE AGREEMENT** and click on **Next** to continue.

5. Supply the FQDN of the machine on which the installer is being run. The installer is programmed to autofill this information, but in case it doesn't enter the FQDN manually. Click on **Next** to continue:

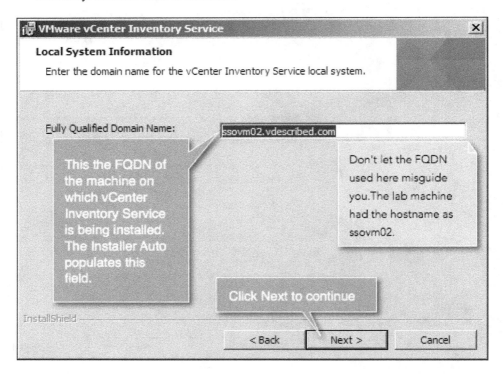

6. Modify the default ports *only* if necessary. In this case, we are leaving them unchanged. Click on **Next** to continue:

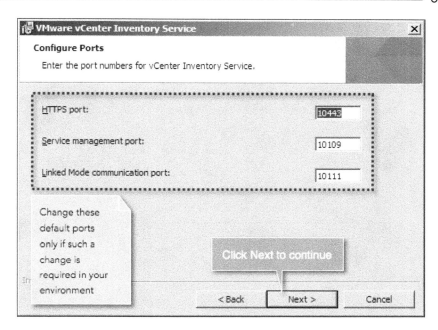

7. Specify the inventory size in terms of the number of ESXi hosts and virtual machines that will be added to the inventory. The inventory size dictates the JVM memory settings. Select one of the three options and click on **Next** to continue. If you choose to increase the size of the JVM, the virtual machine should be sized for the increase in memory usage as well:

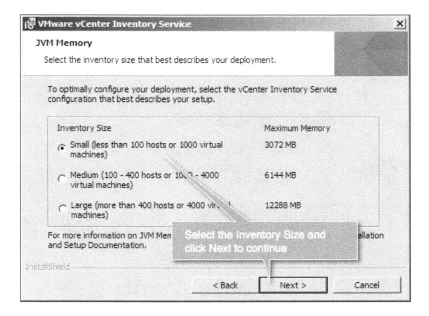

8. Supply the SSO administrator password so that vCenter Inventory Service can be registered as a client to the SSO server. Then click on Next:

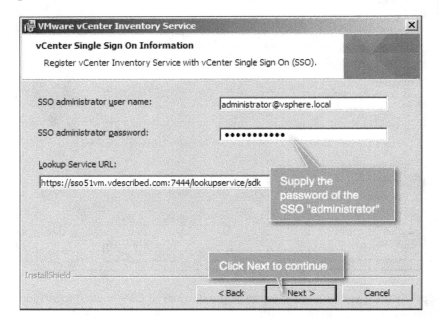

9. You might be prompted to accept the SSO Lookup Service certificate. Click on **Yes** to continue:

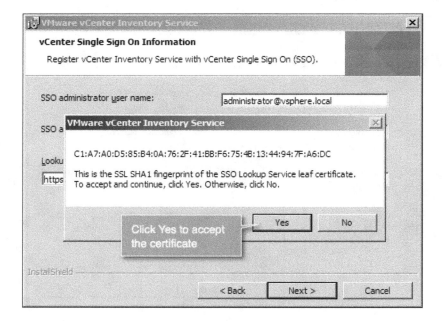

10. On the **Ready to Install** screen, click on **Install** to start the installation.

11. Once the installation is complete, click on **Finish** to exit the wizard.

Performing an upgrade of vCenter Server

An upgrade of vCenter Server can be done either using the vCenter 5.5 Simple Installer or by initiating the vCenter Server's installer separately (recommended). It can be performed only if the previous version of vCenter is on a supported 64-bit Windows operating system.

The following Windows operating systems are supported by VCenter:

▸ Windows Server 2008 x64 Service Pack 2

▸ Windows Server 2008 x64 R2 Service Pack 1

▸ Windows Server 2008 x64 R2 Service Pack 2

▸ Windows Server 2012 x64

 Starting with vCenter 5.5, Windows 2003 is no longer supported.

Only the following releases, if installed on any of the preceding operating systems, are eligible for an in-place upgrade:

▸ vCenter Server 4.0 Update 4

▸ vCenter Server 4.1

▸ vCenter Server 5.0

▸ vCenter Server 5.1

How to do it...

To perform an in-place upgrade of the current vCenter installation to Version 5.5, you will need to initiate the installer for vCenter Server. You can choose to either start a simple install or initiate the installer corresponding to vCenter Server separately. What you end up choosing will depend on your design.

Here are a few scenarios that you might encounter in your environment:

▸ vCenter Server 5.1 with SSO, Inventory Service, and Web Client in the same box

▸ vCenter Server 5.1 with SSO, Inventory Service, and Web Client server segregated onto different machines

▸ vCenter 5.0.x or vCenter 4.0.x (you want to segregate the SSO), Inventory Service, and Web Client installed on different machines when upgrading to vCenter 5.5

This is demonstrated in the following diagram:

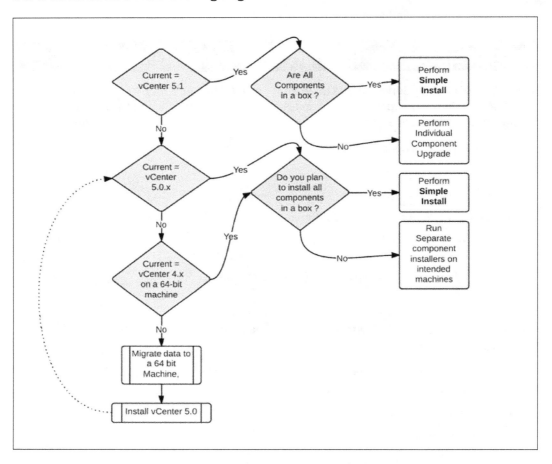

An upgrade using the Simple Installer is straightforward but harder to troubleshoot. I will familiarize you with the Simple Installer wizard screens in *Chapter 2, Performing a New Installation of vSphere 5.5*. As we have already covered the installation of vCenter Single Sign-On 5.5 and vCenter Inventory Service in this chapter, in this section we will use the vCenter 5.5 Installer.

The following procedure will guide you through the steps required to upgrade vCenter server to Version 5.5:

1. Back up the vCenter Server database.

2. Launch the **vCenter Server** installer from the vSphere Installation DVD's Welcome Screen.

3. The first screen of the installer wizard will indicate the presence of an earlier version of vCenter Server on the same machine. Click on **Next** to continue.

4. Accept the **VMWARE END USER LICENSE AGREEMENT** and click on **Next** to continue.

5. Enter the **License Key** if you have it handy. If not just click on **Next** to install vCenter Server in evaluation mode (90 days) and enter the license key later:

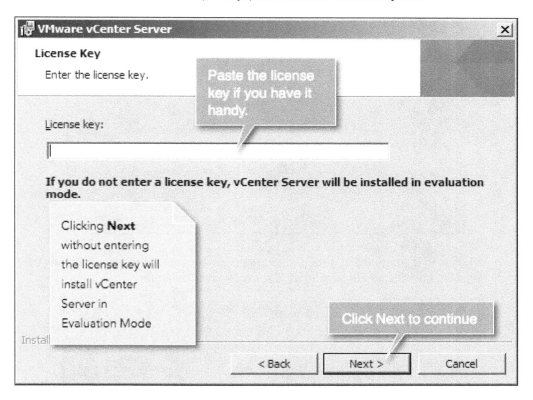

6. The installer will auto-detect the DSN and the authentication. This might not be the case if you use SQL authentication or an Oracle DB. Click on Next to continue:

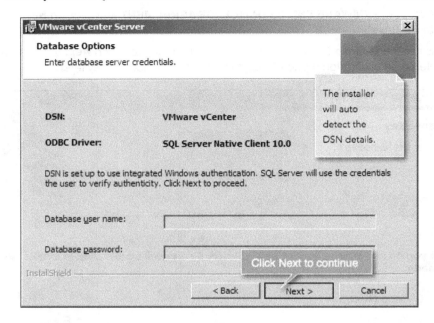

7. Choose to upgrade the vCenter Server database and check the box confirming that the SSO certificates are backed up. Click on **Next** to continue:

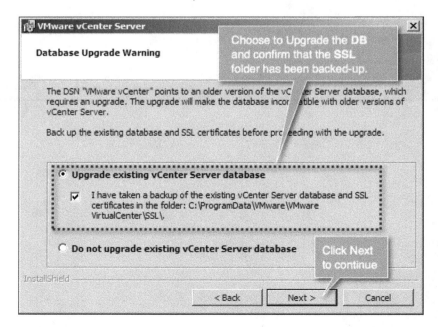

8. Choose the vCenter Agent Upgrade method (**Automatic/Manual**). In this case, we have chosen **Automatic**. Click on **Next** to continue:

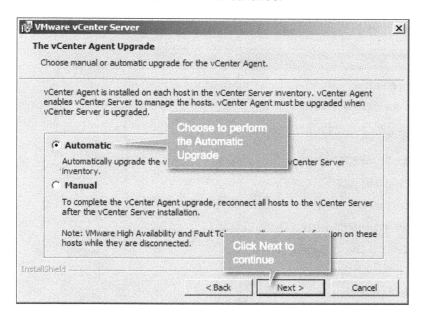

9. Supply the service account credentials or choose to use the local account. In this case, we have chosen to use the local account by selecting the checkbox **Use Windows Local System Account**. Click on **Next** to continue:

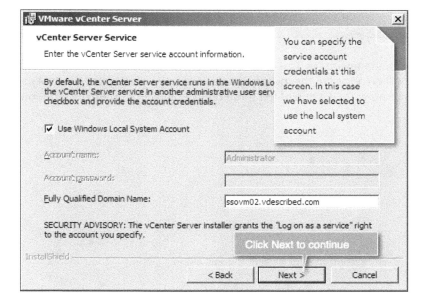

10. Change the default ports only if necessary. We are leaving them unmodified for this example. On the same screen, you could also choose to increase the number of ephemeral ports for the vCenter instance. Make the decision and click on **Next** to continue:

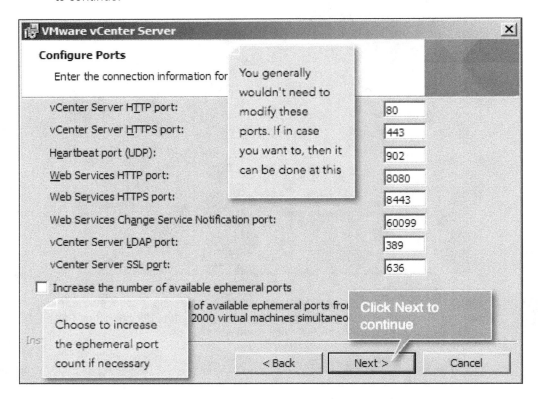

11. Specify the **Inventory Size** in terms of the number of ESXi hosts and virtual machines that will be added to the inventory. The inventory size dictates the JVM memory requirement. Select one of the three options and click on **Next** to continue:

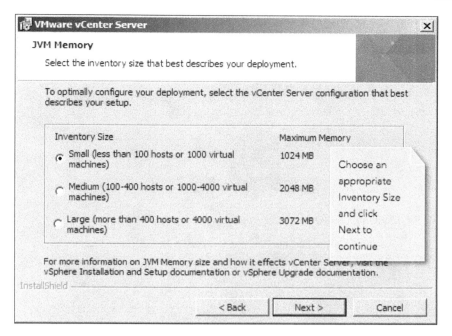

12. Supply the SSO administrator password so that vCenter Inventory Service can be registered as a client to the SSO server, then click Next:

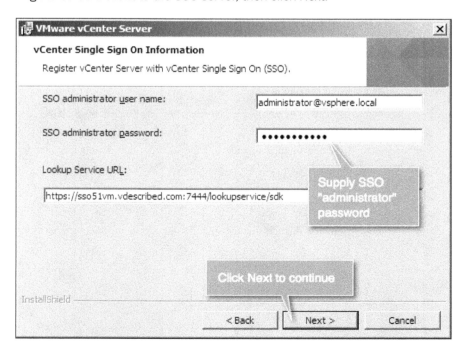

13. You might be prompted to accept the SSO Lookup Service certificate. Click on **Yes** to continue:

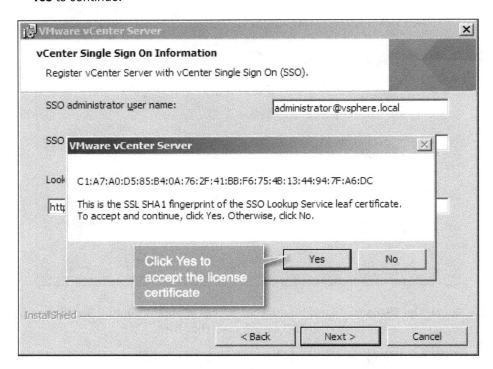

14. Supply the vCenter Inventory Service URL. If the installer does not autopopulate this information, then it will have to be supplied manually. Click on **Next** to continue:

Syntax:

```
https://<FQDN or IP of vCenter Inventory Service Machine>:10433
```

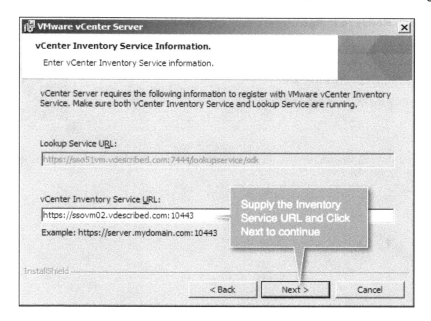

15. Change the installation folder if necessary. In this case, we are using the default folder location.

16. Click on **Next** to continue:

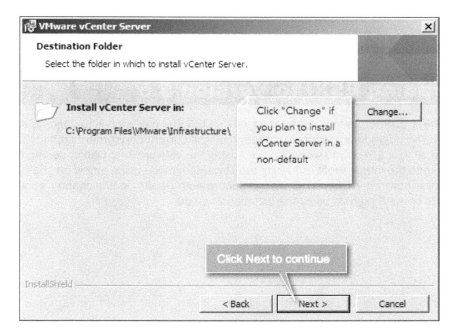

17. On the **Ready to Install** screen, click on **Install** to start the installation:

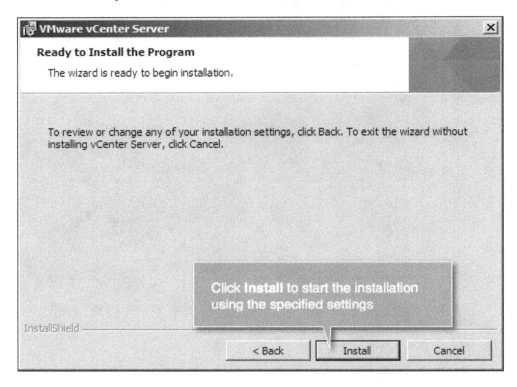

18. Once the installation is complete, click on **Finish** to exit the wizard.

Upgrading ESXi to Version 5.5

Once you have vCenter Server upgraded to Version 5.5, the next step is to upgrade the ESXi hosts. The upgrade procedure will depend on the current deployment architecture. For instance, if all your ESXi hosts were deployed using the VMware Auto Deploy server, then you'll have to update the Image Profile sourcing the streamed image using a new off-line bundle. As Auto Deploy is covered in *Chapter 5, Using vSphere Auto Deploy*, in this chapter we will cover the upgrade of the ESXi host using the installation media.

Getting ready

Before you begin any upgrade, it is very important to plan for it. So what would you need to do to perform an upgrade of ESXi? You would, of course, need the ISO image downloaded from VMware's website, but you would also need a method to present the ISO to the physical machine so that it can boot from it. Most of the modern server equipments have a methodology to avoid the need to burn ISO to a physical DVD medium and then insert it in the DVD drive of the physical machine. If you are an administrator, you might already be aware of terms such as ILO (HP), DRAC (Dell), and KVM Manager (Cisco). These are web-based tools that will connect to an RAC on the server and enable remote access to the server's console via the Web. Enough said on what is available out there; let's make a list of what you need to begin the upgrade:

- The ESXi hypervisor DVD image downloaded from VMware's website
- Access to the remote console of the server on which the upgrade will be performed

To download the DVD image, follow these instructions:

1. Go to the downloads page available at `https://my.vmware.com/web/vmware/downloads`.
2. Click on the **Download Product** hyperlink corresponding to **VMware vSphere**.
3. On the **Download VMware vSphere** webpage, locate **VMware ESXi 5.5** under the needed license category.
4. Click on the **Go to Downloads** URL corresponding to the ESXi entry to reach the web page titled **Download VMware ESXi 5.5**.
5. Download the ESXi ISO image, which includes VMware Tools.

How to do it...

The following procedure will guide you through the steps required to upgrade ESXi to Version 5.5:

1. Boot the machine using the ESXi Installation DVD.
2. Choose the **ESXi-5.5.0 Standard Installer** from the standard boot menu and hit *Enter*:

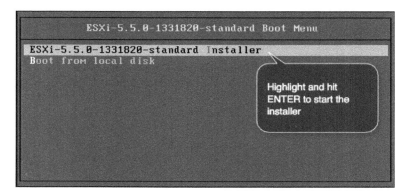

3. At the **Welcome to the VMware ESXi 5.5.0 Installation** screen, hit *Enter*:

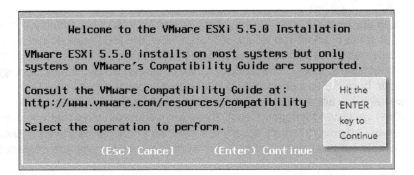

4. Hit the function key (*F11*) to accept the EULA:

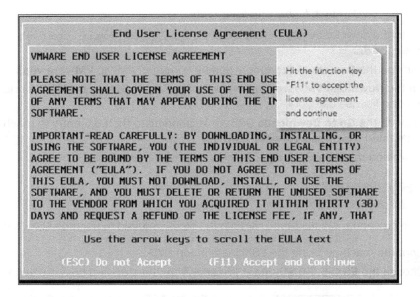

5. Select the storage device that has the previous installation of ESXi and hit *F1* to view the disk details. In this case, it has detected an ESXi 5.1 installation. Next, hit *Enter*:

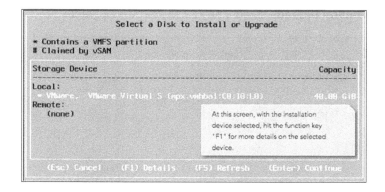

On hitting F1 you will be presented with the Disk Details". Don't make it a bullet though.

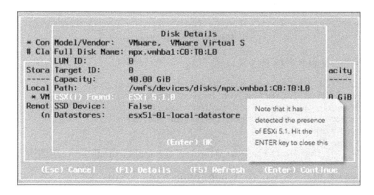

6. On the **ESXi and VMFS Found** screen, choose the option **Upgrade ESXi, preserve VMFS datastore**:

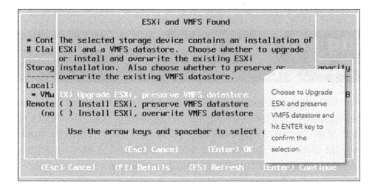

7. On the **Confirm Upgrade** screen, hit *F11* to start the upgrade:

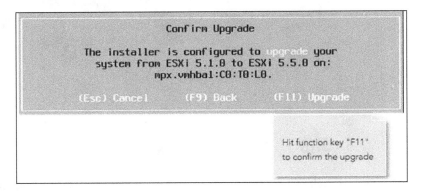

8. Once the upgrade is complete, hit *Enter* to reboot:

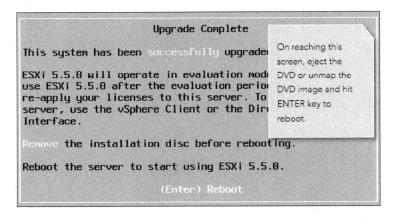

9. After a successful reboot, you will be at ESXi DCUI's welcome screen.

Upgrading vCenter Server Appliance to Version 5.5

If there are **vCenter Server Appliances** (**VCSAs**) managing subsets of your environment, then the upgrade of the appliance is necessary prior to upgrading the ESXi hosts managed by it. There is no concept of an in-place upgrade of a VCSA to a major version, meaning that the upgrade can't really be directly applied to the appliance itself. A new appliance is deployed and the configuration is imported from the existing appliance.

You can download the latest available VCSA 5.5 appliance from VMware's download portal:

1. Go to the download page using the following URL (`https://my.vmware.com/web/vmware/downloads`).

2. Click on the **Download Product** hyperlink corresponding to **VMware vSphere**.

3. On the **Download VMware vSphere** webpage, locate VMware vCenter under the needed license category.

4. Click on the **Go to Downloads** URL corresponding to the vCenter entry to reach the web page titled **Download VMware vCenter Server**.

5. Download the vCenter Server Appliance ZIP bundle.

How to do it...

The following procedure will guide you through the steps required to upgrade the appliance to Version 5.5:

1. Create a snapshot on the source (old) VCSA.

2. Download and deploy the new VCSA 5.5 OVF.

3. After a successful first boot, you will be presented with the **Welcome to VMware vCenter Server Appliance** console screen. Make a note of the current access URL under the **Quick Start Guide** section of the welcome screen:

```
VMware vCenter Server Appliance 5.5.0.5201 Build 1476389

To manage your appliance please browse to https://192.168.70.204:5480/

Welcome to VMware vCenter Server Appliance

Quickstart Guide: (How to get vCenter Server running quickly)
    1 - Open a browser to: https://192.168.70.204:5480/      Use this URL to connect
    2 - Accept the EULA                                        to the appliance using a
    3 - Select the desired configuration mode or upgrade       browser
    4 - Follow the wizard

    The configured appliance will be ready to use.
    In case of upgrade the appliance will reboot and may change
    its network address.

SSL thumbprints
vCenter Server: 82:EA:7C:1C:54:C1:85:6B:65:1C:1C:F2:18:18:D3:45:88:92:3F:57
Lookup service: unconfigured

 Login                                Use Arrow Keys to navigate
    Timezone     (Current:UTC)         and <ENTER> to select your choice.
```

4. Use a browser to connect to the URL `https://IPAddress:5480`. In this case, it is `https://192.168.70.204:5480`.

5. Log in with the default credentials `root/vmware`.

6. After the login, you will be presented with the **vCenter Server Setup** wizard screen. Accept the license agreement and click on **Next** to proceed.

7. On the next screen (**Configure Options**), select the radio button **Upgrade from previous version**, and click on **Next** to continue:

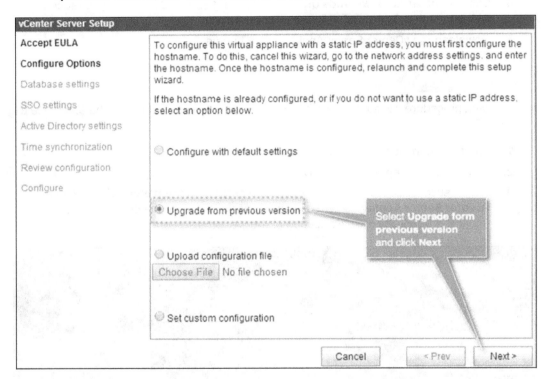

8. The next screen will show you the pre-generated import key. Right-click on the key and copy it:

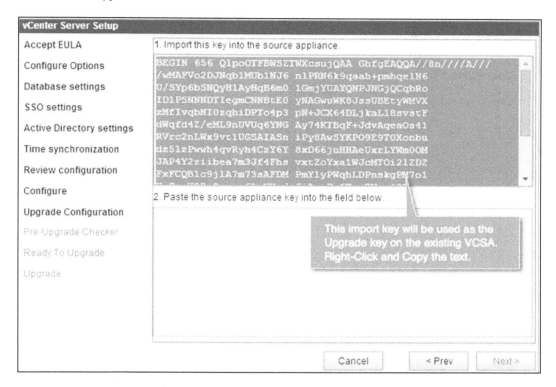

9. Go the management interface of the existing VCSA, using its management URL `https://IPAddress:5480`, and navigate to the **Upgrade** tab.

10. Paste the copied import key into the **Upgrade key** area, and click on **Import key and stop vCenter Server**:

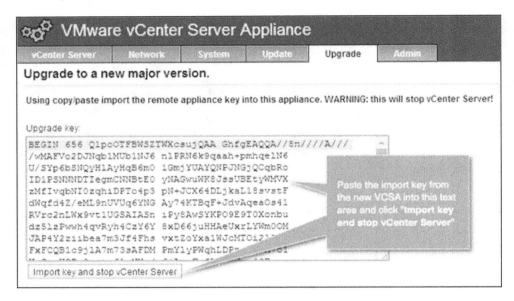

11. Once the import is successful, you'll be informed and the **Upgrade key** text area will now have a new key generated by the existing VCSA. Select and copy the key:

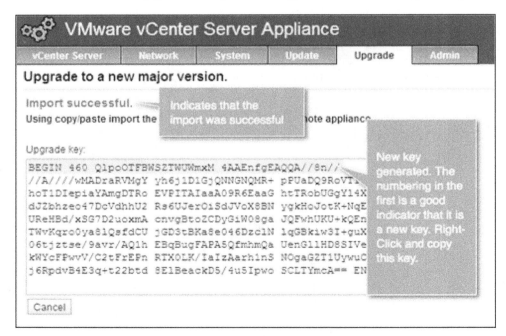

12. Go to the new appliance and paste the copied upgrade key into the source appliance key text area:

13. On the next screen, choose to replace the SSL certificates and click on **Next** to continue:

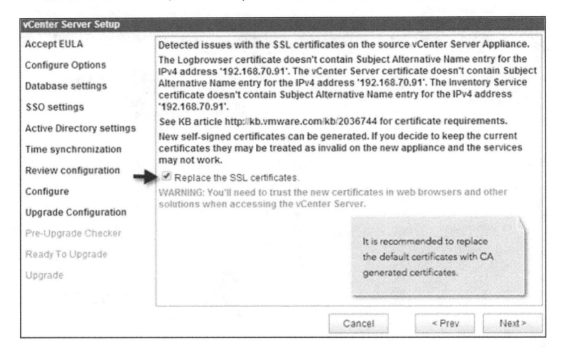

 It is recommended to replace the default self-signed certificates with CA-generated certificates.

14. On the next screen, specify a new password for the SSO administrator and click on **Next**:

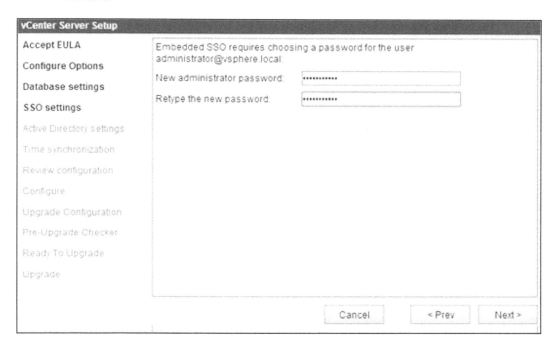

15. The next screen will show a list of ESXi hosts managed by the existing VCSA. Click on **Next** to run the pre-upgrade checker.

16. Once the pre-upgrade check is complete, the next screen will seek confirmation on whether or not you have taken a snapshot of the existing (source) vCenter Server Appliance. Select the checkbox **I confirm that I have made a backup/snapshot of the source vCenter Server Appliance and the external database.**, and click on **Start** to begin the upgrade:

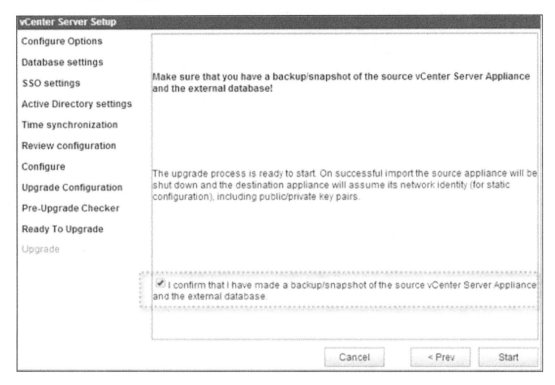

17. The upgrade process will take a few minutes to complete. Once done, it should confirm the same and automatically reboot the appliance VM. At this point, you can click on **Close** to exit the setup wizard:

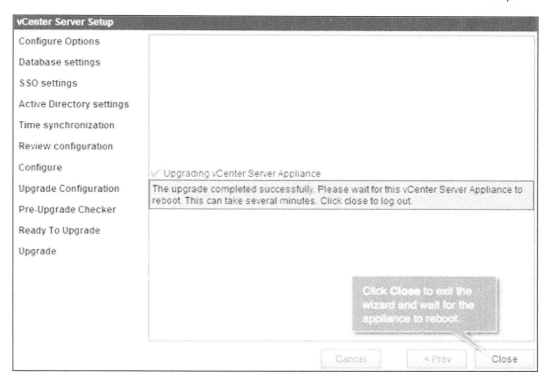

Once the reboot is complete, use the IP address of the source (old) VCSA to connect to the new appliance. This is possible because the new appliance has imported the entire configuration, including networking from the source appliance.

How it works...

Upgrading the appliance is not similar to the in-place upgrade that can be performed for a vCenter Server running on a Windows machine. The newly deployed appliance needs to be paired with an existing VCSA by exchanging SSL keys.

The destination (new) VCSA will have a pre-generated SSL key, which is used by the source (existing) VCSA to generate a new upgrade key. The source VCSA is powered off during the process of generating a new upgrade key.

The upgrade key is then supplied as a source key to the destination VCSA. The vCenter Startup wizard on the new VCSA will then fetch the configuration information from the existing VCSA over the network:

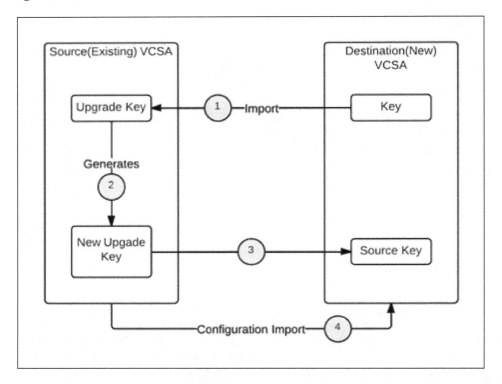

Upgrading VMware Tools

Once the hypervisor has been upgraded, you can start migrating virtual machines on the machine; but not everything has been upgraded to Version 5.5 yet. VMware Tools running inside the virtual machines can be upgraded as well to get the most out of the new hypervisor. The virtual machines, however, can continue to run with the older version of VMware Tools.

VMware Tools include the following:

- ▶ VMware device drivers for the virtual machine hardware
- ▶ The VMware Tools control panel
- ▶ A VMware balloon driver (memctl)

VMware Tools for all supported guest operating system types are packaged with ESXi. For Linux, they are also available as **VMware Operating Specific Packages** (**OSPs**) for download from the repository URL: `http://packages.vmware.com/tools`.

In this recipe, we will learn how to upgrade VMware Tools on virtual machines.

Getting ready

The virtual machine will require a reboot for the successful completion of the VMware Tools upgrade. So, plan for a scheduled downtime to perform this task on the production virtual machines. Also, take a snapshot of the virtual machine before the tools are upgraded.

How to do it...

The VMware Tools upgrade can be done using either vSphere Web Client or the vSphere Client on a powered-on virtual machine or even using the Upgrade Manager. In this section, we will be using vSphere Web Client to achieve the same.

Connect to vCenter Server using the vSphere Web Client:

1. Navigate to the **VMs and Templates Inventory** view.
2. Locate the VM and make sure it is powered on and running.
3. Right-click on the VM and navigate to **All vCenter Actions | Guest OS | Install VMware Tools**:

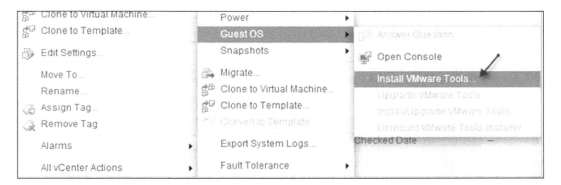

4. Choose the **Automatic Upgrade** option and then click on **Upgrade** to initiate the upgrade:

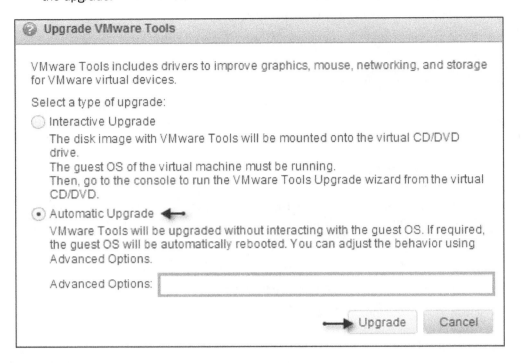

How it works...

The **Automatic Upgrade** option requires no user interaction. It will do the following:

▶ Automatically uninstall the older version of VMware Tools

▶ Install the new version from the ISO that gets mounted

▶ Reboot the **Guest Operating System** (**GOS**) to finish the tools upgrade

To verify that the tools upgrade has successfully completed, log-on to the guest operating system, right-click on the system tray icon for VMware Tools, and click on **About VMware Tools**, which should show you the VMware Tools version:

On selecting **About VMware Tools**, a dialog box showing the version number should come up:

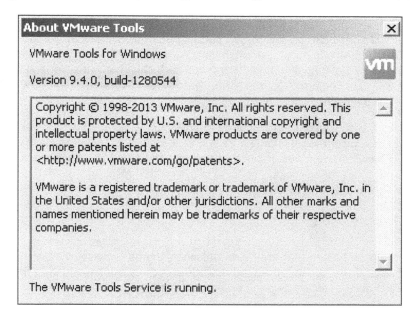

For Linux machines, this verification can be done by running the following command demonstrated in the screenshot that follows later:

```
# vmware-toolbox-cmd -v
```

You can also check the virtual machine's tool version by navigating to **vCenter Servers** | **Clusters** | **Related Objects** | **Virtual Machines**. This will list all the virtual machines and their VMware Tool version status. The VMware Tools version status column is not enabled by default; you will have to enable it manually.

Upgrading the virtual machine hardware

Once VMware Tools has been upgraded, you can upgrade the virtual hardware for the virtual machines. The virtual hardware will determine the BIOS/EFI used, CPU and memory maximums for the virtual machine, and other features. Virtual hardware Version 10 was released with ESX 5.5. The new features of hardware Version 10 are covered in *Chapter 10, Creating and Managing Virtual Machines*.

In this recipe, I will discuss the steps required to upgrade the virtual machine hardware. Once you upgrade to the current virtual hardware version, you cannot downgrade it. If you have a multiversion ESX cluster, then make sure that the VM version (virtual hardware version) is at a level supported by all the participating hosts in the cluster. Also, for the upgrade to complete, the virtual machine requires a downtime.

Getting ready

Gracefully shut down the virtual machine on which you intend to perform the virtual machine hardware upgrade. If you cannot afford the downtime of the virtual machine at the moment, then you could choose to schedule an upgrade during the next restart.

How to do it...

The virtual hardware upgrade can be done either using vSphere Web Client or vSphere Client. I will show you how to perform the task using vSphere Web Client:

1. Connect to the vCenter Server using the Web Client.
2. Navigate to the **VMs and Templates Inventory** view.
3. Locate the VM and perform a graceful shutdown of the Guest Operating System (GOS) if you intend to perform the upgrade now.
4. Right-click on the VM and navigate to **All vCenter Actions | Compatibility | Upgrade VM Compatibility...**:

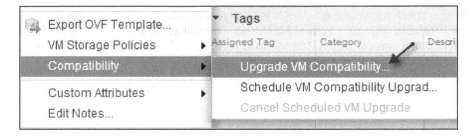

5. You will be prompted to confirm the operation. Click on **Yes**:

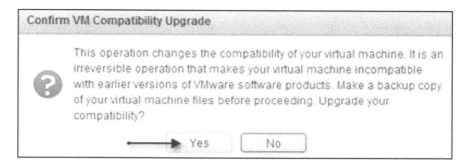

6. In the **Configure VM Compatibility** dialog box, select the ESXi version you upgraded the server to and click on **OK** to finish reconfiguring the VM:

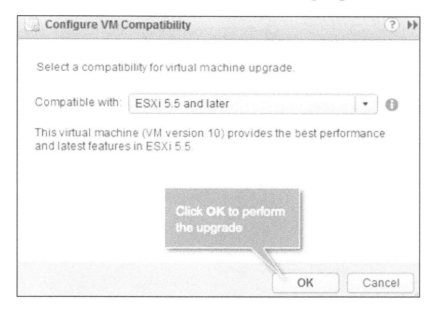

Scheduling the virtual machine hardware upgrade

We cannot finish the virtual hardware upgrade while the virtual machine is powered on. Hence, we need to power off the virtual machine for an immediate upgrade. If you have a large number of virtual machines, then you can schedule the virtual hardware upgrade to happen during the next reboot of the virtual machine; for example, a reboot during the next patch cycle.

Getting ready

Prepare a list of virtual machines you would like to perform the virtual machine hardware upgrade on.

How to do it...

The following procedure will walk you through the steps required to schedule a VM hardware upgrade:

1. Select the virtual machine(s) to perform the VM hardware upgrade on and navigate to **Actions | All vCenter Actions | Compatibility | Schedule VM Compatibility Upgrade**:

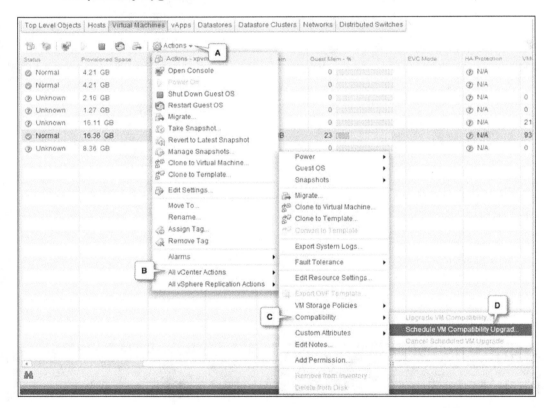

2. You will be prompted to confirm the scheduling operation. Click on **Yes** to confirm and bring up the **Schedule VM Compatibility Upgrade** window:

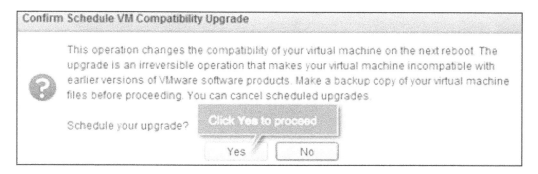

3. In the **Schedule VM Compatibility Upgrade** window, set the compatibility by selecting an ESXi version. In this case, as we have upgraded the ESXi hosts to Version 5.5, we have selected **ESXi 5.5 and later**:

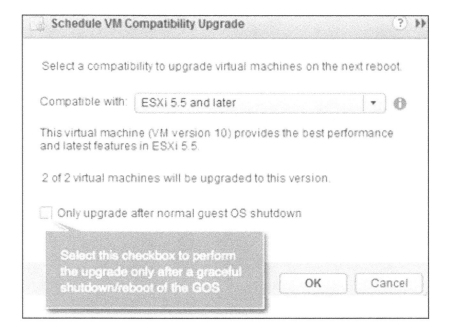

4. Also, to make sure that the hardware upgrade is performed only after a graceful shutdown of the Guest Operating System (GOS), select the checkbox **Only upgrade after normal guest OS shutdown** and click on **OK**.

2
Performing a New Installation of vSphere 5.5

In this chapter, we will cover the following recipes:

- ▶ Installing ESXi 5.5
- ▶ Configuring the ESXi Management Network
- ▶ Installing vCenter 5.5
- ▶ Adding an additional Identity Source to the SSO server
- ▶ Assigning users/groups to the vCenter Server
- ▶ Deploying SSO for the vCenter Linked Mode
- ▶ Creating a vCenter Linked Mode group
- ▶ Deploying vCenter Server Appliance 5.5

Introduction

In *Chapter 1, Upgrading to vSphere 5.5*, we learned how to upgrade our current VMware infrastructure to vSphere 5.5. However, in this chapter, we will focus on performing a fresh/new installation of the same components.

Installing ESXi 5.5

The very first component that you will install in a fully virtualized VMware environment is the **ESXi hypervisor**. It is a bare-metal installation of VMware's hypervisor on the server hardware.

Getting ready

The installation of ESXi 5.5 is pretty straightforward. It is recommended that you refer to the *VMware Compatibility Guide* web page to verify whether the server hardware is compatible with ESXi 5.5; this is available at http://www.vmware.com/resources/compatibility/search.php.

For a complete list of hardware requirements, refer to the *ESXi Hardware Requirements* section on page 13 of the *vSphere Installation and Setup* guide, available at http://bit.ly/vSphere55_install_guide.

Follow these steps to download the DVD image:

1. Go to the downloads page using the URL https://my.vmware.com/web/vmware/downloads.
2. Click on the **Download Product** hyperlink corresponding to VMware vSphere.
3. On the **Download VMware vSphere** web page, locate VMware ESXi 5.5 under the needed license category.
4. Click on the **Go to Downloads** URL corresponding to the ESXi entry to reach the web page titled **Download VMware ESXi 5.5**.
5. Download the ESXi ISO image, which includes VMware Tools.

Also, create a DNS entry (DNS-A and PTR records) for the hostname.

How to do it...

The following procedure will guide you through the steps required to perform a new installation of the ESXi server using the ESXi 5.5 installation DVD:

1. In the ESXi 5.5.0 standard boot menu, select the item **ESXi-5.5.0-01331828-standard Installer** and hit *Enter* to continue:

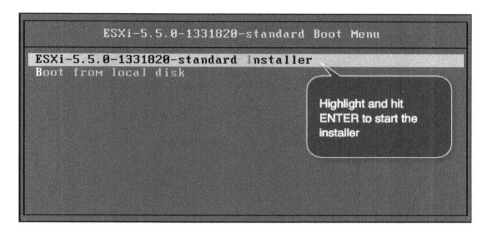

2. On the **Welcome to the VMware ESXi 5.5.0 Installation** screen, hit *Enter* to continue:

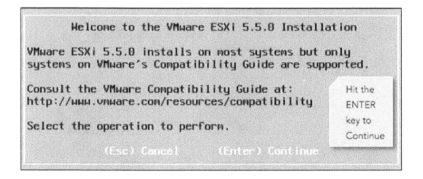

3. Hit *F11* to accept the EULA and continue:

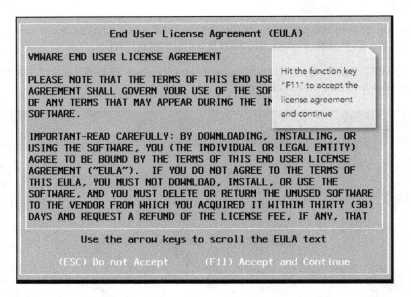

4. On the **Select a Disk to Install or Upgrade** screen, select a storage device to install ESXi on it. In this case, the installer has only detected a device attached to the local controller. If necessary, you could hit *F1* to fetch more details about the device. Hit *Enter* to confirm the selection and continue:

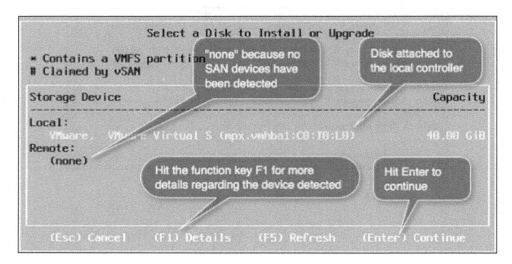

5. Select the keyboard layout and hit *Enter* to continue. The default is **Use Default**.

6. Supply a root password and hit **Enter** to continue:

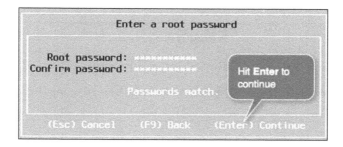

7. At the **Confirm Install** screen, hit *F11* to start the installation:

8. You will now see the **Installing ESXi 5.5.0** screen showing the progress of the installation. This will take a few minutes to complete:

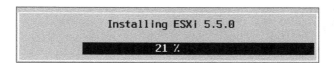

9. Once the installation is complete, you will be presented with an **Installation Complete** message screen. At this point, eject or unmount the CD/DVD drive or image, and hit *Enter* to reboot the machine:

10. A **Rebooting Server** message is displayed, indicating that the server is about to be rebooted. There is nothing that you have to do on this screen:

```
                      Rebooting Server

The server will shut down and reboot.

The process will take a short time to complete.
```

11. Once the reboot is complete, you will be at the main screen for ESXi 5.5.0:

```
VMware ESXi 5.5.0 (VMKernel Release Build 1331820)

VMware, Inc. VMware Virtual Platform

2 x Intel(R) Core(TM) i7 CPU 960 @ 3.20GHz
4 GiB Memory




Download tools to manage this host from:
http://192.168.193.24/ (DHCP)
http://[fe80::20c:29ff:fea4:4d2f]/ (STATIC)
```

12. Once the installation is complete, you will need to supply the basic network configuration. The next recipe, *Configuring the ESXi Management Network*, covers this.

There's more...

ESXi can also be provisioned using vSphere Auto Deploy.

See also

▸ *Chapter 5, Using vSphere Auto Deploy*

Configuring the ESXi Management Network

After the ESXi installation is complete, it is essential to configure its management network before it can be accessed. The management network is what makes the ESXi become a part of a network. It is backed by a VMkernel network interface. We will learn more about these in the networking chapter. The ESXi hypervisor runs a DHCP client, so it does procure a DHCP address if there is a DHCP server on its network; but, in most cases, that is not enough. For instance, if your management network is on a VLAN, then you will need to configure the VLAN ID. Also, it is recommended that the ESXi hosts be assigned with a static IP address. Hence, it becomes important to configure the management network of an ESXi host after it is installed. In this recipe, we will use **Direct Console User Interface** (**DCUI**) to achieve this.

Getting ready

You will need access to the host's console via its IPMI interface DRAC/ILO/KVM, the root password, and the TCP/IP configuration that you would like to assign to the ESXi Management Network.

How to do it...

The following procedure will walk you through the steps required in setting the TCP/IP configuration for the ESXi's Management Network:

1. Connect to the console of an ESXi host.

2. Hit the function key (*F2*) to log in to the DCUI by supplying the root password:

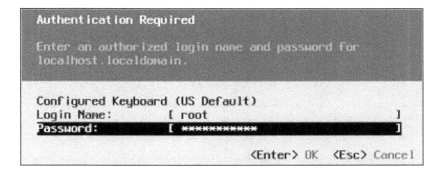

3. Once you are in the **System Customization** view of the DCUI, select **Configure Management Network** and hit *Enter*:

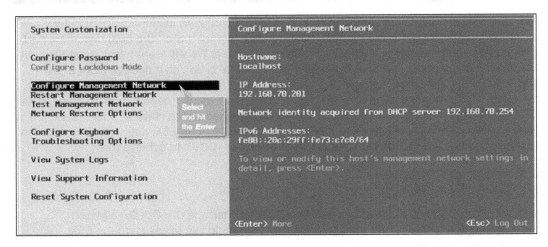

4. In the **Configure Management Network** view, select **VLAN (optional)** and hit *Enter*:

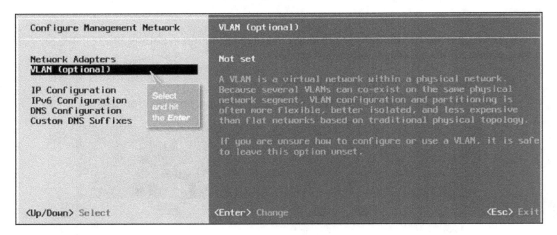

5. In the next dialog box, enter the VLAN ID and hit *Enter*:

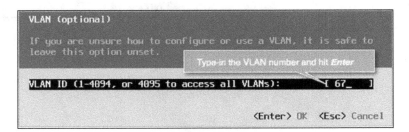

6. Now you will be back in the **Configure Management Network** screen. Select **IP Configuration** and hit *Enter*:

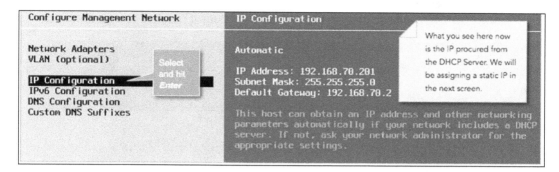

7. In the **IP Configuration** screen, select **Set static IP address and network configuration** to enable manual entry of the IP address, **Subnet Mask**, and **Default Gateway**. Supply the values and hit *Enter*:

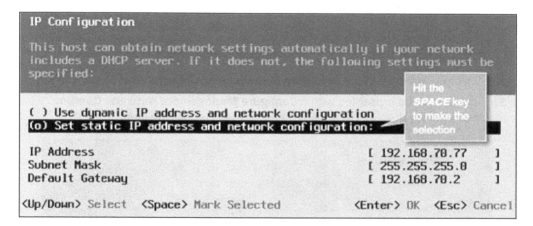

8. You will now be back in the **Configure Management Network** screen again. Select **DNS Configuration** and hit *Enter*:

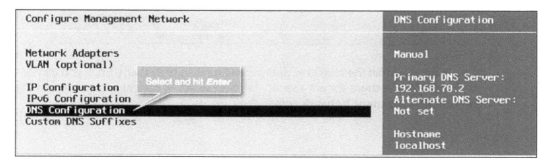

9. You will see that the DNS server entries have already been procured from the DHCP server; change them if need be. However, you will need to supply a hostname, **fully qualified domain name** (**FQDN**), for the host. It will be `localhost` by default. Type in the FQDN for the host, change the DNS server values if needed, and hit *Enter*:

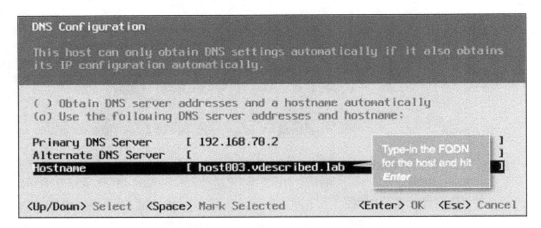

If you do not supply an FQDN, then make sure you configure a custom DNS suffix. The option to do so is available on the **Configure Management Network** screen.

10. Once you are back to the **Configure Management Network** view, hit the *Esc* key.

11. You now will be presented with a **Configure Management Network: Confirm** message. Hit the *Y* key to apply the changes and reboot the host:

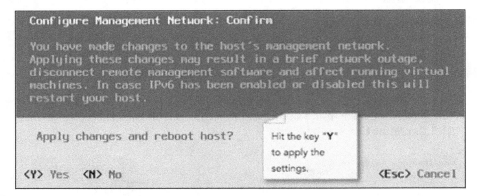

Hitting *N* will revert all the changes, and you will have to redo them. So, if you do not want to apply the settings for any reason, hit the *Esc* key to cancel and go back to the **Configure Management Network** screen.

12. The ESXi host will now reboot to take up the new management network configuration. The DCUI main screen should now show the new hostname and IP address:

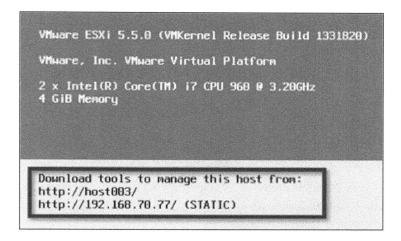

There's more...

IPv6 is enabled by default. If you do not intend to use Version 6, then it can be disabled from the **Configure Management Network** screen.

Select IPv6 Configuration and hit *Enter* to bring up the **IPv6 Configuration** window. Hit the spacebar to disable the selection, and then hit *Enter*. You will need to restart the ESXi host for the changes to be applied:

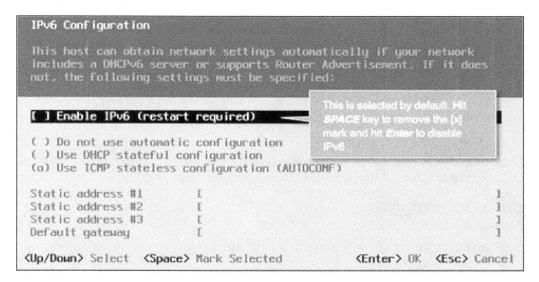

Installing vCenter 5.5

The installation of vCenter 5.5 on a Windows machine is done using the installer available on the vCenter Installation DVD. The installer can be initiated separately or run as part of the simple installation process.

In this chapter, we will be using the simple installer to perform a new installation of vCenter Server.

Getting ready

Let's take a look at the pre-install checks that need to be performed:

1. Check the vCenter Server software requirements.
2. Check ESXi compatibility.
3. Check database compatibility.
4. Take a snapshot of your vCenter VM so that you can revert to a clean VM in the event of the install failing.

We won't be discussing these checks here, as these were discussed in the *Performing an upgrade of vCenter Server* section in *Chapter 1, Upgrading to vSphere 5.5*.

You can download the vCenter Server installation bundle from VMware's product downloads page. For instructions on how to get there, read the *Downloading vCenter 5.5* section in *Chapter 1, Upgrading to vSphere 5.5*.

If you start the installation on a Windows machine that already has a previous version of vCenter Server installed, then the installation wizard will not provide you with an option to perform a fresh/new installation of vCenter Server. It will always be an upgrade, unless you manually uninstall the existing version of vCenter Server. (See *Chapter 15, Monitoring the Performance of a vSphere Environment*.)

To uninstall the existing version of vCenter Server from your machine, perform the following steps:

1. Stop vCenter and component services.
2. Uninstall vCenter Server using Add/Remove Programs. (In Windows 2008, navigate to **Control Panel | Programs | Programs and Features**.)

How to do it...

The process of performing a new installation of vCenter Server involves two tasks:

1. Creating a 64-bit DSN for the SQL database for vCenter Server.
2. Performing a new installation of vCenter Server.

Creating a DSN for the SQL database for vCenter Server

For the installation to complete, vCenter Server should be configured to use a database. The SQL Express DB bundled with the installation should only be used in small/development environments. It is not supported by VMware in production environments. It supports only up to 5 ESXi hosts and 50 virtual machines; also, the database size cannot exceed 4 GB. We will not be discussing the procedure for manually preparing a SQL database for vCenter Server. The procedure has been detailed in the *Configure Microsoft SQL Server Databases* section on page 32 in the *vSphere Installation and Setup* guide. For Oracle databases, read the *Configure Oracle databases* section on page 42. You can find these at `http://pubs.vmware.com/vsphere-55/topic/com.vmware.ICbase/PDF/vsphere-esxi-vcenter-server-55-installation-setup-guide.pdf`.

The following procedure will guide you through the steps required to create a DSN. This procedure has to be performed on the machine where vCenter Server is being installed:

1. Download and install the SQL Server Native Client compatible with your SQL Server.

2. Navigate to **Start | Administrative Tools | Data sources (ODBC)** to bring up the ODBC data sources snap in.

3. Click on the **System DSN** tab and click on **Add** to bring up the **Create New Data Source** window:

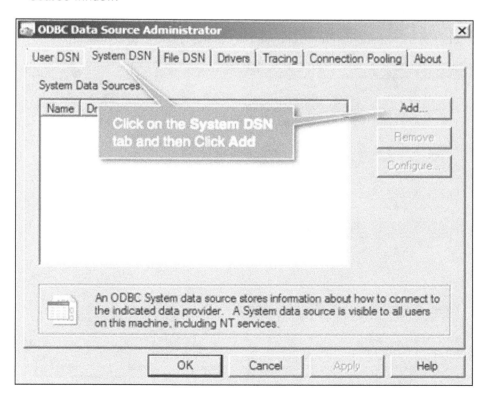

4. Select **SQL Server Native Client 10.0** as the driver and click on **Finish** to bring up the **Create a New Data Source to SQL Server** window:

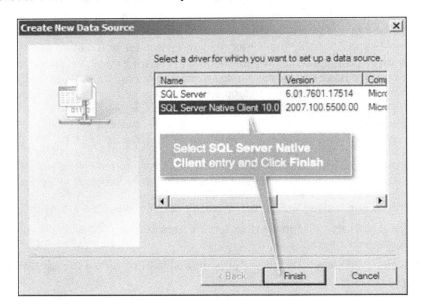

5. Specify a data source name, choose the database server to connect to:

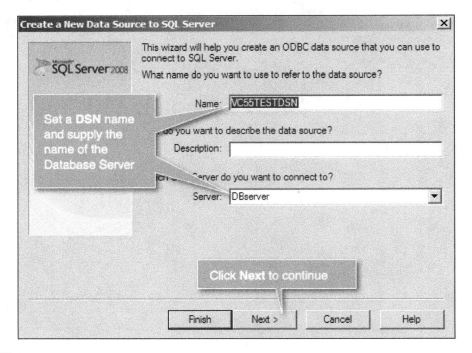

6. Choose the authentication method. Although is not recommended, for the sake of simplicity we are using the SQL **sa** user. Make sure you have a separate user for database connectivity. Click on **Next** to continue:

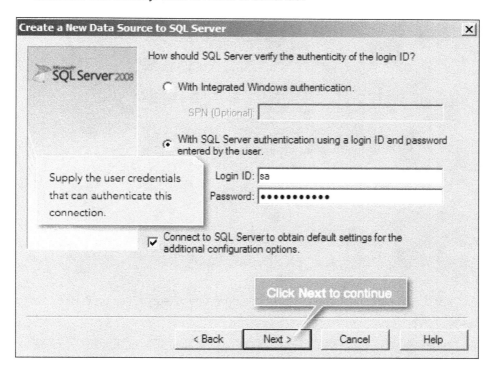

7. Select the **Change the default database to** checkbox and set the precreated vCenter database as the default database for this DSN. Click on **Next** to continue:

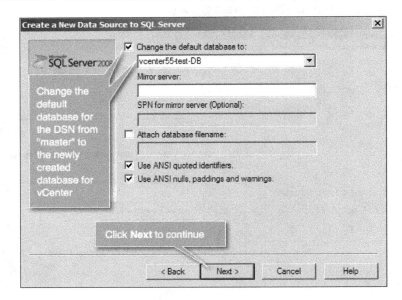

8. On the next screen, change the options only if necessary. Click on **Finish** to create the DSN:

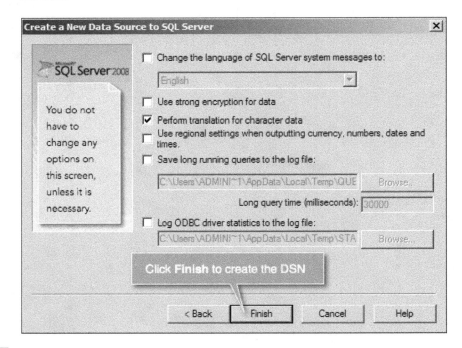

9. On the **ODBC Microsoft SQL Server Setup** window, click on **Test Data Source** to make sure that the DSN can be used to establish a connection with the database. It should read **TESTS COMPLETED SUCCESSFULLY** if the connection attempt was successful. Click on **OK** to close the **SQL Server ODBC Data Source Test** window.

10. Click on **OK** again to close the **ODBC Microsoft SQL Server Setup** window.

11. The newly created DSN should now be listed under the **System DSN** tab. Click on **OK** to close the **ODBC Data Source Administrator** window:

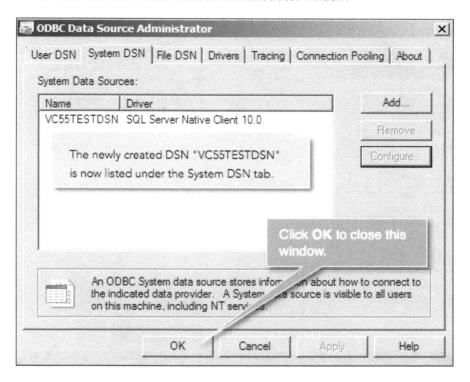

Performing a new installation of vCenter Server

The following procedure will guide you through the steps required to perform a new installation of vCenter 5.5:

1. Select the **Simple Install** option from the vSphere Installation Welcome DVD and click on the **Install** button to start the installer:

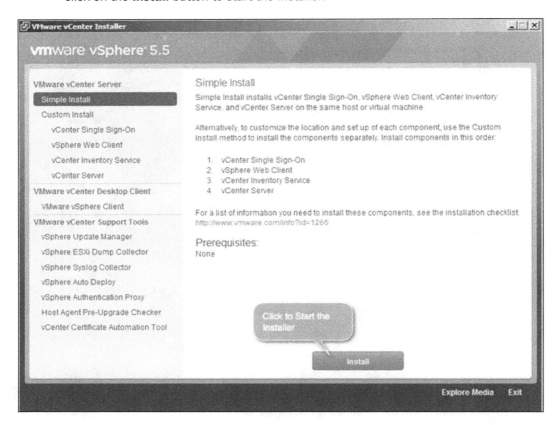

2. On the **Welcome to the vCenter Single Sign-On Setup** screen, click on **Next** to continue:

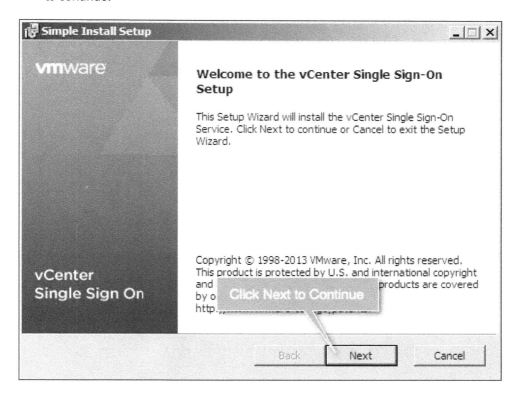

3. Select the checkbox, **I accept the terms in the License Agreement** and click on **Next** to continue.

4. The next screen will show the results of the prerequisites check run by the installer for the vCenter Single Sign-On component. Click on **Next** to continue:

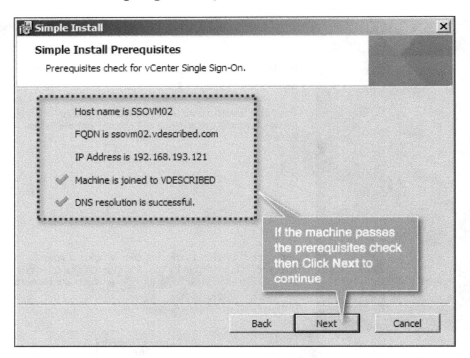

[If any of these checks fail, they need to be fixed before you continue.]

5. Set a complex password for the Single Sign-On server component and click on **Next** to continue:

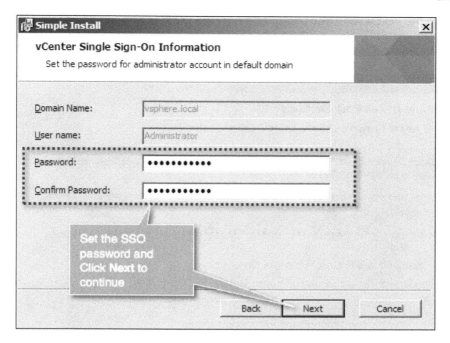

6. Set the site name for this SSO instance. The default site name is **Default-First-Site**. You can specify an intended site name and click on **Next** to continue:

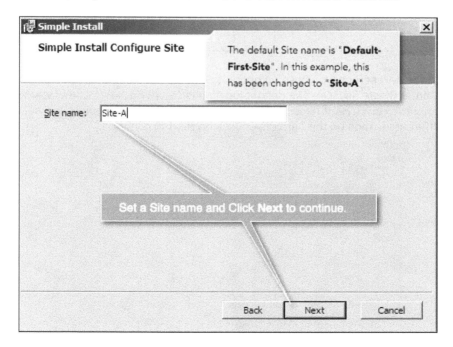

7. On the next screen, you could set the HTTPS port for vCenter Single Sign-On. The default port number is **7444**. Change the port number only if your environment requires you to do so. Click on **Next** to continue:

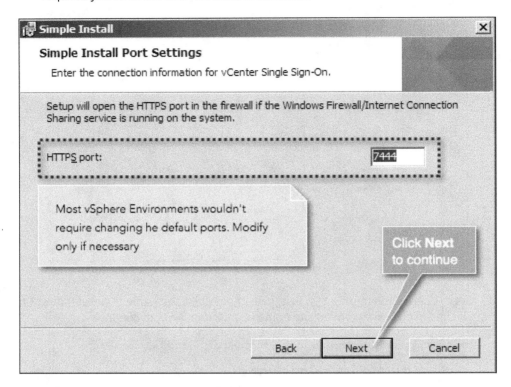

8. On the next screen, you have an option to change the installation location for vCenter Single Sign-On. The default location is `C:\Program Files\VMware\Infrastructure`. If necessary, you can click on **Change** to select and set a different location on the hard drive. Click on **Next** to continue:

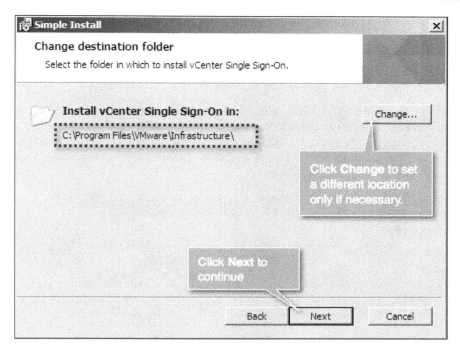

9. Review the install options that you have set and click on **Install** to start the installation:

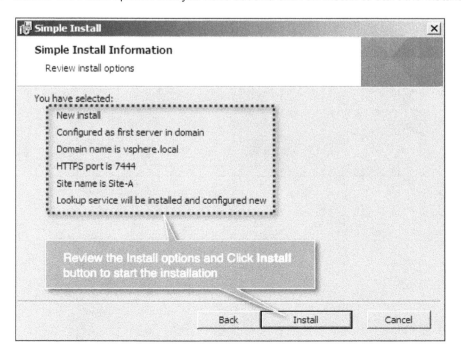

Once the SSO installation is complete, it will automatically start the installer for the vSphere Web Client, finish it, and then finish the Inventory Service. Both the installations require no manual intervention, but make sure that the web client is installed in the default location due to the known issues outlined in the VMware Knowledge Base article KB#2044953 at `http://kb.vmware.com/kb/2044953`.

10. Once the vSphere Web Client and vCenter Inventory Service installations are complete, the wizard automatically starts the vCenter Server installer and prompts for the license key. At this point, you can either enter a license key or just click on **Next**, leaving the **License key** field blank to install vCenter Server in evaluation mode (60 days) and enter a valid key later:

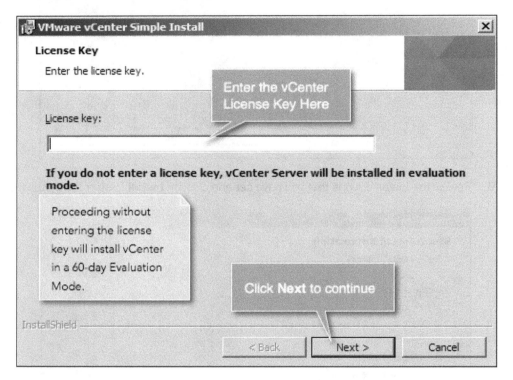

11. On the next screen, select the **Use an existing supported database** option and select the DSN that points to the precreated vCenter database. Click on **Next** to continue:

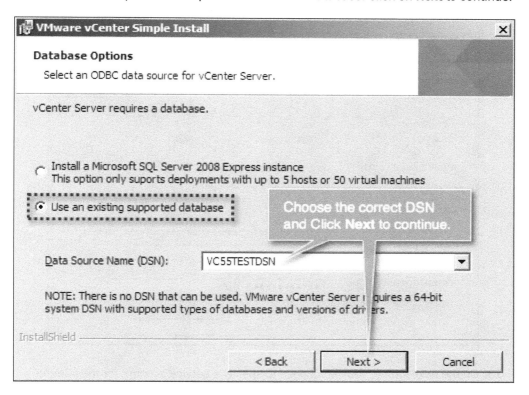

12. Supply the database user credentials and click on **Next** to continue. Keep in mind that although we use the **sa** account in this example, it is not recommended to do so. Create a separate account for database connectivity:

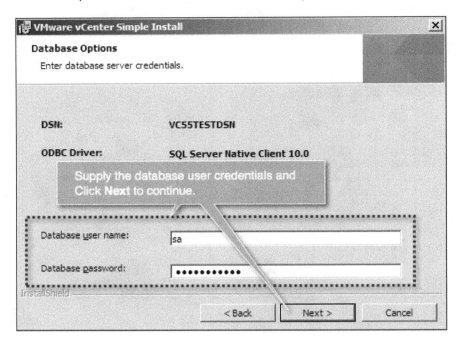

13. On the next screen, you can choose to specify a service account for the vCenter Server service. By default, it uses the local system account. In this example, we have chosen to continue with the default account. Click on **Next** to continue:

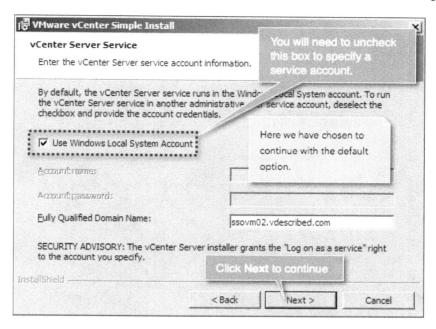

14. On the **Configure Ports** screen, you can supply nondefault port numbers if such a change is required in your environment. Else, leave them at their default values. You can also choose to increase the number of ephemeral ports by selecting the checkbox **Increase the number of available ephemeral ports**. Click on **Next** to continue:

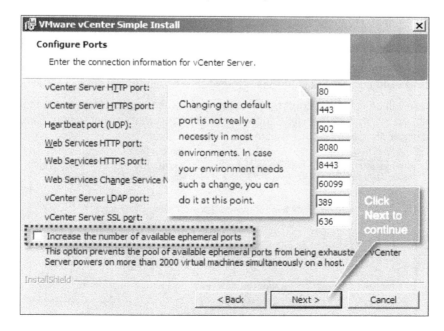

For more information on Ephemeral ports, read VMware KB# 1022312 at http://kb.vmware.com/kb/1022312.

15. Select the Inventory Size and click on **Next** to continue:

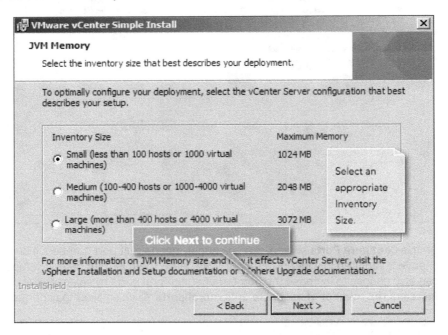

16. On the **Ready to Install** screen, click on **Install** to start the vCenter installation.

17. Once the installation completes, you will be presented with the **Installation Completed** screen. Click on **Finish** to exit the installation wizard.

18. There will be a further confirmation message indicating that the simple installer has finished the installation of SSO, the web client, inventory service, and vCenter Server successfully. Click on **OK** to close the message box:

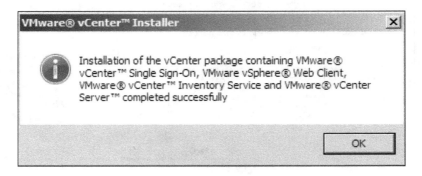

How it works...

Simple Install does a new installation of all the components. It automatically initiates the installers of all the necessary components in the following order:

- ▶ vCenter Single Sign-On
- ▶ vSphere Web Client
- ▶ vCenter Inventory Service
- ▶ vCenter Server

Unlike the case with the standalone installer of SSO, during a simple install you don't get an option to select the placement type. If you want to replicate data from an existing SSO server, then you will have to initiate the SSO installer separately. Once the SSO installation is complete, it will automatically start the installer for vSphere Web Client, vCenter Inventory Service, and then vCenter Server.

If you have an existing vCenter Server installation using a database hosted on a SQL Express database server and you have already hit the 5 hosts/50 VMs/4GB DB limits, then you should be migrating the database to a full-blown SQL database server.

The migration procedure is documented in the VMware Knowledge Base article number 1028601 at `http://kb.vmware.com/kb/1028601`.

Adding an additional Identity Source to the SSO server

An identity source is nothing but a repository of users and groups. These can be the local operating system users, active directory, or open LDAP and VMDir sources.

Here, VMDir is short for VM Directory which is SSO's LDAP-based internal directory that stores identity sources, SSO users, and policies. It is the source of truth for the vsphere.local domain.

Read the *Upgrading the Single Sign-On (SSO) component* recipe in *Chapter 1, Upgrading to vSphere 5.5*, for more information.

In this section, we will learn how to add identity sources to the SSO server.

How to do it...

The following procedure will guide you through the steps required to add Identity Sources to the SSO server:

1. Use vSphere Web Client to connect to vCenter Server. The URL will use the following syntax:

   ```
   https://<IP Address or FQDN>:9443/vsphere-client
   ```

   Here are a few examples:

   ```
   https://localhost:9443/vsphere-client
   https://vcenterhost001.vdescribed.lab:9443/vsphere-client
   ```

2. Log in using the default SSO administrator and its domain (`administrator@vsphere.local`):

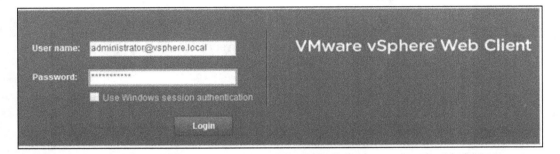

3. Click on **Administration** from the left pane to bring up the **Administration** page:

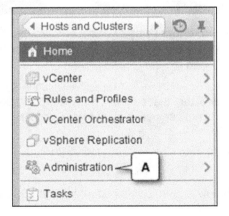

4. Click on **Configuration** from the left pane and go to the **Identity Sources** tab.

    The **Identity Sources** tab will show the current identity sources, **Local OS** being the default. The Local OS is the source for local Windows users on the machine to know if SSO is installed:

5. Click on the **+** icon to bring up the **Add identity source** window:

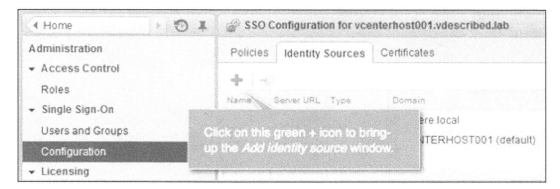

6. Select an identity source type. The user inputs required vary based on the type selected. In this case, we have selected **Active Directory as a LDAP Server**; we supply the details requested and click **Test Connection** to verify when a connection can be established using the details provided.

The following is a sample input set for a domain `vdescribed.lab`:

Identity source settings	Values
Name	vdescribed.lab
Base DN for users	DC=vdescribed, DC=lab
Domain name	vdescribed.lab
Domain alias	VDESCRIBED
Base DN for groups	DC=vdescribed, DC=lab
Primary server URL	ldap://dc2012.vdescribed.lab
Username	domuser@vdescribed.lab
Password	Password of domain user account

Here, the domain user `domuser` is a member of the AD groups domain users and read-only domain controllers:

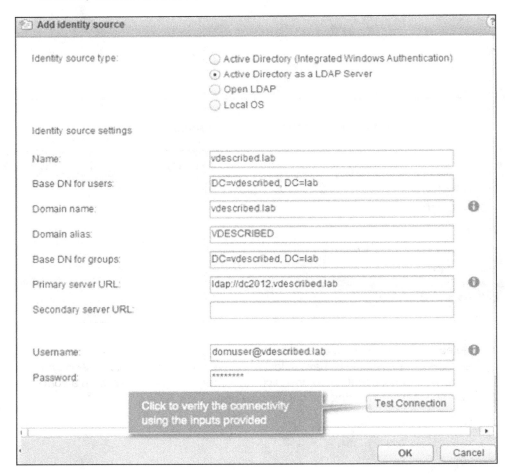

7. If the test works, then you should see a message confirming this. Click on **OK** to close the message and return to the **Add identity source** window:

8. In the **Add identity source** window, click on **OK** to begin adding the identity source. Once added, the new identity source will be listed in the **Identity Sources** tab:

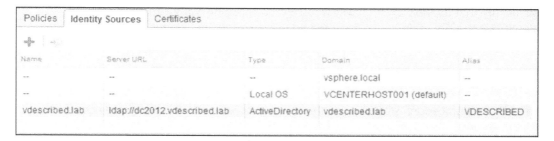

How it works...

Once the identity source is added, authentication requests can be processed against it to issue tokens using **Secure Token Service** (**STS**).

When you try to add an identity source, you are presented with the following identity source types:

- **Active directory (Integrated Windows Authentication)**: This can be used when your active directory is in **Native** mode. With this identity source type selected, you can either use the current local machine account as the **Service Principal Name** (**SPN**) or choose to specify a different SPN. For more information, refer to the VMware Knowledge Base Article KB#2058298 at `http://kb.vmware.com/kb/2058298`.

- **Active directory as an LDAP server**: This is primarily used for backward-compatibility.

- **Open LDAP**: This is used when you have an open LDAP-only-based directory service in your environment.

- **Local OS**: This will become the source for local operating system users on the machine where SSO is installed (not vCenter Server).

Assigning users/groups to the vCenter Server

Be it a simple installation or component installation, you will only able to connect to vCenter Server using the SSO administrator (`administrator@vsphere.local`) after the installation. This is because, by default, the SSO administrator is assigned the vCenter administrator role. Most environments require other users to be able to connect to vCenter Server. To make this possible, you will need to manually assign an access role to a user/group you would like to provide access to.

Getting ready

Make sure that the domain from which you will be selecting a group/user is added as an identity source. For instructions, read the *Adding an additional Identity Source to the SSO Server* recipe.

How to do it...

The following procedure will guide you through the steps required in assigning access roles to a user/group:

1. Using Web Client, connect to vCenter Server as the SSO administrator and navigate to the vCenter inventory home:

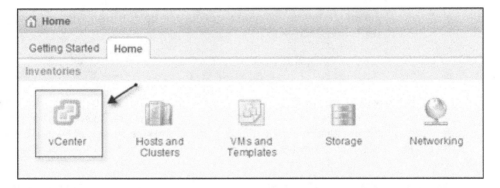

2. At vCenter Home, click on **vCenter Servers** under the **Inventory Lists** category:

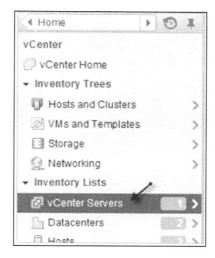

3. Then, with the vCenter Server selected, navigate to **Manage | Permissions** and click on the **+** icon to bring up the **Add Permission** window:

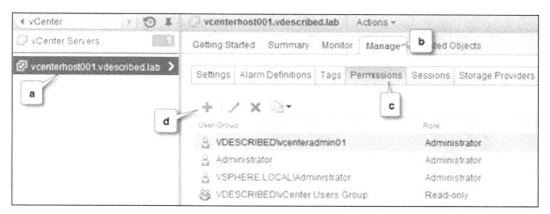

4. Click on the **Add** button to bring up the **Select Users/Groups** window:

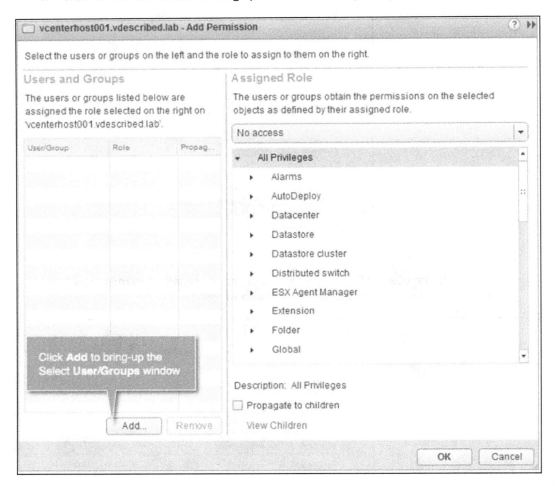

5. Select the domain you would like to add a group/user from, use the search box to filter the search, select the group/user, hit *Enter* to find the user/group, select and click on **Add** to make the selection, and click on **OK** to return to the **Add Permission** window:

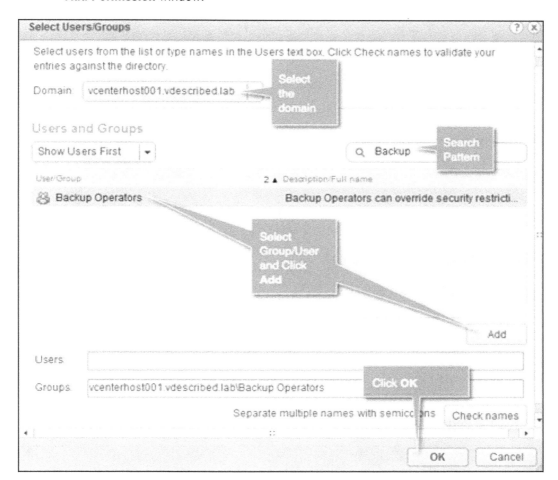

6. In the **Change Role On Permission** window, with the user selected, assign an intended role. Click on **OK** to add the permission:

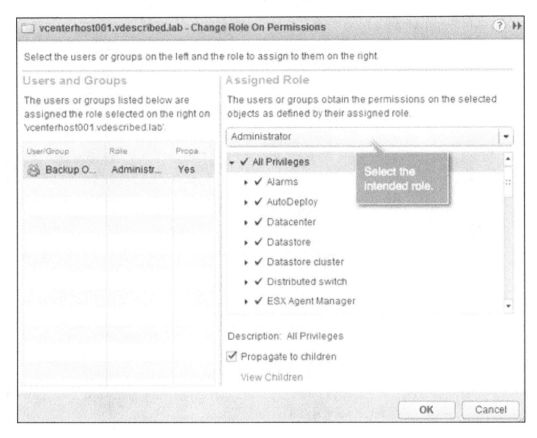

7. The **Permissions** tab will now show the newly added group/user:

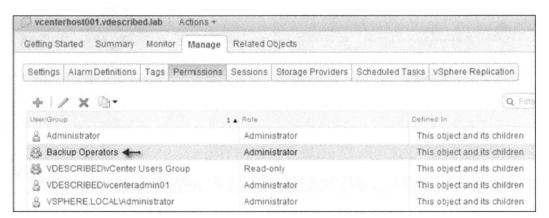

You should now be able to use vSphere Client, vSphere Web Client, or any other connection type (API) to connect to vCenter Server using the added user.

Deploying SSO for the vCenter Linked Mode

For two vCenter Servers to be in Linked Mode, they should share the same SSO security domain. This is achieved by using two available SSO deployment modes:

- ▶ vCenter Single Sign-On for an additional vCenter Server in an existing site
- ▶ vCenter Single Sign-On for an additional vCenter Server with a new site

These options are only made available when you start the SSO installer separately. The SSO installer initiated during the Simple Install doesn't expose these options for an obvious reason—that is, to keep the installation simple.

Deployment mode	Site name	Use case
SSO for an additional vCenter in an existing site	The same as the first site	Linked Mode—vCenters at the same site
SSO for an additional vCenter with a new site	A new site name	Linked Mode—vCenters at different sites

Getting ready

Before you begin the SSO installation, you need to do the following:

- ▶ Decide on the deployment mode based on how your environment is designed.
- ▶ Make sure that you have static IP addresses assigned and DNS entries created for the SSO VMs. The forward/reverse lookup of the FQDNs should also be verified.
- ▶ Make sure that SSO VMs are joined to the domain.

How to do it...

The following procedure will guide you through the steps required to deploy an SSO server in a way that enables support for the vCenter Linked Mode:

1. Start the vCenter Single Sign-On individual installer and click on **Next** to continue.
2. Accept the license agreement and click on **Next** to continue.

3. Review the prerequisites, check the results, and click on **Next** continue:

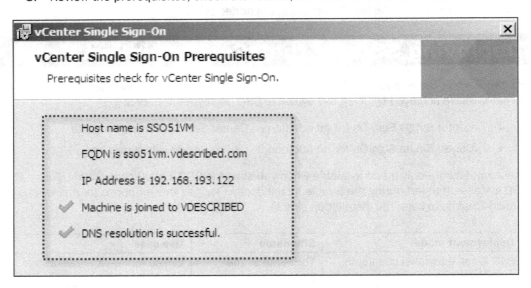

4. Choose a deployment mode and click on **Next** to continue:

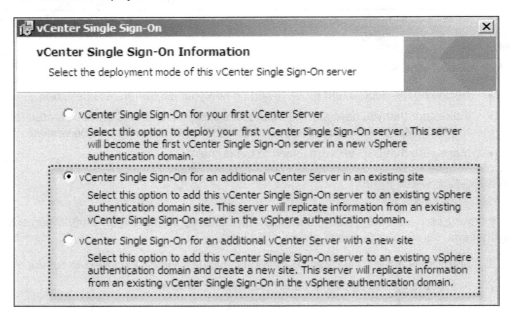

5. Enter the partner hostname, which is nothing but the IP address /FQDN of an existing SSO server. Also, supply the administrator's password for the SSO domain `vsphere.local`. Click on **Next** to continue:

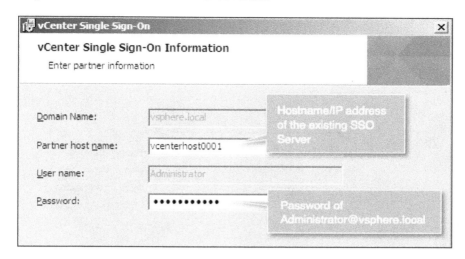

6. The next screen will prompt you to confirm that you accept the partner SSO server's certificate. Click on **Continue** to proceed:

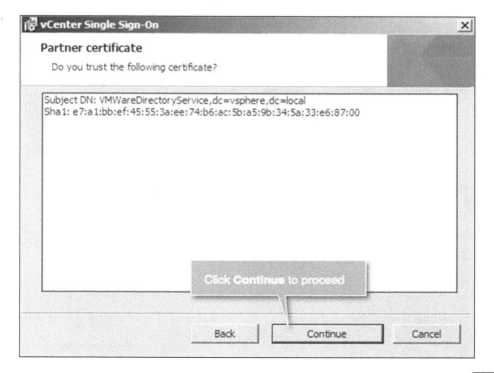

7. The inputs prompted on the next screen will depend on the SSO deployment mode selected.

It will prompt you to supply a new site name if the selected deployment mode is **vCenter Single Sign-On for an additional vCenter Server with a new site**:

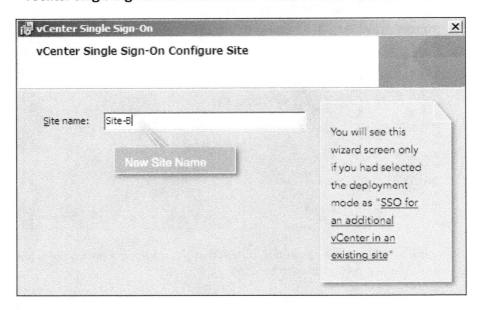

The wizard will ask for a site to join if you opted for the deployment mode to be **vCenter Single Sign-On for an additional vCenter Server in an existing site**:

8. On the Single Sign-On port settings' screen, you could change the default port if necessary; otherwise, click on **Next** to continue with the default port.

9. On the next screen, you can change the installation location by choosing a different destination folder if necessary; otherwise, click on **Next** to continue.

10. Review the install options and click on **Install** to begin the installation. Note that the decision to deploy a new lookup service will depend on the deployment type chosen. The following are the two possible final screens:

    If you chose vCenter Single Sign-On for an additional vCenter Server with a new site, the following screen appears:

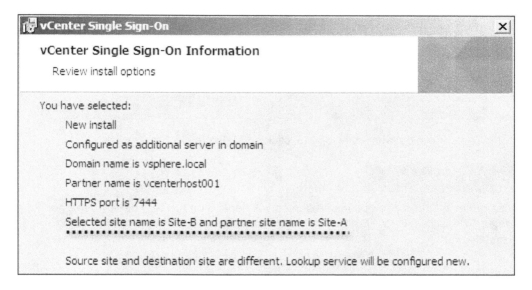

If you chose vCenter Single Sign-On for an additional vCenter Server in an existing site, the following screen appears:

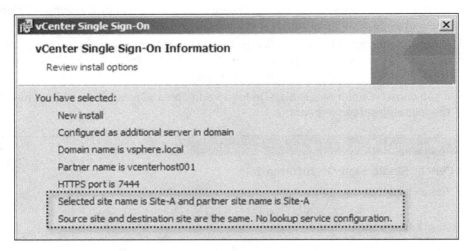

11. Once the installation is complete, click on **Finish** to exit the installer.

How it works...

During the installation, the options presented will depend on the SSO deployment mode selected. The following flowchart will depict the conditional options presented during the installation:

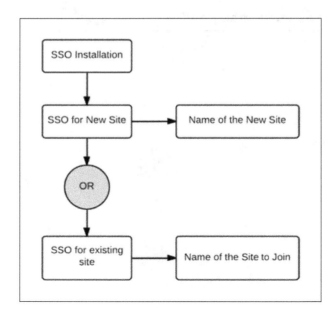

Once the installation is complete, the SSO instances will synchronize their directory `VMDir` between the partner instances. SSO partners in the same site can be configured for a failover using third-party load balancers. This is, however, not possible with SSO partners at two different sites.

Creating a vCenter Linked Mode group

The information in the previous section will help you deploy your SSO servers in a mode compatible with vCenter Linked Mode. Linked Mode provides a single pane of glass for administration when you have more than one vCenter Server in your environment. Keep in mind, though, that you can only include up to 10 vCenter Servers in a Linked mode group.

Getting ready

The vCenter Servers that you intend to link should be registered to the same Single Sign-On server domain. If it isn't, and if you want to register the vCenter components to the SSO server, use the instructions in the VMware Knowledge Base article KB#2033620 at `http://kb.vmware.com/kb/2033620`.

For instructions on how to deploy SSO for Linked Mode, read the *Deploying SSO for the vCenter Linked Mode* recipe.

To verify your current deployment mode, refer to the instructions in the article KB#2035817 at `http://kb.vmware.com/kb/2033620`.

There are several other prerequisites for the Linked Mode to work, and those are outlined in the *Linked Mode Prerequisites for vCenter Server* section of the *vSphere 5.5 Upgrade Guide*.

How to do it...

The following procedure will guide you through the steps required to create a vCenter Linked Mode group:

1. Exit all instances of the vSphere C# client. The vSphere Web Client session can remain active.
2. On the machine where you have vCenter installed, navigate to **Start | All Programs | VMware | vCenter Linked Mode Configuration** to bring up the vCenter installation wizard. Click on **Next** to continue.

3. Next, on the **Program Maintenance** screen, the option **Modify Linked Mode Configuration** is preselected. Click on **Next** to continue:

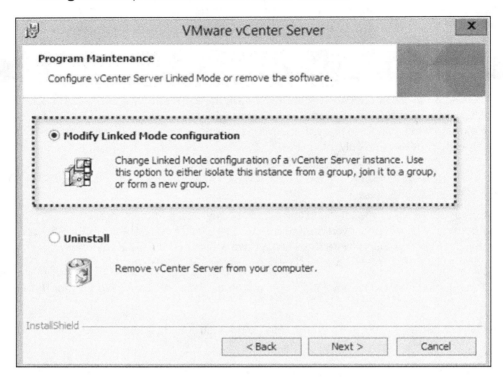

4. On the **Linked Mode configuration** screen, you will see **Join vCenter Server instance to an existing Linked Mode group or another instance** preselected. Click on **Next** to continue. Note that, if the current vCenter is not already part of the Linked Mode group, you will see **Isolate this vCenter Server instance from Linked Mode group** grayed out:

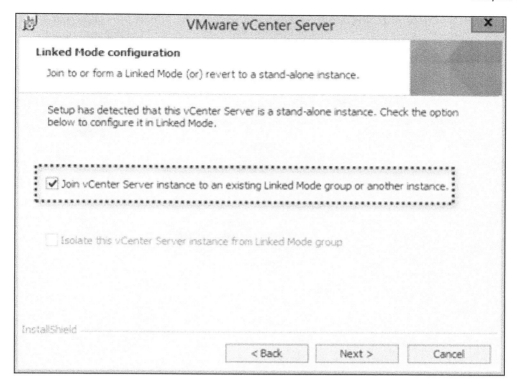

5. As stated earlier, the vCenter version should be the same for the Linked Mode configuration. Hence, there will be a warning informing you of this. Click on **OK** to exit the warning message:

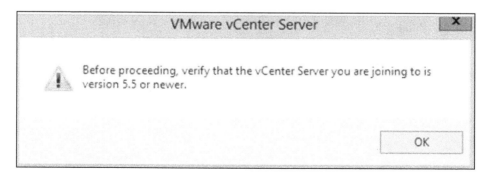

6. In the **Connect to a vCenter Server instance** window, supply the FQDN of the second vCenter instance and the LDAP port number 389. Click on **Next** to continue:

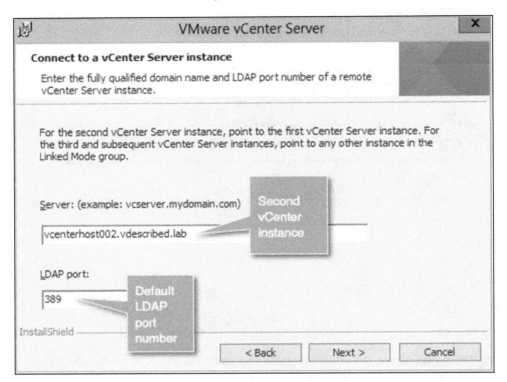

 The default ports for vSphere 5.5 can be found in the VMware Knowledge Base article KB#2051575 at http://kb.vmware.com/kb/2051575.

7. On the **Ready to modify Linked Mode settings** window, click on **Continue** to begin the configuration:

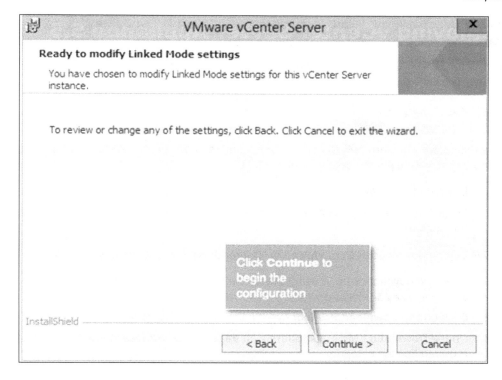

8. Once the configuration is complete, you will see the **Installation Completed** screen. Click on **Finish** to exit the wizard.

9. You should now be able to log in to any of the vCenters in the Linked Mode group and see all the other vCenters:

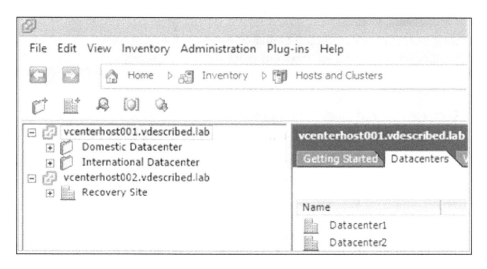

Deploying vCenter Server Appliance 5.5

The vCenter Server Appliance can either be downloaded as a single OVA, an ISO, or a ZIP package. The OVF, system disk, and data disk are also available as separate downloads.

Getting ready

In this recipe, we will learn how to deploy vCSA using the OVA. Here is a list of tasks that have to done before you begin the deployment of vCSA:

1. Download the OVA.
2. Create a DNS entry (DNS-A and PTR records) for the hostname that will be given to the appliance.

The OVA can be downloaded from VMware's vCenter Server downloads page:

1. Go to the downloads page using the following URL `https://my.vmware.com/web/vmware/downloads`.
2. Click on the **Download Product** hyperlink corresponding to VMware vSphere.
3. On the **Download VMware vSphere** web page, locate VMware vCenter under the required license category.
4. Click on the **Go to Downloads** URL corresponding to the vCenter entry to reach the web page titled **Download VMware vCenter Server**.
5. Download the vCenter Server OVA image.

How to do it...

The following procedure will guide you through the steps involved in deploying and configuring the VCSA. Let's assume you do not have any other vCenter managing your environment. In that case, you will be using the vSphere C# client to connect directly to an ESXi host and then deploy the OVF on to it.

1. Connect to an ESXi host using vSphere C# client.
2. Navigate to **File | Deploy OVF Template** to bring up the **Deploy OVF Template** wizard.
3. Browse and locate the downloaded OVF file and click on **Next** to continue.
4. On the next screen, review the details of the OVF template and click on **Next** to continue.
5. Supply a name for the appliance and click on **Next** to continue.
6. In the next screen, choose a datastore and also the disk provisioning method. The default is **Thick Provision Lazy Zeroed**. Click on **Next** to continue.

7. Select a virtual switch port group for the virtual appliance machine to connect to and then click on **Next** continue:

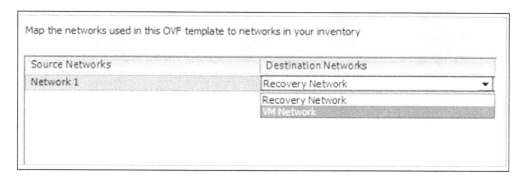

8. In the **Ready to Complete** screen, review the deployment settings and click on **Finish** to begin deploying the OVA.

9. Power on the VCSA VM after deployment. Once the bootup is complete, you will be presented with the VCSA welcome screen in the VM console. The management URL for the appliance can be accessed using the static IP address that was supplied to the deployment wizard:

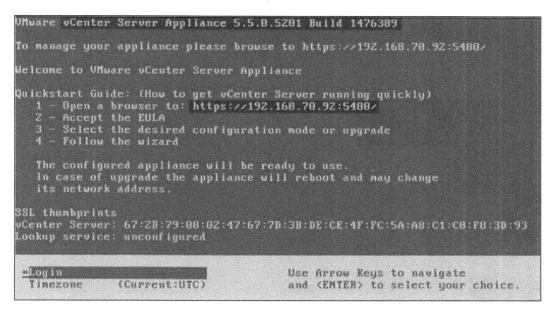

10. Connect to the appliance management URL `https://IPaddress:5480/`. You will be presented with a login screen for vCSA. The default credentials are `root` and `vmware`. Enter the credentials and click on **Login**:

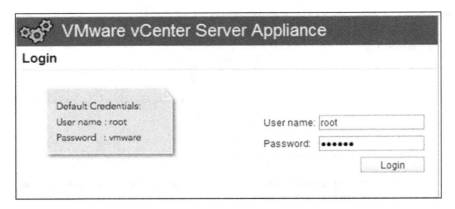

11. The moment you log in for the first time, you will be presented with the **vCenter Server Setup** wizard. Accept the license agreement and click on **Next** to continue.

12. In the **Configure Options** page, select **Set custom configuration** and click on **Next**:

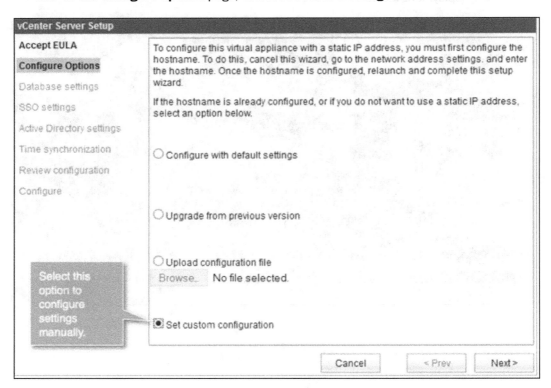

13. In the **Database settings** screen, select the database type as **embedded**. You can choose **Oracle** if you have prepared an Oracle database for use with vCSA. **MS SQL** is not supported by the appliance. Click on **Next** to continue:

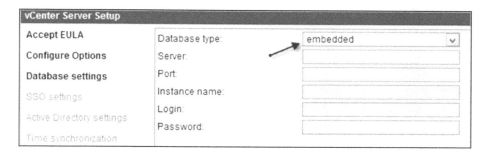

14. In the **SSO settings** screen, you could choose between using an embedded SSO or an external one. The inputs required will depend on the SSO deployment type (embedded or external) selected. For now, I have selected embedded. You will need to supply a password for the SSO administrator. Once done, click on **Next** to continue:

15. In the **Active Directory settings** screen, select **Active Directory Enabled** and supply the domain administrator/joiner user credentials:

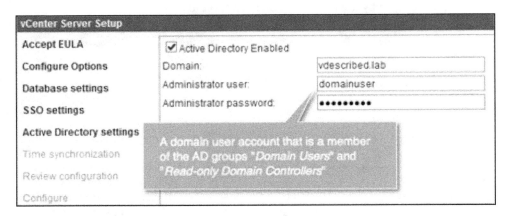

16. In the next screen, review the details and click on **Start** to begin the configuration:

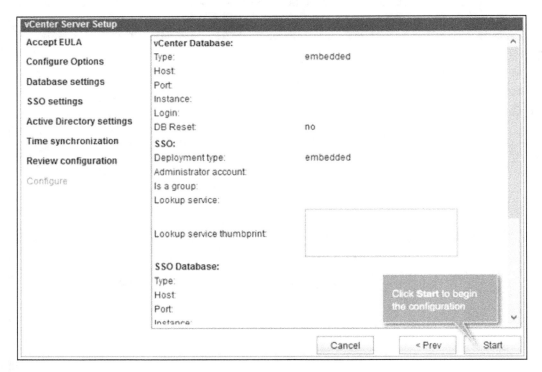

17. Once the configuration is complete, you should be able to connect to the vCenter Server using the SSO administrator user.

3
Using vSphere Host Profiles

In this chapter, we will cover the following recipes:

- ▶ Preparing a reference host
- ▶ Creating a Host Profile
- ▶ Exporting a Host Profile
- ▶ Importing a Host Profile
- ▶ Duplicating a Host Profile
- ▶ Attaching/detaching ESXi hosts to/from a Host Profile
- ▶ Verifying the profile compliance of an ESXi host
- ▶ Remediating an ESXI host for profile compliance
- ▶ Using Host Profiles to push a new configuration change

Introduction

It is of prime importance to make sure that every ESXi host in a cluster is configured identically to achieve operational efficiency at the cluster level. There is a lot of configuration that would go into an ESXi host after it is deployed. These include the general/advanced settings, storage and networking configuration, licensing, and so on. With the number of ESXi hosts that can be part of a cluster or vCenter increasing with every release of vSphere, the amount of work to be done manually will also increase.

With vSphere 4.1, VMware introduced a method to extract the configuration from an ESXi host and form a configuration template often referred to as a blueprint or golden image. Such a configuration template is called a vSphere Host Profile. Host Profiles help an administrator to maintain compliance of configuration standards on a set of ESXi hosts. They can also be used to make a configuration change to be pushed to all the hosts attached to the template, without the need to make the change on each of the hosts manually. For instance, if the NTP time source for environment has changed, then there is a need to make this change on every host using the time source. Such a change can be pushed via a Host Profile. Another example would be a change in the VLAN ID for the virtual machine network on a cluster of ESXi hosts configured with standard vSwitches. Since the hosts are using standard vSwitches, the VLAN ID should be manually changed on the virtual machine port group on each of the hosts in the cluster. This manual work can be avoided by editing the Host Profile and then pushing the VLAN ID change to the entire cluster.

So, what does a Host Profile look like, and what does it contain? Host Profiles once created are presented to the user as GUI objects in the vCenter Server. Host Profiles contain configuration policies that are either fetched from the reference host, or added to the Host Profile at a later stage.

A Host Profile can contain the following information:

- ▸ Advanced configuration settings
- ▸ General system settings
- ▸ Networking configuration
- ▸ Security and services
- ▸ Storage configuration

In this chapter, we will learn how to use the vSphere Host Profile to make the configuration of the ESXi host easier.

Preparing a reference host

A reference host is prepared so that its configuration can be extracted and saved to a Host Profile, which becomes the golden image. It is important that you take extra care in configuring the reference host since this configuration will be applied to the rest of the hosts in the cluster/environment. The following flow chart provides an overview of the procedure:

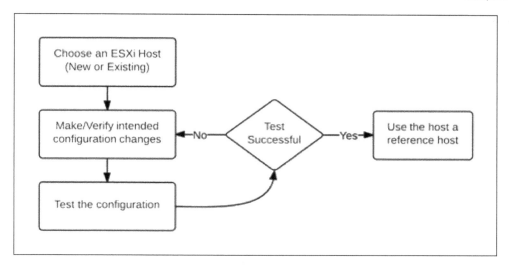

Getting ready

We need an ESXi host that is managed by the vCenter. This could be a newly installed ESXi or an existing ESXi host.

How to do it...

The following procedure will help you prepare a reference host for generating a Host Profile:

1. You can deploy a new ESXi host or use an existing host for this purpose.
2. Configure the basic/advanced/storage/network settings on your chosen host, as you will need them on all the other ESXi hosts.
3. Deploy and run a few virtual machines on the reference ESXi hosts and make sure that everything is functioning as expected. For instance, verify whether the VMs are reachable over the network.
4. If everything works as you want it to, then you have the reference host ready.

How it works...

A Host Profile, once created, would still be related to the reference host. New configuration changes can be made to the reference host and pushed to the Host Profile. Read the section *Using the Host Profile to push a new configuration change* for more details.

Creating a Host Profile

The Host Profile is created by extracting the host configuration information from the reference host. Once created, it will be listed as an object of the type Host Profile in the Host profiles **Objects** tab. Keep in mind that you will need access to a vCenter server to create Host Profiles.

Getting ready

Before you begin, make sure that you have identified a reference host to extract the configuration and form a template. For instructions on how to prepare a reference host, read the previous recipe *Preparing a reference host*.

How to do it...

The following procedure will guide you through the steps required to create a Host Profile:

1. Connect to the vCenter Server using the vSphere Web Client.

2. Go to the **Inventories** Home and navigate to **Rules and Profiles**.

3. Click on **Host Profiles** to bring up the Host Profile objects page.

4. Click on the Green **+** icon to start the **Extract Host Profile** wizard:

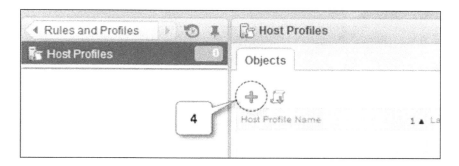

5. On the **Extract Host Profile** wizard screen, select the reference ESXi host, which will be used to form the Host Profile and click on **Next** to continue:

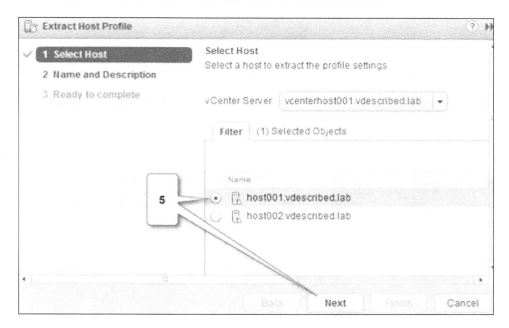

6. Supply a **Name** for the Host Profile and an optional **Description** and click on **Next** to continue:

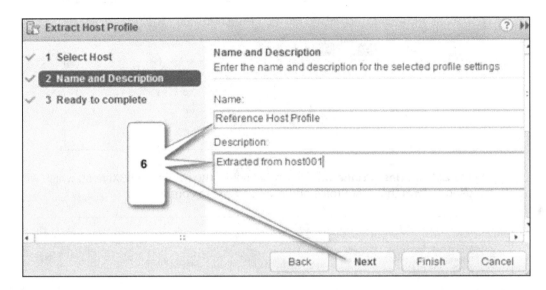

7. On the **Ready to complete** screen, click on **Finish** to create the Host Profile:

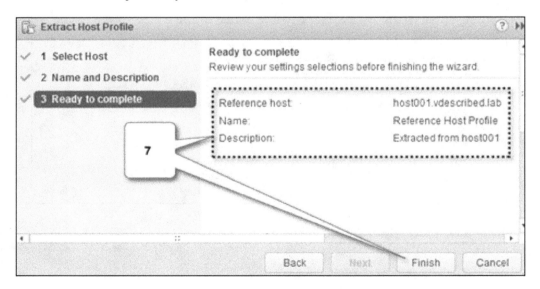

8. The **Recent Tasks** pane should show an **Extract Host Profile** task in progress and a **Create a Host Profile** task completed successfully.

How it works...

As mentioned previously, you can only create Host Profiles using the vCenter. This is because the object data corresponding to the Host Profiles created are saved in the vCenter server database.

Exporting a Host Profile

The vSphere Host Profiles can be exported to back up or transport the configuration. The exported data is stored in an XML data file with the extension (.vpf). Since this is an XML file, the contents of the file can be viewed using any text editor, so the passwords are not exported into this file.

How to do it...

The following procedure will guide you through the steps required to export or import Host Profiles:

1. Connect to the vCenter server using the vSphere Web Client.

2. Go to the vCenter Inventory **Home** tab and navigate to **Rules and Profiles | Host Profiles**.

3. Right-click on the Host Profile that you intend to export and go to **All vCenter Actions | Export Host Profile**.

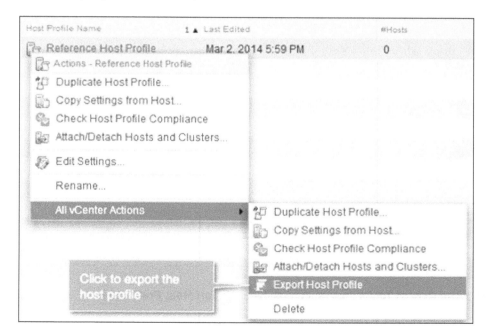

4. It should display a message window informing you that the administrator passwords have not been exported for security reasons. Click on **Save** and choose a location to the save the profile:

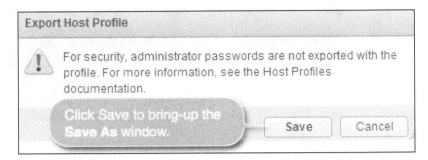

5. Choose the location and click on **Save** to save the file:

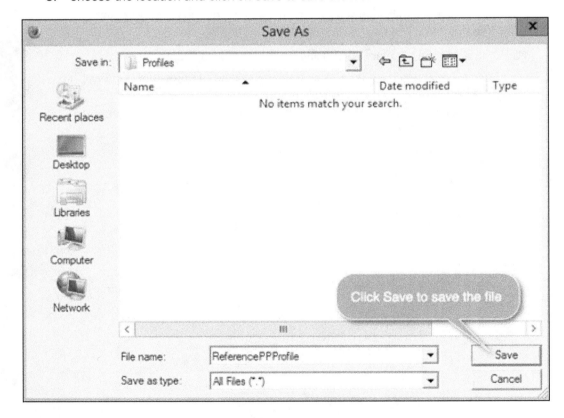

6. The **Recent Tasks** pane should show an **Export Host Profile** task completed successfully.

How it works...

When the export operation is initiated, it will extract the profile data and dump it into an XML data file with the extension (.vpf):

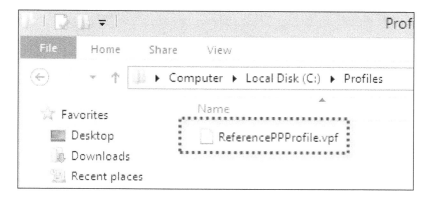

This file can then be imported into the vCenter Server as a Host Profile object.

 During the export operation, the newly formed Host Profile file (*.vpf) loses its association with the reference host it was originally extracted from.

Importing a Host Profile

The already exported Host Profile (.vpf) files can be imported into the vCenter. For instance, if you were to build a new data center in your environment which will be managed by a new vCenter and if the hosts in the new data center should be configured identically to an existing data center host, then a Host Profile from the existing data center can be exported and then imported into the new vCenter so that it can be applied to the new hosts.

How to do it...

The following procedure will guide you through the steps required to import a VPF file as a Host Profile object into the vCenter server:

1. Connect to the vCenter server using the vSphere Web Client.

2. Go to the vCenter Inventory Home tab and navigate to **Rules and Profiles | Host Profiles**.

3. Click on the Import a Host Profile icon to bring up the **Import Host Profile** window:

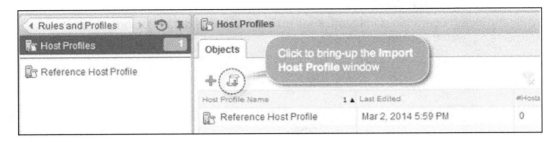

4. In the **Import Host Profile** window, click on **Browse** to locate and select the `.vpf` file. Specify a name and an optional description for the Host Profile and click on **OK** to begin importing the profile:

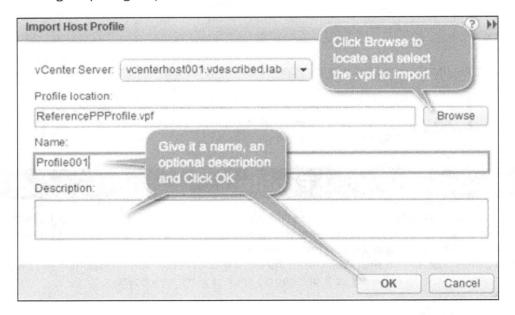

5. The **Recent Tasks** pane should show a **Create a Host Profile** task completed successfully.

How it works...

The import operation is similar to a create profile operation, the only difference being that in this case the configuration information is being fetched from an XML data file, instead of a running ESXi host. You will see an **Import a Host Profile** task in progress and a subsequent **Create a Host Profile operation** in the **Recent Tasks** pane. Unlike a Host Profile that is created from the reference host the imported Host Profile will not have a reference host associated with it.

Duplicating a Host Profile

An existing Host Profile can be cloned to create a duplicate of the same. This can be achieved by using the "Duplicate Host Profile" operation. Keep in mind that only a Host Profile with a reference host associated with it can be duplicated.

How to do it...

The following procedure will guide you through the steps required to duplicate an existing Host Profile:

1. Connect to the vCenter server using the vSphere Web Client.

2. Go to the vCenter Inventory Home tab and navigate to **Rules and Profiles** | **Host Profiles**.

3. Select the Host Profile that you intend to duplicate and click on the Duplicate Host Profile icon:

4. On the **Duplicate Host Profile** wizard screen, supply a name and an optional description for the duplicate profile and click on **Next** to continue:

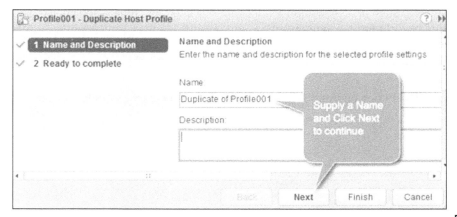

5. On the **Ready to complete** screen, click on **Finish** to create the duplicate Host Profile.

6. The **Recent Tasks** pane should show a **Duplicate Host Profile** task in progress and a subsequent **Create a Host Profile** task completed successfully.

How it works...

The Host Profile duplicate operation will create an exact duplicate of the original profile. Unlike the export operation, which discards the password data, the duplicate operation includes it. This is because the duplicate operation doesn't export the contents to a file.

Imported Host Profiles cannot be duplicated since they don't have a reference host associated with them. Attempts to do so will throw a warning indicating the same, as shown in the following screenshot:

However, copying the settings to it from a reference host creates the association so it can be duplicated.

Attaching/detaching ESXi hosts to/from a Host Profile

The whole purpose of creating a Host Profile is to automate large-scale configuration of ESXi hosts. Before you can apply a Host Profile to any ESXi host, there should be a way to associate the host with the Host Profile. This is done in the vCenter by attaching the ESXi hosts to the Host Profile. Such an association is subsequently used for compliance checks and remediating new configuration changes.

If for any reason, you decide not to associate a host with a particular Host Profile, then you could choose to detach the host from the Host Profile.

Both the attach/detach operations are performed using the same workflow wizard.

How to do it...

The following procedure will guide you through the steps required to attach/detach ESXi hosts' to/from a Host Profile:

1. Connect to the vCenter server using the vSphere Web Client.

2. Go to the vCenter Inventory **Home** tab and navigate to **Rules and Profiles | Host Profiles**.

3. Select the Host Profile to which you would like to attach the hosts and click on the Attach/Detach Hosts and Clusters icon, to bring up the **Attach/Detach Hosts and Clusters** wizard.

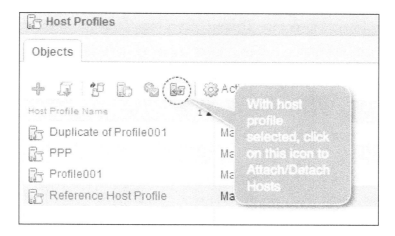

4. On the **Attach/Detach Host and Clusters** wizard screen, you can choose to attach an entire cluster of hosts or individual hosts and click on the **Attach** button to move the selection to the right pane. Detaching would require the items to be moved to the left pane:

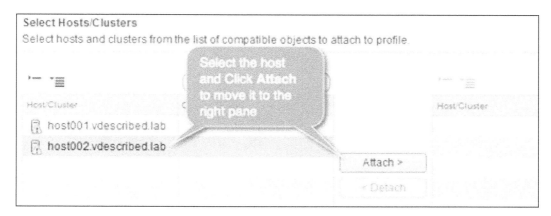

5. Move the selected hosts to the right pane and click on **Next** to continue.

6. In the **Customize host** screen, verify and modify the host specific information, if necessary. Once done, click on **Finish** to attach the selected host/cluster to the Host Profile.

7. You should see an **Attach Host Profile** task completed successfully in the **Recent Tasks** pane.

Verifying the profile compliance of an ESXi host

Once you have the ESXi hosts associated (attached) with a Host Profile of your choice, the host can be checked for compliance. The compliance check is done in the vCenter server.

In this section, you will learn how to check an ESXi host for compliance against an associated Host Profile.

How to do it...

The following procedure will guide you through the steps required to check an ESXi host for compliance:

1. Connect to the vCenter server using the vSphere Web Client.

2. Go to the vCenter Inventory **Home** tab and navigate to **Rules and Profiles | Host Profiles**.

3. Click on the Host Profile, to bring up the Host Profile specific page.

4. Navigate to **Monitor | Compliance** to see a list of ESXi hosts attached to the profile and their compliance status. If the compliance status of a host is **Unknown**, then it means it hasn't been checked for compliance yet:

5. Select the host and click on the Check Host Profile Compliance icon, to start the compliance check:

6. You should see a **Check Host Profile Compliance** task completed successfully in the **Recent Tasks** pane and the **Host Compliance** column should now indicate whether the host is compliant or non-compliant.

How it works...

Checking a host for compliance against an associated Host Profile will compare the host configuration with the configuration settings in the Host Profile. If any of the configuration policy/settings in the Host Profile are not present on the host, the host is tagged as non-compliant. Non-compliant hosts can be remediated to meet the configuration requirements.

You could also create a scheduled task to periodically run a Host Profile's compliance check on the hosts or the cluster attached to a Host Profile. This is done by selecting a Host Profile and then navigating to the **Manage | Scheduled Tasks** tab and creating a new scheduled task as shown in the following screenshot:

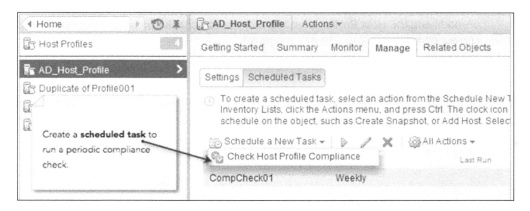

Remediating an ESXi host for profile compliance

An existing ESXi host or a newly added ESXi host, that is found to be noncompliant with a Host Profile, to which it has been attached, needs a configuration change to make it compliant. Such changes are automated with the help of the remediate operation. The remediate operation adds/removes/changes the configuration of the host to match the profile.

The following flow chart shows a general overview of the remediation process:

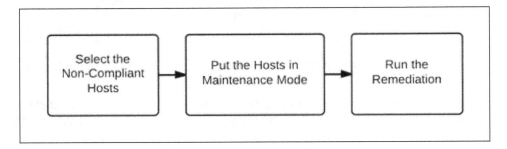

How to do it...

The following procedure will guide you through the steps required to remediate non-compliant ESXi hosts:

1. Connect to the vCenter server using the vSphere Web Client.

2. Go to the vCenter Inventory **Home** tab and navigate to **Rules and Profiles** | **Host Profiles**.

3. Click on the Host Profile, to bring up the Host Profile specific page.

4. Navigate to **Monitor | Compliance**, to see a list of ESXi hosts attached to the profile and their compliance status. If the host wasn't scanned for compliance attaching or modifying the Host Profile, then the compliance check should be initiated for the correct compliance status to the displayed.

5. Select the noncompliant host(s) and click on the Enter Maintenance Mode icon to put the host in maintenance mode.

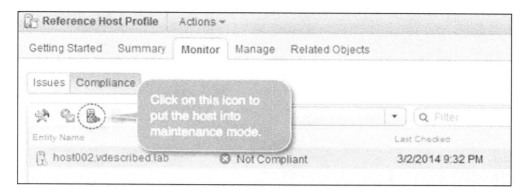

6. You will be prompted to confirm the maintenance mode operation. Click on **OK** to confirm:

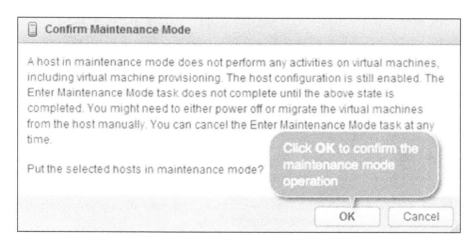

You should see an Enter maintenance mode operation completed successfully in the **Recent Tasks** pane.

7. Once in maintenance mode, click on the Remediate icon to bring up the remediation wizard:

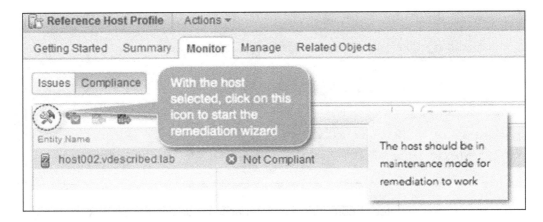

8. In the **Remediate host based on Host Profile** wizard, use the **Customize hosts** section to make host-specific changes only if necessary, and click on **Next** to continue.

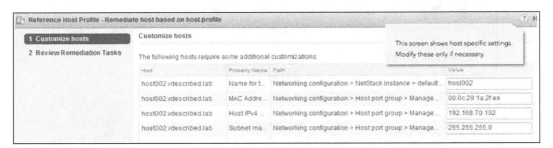

9. In the **Review Remediation Tasks** section, click on the host name to expand and review the changes that will be made to the host:

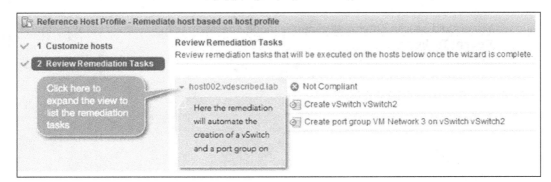

10. Click on **Finish** to begin the remediation.

11. The **Recent Tasks** pane should list an **Apply host configuration** and a **Check compliance** task completed successfully, and also list the host as compliant.

Using Host Profiles to push a new configuration change

The whole purpose of using Host Profiles is to effortlessly push the required configuration on to the ESXi hosts without the need for a manual configuration activity per ESXi host. This would not just come in handy when you deploy a new infrastructure but also when you want to push a new configuration to all the ESXi hosts.

The following flow chart shows a high— level overview of the whole procedure:

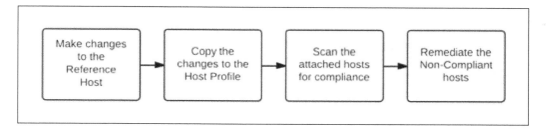

How to do it...

The following procedure will guide you through all the steps that have to be performed on the vCenter server to push a new configuration change, using Host Profiles:

1. Connect to the vCenter server managing the reference ESXi host and make the intended changes on the reference host. This can also be achieved by directly connecting to the ESXi host using the vSphere Web Client. However, since all the Host Profile activities are done using the vCenter server, I would suggest using it to avoid switching between the clients.

2. Go to the vCenter Inventory Home tab and navigate to **Rules and Profiles | Host Profiles**.

3. Select the Host Profile and click on the Copy settings from host icon to bring up the copy settings from host window containing a list of ESXi hosts to select from.

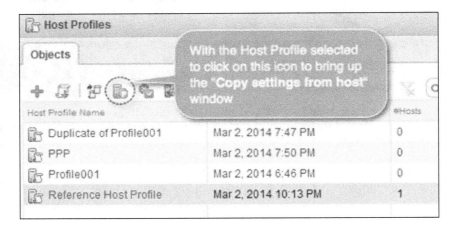

4. In the **Copy settings from host** window, select your reference host from the list and click on **OK**.

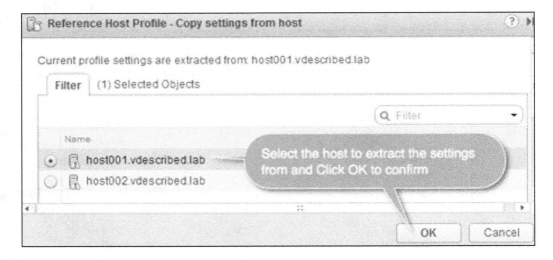

The **Recent Tasks** pane should show a **Copy settings from host** task in progress and eventually show an **Update Host Profile** task completed successfully.

5. Click on the Host Profile and navigate to its **Monitor | Compliance** tab to list all the hosts attached to it. The hosts will appear as compliant if they have been already remediated to match the original Host Profile.

6. Since we are pushing new changes, you will need to scan the hosts again for compliance. So, select the hosts and click on the **Check Host Profile Compliance** icon to run the compliance check.

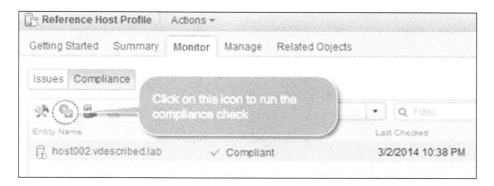

7. Once the compliance check completes, it should show that the hosts are non-compliant since we are pushing a new change to the hosts.

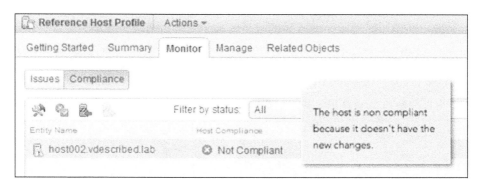

8. Plan and choose the host(s) that you want to remediate and put them in maintenance mode by clicking on the **Enter Maintenance Mode** icon.

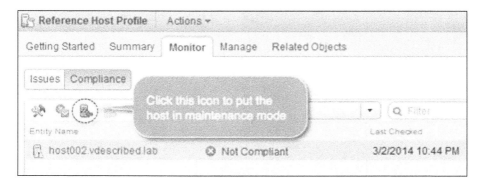

9. In the **Confirm Maintenance Mode** window, click on **OK**. The **Recent Tasks** pane should show an **Enter Maintenance Mode** task completed successfully.

10. Once the host is in maintenance mode, use the Remediate host icon to start the remediation wizard.

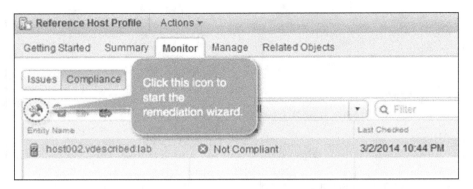

11. In the **Customize host** section, modify any specific host only if necessary. This section is particularly useful when you are applying a newly deployed ESXi host. Otherwise, leave the values unchanged and click on **Next** to continue.

12. In the **Review Remediate Tasks** section, click on the host name to expand the view to list all the changes that will be made to the host. Review them to make sure that those are changes you planned and click on **Finish** to begin the remediation.

13. You should see an **Apply host configuration** and a **Check compliance** task completed successfully in the **Recent Tasks** pane. If all the changes were successful, then the host should be listed as compliant.

4
Using ESXi Image Builder

In this chapter, we will cover the following recipes:

- ▸ Downloading an ESXi offline bundle
- ▸ Creating an image profile by cloning a predefined profile
- ▸ Removing an ESXi image profile
- ▸ Adding a VIB (software package) to an image profile
- ▸ Adding the HA VIB to the image profile
- ▸ Exporting an image profile as an ISO or offline bundle
- ▸ Creating an image profile from scratch
- ▸ Applying an image profile to the host

Introduction

As the name suggests, the ESXi Image Builder is used to build ESXi bootable images. It is particularly useful when there is a need to custom-build an ESXi image. For example, it can be used to custom-build ESXi images with an updated device driver and that can be used in your vSphere environment. The VMware Auto Deploy leverages the ability of the ESXi Image Builder to deploy stateless/stateful ESXi hosts. Read *Chapter 5*, *Using vSphere Auto Deploy* for more details.

The Image Builder requires the following data to proceed:

- ▸ An offline bundle of the ESXi packages
- ▸ Driver/software offline bundles from the vendor-partners you want to integrate
- ▸ VMware PowerCLI

Once you have all the required data software downloaded, you can use the ESXi Image Builder cmdlets to create an image profile using the ESXi offline depot.

The ESXi Image Builder doesn't need a separate installation. The vSphere PowerCLI has the Image Builder snap-in built into it. You should be ready to go once you have VMware vSphere PowerCLI 5.5 installed.

vSphere Installation Bundle

A **vSphere Installation Bundle** (**VIB**) is a packaged archive that contains a file archive, an XML configuration file, and a signature file. Most of the hardware OEMs package their device driver bundles as VIBs.

Image profiles

An image profile is a predefined or custom-defined set of VIBs that can be addressed as a package. All the VMware ESXi offline bundles will have more than one VMware-defined image profile. The image profiles are primarily used to deploy, upgrade, and patch auto-deployed ESXi servers. You will learn how to auto-provision ESXi hosts, in *Chapter 5, Using vSphere Auto Deploy*.

Offline bundles

An offline bundle is an archive that can either be the entire ESXi image or a driver bundle. It is a collection of VIBs and the corresponding metadata. It is the first thing that the Image Builder will need to perform any of its tasks. It is also referred to as a software depot by the vSphere PowerCLI. Refer to the following image:

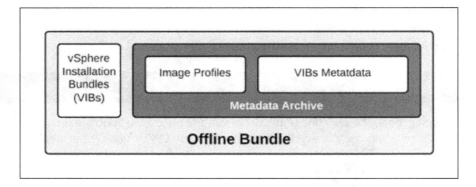

The metadata archive is a ZIP bundle containing the image profiles available with the bundle and the metadata for each of the VIBs included in the bundle.

An offline bundle is available for download from VMware or from the OEM's website for use with ESXi Image Builder.

Downloading an ESXi offline bundle

To auto-deploy an ESXi server, we need to have the ESXi offline bundle ready. The vanilla version of the offline bundle can be downloaded from VMware's website. Customized offline bundles from the server vendors are available for download from the vendor's website. They are also available at VMware's download page, under the **Drivers & Tools** tab and listed under the category **OEM Customized Installer CDs**.

How to do it...

You can download the ESXi 5.5 offline bundle from the VMware downloads page, under the VMware vSphere product category. Perform the following steps:

1. Go to the URL `http://myvmware.com/`.

2. Navigate to **Downloads | vSphere**.

3. Click on the **Go to downloads** hyperlink corresponding to the VMware ESXi 5.5 entry listed under your licensing type category.

   The following screenshot shows an offline bundle download entry. This one is for ESXi 5.5 Update 1:

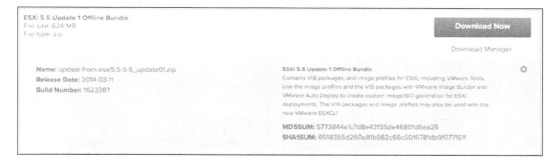

4. Copy the downloaded offline bundle (`.zip`) to a hard disk location in the virtual machine where vSphere PowerCLI is installed.

Creating an image profile by cloning a predefined profile

All the predefined image profiles available in an offline bundle are read-only. To customize such image profiles, you will need to clone them to form new image profiles. In this recipe, we will learn how to create a new image profile by cloning a predefined image profile.

How to do it...

The following procedure will guide you through the steps required to clone a predefined ESXi image profile available from an ESXi offline bundle.

It is a three-step process:

1. Adding an ESXi software depot.
2. Listing available ESXi image profiles.
3. Cloning a predefined ESXi image profile to form a new one.

Adding an ESXi software depot

The metadata of an ESXi offline bundle will have the definitions for the predefined image profiles contained in it. To be able to use the image profiles available in an offline bundle, it needs to be presented to a vSphere PowerCLI session as a software depot, which is nothing but PowerCLI's term for an offline bundle. The procedure to be followed is given next.

Before you begin, it is important to verify whether there are any software depots defined in the current session. This is recommended if you were about to use an already running PowerCLI session. If you have started a new PowerCLI session for the purpose of this task, then you won't have to do this verification.

To verify whether there are any existing software depots defined in the current PowerCLI session, issue the following command:

`$DefaultSoftwareDepots`

The output is as shown:

Note that the command has not returned any values, meaning that there are no software depots defined in the current session. If the needed software depot has already been added, then the command output will list the depot.

Before you add a software depot, make sure that you have the offline bundle saved to your local disk. The offline bundle can be downloaded from VMware's website or from the OEM's website. The bundle can either be an ESXi image or a driver bundle.

We already have the offline bundle downloaded to the `C:\Offline Bundles` directory as shown:

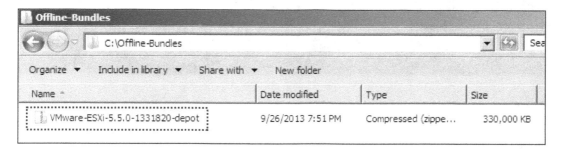

To add the downloaded software depot, issue the following command:

```
Add-EsxSoftwareDepot -DepotUrl C:\Offline-Bundles\VMware-ESXi-5.5.0-
1331820-depot.zip
```

The output is as follows:

```
PowerCLI C:\>
PowerCLI C:\>
PowerCLI C:\> Add-EsxSoftwareDepot -DepotUrl C:\Offline-Bundles\VMware-ESXi-5.5.
0-1331820-depot.zip  <—

Depot Url

zip:C:\Offline-Bundles\VMware-ESXi-5.5.0-1331820-depot.zip?index.xml

PowerCLI C:\>
```

Once the software depot has been successfully added to the PowerCLI session, the command `$DefaultSoftwareDepots` should list the newly added software depot as shown in the following screenshot:

```
PowerCLI C:\> $DefaultSoftwareDepots

Depot Url

zip:C:\Offline-Bundles\VMware-ESXi-5.5.0-1331820-depot.zip?index.xml

PowerCLI C:\> _
```

You could also just issue the command `Get-EsxSoftwareDepot` to list all the added depots (offline bundles). Here, you could use the newly added ESXi 5.5 bundle and a be2net driver bundle depot added as shown:

```
PowerCLI C:\>
PowerCLI C:\> Get-EsxSoftwareDepot

Depot Url
---------
zip:C:\Offline-Bundles\VMware-ESXi-5.5.0-1331820-depot.zip?index.xml
zip:C:\AutoDeploy-VIBS\DriverVIBS\be2net-4.4.231.0-offline_bundle-1028063.zi...


PowerCLI C:\>
```

Listing available image profiles

Once the software depot has been added, the next step is to list all the currently available image profiles from the depot by issuing the following command:

`Get-EsxImageProfile`

The output is as follows:

```
PowerCLI C:\>
PowerCLI C:\> Get-EsxImageProfile

Name                           Vendor         Last Modified    Acceptance Level
----                           ------         -------------    ----------------
ESXi-5.5.0-1331820-standard    VMware, Inc.   9/19/2013 6:...  PartnerSupported
ESXi-5.5.0-1331820-no-tools    VMware, Inc.   9/19/2013 6:...  PartnerSupported


PowerCLI C:\>
```

We see that there are two image profiles that the ESXi offline bundle offers. One is an ESXi image, with no VMware Tools ISOs bundled with it, and the other is the standard image with the VMware Tools ISOs bundled with it.

Cloning a predefined ESXi image profile to form a new one

Now that we know there are two image profiles available, the next step will be to clone the required image profile to form a new one. This is achieved by using the `New-ESXImageProfile` cmdlet. The cmdlet can be supplied with the name of the image profile as an argument. However, in most cases remembering the names of the image profiles available would be difficult. So, the best way to work around this difficulty is to define an array variable to hold the names of the image profiles and then the array elements (image profile names) can be easily and individually addressed in the command.

In this example, we will be using a user defined array variable `$profiles` to hold the output of the command `Get-EsxImageProfile`.

The following expression will save the output of the Get-ESXImageProfile command to the variable $profiles:

```
$profiles = Get-EsxImageProfile
```

The $profiles variable now holds the two image profile names as array elements [0] and [1] sequentially. Refer to the following screenshot:

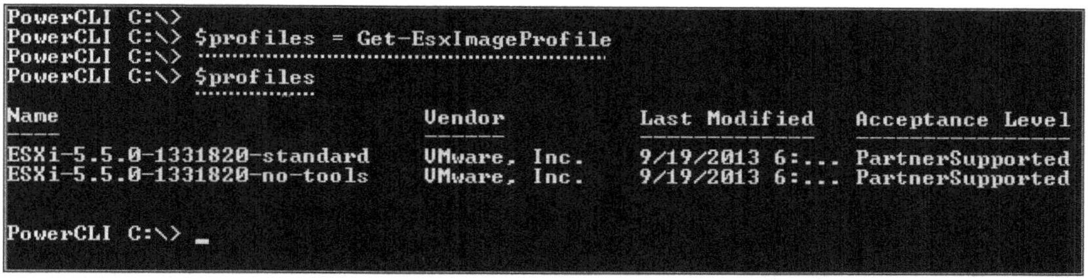

```
PowerCLI C:\>
PowerCLI C:\> $profiles = Get-EsxImageProfile
PowerCLI C:\> ........................................
PowerCLI C:\> $profiles
.............

Name                          Vendor          Last Modified   Acceptance Level
----                          ------          -------------   ----------------
ESXi-5.5.0-1331820-standard   VMware, Inc.    9/19/2013 6:... PartnerSupported
ESXi-5.5.0-1331820-no-tools   VMware, Inc.    9/19/2013 6:... PartnerSupported


PowerCLI C:\> _
```

Now the following command can be issued to clone the array element [0] ESXi-5.5.0-1331820-standard to form a new image profile, with the user-defined name Profile001:

```
New-EsxImageProfile -CloneProfile $profiles[0] -Name "Profile001" -Vendor
VMware
```

Once the previous command has been successfully executed, you can issue the Get-EsxImageProfile command to list the newly created image profile, as shown:

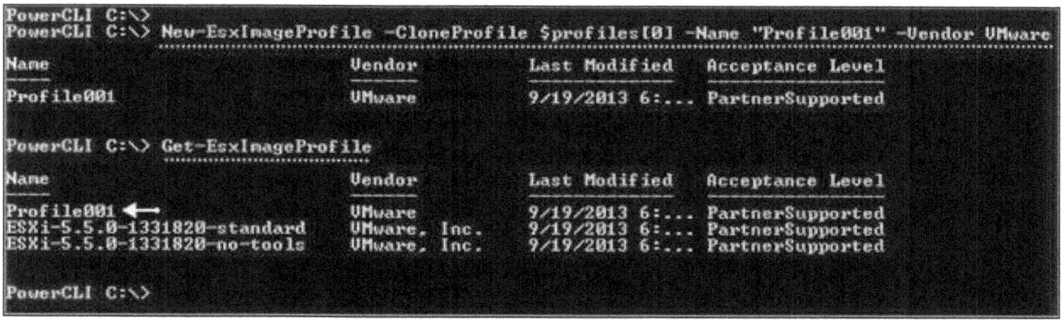

```
PowerCLI C:\>
PowerCLI C:\> New-EsxImageProfile -CloneProfile $profiles[0] -Name "Profile001" -Vendor VMware
.................................................................................................

Name                          Vendor          Last Modified   Acceptance Level
----                          ------          -------------   ----------------
Profile001                    VMware          9/19/2013 6:... PartnerSupported


PowerCLI C:\> Get-EsxImageProfile
.................................

Name                          Vendor          Last Modified   Acceptance Level
----                          ------          -------------   ----------------
Profile001 ◄───               VMware          9/19/2013 6:... PartnerSupported
ESXi-5.5.0-1331820-standard   VMware, Inc.    9/19/2013 6:... PartnerSupported
ESXi-5.5.0-1331820-no-tools   VMware, Inc.    9/19/2013 6:... PartnerSupported


PowerCLI C:\>
```

How it works...

The PowerCLI session will have a list of image profiles available from the added offline bundle. During the process of creating a new Image profile, you verify whether a software depot is already added to the PowerCLI session using the $DefaultSoftwareDepots command. If there are no software depots added, then the command will silently exit to the PowerCLI prompt. If there are software depots added, then it will list the depots added and show the path to its XML file. This is referred to as a depot URL.

The process of adding the software depot is pretty straightforward. First, you need to make sure that you have downloaded the required offline bundles to the server where you have PowerCLI installed. In this case, they were downloaded and saved to the `C:\AutoDeploy-VIBs` folder. Once the offline bundle is downloaded and saved to an accessible location, you can then issue the command `Add-EsxSoftwareDepot` to add the offline bundle as a depot to the PowerCLI session.

Once the software has been added, you can then list all the image profiles available from the offline bundle. Then the chosen image profile is cloned to form a new image profile that can then be customized by adding/removing VIBs. It can then be published as an offline bundle or an ISO. Now, there is a reason why we clone an image profile to customize it. The reason is that all predefined image profiles are read-only, hence they cannot be modified. Let's view the properties of a standard image profile:

```
PowerCLI C:\> Get-EsxImageProfile | Format-List

Name              : ESXi-5.5.0-1331820-standard  ◄──
Vendor            : VMware, Inc.
Author            :
Description       : The general availability release of VMware ESXi Server 5.5.0 brings whole new
                    levels of virtualization performance to datacenters and enterprises.
CreationTime      : 9/19/2013 6:07:00 AM
ModifiedTime      : 9/19/2013 6:07:00 AM
ReadOnly          : True  ◄──
VibList           : {misc-cnic-register 1.72.1.v50.1i-1vmw.550.0.0.1331820, scsi-lpfc820 8.2.3.1-1
                    29vmw.550.0.0.1331820, esx-base 5.5.0-0.0.1331820, esx-xlibs 5.5.0-0.0.1331820
                    ...}
AcceptanceLevel   : PartnerSupported
Guid              : b267d26c20f111e39d2e0050568dce39
Rules             :
StatelessReady    : True
```

Note that it shows that the `ReadOnly` attribute/property of the image profile is set to `True`. This is generally the case with all the default/predefined image profiles in an offline bundle. For this purpose, in this task you will need to clone the predefined profile to form a new one.

However, the cloned image profiles will have the `ReadOnly` property set to `False` by default, as shown in the following screenshot:

```
PowerCLI C:\> $profiles = Get-EsxImageProfile
PowerCLI C:\> $profiles[0] | Format-List

Name              : Profile001  ◄──
Vendor            : VMware
Author            :
Description       : The general availability release of VMware ESXi Server 5.5.0 brings whole new
                    levels of virtualization performance to datacenters and enterprises.
CreationTime      : 9/19/2013 6:07:00 AM
ModifiedTime      : 9/19/2013 6:07:00 AM
ReadOnly          : False  ◄──
VibList           : {misc-cnic-register 1.72.1.v50.1i-1vmw.550.0.0.1331820, scsi-lpfc820 8.2.3.1-1
                    29vmw.550.0.0.1331820, esx-base 5.5.0-0.0.1331820, lsi-msgpt3 00.255.03.03-1vm
                    w.550.0.0.1331820...}
AcceptanceLevel   : PartnerSupported
Guid              : da866dcf-5256-49ac-b580-7a3042e3d87e
Rules             :
StatelessReady    : True
```

See also

> ▸ For instructions on how to export an image profile, read the recipe *Exporting an image profile as an ISO or offline bundle*

Removing an ESXi image profile

Starting with the vSphere Image Builder 5.1, there is a cmdlet `Remove-EsxImageProfile` to remove an image profile. The command and its syntax remain the same with vSphere Image Builder 5.5 as well.

How to do it...

The following procedure will guide you through the steps required to remove/delete image profiles:

1. Issue the command `Get-EsxImageProfile` to list all the available image profiles.

```
PowerCLI C:\> Get-EsxImageProfile
..................................
Name                           Vendor          Last Modified      Acceptance Level
----                           ------          -------------      ----------------
Profile001                     VMware          9/19/2013 6:...    PartnerSupported
ESXi-5.5.0-1331820-standard    VMware, Inc.    9/19/2013 6:...    PartnerSupported
ESXi-5.5.0-1331820-no-tools    VMware, Inc.    9/19/2013 6:...    PartnerSupported
```

2. Identify the image profile to be deleted. In this example, we will delete the image profile `Profile001`.

3. Issue the `Remove-EsxImageProfile` command to delete the image profile:

   `Remove-EsxImageProfile -ImageProfile "Profile001"`

```
PowerCLI C:\>
PowerCLI C:\> Remove-EsxImageProfile -ImageProfile "Profile001"
PowerCLI C:\> ...........................................................
PowerCLI C:\> Get-EsxImageProfile
..................................
Name                           Vendor          Last Modified      Acceptance Level
----                           ------          -------------      ----------------
ESXi-5.5.0-1331820-standard    VMware, Inc.    9/19/2013 6:...    PartnerSupported
ESXi-5.5.0-1331820-no-tools    VMware, Inc.    9/19/2013 6:...    PartnerSupported

PowerCLI C:\> _
```
The Image Profile "Profile001" is no longer listed, confirming the deletion.

How it works...

The `Remove-EsxImageProfile` command will only delete the image profile from the current vSphere PowerCLI session. However, it is important to know that you can't remove an image profile from a read-only software depot. For example, the predefined image profiles available in the ESXi offline bundle cannot be removed.

Adding a VIB (software package) to an image profile

When there is a need to patch an auto-deployed ESXi server with a newer device driver version, you will have to modify an image profile in use so you can add an updated driver to it. Once the driver VIBs have been added to the image profile, it can then be used to redeploy the same ESXi servers.

Getting ready

To add VIBs to an ESXi image profile, the image profile should meet the following requirements:

- ▶ The image profile should not be set to read-only.
- ▶ The image profile should not be assigned to hosts. This is because the image profiles assigned to hosts are locked and thus do not allow you to add VIBs to them.
- ▶ The VIBs shouldn't conflict with any of the existing VIBs in the profile. If there is such a conflict, the addition of the VIB to the profile will not be allowed and a message indicating this will be displayed in the PowerCLI console.
- ▶ Install VIBs from only one OEM vendor at a time.

Image Builder will perform a validation when VMware VIBs are added. However, it does not perform any validation when partner VIBs are added.

The following flowchart depicts the procedure involved in adding a driver VIB to an ESXi image profile:

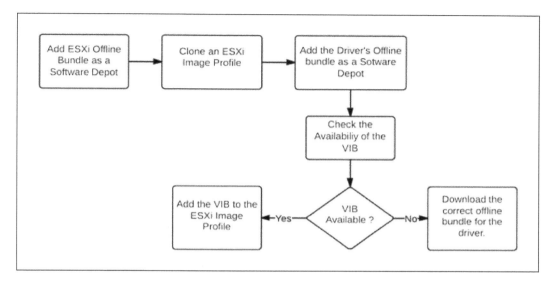

How to do it...

The following procedure will guide you through the PowerCLI procedure to add a VIB to an ESXi image profile:

1. Add the ESXi offline bundle as a software depot to the PowerCLI session. This is done using the following command:

   ```
   Add-EsxSoftwareDepot -DepotUrl C:\AutoDeploy-VIBS\ESXi500-
   201111001.zip
   ```

2. Keep in mind that all predefined image profiles are read-only, hence they cannot be modified. Clone the intended predefined image profile. Cloned image profiles will have the ReadOnly flag set to False. For instructions on how to clone an image profile, read the recipe *Creating an image profile by cloning a predefined profile*.

3. To add the driver's VIBs to an image profile, you need to procure the driver's offline bundle and present that to the PowerCLI session using the Add-ESXSoftwareDepot command.

4. In this example, we will be adding the offline bundle containing the network function driver for the Emulex OneConnect OCe10102 10GbE adapter. The driver's offline bundle has been downloaded and saved to the `C:\AutoDeploy-VIBS\DriverVIBS` folder.

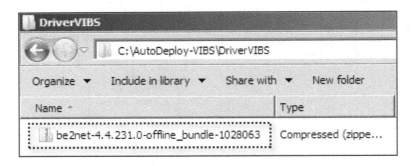

5. Now, add this driver's offline bundle to the software depot by issuing the following command:

```
Add-EsxSoftwareDepot -DepotUrl C:\AutoDeploy-VIBS\DriverVIBS\
be2net-4.4.231.0-ofline_bundle-1028063.zip
```

6. Once the driver's offline bundle has been presented to the PowerCLI session as a software depot, the next step is to check whether the offline bundle has the required VIBs (in this case, the Emulex driver) in it. This can be achieved by issuing the following command:

```
Get-EsxSoftwarePackage -Vendor "Emulex"
```

```
PowerCLI C:\> Get-EsxSoftwarePackage -Vendor "Emulex"

Name                    Version                        Vendor    Creation Date

net-be2net              4.4.231.0-10EM.500.0.0.472560  Emulex    1/12/2013 2:4...

PowerCLI C:\>
```

7. Now it is very important to be aware of any package dependencies or conflicts. This information pretty much helps you decide whether to go ahead with the inclusion of the VIB in the ESXi image profile or not.

Information regarding that can be obtained by issuing the following command:

```
Get-EsxSoftwarePackage -Name net-be2net -Vendor "Emulex" | Format-List
```

The output obtained is as follows:

8. Once you have verified that there aren't any dependencies or conflicts that can affect the functioning of the driver/hypervisor, you then decide to go ahead with including the package in the image profile. We can issue the following command to add the VIB to the image profile:

```
Add-EsxSoftwarePackage -ImageProfile Profile001 -SoftwarePackage net-be2net
```

The output is as follows:

9. It is important to verify that the VIB (driver package) has been added successfully to the ESXi image profiles. This can be achieved by issuing the following script:

```
Get-EsxImageProfile "Profile001" | Select -ExpandProperty viblist
| where { $_.Name -like "net-be2net"}
```

```
PowerCLI C:\> Get-EsxImageProfile "Profile001" | Select -ExpandProperty viblist | where ( $_.Name
-like "net-be2net")

Name                    Version                         Vendor      Creation Date
----                    -------                         ------      -------------
net-be2net              4.6.100.0v-1vmw.550.0.0.133...  VMware      9/19/2013 6:0...

PowerCLI C:\> _
```

We can see that net-be2net, the Emulex driver package (VIB), is now part of the ESXi Image profile Profile001.

> Running the command Get-EsxImageProfile "Profile001" | Select -ExpandProperty viblist will list all the VIBs in the image profile.

10. Do not exit the PowerCLI session at this stage. If you do so, you will lose the newly formed image profile, as it is still in memory. You should export the new image profile as an ISO or as an offline bundle for future use. Read the recipe *Exporting an image profile as an ISO or offline bundle* for more instructions.

There's more...

To remove a VIB from an image profile, issue the following command:

```
Remove-EsxSoftwarePackage -ImageProfile Profile001 -SoftwarePackage net-
be2net
```

Adding the HA VIB to the image profile

If you are deploying stateless ESXi hosts using vSphere Auto Deploy, then you should be packaging the vSphere HA FDM VIB into the image profile; otherwise, you won't be able to enable HA on the auto-deployed hosts.

How to do it...

The following procedure will guide you through the steps required in adding the FDM VIB to the image profile:

1. Use the cmdlet `Connect-VIServer` to add the vCenter server to the PowerCLI session:

    `Connect-VIServer -Server vcenterhost001 -User Administrator -Password pass123`

2. Add the ESXi offline bundle to the session:

    `Add-EsxSoftwareDepot -DepotUrl C:\Offline-Bundles\VMware-ESXi-5.5.0-1331820-depot.zip`

3. Add the vSphere HA depot to the session. The vSphere HA depot is at `http://IP or FQDN of the vCenterhost/vSphere-HA-depot`:

    `Add-EsxSoftwareDepot http://vcenterhost001/vSphere-HA-depot`

4. Clone and create a new image profile to customize. Read the recipe *Creating an image profile by cloning a predefined profile* for instructions.

5. Add the FDM VIB `vmware-fdm` to the new image profile:

    `Add-EsxSoftwarePackage "vmware-fdm" -ImageProfile Profile001`

6. Export the image profile to a ZIP archive, so that the customization is not lost when you exit the Power CLI Session. Read the recipe *Exporting an image profile as an ISO or offline bundle*.

7. The image profile can now be used in an Auto Deploy rule. For instructions on how to create auto deploy rules, read *Chapter 5, Using vSphere Auto Deploy*.

Exporting an image profile as an ISO or offline bundle

The VMware PowerCLI session will not retain the image profile details upon its exit. If you need to preserve a customized profile that you created, you will have to export it as an offline bundle (ZIP or ISO). When you start a new VMware PowerCLI session, you can just add the offline bundle back to the software depot.

How to do it...

The following procedures will guide you through the steps required to export an image profile to an ISO or a ZIP archive:

1. To export an existing image profile to an ISO, issue the following command:

   ```
   Export-EsxImageProfile -ImageProfile "Profile001" -ExportToIso
   -FilePath C:\AutoDeploy-VIBS\Exported\Profile001.iso
   ```

2. To export an existing image profile to an offline bundle, issue the following command:

   ```
   Export-EsxImageProfile -ImageProfile "Profile001" -ExportToBundle
   -FilePath C:\AutoDeploy-VIBS\Exported\Profile001.zip
   ```

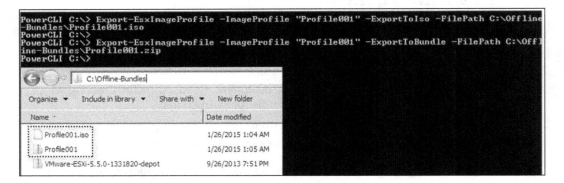

How it works...

Exporting to an ISO is used when you want to use the customized ESXi image to build an ESXi host by booting off that ISO. The export to ZIP option is used if you want to use the customized image as an offline bundle. Keep in mind that only ZIP bundles can be imported as software depots into a PowerCLI session.

Creating an image profile from scratch

When creating an image profile from scratch, you will have to identify the software packages you need to be part of the image. This means that, unlike customizing an existing image, you will create a new one with only what you need, so that you don't have to go through the process of removing software packages from an image profile.

 Pay careful attention to dependencies and acceptance levels when you create an image profile from scratch.

Getting ready

Read the recipes *Downloading an ESXi offline bundle, Creating an image profile by cloning a predefined image profile*, and *Adding a VIB (software package) to an image profile* as a preparation before you start learning how create an image from scratch.

How to do it...

The following procedure will guide you through the steps required to create an image profile from scratch:

1. Use the `Add-EsxSoftwareDepot` cmdlet to add all the needed offline bundles to the vSphere PowerCLI session.

   `Add-EsxSoftwareDepot C:\AutoDeploy-VIBS\ESXi500-201111001.zip`

2. Issue the `Get-EsxSoftwareDepot` cmdlet to verify that the offline bundles have been added successfully.

3. Assign the output of the `Get-EsxSoftwareDepot` command to a user-defined variable:

   `$softdepot = Get-EsxSoftwareDepot`

4. Use the `Get-EsxSoftwarePackage` cmdlet to list the needed software packages from the correct depot. Filter the results as needed and assign them to a variable. In this example, let's list all the packages released after 1/5/2013 (mm/dd/yyyy) by issuing the following command:

   `Get-EsxSoftwarePackage -SoftwareDepot $softdepot[0] -CreatedAfter 1/5/2013`

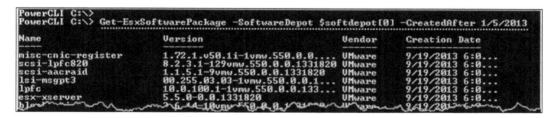

5. Assign this output to a user-defined variable:

   `$afterMay2013 = Get-EsxSoftwarePackage -CreatedAfter 1/5/2013 -SoftwareDepot $softdepot[0]`

6. Use the `New-EsxImageProfile` cmdlet to create a new image profile by supplying `Name`, `Vendor`, and `AcceptanceLevel`:

```
New-EsxImageProfile -NewProfile -Name "PostMay2013" -Vendor
"vDescribed" -SoftwarePackage $afterMay2013 -AcceptanceLevel
CommunitySupported
```

```
PowerCLI C:\>
PowerCLI C:\> New-EsxImageProfile -NewProfile -Name "PostMay2013" -Vendor "vDescribed" -SoftwareP
ackage $afterMay2013 -AcceptanceLevel CommunitySupported

Name                          Vendor           Last Modified     Acceptance Level
----                          ------           -------------     ----------------
PostMay2013                   vDescribed       1/26/2015 1:...   CommunitySupported


PowerCLI C:\>
```

7. Export the image profile to an ISO or offline bundle:

```
Export-EsxImageProfile -ImageProfile "PortMay2013" -ExportToBundle
-FilePath C:\Offline-Bundles\PostMay2013.zip.
```

How it works...

It creates an ESXi image from scratch and helps to reduce the amount of data in terms of unnecessary drivers and software packages.

See also

▶ For information regarding the structure of an image profile, read the section *Structure of ImageProfile, SoftwarePackage, and ImageProfileDiff Objects in the vSphere Installation and Setup* Guide for vSphere 5.5 at page 228; this document can be found at `http://bit.ly/vSphere55_install_guide`

Applying an image profile to the host

The whole purpose of creating an image profile is to assign it to a host and apply it. This is particularly useful when performing upgrades or driver updates on auto-deployed ESX servers.

Getting ready

Read the recipes *Downloading an ESXi offline bundle, Creating an image profile by cloning a predefined image profile*, and *Adding a VIB (software package) to an image profile* as a preparation before you start learning how to apply an image profile to an ESXi host.

How to do it...

The following procedure will guide you through the steps required to assign and apply an image profile to an ESX server:

1. Use the cmdlet `Connect-VIServer` to add the vCenter server to the PowerCLI session:

    Connect-VIServer -Server vcenterhost001 -User Administrator -Password pass123

2. Use the `Get-VMHost` cmdlet to fetch a list of ESX servers in `Maintenance` mode:

    Get-VMHost -State Maintenance

3. Save the output of the `Get-VMHost` command to a user-defined variable:

    $esxhost = Get-VMHost -State Maintenance

4. Use the `Apply-EsxImageProfile` cmdlet to apply the image profile to the ESX servers:

    Apply-ESXImageProfile -ImageProfile "Profile001" -Entities $esxhost

```
PowerCLI C:\>
PowerCLI C:\> Apply-ESXImageProfile -ImageProfile "Profile001" -Entities $esxhost
Downloading tools-light 5.5.0-0.0.1331820
Download finished, uploading to AutoDeploy...
Upload finished.
PowerCLI C:\>
```

5. Check whether the auto deployed ESX server is compliant with the created profile:

    Test-DeployRuleSetCompliance -VMHost $esxhost

6. If there are servers that are non-compliant, assign the compliance test output to a user-defined variable and then use that to do the repair (remediate) operation:

    $compliance_result = Test-DeployRuleSetCompliance -VMHost $esxhost

7. Once done, use the cmdlet `Repair-DeployRuleSetCompliance` to remediate the ESXi server:

    Repair-DeployRuleSetCompliance $compliance_result[0]

8. Once you are done with working on the vCenter server, it is important to make sure that you disconnect the session as a best practice and to clear idle sessions:

    Disconnect-VIServer -Server vcenterhost001

How it works...

Applying an image profile to an ESXi host is a way to update software changes, such as a driver update. The ESXi hosts need to be in maintenance mode for this to be done. Although the host is checked for compliance and remediated, the software change (for example, the inclusion of a newer device driver version) is not immediately seen by the ESXi host. The ESXi host will load the updated image into memory only during its next reboot.

5
Using vSphere Auto Deploy

In this chapter, we will cover the following recipes:

- ▸ Installing an Auto Deploy server
- ▸ Configuring a TFTP server with Auto Deploy files
- ▸ Configuring the DHCP server for PXE boot
- ▸ Testing the PXE boot configuration
- ▸ Preparing VMware PowerCLI for first use
- ▸ Preparing vSphere Auto Deploy for provisioning
- ▸ Choosing an ESXi Image Profile to deploy
- ▸ Creating a Host Profile
- ▸ Creating a deploy rule
- ▸ Activating a deploy rule
- ▸ Testing Auto Deploy
- ▸ Enabling Stateless Caching
- ▸ Performing an Auto Deploy stateful install

Introduction

In a large environment, deploying and upgrading ESXi hosts is an activity that requires a lot of planning and manual work. For instance, if you were to deploy a set of 50 ESXi hosts in an environment, then you might need more than one engineer assigned to perform this task. The same would be the case if you were to upgrade or patch ESXi hosts. The upgrade or the patching operation should be done on each host. Of course, you have vSphere update manager that can be configured to schedule, stage, and remediate hosts, but again the process of remediation would consume considerable amount of time, depending on the type and size of the patch. VMware have found a way to reduce the amount of manual work and time required for deploying, patching, and upgrading ESXi hosts. They call it vSphere Auto Deploy. In this chapter, you will learn not only to design, install, and configure the vSphere Auto Deploy solution, but also to provision ESXi hosts using it.

vSphere Auto Deploy architecture

vSphere Auto Deploy is a web server component which once configured can be used to quickly provision a large number of the ESXi hosts without the need to use the ESXi installation image to perform an installation on the physical machine. It can also be used to perform the upgrade or patching of the ESXi hosts without the need for vSphere update manager. Now, how is this achieved? vSphere Auto Deploy is a centralized web server component that lets you define rules that govern how the ESXi servers are provisioned. It however cannot work on its own. They are a few other components that play a supporting role for Auto Deploy to do its magic.

So, let's review the following components that play a role in an Auto Deployed infrastructure:

-   DHCP server (with the scope options 66 and 67 configured)
-   TFTP Server
-   Auto Deploy Server
-   Hosts with Network Boot (PXE) Enabled in the BIOS

It is important to have a brief understanding about how Auto Deploy works:

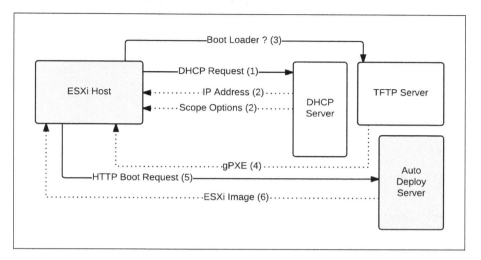

The **ESXi Host** first begins to network boot by requesting for an IP address from the **DHCP Server**. The **DHCP Server** responds with an IP address and the DHCP scope options providing the details of the **TFTP Server**. The **ESXi Host** then loads the **gPXE** boot image from the **TFTP Server** to bootstrap the machine and subsequently sends an **HTTP Boot Request** to the **Auto Deploy Server**, to load an **ESXi Image** into the host's memory. The image is chosen based on the rules created at the **Auto Deploy Server**.

Preparing a vSphere environment for vSphere Auto Deploy

Like with any other solution, it is important to lay the foundation, so that the implementation of the solution would go as planned. In this section, we will discuss the steps required to prepare a vSphere environment to support the use of vSphere Auto Deploy.

We need the following components configured for an ESXi host to be auto deployed:

- ▸ vSphere Auto Deploy Server
- ▸ Servers with PXE-enabled BIOS (and NICs)
- ▸ A DHCP server
- ▸ A TFTP Server
- ▸ vSphere Host Profiles configured at the vCenter Server.

Installing an Auto Deploy server

VMware vSphere Auto Deploy server as a solution is not available as a separate download. It is packaged with the vCenter installation image. The Auto Deploy server can be installed either on the same machine running the vCenter server, or on a separate machine deployed specifically for its purpose.

How to do it...

The following procedure will guide you through the steps required to install Auto Deploy server:

1. You can start the installation wizard by clicking on the **Install** button on the vSphere installation DVD welcome screen, to bring up the **vSphere Auto Deploy** install wizard.

2. The installer extracts the MSI package and presents you with the **Welcome to the Installation Wizard for vSphere Auto Deploy** window. Click on **Next** to continue.

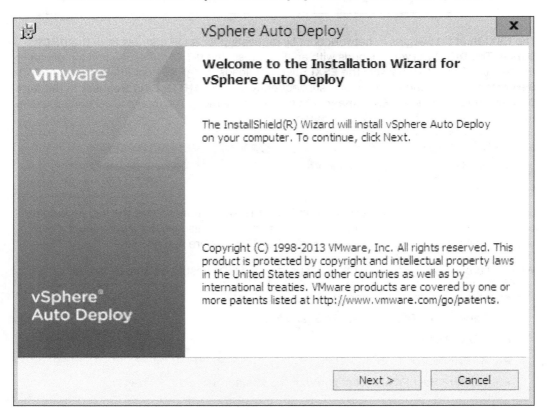

3. Accept the VMware End User License Agreement and click on **Next** to continue.

4. In the **Destination Folder** wizard screen, you can choose alternative locations for the installation directory and the Auto Deploy repository directory:

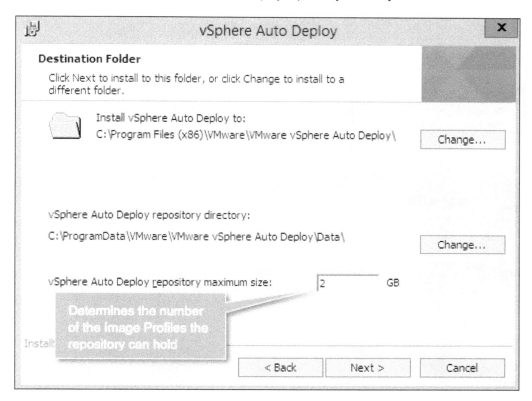

 The default size of the Auto Deploy repository is 2 GB, which is as per the best practice to allow enough room in the repository for four image profiles. Each image profile requires approximately 350 MB of free repository space.

5. You can choose to change these settings on this screen during the installation. In this example, I will proceed with the default settings. Click on **Next** to continue.

6. On the next screen, supply the vCenter server's IP/FQDN and its credentials. In this case, I have used the administrator's credentials, but it is recommended to use a service account. Click on **Next** to continue.

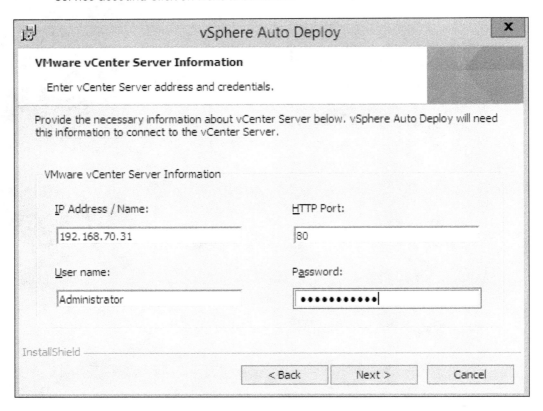

7. If you are prompted to trust the SSL certificate, then click on **Yes**.

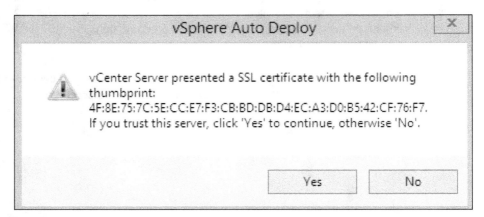

8. The default Server Port and Management Port numbers can be modified if required; otherwise, leave them at their default values and click on **Next** to continue.

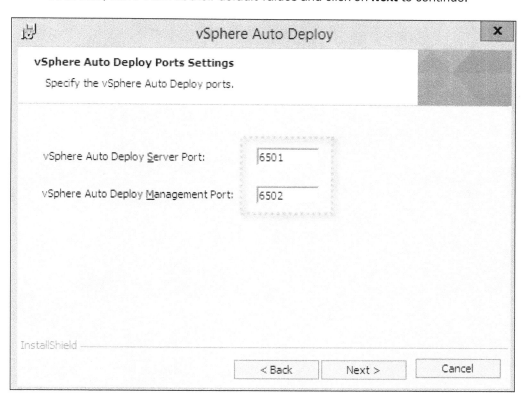

9. Specify how vSphere Auto Deploy should be identified on the network. You can choose between the IP address or FQDN of the vCenter server. Click on **Next** to continue.

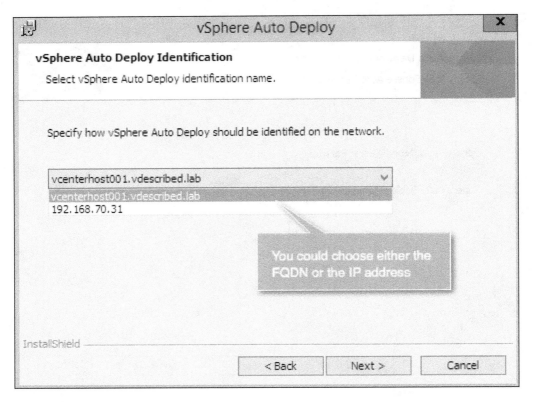

10. On the next screen, click on **Install** to begin the installation.

11. Once the installation is complete, connect to the vCenter server using the vSphere Client. The Inventory Home screen will show **Auto Deploy** under **Administration** as shown in the following screenshot:

 Note that Auto Deploy cannot be accessed from the vSphere Web Client.

Configuring a TFTP Server with Auto Deploy files

Trivial File Transfer Protocol (**TFTP**) is primarily used to exchange configuration or boot files between machines in an environment. It is relatively simple and provides no authentication mechanism. The TFTP server component can be installed and configured on a Windows or Linux machine.

Getting ready

There are many freeware TFTP servers on the Internet to choose from. I have deployed WinAgents TFTP server manager available at `http://www.winagents.com/en/products/tftp-server/`.

The installation of the TFTP server manager is pretty straightforward. Make sure it is installed on a Windows machine, which is in the same subnet as the intended management network for the ESXi hosts. Also make sure that the service is started before you begin.

How to do it...

The following steps will help you configure the TFTP server to facilitate PXE booting:

1. Deploy the WinAgents TFTP server, by installing it on a Windows machine.

2. Click on the Auto Deploy icon to bring up the configuration screen at the vCenter Inventory Home.

3. Make a note of the BIOS DHCP file name **undionly.kpxe.vmw-hardwired** that will be used as the string value to the DHCP scope option-67 (boot file name) and then download the TFTP boot ZIP (`deploy-tftp.zip`) file.

4. If there is a security alert not letting you download the file, then enable the **File |
Download** option in the security settings.

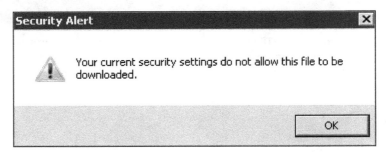

5. Here are the steps to enable file download and retry downloading the TFTP boot ZIP:

   1. Go to **Control Panel**.

   2. Bring up **Internet options**.

   3. Navigate to the **Security** tab.

   4. Select the appropriate zone. In most cases, it is the **Internet**.

   5. Click on the **Custom Level** button and scroll down to the
   Downloads category.

   6. Enable **File download** and retry the download of the TFTP Boot ZIP file.

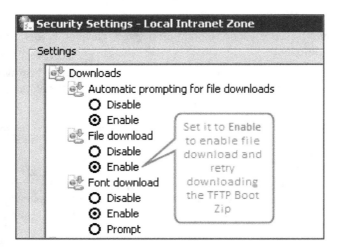

6. The following screenshot shows the contents of the TFTP boot ZIP file:

Name	Type	Compressed size
snponly64.efi	EFI File	1 KB
snponly64.efi.vmw-hardwired	VMW-HARDWIRED File	1 KB
tramp	File	1 KB
undionly.0	0 File	112 KB
undionly.kpxe	KPXE File	112 KB
undionly.kpxe.debug	DEBUG File	82 KB
undionly.kpxe.debugmore	DEBUGMORE File	88 KB
undionly.kpxe.vmw-hardwired	VMW-HARDWIRED File	113 KB

7. Extract `deploy-tftp.zip` and then drag-and-drop its contents onto the TFTP server virtual root (\) folder of the WinAgents TFTP server.

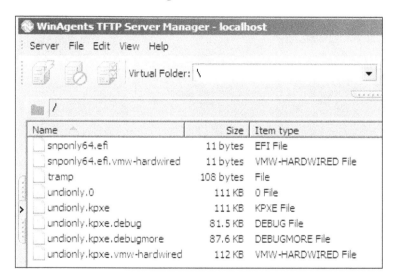

How it works...

More details on TFTP and a protocol walkthrough are available in the RFC 1350 available at `https://www.ietf.org/rfc/rfc1350.txt`.

Auto Deploy uses the TFTP server as a remote storage to store configuration or boot files, required to PXE boot the ESXi hosts. The TFTP server will be contacted during the Auto Deploy process for PXE-booting the server on which ESXi hypervisor will be deployed. Hence, we need to deploy a TFTP server and configure it with a gPXE boot image and the configuration files.

Configuring the DHCP server for PXE boot

Once you have the TFTP server configured, the next step is to configure the DHCP server with the scope options 66 and 67.

Getting ready

Configure the TFTP server as explained in the recipe *Configuring a TFTP Server with Auto Deploy files*. Also, you will need a DHCP server available in the subnet of which the ESXi hosts' management network will be a part of.

How to do it...

The following steps will help you create a new DHCP scope and configure it with the TFTP information. However, if you already have an existing scope servicing the subnet, then you could start at step 12, to configure the scope options. Perform the following steps:

1. On a Windows based DHCP server, bring up the DHCP Snap-in, right-click on **IPv4**, and click on **New Scope**.

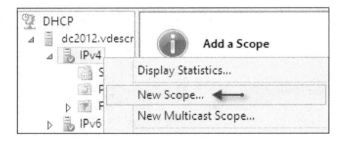

2. In **New Scope Wizard**, click on **Next**, specify a name and an optional description, and click on **Next**.

3. On the next screen, choose the IP address range for the scope by specifying the start and the end IP address of the range.

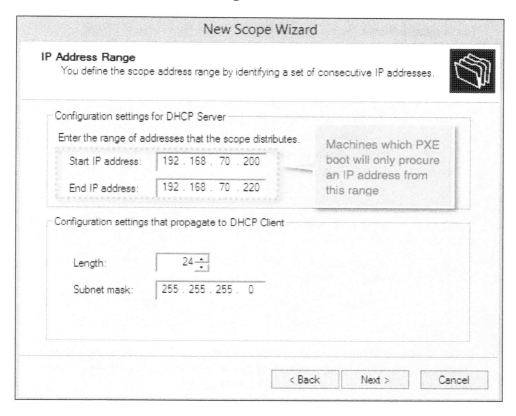

4. On the next screen, add an optional exclusion range or a DHCPOFFER delay, if required. Otherwise, just click on **Next** to continue.

5. Choose a DHCP lease duration and click on **Next**.

6. **New Scope Wizard** will now prompt you to choose whether to configure the additional information such as the default gateway, DNS servers, and so on. Select **Yes, I want to configure these options now** and click on **Next**.

7. At the **Router (Default Gateway)** wizard page, add the IP address of the default gateway and click on **Next**.

8. Specify the parent domain, resolve the DNS servers IP address, add it, and click on **Next** to continue.

9. WINS details are required to be filled for Auto Deploy .Click on **Next** to continue.

10. On the next screen, choose the option **Yes, I want to activate the scope now** and click on **Next** to continue.

11. Click on **Finish** to create and activate the scope. Once done, the scope will be listed in the inventory.

12. Right-click on **Scope Options** and click on **Configure Options** as shown in the following screenshot:

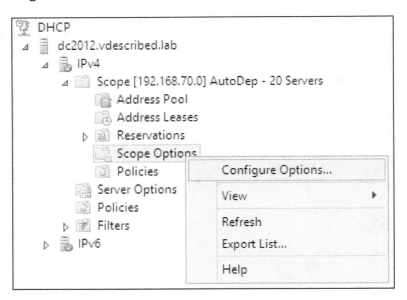

13. Under the **General** tab of the **Scope Options** window, scroll down and select the check box against the option **066 Boot Server Host Name**; and supply the string value with the FQDN or IP address of the TFTP server.

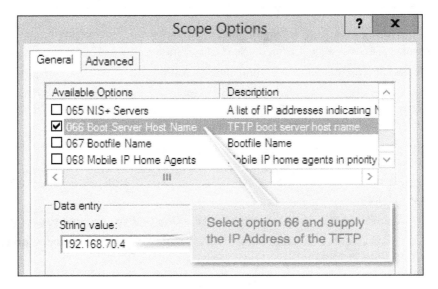

14. Next, select **067 Bootfile Name** and supply the string value `undionly.kpxe.` `vmw-hardwired`, which we made a note of from the Auto Deploy plugin page at the vCenter Server.

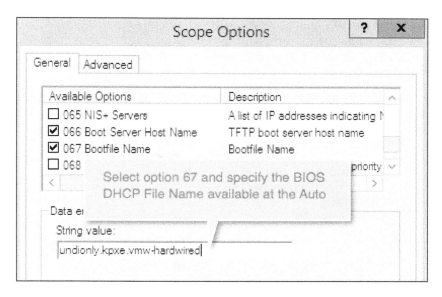

15. Click on **Apply** and **OK** to save the scope options specified.

How it works...

When a machine is chosen to be provisioned with ESXi and is powered-on, it does a PXE boot by fetching an IP address from the DHCP server. The DHCP scope configuration option 66 and 67 will direct the server to contact the TFTP server and load the bootable gPXE image and an accompanying configuration file.

There are three different ways in which you can configure the DHCP server for the Auto Deployed hosts:

1. Create a DHCP scope for the subnet to which the ESXi hosts will be connected to. Configure scope options 66 and 67.

2. If there is already an existing DHCP scope for the subnet, then edit the scope options 66 and 67 accordingly.

3. Create a reservation under an existing or a newly created DHCP scope using the MAC address of the ESXi host.

Large-scale deployments avoid creating reservations based on the MAC addresses, because that adds a lot of manual work; whereas the use of DHCP scope without any reservations is much preferred.

Testing the PXE boot configuration

Once you have configured the TFTP and the DHCP servers, it is a best practice to verify whether the servers can PXE boot successfully. If you haven't already configured the TFTP and DHCP servers, then follow the instructions in the *Configuring a TFTP Server with Auto Deploy files* and *Configuring a DHCP server for PXE boot* recipes before proceeding with testing the PXE configuration.

Although we don't specify the ESXi image the server should boot from, while configuring the TFTP or DHCP servers, the PXE boot process should be able to reach a point to confirm that the PXE boot is working and all it would need is an ESXi image to proceed further.

The *How to do it...* section of this recipe will guide you through the procedure required to test the PXE boot configuration.

Getting ready

Configure the BIOS of the machine for PXE/Network boot. See the following screenshot:

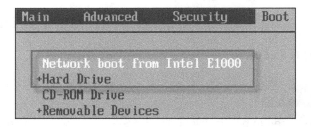

Keep in mind that there is no support for VLANs during a PXE boot. If the intended management network is a VLAN and if the machine's physical adapter is cabled to a switch port which is in trunk mode for multiple VLANs, then you will need to configure the VLAN corresponding to the management network as the native VLAN. The rationale behind this is the fact that all the untagged packets belong to the native VLAN.

For example, let's assume that the machine is cabled to a physical switch port which is trunked for VLANs 25, 30, 45, and 50. Of those VLANs, VLAN-45 is for ESXi's management network. Now for PXE to work, you will need to set VLAN-45 as the native VLAN.

How to do it...

The following procedure will help you test the PXE boot configuration:

1. Configure the BIOS of the server so that it will attempt a network boot (PXE boot) during every boot-up.

2. Make sure the server is connected to a segment that has an active DHCP scope. The DHCP scope options 66 and 67 should already be configured correctly.

3. Boot-up the server to check if its network boots.

How it works...

On the first screen during the PXE boot (network boot) process, note that the server does procure an IP address 192.168.193.25 from the scope we created at the DHCP server. The scope that we defined was of the range 192.168.193.21 to 192.168.193.27.

```
Copyright (C) 2003-2008  VMware, Inc.
Copyright (C) 1997-2000  Intel Corporation

CLIENT MAC ADDR: 00 0C 29 D1 AE 17  GUID: 564DD94B-F749-25CC-8BDF-654370D1AE17
CLIENT IP: 192.168.70.200  MASK: 255.255.255.0  DHCP IP: 192.168.70.3
GATEWAY IP: 192.168.70.2
PXE->EB: !PXE at 9E95:0070, entry point at 9E95:0106
        UNDI code segment 9E95:0BDE, data segment 98FF:5960 (611-638kB)
        UNDI device is PCI 02:01.0, type DIX+802.3
        611kB free base memory after PXE unload
iPXE initialising devices...ok
```
IP Configuration procured from the DHCP Server

```
VMware Build: 756170 undionly.kpxe.vmw-hardwired
iPXE 1.0.0+ -- Open Source Network Boot Firmware -- http://ipxe.org
Features: HTTP HTTPS iSCSI DNS TFTP AoE bzImage COMBOOT ELF MBOOT PXE PXEXT

net0: 00:0c:29:d1:ae:17 on UNDI (open)
  [Link:up, TX:0 TXE:0 RX:0 RXE:0]
DHCP (net0 00:0c:29:d1:ae:17).... ok
net0: 192.168.70.200/255.255.255.0 gw 192.168.70.2
Next server: 192.168.70.4
Filename: tramp
tftp://192.168.70.4/tramp.https://192.168.70.31:6501/vmw/rbd/tramp./vmw/rbd/host
-register?bootmac=00:0c:29:d1:ae:17._
```
The TFTP Boot Image Being loaded

"IP address: Port" of the vSphere Auto Deploy Server

Since we had supplied option 66 and option 67 to the DCHP scope, it knows the IP address of the TFTP server and the UNDI driver to be used. Subsequently, it boots using the tramp file, located on the virtual root of TFTP server. It is part of the deploy-tftp.zip bundle. If you examine the contents of the tramp file, you will see that it has the IP address of the machine where Auto Deploy was installed.

tramp - Notepad

File Edit Format View Help

```
#!gpxeset filename https://192.168.70.31:6501/vmw/rbd/trampchain
https://192.168.70.31:6501/vmw/rbd/tramp
```

Now, an HTTP Boot Request (with the machine attributes) is sent to the Auto Deploy server. Since the Auto Deploy server doesn't have any image profile or rule created to match the attributes, the PXE boot doesn't proceed any further.

```
* However, there is no ESXi image associated with this host.
*
* Detail: No rules containing an Image Profile match this host.
* You can create a rule with the New-DeployRule PowerCLI cmdlet
* and add it to the rule set with Add-DeployRule or Set-DeployRuleSet.
* The rule should have a pattern that matches one or more of the
* attributes listed below.
*
* Machine attributes:
* . asset=No Asset Tag
* . domain=vdescribed.lab
* . hostname=
* . ipv4=192.168.70.200
* . mac=00:0c:29:d1:ae:17
* . model=VMware Virtual Platform
* . oemstring=[MS_VM_CERT/SHA1/27d66596a61c48dd3dc7216fd715126e33f59ae7]
* . oemstring=Welcome to the Virtual Machine
* . serial=VMware-56 4d d9 4b f7 49 25 cc-8b df 65 43 70 d1 ae 17
* . uuid=564dd94b-f749-25cc-8bdf-654370d1ae17
* . vendor=VMware, Inc.
*
* Sleeping for 5 minutes and then rebooting...
*****************************************************************************
```

These are the machine attributes that can be used when creating vSphere Auto Deploy Rules

Preparing VMware PowerCLI for first use

All the tasks performed on the Auto Deploy server will be done using VMware PowerCLI commands. Hence, it is a requirement to have VMware vSphere PowerCLI installed and configured for use.

At the time of writing this book, the latest available version was VMware-PowerCLI version 5.5.

Download and install VMware PowerCLI from www.vmware.com/go/powercli.

The installation of PowerCLI is pretty straightforward. Just go through the wizard defaults and finish the installation. Once the installation is complete, it needs to be configured so that it can be used in your environment.

How to do it...

The following procedure will help you configure VMware PowerCLI for first use and also add the vCenter server that will be used to manage the ESXi servers, which you plan to deploy in your environment:

1. If VMware PowerCLI is being installed for the first time, you need to make sure that you issue the command to set the execution policy to either `RemoteSigned`, or `Unrestricted`, by issuing any of the following commands:

   `Set-ExecutionPolicy Unrestricted`

   Or

   `Set-ExecutionPolicy RemoteSigned`

2. Close the PowerCLI window and reopen it. You should see the vSphere PowerCLI welcome screen as shown in the following screenshot:

3. Connect the vCenter server to VMware PowerCLI, by issuing the following command:

   Syntax:

   `Connect-VIServer FQDN or IP address of the vCenter`

   Example:

   `Connect-VIServer vcenterhost001.vdescribed.lab`

How it works...

VMware PowerCLI is a set of cmdlets based on Microsoft Power Shell.

The Set-Execution policy cmdlet will determine what type of PowerCLI commands/scripts are allowed to run from the computer where VMware PowerCLI is installed. There are four types of execution policies, namely `Restricted`, `AllSigned`, `RemoteSigned`, and `Unrestricted`.

The default execution policy is `Restricted`, which does not allow running any scripts:

► Setting it to `RemoteSigned` will allow running scripts/cmdlets signed by a trusted publisher, in this case VMware Inc.

► Setting it to `Unrestricted` will impose no restrictions.

The `Connect-VIServer` cmdlet can be used to connect either the vCenter Server, or the ESXi host. However, for you to be able to address clusters, folders, and host profiles when creating a deploy rule, you will need vCenter level access. Therefore, you will need to connect to the vCenter server and not the ESXi server.

Disconnect –vi -> idle sessions

Preparing vSphere Auto Deploy for provisioning

Now that we have the offline bundle downloaded, there is a series of procedures to prepare vSphere Auto Deploy server for stateless provisioning of the ESXi hosts. Most of the procedures are done using vSphere PowerCLI, except for the creation of the host profile which should be done at the vCenter Server where Auto Deployed ESXi host will eventually be added.

The following flowchart depicts the sequence of the procedures involved:

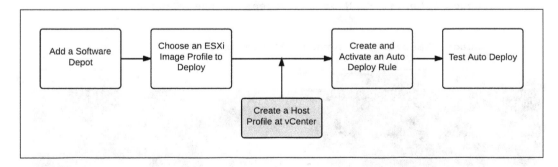

Adding a Software Depot

Once we have the offline bundle downloaded on the VMware PowerCLI machine, the next step is to present the offline bundle to the vSphere PowerCLI session. It is a requirement that the offline bundle should be accessible on the machine where PowerCLI is installed. vSphere PowerCLI refers to an offline bundle as a software depot.

How to do it...

The following command will add the offline bundle as a Software Depot to the active vSphere PowerCLI session:

- ▶ Syntax:

  ```
  Add-ESXSoftwareDepot <File name inclusive of the location of the
  bundle >
  ```

- ▶ Example:

  ```
  Add-EsxSoftwareDepot 'C:\Offline Bundles\VMware-ESXi-5.5.0-
  1331820-depot.zip'
  ```

```
PowerCLI C:\Program Files (x86)\VMware\Infrastructure\vSphere PowerCLI>
 Add-EsxSoftwareDepot 'C:\Offline Bundles\VMware-ESXi-5.5.0-1331820-depot.zip'

Depot Url
---------
zip:C:\Offline Bundles\VMware-ESXi-5.5.0-1331820-depot.zip?index.xml


PowerCLI C:\Program Files (x86)\VMware\Infrastructure\vSphere PowerCLI> _
```

How it works...

On successful execution of the `Add-EsxSoftwareDepot` command, it imports the metadata of the offline bundle and stores it in the memory for use with the current session. This in-memory information is lost when you exit the PowerCLI session, but it can be reimported by running the same command again.

The metadata contains the information such as the version of ESXi, the details of the individual VIBs in the bundle, and the image profiles available for the bundle.

Every offline bundle will have its metadata information in a ZIP bundle. You could manually navigate into the offline bundle to find a ZIP bundle `xxxxx-metadata.zip`. The following screenshot shows the contents of an offline bundle. Here, `vmw-ESXi-5.5.0-metadata.zip` is the metadata bundle:

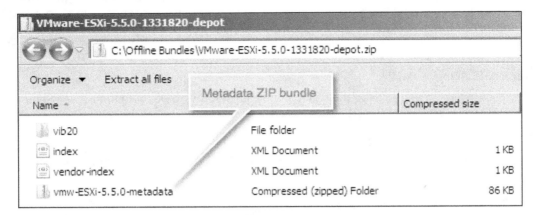

On further delving into the metadata bundle, you would see separate metadata folders for the VIBs and the profiles. The `vibs` directory will contain an XML metadata file for every VIB in the bundle:

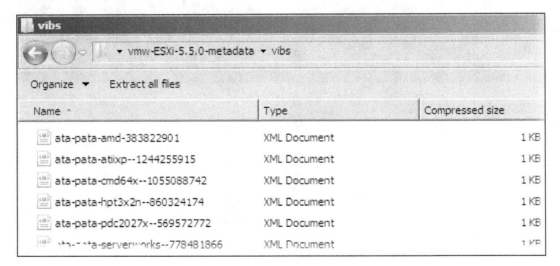

The `profiles` directory will contain a file each for the image profiles available for the bundle:

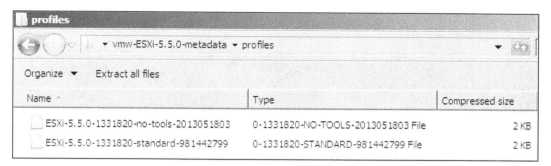

Choosing an ESXi Image Profile to deploy

Every offline bundle will have one or more predefined image profiles. An image profile defines what **vSphere Installation Bundles** (**VIBs**) should be included in an image deployed using it. For creating an Auto Deploy rule, you will need to make a decision on which of the available image profiles to use.

How to do it...

The following procedure will help you list all the image profiles imported from an offline bundle, and assign the list to an array variable, so that they can be easily referenced in any of the future commands executed in the current PowerCLI session:

1. Display all the ESXi image profiles available in the current session, by issuing the command `Get-EsxImageProfile`:

```
PowerCLI C:\Program Files (x86)\VMware\Infrastructure\vSphere PowerCLI>
 Get-EsxImageProfile

Name                        Vendor          Last Modified       Acceptance Level
----                        ------          -------------       ----------------
ESXi-5.5.0-1331820-standard  VMware, Inc.    9/19/2013 6:...     PartnerSupported
ESXi-5.5.0-1331820-no-tools  VMware, Inc.    9/19/2013 6:...     PartnerSupported
```

2. Save the output of the `Get-EsxImageProfile` command to an array variable for easy subsequent reference in the session, by issuing the following command:

   ```
   $image_profile_array=Get-EsxImageProfile
   ```

3. Try viewing each of the array elements by performing an individual listing on them:

```
$image_profile_array[0].name

$image_profile_array[1].name
```

```
PowerCLI C:\Program Files (x86)\VMware\Infrastructure\vSphere PowerCLI>
$image_profile_array[0].name
ESXi-5.5.0-1331820-standard
PowerCLI C:\Program Files (x86)\VMware\Infrastructure\vSphere PowerCLI>
$image_profile_array[1].name
ESXi-5.5.0-1331820-no-tools
PowerCLI C:\Program Files (x86)\VMware\Infrastructure\vSphere PowerCLI> _
```

Creating a Host Profile

ESXi hosts deployed using vSphere Auto Deploy run a stateless ESXi image in the machine memory with host specific configuration applied to it. However, when you create a deploy rule, which you will learn in the next section, you have an option to associate a host profile to the hosts that will be provisioned using the deploy rule. Hence, it is important to create a host profile prior to creating a deploy rule. To learn more about creating host profiles, read the recipe *Creating a Host Profile*, in *Chapter 3, Using vSphere Host Profiles*.

In order to make sure that you do not have to jump between chapters to achieve the task, I have included a summary of the steps required to create a host profile.

How to do it...

Let's have a look at the following procedure:

1. Navigate to the **Inventory Home** tab and go to Host Profiles listed under the **Monitoring** section.

2. At the **Host Profiles** page, click on the + sign to bring up the **Extract Host Profiles** wizard.

3. On the **Extract Host Profile** wizard screen, select the reference host from the list and click on **Next** to continue.

4. On the next screen, enter a name for the Host Profile and an optional description; click on **Next**.

5. On the **Ready to Complete** screen, click on **Finish** to generate the profile, which will generate a profile and list it under the host profile objects.

Creating a deploy rule

A deploy rule is created to deploy a chosen ESXi image onto a server or group of servers chosen based on a supported pattern. Without a deploy rule, Auto Deploy server will not be able to associate an ESXi image with a server to boot.

The pattern used to choose a server for deploying ESXi uniquely identifies the machine or a group of machines. The pattern can be an IPv4 address range, a MAC address, hardware vendor name, asset tag, domain name, server model, serial number, and so on.

Getting ready

Prior to creating a deploy rule, it is a prerequisite to connect to the vCenter server to which Auto Deploy is registered to, using the `Connect-VIServer` cmdlet. Unless this is done, you will not be able to create a new deploy rule.

How to do it...

To create a new deploy rule, the PowerCLI cmdlet `New-DeployRule` is used. The command can accept different patterns:

- Syntax:

  ```
  New-DeployRule -Name "<Name of the Rule>" -Item <Image Profile>,
  "<Name of the Cluster>", "<Host Profile>" -pattern "ipv4/mac/
  vendor=<IP Address Range or MAC Address or Vendor>"
  ```

- Example:

  ```
  New-DeployRule -Name "Rule001" -Item $image_profile_array[1],
  "SiteA-Cluster" -Pattern "ipv4=192.168.70.200-192.168.70.220"
  ```

```
PowerCLI C:\Program Files (x86)\VMware\Infrastructure\vSphere PowerCLI>
 New-DeployRule -Name "Rule001" -Item $image_profile_array[1], "SiteA-Cluster"
 -Pattern "ipv4=192.168.70.200 - 192.168.70.220"
Downloading misc-cnic-register 1.72.1.v50.1i-1vmw.550.0.0.1331820
Download finished, uploading to AutoDeploy...
Upload finished.
Downloading scsi-lpfc820 8.2.3.1-129vmw.550.0.0.1331820
Download finished, uploading to AutoDeploy...
Upload finished.
Downloading esx-base 5.5.0-0.0.1331820
Downloaded 114,884,608 bytes...
```

Here, `Rule001` is the name of the new Auto Deploy rule that is being created, `$image_profile_array[1]` is the second array item representing `ESXi-5.50-1331820-no-tools` and `SiteA-Cluster` is the host cluster at the vCenter server the host will be part of and `ipv4=192.168.70.200 - 192.168.70.220` is the IP range the rule will be applied to.

It is also possible to attach a host profile to an ESXi server that is auto deployed. This can be achieved by specifying the host profile's name as one of the items:

► Example:

```
New-DeployRule -Name "Rule001-HP" -Item $image_profile_array[1],
"SiteA-Cluster", "AD_Host_Profile" -Pattern "ipv4=192.168.70.220-
192.168.70.220"
```

```
PowerCLI C:\Program Files (x86)\VMware\Infrastructure\vSphere PowerCLI>
 New-DeployRule -Name "Rule001-HP" -Item $image_profile_array[1], "SiteA-Cluster
", "AD_Host_Profile"  -Pattern "ipv4=192.168.70.200-192.168.70.220"


Name          : Rule001-HP
PatternList   : {ipv4=192.168.70.200-192.168.70.220}
ItemList      : {ESXi-5.5.0-1331820-no-tools, SiteA-Cluster, AD_Host_Profile}
```

Here, the item `AD_Host_Profile` is a host profile that will be attached to the host.

How it works...

When the command to create a new deploy rule is executed, it starts uploading the VIBs in the image onto the Auto Deploy's `cache` folder.

The `cache` folder location is as follows:

C:\ProgramData\VMware\VMware vSphere Auto Deploy\Data\cache

The following screenshot shows the Auto Deploy's `cache` folder:

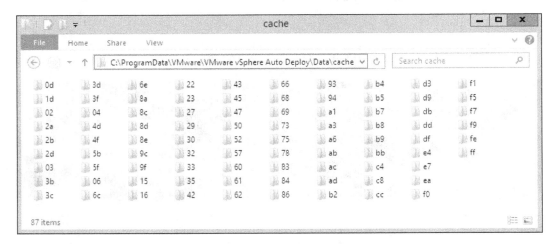

Once the upload is complete, it will finish and display a summary of the rule that was created:

```
VMware vSphere PowerCLI 5.5 Release 2 Patch 1                           _|□|×|
Upload finished.
Downloading ehci-ehci-hcd 1.0-3vmw.550.0.0.1331820
Download finished, uploading to AutoDeploy...
Upload finished.
Downloading esx-dvfilter-generic-fastpath 5.5.0-0.0.1331820
Download finished, uploading to AutoDeploy...
Upload finished.
Downloading net-tg3 3.123c.v55.5-1vmw.550.0.0.1331820
Download finished, uploading to AutoDeploy...
Upload finished.
Downloading mtip32xx-native 3.3.4-1vmw.550.0.0.1331820
Download finished, uploading to AutoDeploy...
Upload finished.
Downloading ata-pata-atiixp 0.4.6-4vmw.550.0.0.1331820
Download finished, uploading to AutoDeploy...
Upload finished.

Name        : Rule001
PatternList : {ipv4=192.168.70.200-192.168.70.220}
ItemList    : {ESXi-5.5.0-1331820-no-tools, SiteA-Cluster}

PowerCLI C:\Program Files (x86)\VMware\Infrastructure\vSphere PowerCLI>
```

Activating a deploy rule

The Auto Deploy rules that you create are not active and can't be used by the Auto Deploy server. Newly created rules must be activated by adding them to a ruleset. A ruleset is nothing but an array of deploy-rules, in which the rules are queued in the order in which they are added.

There are two types of rule sets:

▶ Active ruleset
▶ Working ruleset

How to do it...

Deploy rules can be added to the ruleset by using the `Add-DeployRule` cmdlet:

▶ Syntax:
```
Add-DeployRule -DeployRule "<Name of the Rule>"
```

▶ Example:
```
Add-DeployRule -DeployRule Rule001
Add-DeployRule -DeployRule Rule001-HP -At 0
```

Here, the `-At` is the queue location of the rule in the ruleset. The lower numbered rules are auctioned first by Auto Deploy:

```
PowerCLI C:\Program Files (x86)\VMware\Infrastructure\vSphere PowerCLI>
 Add-DeployRule -DeployRule Rule001

Name       : Rule001
PatternList : {ipv4=192.168.70.200-192.168.70.220}
ItemList    : {ESXi-5.5.0-1331820-no-tools, SiteA-Cluster}


PowerCLI C:\Program Files (x86)\VMware\Infrastructure\vSphere PowerCLI>
 Add-DeployRule -DeployRule Rule001-HP -At 0
                                                   First in the list since it
                                                   was added at 0
Name       : Rule001-HP
PatternList : {ipv4=192.168.70.200-192.168.70.220}
ItemList    : {ESXi-5.5.0-1331820-no-tools, SiteA-Cluster, AD_Host_Profile}

Name       : Rule001
PatternList : {ipv4=192.168.70.200-192.168.70.220}
ItemList    : {ESXi-5.5.0-1331820-no-tools, SiteA-Cluster}
```

How it works...

Only rules in the active ruleset are referenced by the Auto Deploy server when it receives an HTTP boot request. The `Add-DeployRule` command, by default, adds the deploy rule to both the working and active rulesets. When a machine boots for the first time, the Auto Deploy servers select the image profile based on the lowest number deploy rule in the active ruleset. Once the image profile has been identified, it will be cached at the Auto Deploy server and reused during future reboots.

There's more...

A common problem with Auto Deployed servers is that the servers sometimes boot from a wrong image or an image that doesn't contain the latest update. This happens when an image profile/deploy rule corresponding to an Auto Deployed server has been changed, but since the server is booting from the Auto Deploy cache, it remains unaware of the changes. We can resolve this issue by verifying the Auto Deploy cache against the active deploy rule to make sure that the cache is up-to-date and remediate it if necessary.

To verify the Auto Deploy cache against the deploy rule, use the cmdlet `Test-DeployRuleSetCompliance`. To remediate a host or a set of hosts with the updated image profile, use the cmdlet `Repair-DeployRuleSetCompliance`.

Read the *Applying an image profile to the host* in *Chapter 4, Using ESXi Image Builder*, to learn how to use these commands.

Testing Auto Deploy

Now that we have deploy rules created, let's boot up an ESX server in the subnet and check if it is able to fetch and load the image from the Auto Deploy server.

How to do it...

1. Start the machine intended to host the ESXi server. If everything has been configured correctly, then it will PXE-boot and will start loading the VIBs from the cache to the server's memory:

```
                                    Loading VMware ESXi
━━━━
Loading /vmw/cache/d5/08d327484169f32e59313812d567fd/tboot.187776ae0cf918b0193c8ef62904a997
Loading /vmw/cache/52/892c4fa932460ee5d78ef6b180777c/b.03efb9afcb231f58786e5a98a6f0c32b
Loading /vmw/cache/52/892c4fa932460ee5d78ef6b180777c/jumpstrt.03efb9afcb231f58786e5a98a6f0c32b
Loading /vmw/cache/52/892c4fa932460ee5d78ef6b180777c/useropts.03efb9afcb231f58786e5a98a6f0c32b
Loading /vmw/cache/52/892c4fa932460ee5d78ef6b180777c/k.03efb9afcb231f58786e5a98a6f0c32b
Loading /vmw/cache/52/892c4fa932460ee5d78ef6b180777c/chardevs.03efb9afcb231f58786e5a98a6f0c32b
Loading /vmw/cache/d5/08d327484169f32e59313812d567fd/a.187776ae0cf918b0193c8ef62904a997
Loading /vmw/cache/52/892c4fa932460ee5d78ef6b180777c/user.03efb9afcb231f58786e5a98a6f0c32b
Loading /vmw/cache/52/892c4fa932460ee5d78ef6b180777c/sb.03efb9afcb231f58786e5a98a6f0c32b
```

2. Once it is done, it will load all the VIBs into its memory and it will finish booting up the ESXi server:

```
VMware ESXi 5.5.0 (VMKernel Release Build 1331820)

VMware, Inc. VMware Virtual Platform

2 x Intel(R) Core(TM) i7 CPU 960 @ 3.20GHz
4 GiB Memory




Download tools to manage this host from:
http://192.168.70.200/ (DHCP)
http://[fe80::20c:29ff:fed1:ae17]/ (STATIC)
```

3. As per the deploy rule, it should add the host to SiteA-Cluster. You should also see it attaching the host profile AD_Hosts_Profile to the ESXi host.

How it works...

Now that we have learned how to Auto Deploy an ESXi server, it will be beneficial to understand what happens in the background during the first and the subsequent server boot-up operations.

First boot

When a machine chosen to be provisioned with ESXi is powered-on, it does a PXE boot by fetching an IP address from the DHCP server. The DHCP scope configuration option 66 and 67 will direct the server to contact the TFTP server and load the bootable gPXE image and an accompanying configuration file. The configuration will direct the server to send an HTTP boot request to the Auto Deploy server. The HTTP boot request will contain the server attributes such as the IP address, MAC address, vendor details, and so on.

On receipt of the HTTP boot request, the Auto Deploy server will check its rule engine to see if there are any rule criteria that match with the host attributes. If it finds a corresponding rule, then it would use that rule from the active rule set to load an appropriate ESXi image from an image profile.

Subsequent boot

After the host is provisioned and added to the vCenter server, the vCenter server holds the details of the image profile and the host profile associated with the host object, in its database. Hence, during a subsequent reboot, the Auto Deploy server doesn't have to leverage its rule engine again. Instead, it would use the information from the vCenter database.

If, for whatever reason the vCenter server is unavailable, then the Auto Deploy Rule Engine is engaged to determine the image profile and the host profile to be used. Since vCenter is unavailable, the host profile cannot be applied to the server.

Enabling Stateless Caching

ESXi hosts deployed using Auto Deploy requires the Auto Deploy server to be available and reachable every time the host reboots. Prior to vSphere 5.1, if the network boot failed, the server did not have a source to continue the boot process. Starting with vSphere 5.1, you can enable stateless caching that will add a level resiliency in case the network boot (PXE boot) fails. The stateless caching mode can be enabled by editing the host profile associated to the ESX host.

Getting ready

The ESXi host should have local storage for stateless caching to work.

How to do it...

The following procedure will guide you through the steps required to enable stateless caching:

1. Select the host profile and navigate to **Actions | Edit Host Profile**:

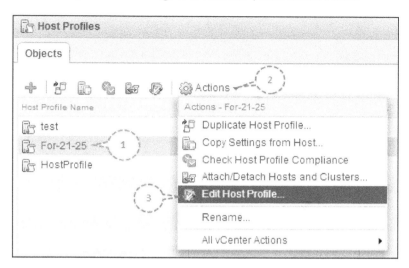

2. At the **Edit Host Profile** wizard, click on **Next** to go to the **Edit Host Profile** page of the wizard.

3. Expand **Advanced Configuration Settings** and then select the **System Image Cache Configuration** checkbox:

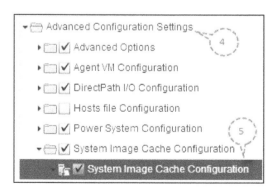

4. On the right pane, use the **System Image Cache Profile Settings** drop-down menu to select **Enable stateless caching on the host** from the list.

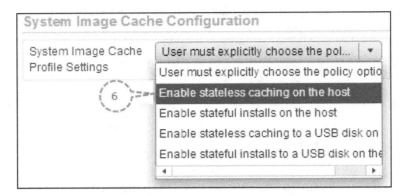

5. Once selected, it will show the arguments for the first local disk as shown in the following screenshot:

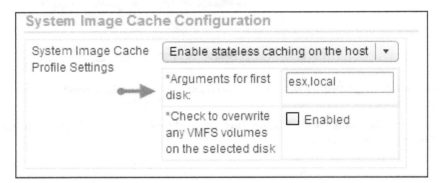

 Usually, there is no need to change this argument, because it auto detects the first local disk available.

6. If required, you could choose to overwrite the VMFS volumes on the selected disk.

7. Click on **Finish** and close the **Edit Host Profile** wizard.

8. Change the boot order in the BIOS of the ESXi machine in a way that it would always attempt to do a network boot first and the fall back to the hard drive if the network boot fails:

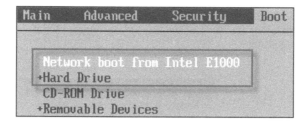

9. Reboot the ESXi host.

How it works...

Once you have enabled stateless caching on the associated host profile and configured the BIOS to always do a network boot first, then during the next reboot of the ESX machine, it performs a network boot and loads the ESXi image from the Auto Deploy server. The server finishes booting and applies (remediates) the host profile. Remediation will dump the ESXi image running in memory to the first disk (the local disk by default) selected during the stateless configuration.

Subsequent to this, if an attempt to network boot the server fails, it will load the image that was cached to the local disk during the previous successful network boot.

Performing an Auto Deploy stateful install

An Auto Deployed ESXi server will always have to perform PXE boot, engage the Auto Deploy server or the vCenter database (if it has the information of the image profile and the host profile). This is because the ESXi image is not stored on the machine but is loaded directly into the server's volatile memory. So, every reboot requires the server to go through the PXE boot procedure to load an ESXi image into its memory. Starting with vSphere 5.1, you can use Auto Deploy to install the ESXi image onto the local disk of the chosen server. This process is referred to as a stateful install.

How to do it...

The following procedure will help you prepare a host for a stateful install:

1. Extract a host profile from a reference host and edit the settings.

2. Expand **Advanced Configuration Settings** and then check the **System Image Cache Configuration** checkbox.

3. On the right pane, use the **System Image Cache Profile Settings** drop-down menu to select **Enable stateful installs on the host** as shown in the following screenshot:

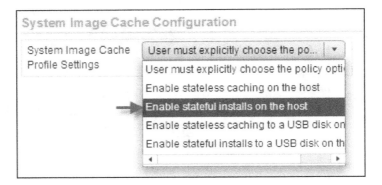

4. Configure an Auto Deploy rule for the intended hosts to use the host profile you created.

5. At the BIOS of a machine on which you intend to perform stateful installs, make sure the boot order is configured in such a way that the server attempts to boot from the local hard drive first and should fall back to network boot if that fails:

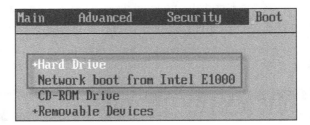

6. Boot the machine. Once the server is booted, it will be automatically placed in Maintenance Mode.

7. Navigate to the **Actions** menu from the server, then go to **All vCenter Actions | Host Profiles | Remediate**:

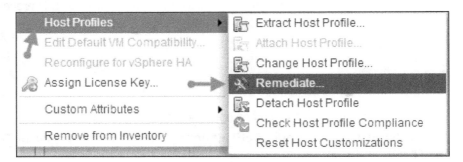

8. It will prompt you for host customization. Supply the needed information and click on **Next** to review the remediation tasks and then click on **Finish** to begin remediation.

9. Reboot the server to load from the local hard disk.

How it works...

With stateful install configured correctly, when you boot a server for the first time, it attempts to boot from the hard drive. Since there is no image on the local disk, it does a network boot and loads the ESXi image from the Auto Deploy server. The rule configured at the Auto Deploy server will attach the host profile to the ESXi server. The ESXi server deployed will be automatically put in maintenance mode.

Now, you will have to manually remediate the hosts, to apply the changes made to the host profile. Remediation will save the ESXi image from the memory to the local hard disk of the ESXi machine. Keep in mind that, even though remediation dumps the image to the local hard drive, the server is still running an image loaded from the memory. The server will have to be rebooted so that a boot from the local hard disk succeeds.

6
Configuring vSphere Networking

In this chapter, we will cover the following recipes:

- ▸ Creating a vSphere Standard Switch
- ▸ Deleting a vSphere Standard Switch
- ▸ Creating a VMkernel interface on a standard vSwitch
- ▸ Deleting a port group from a standard vSwitch
- ▸ Adding an uplink to a standard vSwitch
- ▸ Creating a vSphere Distributed Switch
- ▸ Creating a distributed port group
- ▸ Adding hosts to a vSphere Distributed Switch
- ▸ Migrating a virtual machine network from a vSphere Standard Switch to a vSphere Distributed Switch
- ▸ Mapping a physical adapter (vmnic) to a dvUplink
- ▸ Configuring security, traffic shaping, teaming and failover on a vSwitch and a VDS
- ▸ Migrating VMkernel interfaces between a standard vSwitch and a VDS
- ▸ Creating additional VMkernel interfaces on a VDS
- ▸ Creating a backup of a VDS
- ▸ Restoring a VDS configuration
- ▸ Importing a VDS into the data center from a backup
- ▸ Creating Network Resource Pools on a VDS
- ▸ Enabling port mirroring on a VDS
- ▸ Enabling NetFlow on a VDS
- ▸ Configuring private VLANs on a VDS

Introduction

Networking is the backbone of any infrastructure, be it virtual or physical. It enables connection between various infrastructure components. In this chapter, we will learn how to create and configure the basic switching constructs of a vSphere network.

Before we start learning how to create these constructs, it is important to have a brief understanding of them, discussed as follows:

> ▶ **vSphere Standard Switch (vSwitch)**: This is a software switching construct local to each ESXi host that provides a network infrastructure for the virtual machines running on that server. Unlike a physical switch, a vSphere Standard Switch is not a managed switch. It doesn't learn MAC addresses and build a **Content Addressable Memory** (**CAM**) table like a physical switch, but it does know the MAC addresses of the virtual machine vNICs connected to it. Refer to the following diagram:

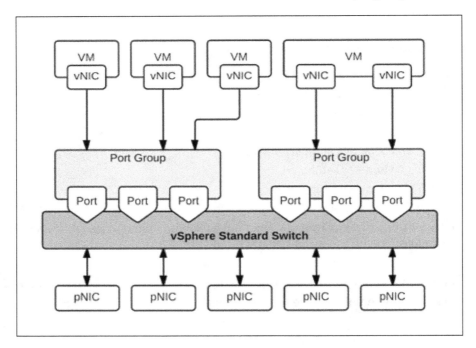

The vSwitch has logical ports to which a virtual machine's virtual NIC connects.

 The logical ports themselves cannot be chosen during the configuration; it is always a port group "label" that a virtual machine's vNIC would be configured to use.

- **vSphere Distributed Switch (VDS)**: This is a software switching construct that spans across multiple ESXi hosts. It is not locally managed at the ESXi host. It requires VMware vCenter Server for configuration and management. VDS is only available with the vSphere Enterprise Plus License. It has a control plane which resides at the vCenter Server and a data plane which resides on an ESXi host that is connected to the VDS. Refer to the following diagram:

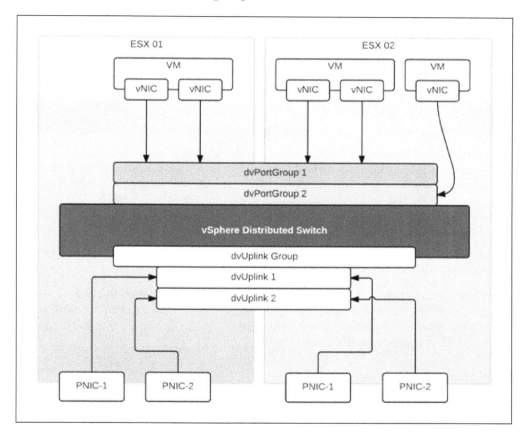

- **Port group** or **dvPortGroup**: This is a way to group a set of virtual ports on a VSS or VDS under a common configuration umbrella.

- **The VMkernel port**: This is a virtual adapter, which would act as a network interface for VMkernel. There are many services that mandate the presence of this interface, including vMotion, iSCSI, and management.

- **dvUplink**: With VDS, you can no longer apply teaming, load balancing, or failover policies directly for physical NICs. Instead, we now have an additional layer of abstraction called a dvUplink, which can be mapped to a physical NIC. The dvUplink count dictates the number of physical NICs from each host that can participate in the network configuration.

vSphere networking also provides advanced functionalities such as NetFlow, port mirroring, and ingress/egress traffic shaping, making a very feature-rich software switch. Keep in mind you can also use a Cisco Nexus 1000v, which provides more advanced functionalities and a familiar administration interface for network administrators. It comes with an additional cost of course.

 For more information on the new and enhanced networking features introduced with vSphere 5.5, read the *What's New in VMware vSphere 5.5 Networking* technical whitepaper at:

`http://www.vmware.com/files/pdf/techpaper/VMware-Whats-New-in-VMware-vSphere-Networking.pdf`

Creating a vSphere Standard Switch

A **vSphere Standard Switch** (**vSwitch**) operates at the VMkernel layer. By default, a vSwitch—vSwitch0—is created during ESXi installation. In this section, we will learn how to create a new vSwitch using the vSphere Web Client and also the ESXi command-line interface.

How to do it...

To manually create a new vSwitch, you can use the vSphere Web Client GUI, the vSphere Windows Client GUI, or the `esxcli` command on an ESXi server.

There is one fundamental difference in the process of creating a vSwitch using the `esxcfg-vswitch` command. Unlike the **Add Networking** wizard, which requires you to create a port group to proceed with the creation of the vSwitch, the `esxcli` command lets you create a vSwitch with no port groups and with no uplinks.

Using the vSphere Web Client

The following procedure explains how to create a new vSwitch using the vSphere Web Client:

1. From the inventory **Home**, click on **Hosts and Clusters**:

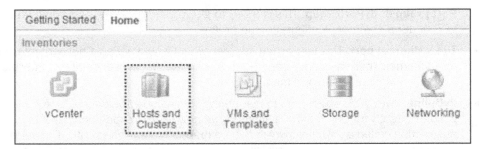

2. Select the ESXi host from the inventory, right-click on it, navigate to **All vCenter Actions**, and click on **Add Networking** to bring up the **Add Networking** wizard.

3. In the **Add Networking** wizard, select the required connection type and click on **Next**. In the following screenshot, we have chosen a connection type of **Virtual Machine Port Group for a Standard Switch**:

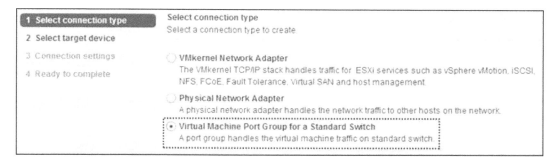

4. Select the **New standard switch** option and click on **Next** as shown in the following screenshot:

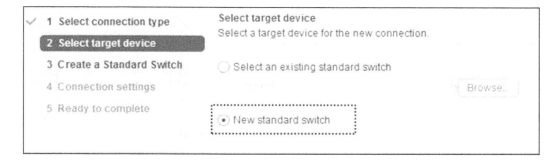

5. On the next screen, click on the green + icon to bring up the **Add Physical Adapters to the Switch** window in order to assign physical adapters (vmnic) to the vSwitch:

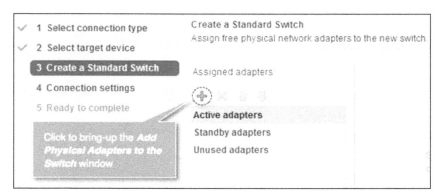

6. Select the vmnic (physical uplink) that is to be added, and click on **OK**:

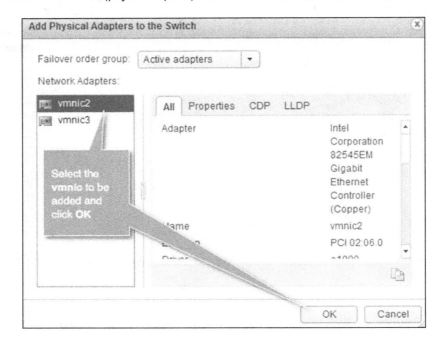

 Keep in mind that if you create a vSwitch with no physical uplinks, then it becomes an internal vSwitch. The traffic between the VMs connected to an internal vSwitch never leave the ESXi host.

7. Review the assigned adapter/adapters and click on **Next** to continue:

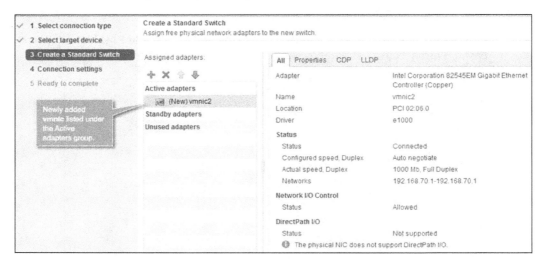

8. Supply **Network label** for the port group that will be created on the vSwitch, and click on **Next**:

9. Review the **Ready to complete** screen and click on **Finish** to create the vSwitch.

10. If the vSwitch has been created successfully, you should see it listed under the **Manage | Networking | Virtual Switches** section for the ESXi host.

Using esxcli

The following procedure guides you through the commands that need to be executed in order to create a new vSphere Standard Switch:

1. SSH to the ESXi host as root, or use a direct console access method such as HP ILO or DRAC and log in as root.

2. List all the available vmnic adapters by issuing the following command:

   ```
   # esxcfg-nics -l
   ```

   Output:

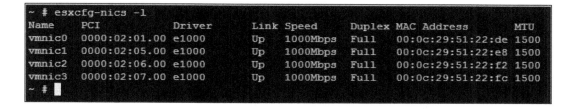

3. Issue the following command to create a new vSphere Standard Switch:

   ```
   # esxcli network vswitch standard add -v <Name of the vSwitch>
   ```

   Example:

   ```
   # esxcli network vswitch standard add -v vSwitch1
   ```

Output:

```
~ # esxcli network vswitch standard add -v vSwitch1
~ #
~ # esxcli network vswitch standard list

vSwitch1
    Name: vSwitch1                      Newly
    Class: etherswitch                  created
    Num Ports: 1536                     vSwitch.
    Used Ports: 1
    Configured Ports: 128
    MTU: 1500
    CDP Status: listen
    Beacon Enabled: false
    Beacon Interval: 1
    Beacon Threshold: 3
    Beacon Required By:
    Uplinks:
    Portgroups:
~ #
```

4. Add an uplink to the new vSwitch, `vSwitch1`, by issuing the following command:

   Syntax:

   ```
   # esxcli network vswitch standard uplink add -u vmnic2 -v vSwitch1
   ```

   Example:

   ```
   # esxcli network vswitch standard uplink add -u vmnic2 -v vSwitch1
   # esxcli network vswitch standard uplink add -u vmnic3 -v vSwitch1
   ```

   Output:

```
~ # esxcli network vswitch standard uplink add -u vmnic2 -v vSwitch1
~ # esxcli network vswitch standard uplink add -u vmnic3 -v vSwitch1
~ #
~ # esxcli network vswitch standard list -v vSwitch1
vSwitch1
    Name: vSwitch1
    Class: etherswitch
    Num Ports: 1536
    Used Ports: 5
    Configured Ports: 128
    MTU: 1500
    CDP Status: listen
    Beacon Enabled: false               Added
    Beacon Interval: 1                  Uplinks
    Beacon Threshold: 3                 vmnic3 and
    Beacon Required By:                 vmnic2
    Uplinks: vmnic3, vmnic2
    Portgroups:
~ #
```

5. Create a port group on the new vSwitch by issuing the following command:

   Syntax:

   ```
   # esxcli network vswitch standard portgroup add -p <Name of the
   port group> -v <Name of the vSwitch>
   ```

   Example:

   ```
   # esxcli network vswitch standard portgroup add -p PG001 -v
   vSwitch1
   ```

   Output:

```
~ # esxcli network vswitch standard portgroup add -p PG001 -v vSwitch1
~ # ................................................................................
~ # esxcli network vswitch standard list -v vSwitch1
vSwitch1
    Name: vSwitch1
    Class: etherswitch
    Num Ports: 1536
    Used Ports: 5
    Configured Ports: 128
    MTU: 1500
    CDP Status: listen
    Beacon Enabled: false
    Beacon Interval: 1
    Beacon Threshold: 3                    Newly
    Beacon Required By:                    created
    Uplinks: vmnic3, vmnic2                Port
    Portgroups: PG001                      Group
~ #
```

How it works...

With vSphere 5.5, you can no longer modify the number of ports on a vSwitch. The default number of ports now is `1536`, as shown in the previous screenshot. The number of ports on a vSwitch is dynamically increased or decreased depending on the number of virtual machines.

This new behavior has been documented in the *VMware KB article – 2064511*, available at `http://kb.vmware.com/kb/ 2064511`.

The properties of a vSwitch at the vSphere Web Client GUI will indicate this new behavior via the **Number of ports** value set to **Elastic**, as demonstrated in the following screenshot:

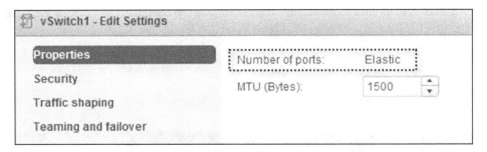

The ESXi CLI command will show the value as `1536` as expected:

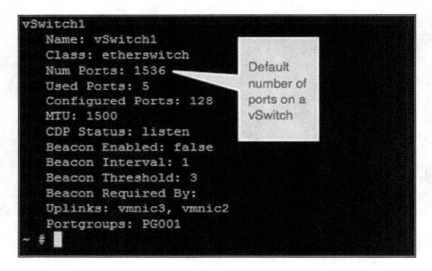

Note that according to the KB, when you view the vSwitch information via the command-line interface, it should show the number of ports as `5632`, which is inaccurate.

However, if you try to view this information using the vSphere C# Client, then it would still show the number of ports as `120`, which is accurate as well.

Deleting a vSphere Standard Switch

When you choose to delete a vSwitch in a production environment, make sure that the virtual machines have been reconfigured to use a port group on another vSwitch, which would provide them with network access.

How to do it...

A vSwitch can be deleted either from the vSphere Web Client GUI or by using the `esxcli` command.

Using the vSphere Web Client

The following procedure explains how to delete a vSwitch by using the vSphere Web Client:

1. Select the ESXi host from the inventory and navigate to **Manage | Networking | Virtual switches**.

2. Select the vSwitch to be deleted and click on the delete (X) icon to remove the vSwitch from the ESXi host:

3. You will be prompted for a confirmation. Click on **Yes** to confirm the removal:

4. You should see the **Update network configuration** and **Remove virtual switch** tasks completed successfully in the **Recent Tasks** pane:

Using esxcli

The following procedure guides you through the commands required to delete a vSwitch:

1. SSH to the ESXi host as root, or use a direct console access method such as HP ILO or DRAC and log in as root.

2. List all the vSwitches on the ESXi server by issuing the following command and identify the vSwitch to be deleted:

    ```
    # esxcli network vswitch standard list
    ```

3. Issue the following command to delete the identified vSwitch:

    Syntax:

    ```
    # esxcli network vswitch standard remove -v <Name of the vSwitch
    to be deleted>
    ```

    Example:

    ```
    # esxcli network vswitch standard remove -v vSwitch1
    ```

4. List all the vSwitches again to verify whether the vSwitch has been deleted.

Creating a VMkernel interface on a standard vSwitch

A VMkernel port group is created when there is a need to create a VMkernel network interface (VMK). It is used for management, FT, iSCSI, NAS, vMotion, and vSphere replication.

There can only be one VMkernel port per subnet. Although it doesn't stop you from creating multiple VMkernel ports per subnet, it will only use one of them. Usually, the VMkernel port that was first created is used. VMkernel traffic can be routed, although this is not advisable for vMotion, as it can cause latency issues. The VMkernel gateway IP address should also be in the same subnet.

 Only one VMkernel default gateway can be configured on an ESXi host.

How to do it...

A VMkernel port group can be created either from the vSphere Web Client GUI or by using the `esxcli` and `esxcfg-vmknic` commands.

Using the vSphere Web Client

The following procedure explains how to create a VMkernel port group using the vSphere Web Client:

1. Select the ESXi host from the inventory, right-click on it, navigate to **All vCenter Actions**, and click on **Add Networking** to bring up the **Add Networking** wizard.

2. In the **Add Networking** wizard, select the connection type as **VMkernel Network Adapter** and click on **Next** to continue:

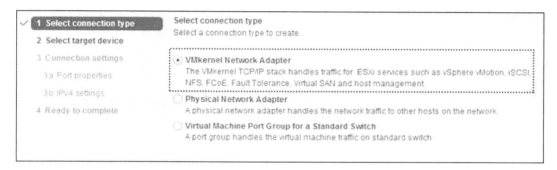

3. Select a dvPortGroup or a vSphere Standard Switch on which you would like the new VMkernel port to be configured, and click on **Next** to continue. Note that you could also choose to create **New standard switch**:

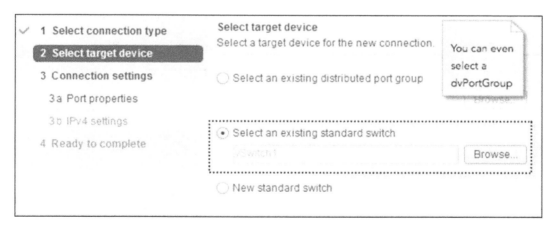

4. On the next screen, supply a value for the **Network label** field and an optional **VLAN ID**, and enable a traffic type for the VMkernel port group. The traffic types available are **vMotion traffic**, **Fault Tolerance logging**, **Management traffic**, and **Virtual SAN traffic**, as indicated in the following screenshot. Click on **Next** to continue.

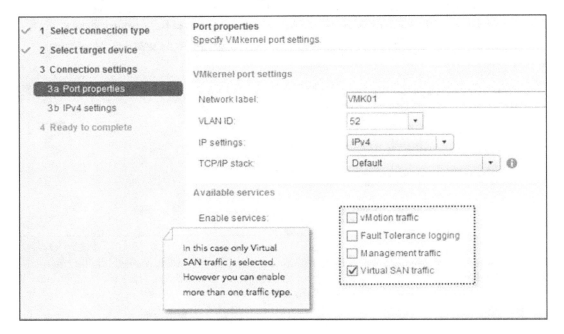

5. Supply the IP configuration for the VMkernel interface and click on **Next**:

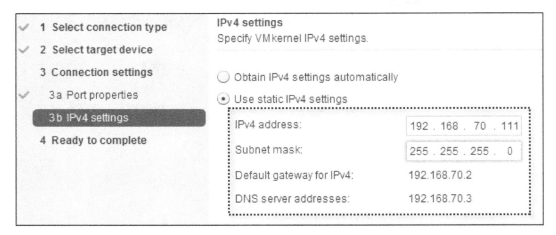

6. On the **Ready to complete** screen, verify the configuration and click on **Finish** to create the VMkernel port group.

Using esxcli and esxcfg-vmknic

The following procedure guides you through the commands needed to create a VMkernel interface on an existing vSwitch:

1. SSH to the ESXi host as root, or use a direct console access method such as HP ILO or DRAC and log in as root.

2. Create a new port group on an existing vSwitch by using the following command:

   ```
   # esxcli network vswitch standard portgroup add -p VMK02 -v
   vSwitch1
   ```

3. Issue either of the following commands in order to add a VMkernel interface to the port group:

   ```
   esxcfg-vmknic -a -i DHCP -p PG001
   ```

   Or:

   ```
   esxcfg-vmknic -a -i 192.168.70.111 -n 255.255.255.0 PG001
   ```

A new VMkernel interface is created as shown in the following screenshot:

There's more...

Although we can have only one VMkernel default gateway on an ESXi host, we can configure static routes to additional gateways. For instructions on how to configure static routes, refer to the *VMware Knowledge Base article 2001426*, available at `http://kb.vmware.com/kb/2001426`.

We could enable vMotion and FT functionalities on a selected VMkernel interface from the command line by using `vim-cmd`.

The corresponding commands are as follows:

```
vim-cmd hostsvc/vmotion/vnic_set vmk1
vim-cmd hostsvc/advopt/update FT.VMknic string vmk1
```

You need to refresh to apply the changes by issuing the following command:

```
vim-cmd hostsvc/net/refresh
```

See also

▶ You can refer to the iSCSI and Jumbo Frames configuration on ESX/ESXi (VMware Knowledge Base article *1007654*, available at `http://kb.vmware.com/kb/1007654`)

Deleting a port group from a standard vSwitch

We learned how to create a port group in the *Using esxcli* section of the recipe *Creating a vSphere Standard Switch*. In this recipe, we will learn how to delete an existing port group.

Getting ready

Reconfigure the powered-on VMs to use a different port group.

How to do it...

A port group can be deleted by using either the vSphere Web Client GUI or the `esxcli` command. We will cover both methods.

Using the vSphere Web Client

The following procedure explains how to delete a port group by using the vSphere Web Client:

1. Select the ESXi host from the inventory, navigate to **Manage | Networking | Virtual switches**, and select the vSwitch you would like to delete the port group from.

2. With the vSwitch selected, identify the port group from the switch diagram, click on the name of the port group, and click on the red delete (X) icon to remove the port group as explained in the following screenshot:

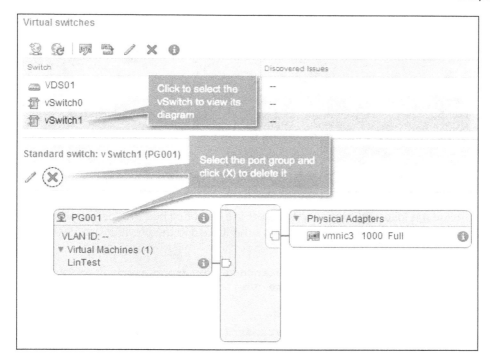

3. You will be prompted for confirmation. Click on **Yes** to proceed with the removal of the port group.

4. The **Recent Tasks** pane should show the **Remove Port Group** task completed successfully.

Using esxcli

The following procedure explains how to remove a port group from the ESXi console:

1. SSH to the ESXi host as root, or use a direct console access method such as HP ILO or DRAC and log in as root.

2. List all the port groups on the ESXi host by issuing the following command and make sure that the intended port group does not have any active clients:

```
# esxcli network vswitch standard portgroup list
```

Output:

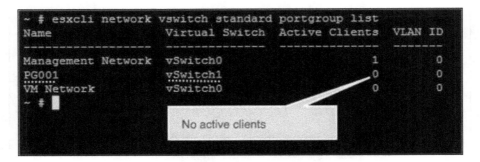

3. Issue the following command to delete the identified port group. For this example, we will be deleting the port group `PG001` mentioned in the previous screenshot.

Syntax:

```
# esxcli network vswitch standard portgroup remove -p <Name of the
Port Group> -v <Name of the vSwitch>
```

Example:

```
# esxcli network vswitch standard portgroup remove -p PG001 -v
vSwitch1
```

As seen in the following screenshot, the desired port group is deleted:

```
~ # esxcli network vswitch standard portgroup remove -p PG001 -v vSwitch1
~ # esxcli network vswitch standard portgroup list
Name                     Virtual Switch  Active Clients  VLAN ID
-----------------------  --------------  --------------  -------
Management Network       vSwitch0                     1        0
VM Network               vSwitch0                     0        0
~ #
```

How it works...

Port group delete operations work differently when performed from the Web Client GUI or `esxcli`. The difference is in how they handle any unintentional delete operations.

When using the Web Client, all it does is prompt you for a confirmation. However, when you use `esxcli`, you will not be able to delete any port group with active clients. The active clients could be powered-on virtual machines with their vNICs connected to the port group, or if it is a VMkernel port group, then they can be the VMkernel interfaces. Active clients prevent the deletion of a port group. This is why it becomes necessary to disconnect the vNICs or reconfigure the VMs to use a different port group.

The following is what you get when you try to delete a port group with active clients:

```
~ # esxcli network vswitch standard portgroup list
Name                  Virtual Switch  Active Clients  VLAN ID
--------------------  --------------  --------------  -------
Management Network    vSwitch0                     1        0
PG001                 vSwitch1                     1        0
VM Network            vSwitch0                     0        0
~ #
~ # esxcli network vswitch standard portgroup remove -p PG001 -v vSwitch1
Unable to delete portgroup "PG001", for the following reasons: 1 active ports
~ #
```

Adding an uplink to a standard vSwitch

There can be situations where you would need to add additional uplinks (physical NICs) for a vSphere Standard Switch. Such an addition is generally done with the intention of enabling the use of teaming and load balancing features. There are different GUI methods to achieve this. You could either use the **Add Networking** wizard or the **Manage Physical Network Adapters** option. For both methods, you start at different places in the GUI. In this recipe, we will use the wizard-driven method.

How to do it...

You can present the uplinks to the vSphere Standard Switch either by using the vSphere Web Client GUI or by using the `esxcfg-vswitch` command.

Using the vSphere Web Client

The following procedure explains how to add an uplink to an existing vSwitch by using the vSphere Web Client:

1. Select the ESXi host from the inventory, right-click on it, navigate to **All vCenter Actions**, and click on **Add Networking** to bring up the **Add Networking** wizard.

2. In the **Add Networking** wizard, select the connection type as **Physical Network Adapter** and click on **Next** to continue.

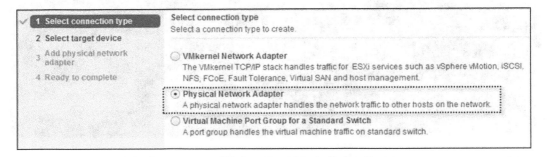

3. On the next screen, click on **Browse** and select the vSwitch you want to add uplinks to, and click on **Next** to continue.

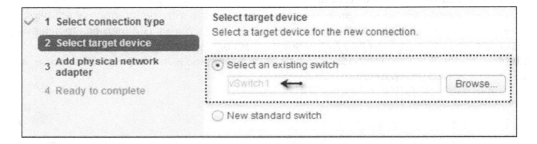

4. On the next screen, click on the green (+) icon to bring up the **Add Physical Adapters to the Switch** window.

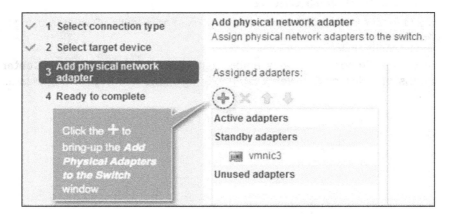

5. Select a vmnic to be added and click on **OK** to exit the **Add Physical Adapters to the Switch** window and return to the wizard screen.

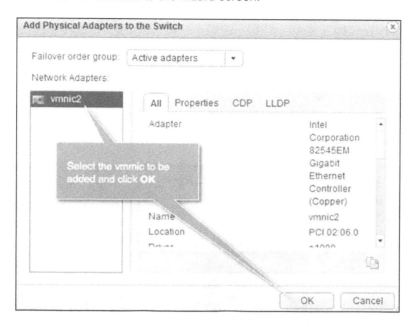

6. Once you are back to the wizard screen, you should see the **Assigned adapters** section populated with the new vmnic as shown in the following screenshot. Click on **Next** to continue.

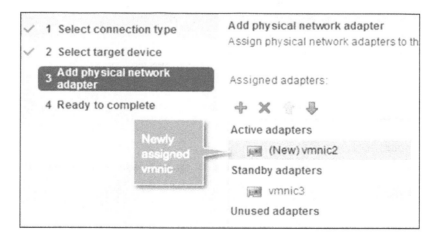

7. On the **Ready to complete** screen, click on **Finish** to complete the configuration.

Using esxcfg-vswitch

The following procedure explains how to link a vmnic (physical NIC) to an existing vSphere Standard Switch by using the command line:

1. SSH to the ESXi host as root, or use a direct console access method such as HP ILO or DRAC and log in as root.

2. View the configuration of the vSwitch you plan to add the uplink to by issuing the following command:

   ```
   # esxcli network vswitch standard list -v vSwitch1
   ```

   The output obtained is as follows:

   ```
   ~ # esxcli network vswitch standard list -v vSwitch1
   vSwitch1
       Name: vSwitch1
       Class: etherswitch
       Num Ports: 1536
       Used Ports: 3
       Configured Ports: 128
       MTU: 1500
       CDP Status: listen
       Beacon Enabled: false
       Beacon Interval: 1
       Beacon Threshold: 3
       Beacon Required By:
       Uplinks: vmnic3
       Portgroups:
   ~ #
   ```

3. Issue the following command to add a vmnic to the vSwitch:

   Syntax:

   ```
   # esxcli network vswitch standard uplink add -u <vmnic> -v
   <vSwitch>
   ```

   Example:

   ```
   # esxcli network vswitch standard uplink add -u vmnic2 -v vSwitch1
   ```

```
~ # esxcli network vswitch standard uplink add -u vmnic2 -v vSwitch1
~ # esxcli network vswitch standard list -v vSwitch1
vSwitch1
    Name: vSwitch1
    Class: etherswitch
    Num Ports: 1536
    Used Ports: 5
    Configured Ports: 128
    MTU: 1500
    CDP Status: listen
    Beacon Enabled: false
    Beacon Interval: 1
    Beacon Threshold: 3
    Beacon Required By:
    Uplinks: vmnic2, vmnic3
    Portgroups:
~ #
```

> vmnic2 has been successfully added. Hence listed as one of the uplinks for **vSwitch1**

You can issue the following command to remove an uplink:
```
# esxcli network vswitch standard uplink add
-u vmnic2 -v vSwitch1
```

Creating a vSphere Distributed Switch

A vSphere Distributed Switch cannot be created on an ESXi host directly. You need to be connected to the vCenter Server either by using the vSphere Client or by using the vSphere Web Client. Also keep in mind that a VDS can only be created at a data center level in the vCenter inventory.

How to do it...

The following procedure explains how to create a new distributed vSwitch by using the vSphere Web Client:

1. From the vCenter inventory, right-click on the data center at which you intend to create the VDS and click on **New Distributed Switch** to bring up the **New Distributed Switch** wizard.

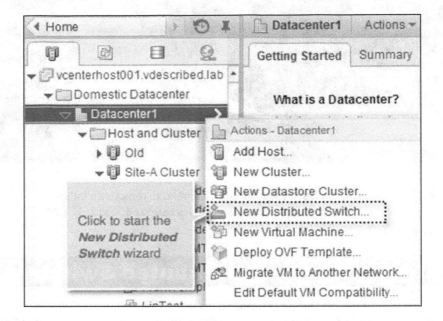

2. In the **New Distributed Switch** wizard, supply a name for the VDS and click on **Next** to continue.

3. On the next screen, select a VDS version. This is an important selection because a newer version of VDS will not be compatible with an older ESXi version. Hence, depending on the version of the ESXi hosts in your environment, choose an appropriate VDS version. Make a selection and click on **Next** to continue.

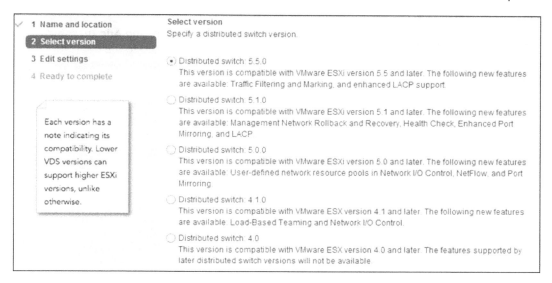

4. On the next screen, specify the number of uplinks the VDS should support. The number of uplinks determines the number of physical NICs you can connect to the VDS from an ESXi host. The default is **4**. You can choose to enable or disable **Network I/O Control** and also create a default port group along with the VDS. Make appropriate selections and click on **Next** to continue.

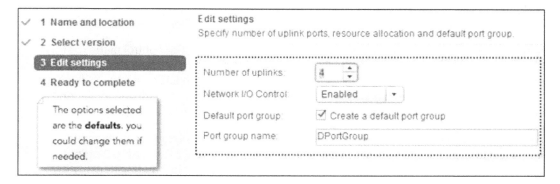

5. The next screen is the **Ready to complete** screen. Review the options selected and click on **Finish** to create the VDS.

6. The **Recent Tasks** pane should show the **Create a vSphere Distributed Switch, Update network I/O control on vSphere Distributed Switch**, and **Add Distributed Port Groups** tasks completed successfully. Also, if you navigate to the network inventory by using the keyboard shortcut *Ctrl + Alt + 6*, you should see the new VDS created, as shown in the following screenshot:

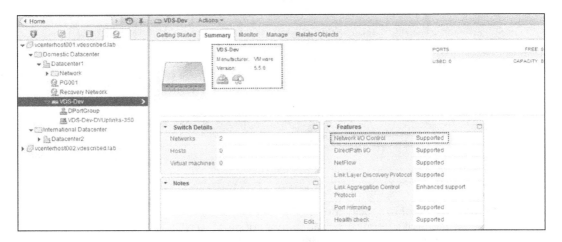

How it works...

A **vSphere Distributed Switch** (**VDS**) is created at the data center level and spans across multiple participating hosts. Therefore, it can only be created by using the vCenter Server.

A VDS will have a single control plane and multiple data planes. The control plane is at the vCenter Server and is used to create and manage the VDS. There will be a data plane created on each of the participating ESXi hosts. This means that all the packet switching will happen at the ESXi hosts. The use of a VDS reduces the administrative complexity of configuring vSphere Standard Switches on individual ESXi hosts in a large environment.

Five different versions of vSphere Distributed Switches were available in this example: 4.0, 4.1.0, 5.0.0, 5.1.0, and 5.5. Choosing Version 5.5 will make the vSphere Distributed Switch incompatible with older versions of the ESXi hosts (if they are managed using the same vCenter Server).

A dvUplink is another layer of abstraction added to reduce the administrative complexity. Every VDS with dvUplink/dvUplinks will have a dvUplinks port group. Every dvPortGroup created will increase the network count by one.

Additional ports will always be consumed by the number of dvUplinks in the dvUplinks port group. This is true regardless of whether or not a dvUplink is backed by a vmnic from the participating ESXi servers.

Creating a distributed port group

A **distributed port group** (**dvPortGroup**) can only be created from the vCenter Server. Every dvPortGroup created has a default of eight available ports. Port allocation is elastic, which means that the port count will automatically increase or decrease as needed.

How to do it...

The following procedure explains how to create a distributed port group:

1. Connect to the vCenter Server using the vSphere Web Client and use the keyboard shortcut *Ctrl + Alt + 6* to go to the **Network Inventory** view.

2. Right-click on the VDS on which you want to create a dvPortGroup and click on the menu item **New Distributed Port Group**, as shown in the following screenshot:

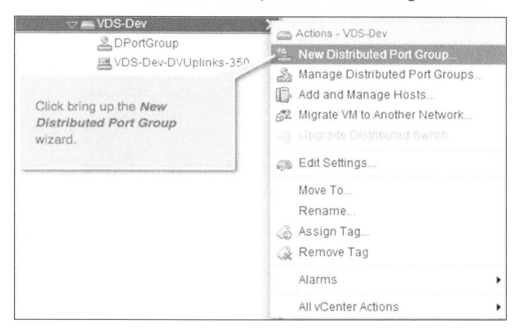

3. In the **New Distributed Port Group** wizard, supply a name for the dvPortGroup and click on **Next** to continue.

4. On the next screen, configure the port group settings (**Port binding**, **Port allocation**, **Number of ports**, **Network resource pool**, and **VLAN type**) as per your requirements, and click on **Next** to continue:

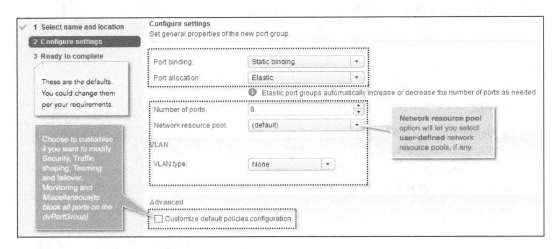

To learn more about network resource pools, read the recipe *Creating Network Resource Pools on a VDS* in this chapter.

5. On the **Ready to complete** screen, review the settings and click on **Finish** to create the dvPortGroup.

6. The **Recent Tasks** pane should show an **Add Distributed Port Groups** task completed successfully. Also, you should see the new dvPortGroup created in the network inventory.

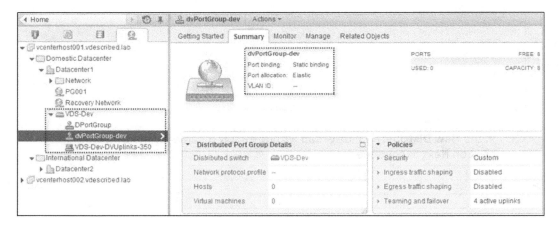

How it works...

Every dvPortGroup created will increase the network count by one and also increase the number of available ports on the VDS. The increase in the number of available ports (referred to as the capacity of the VDS) depends on the number of ports allocated to the dvPortGroup. The dvUplinks port group will also increase the network count by one. The following screenshot explains the summary of the new dvPortGroup created:

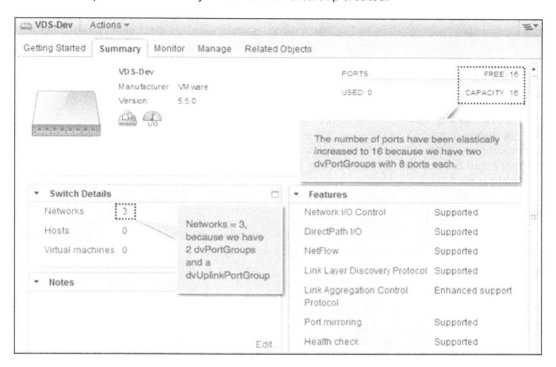

Port binding

Port binding refers to the concept of associating a port of a VDS (dvPort) to a virtual machine's NIC (vNIC).

There are different types of port binding methods available on a VDS:

- ▸ Static binding
- ▸ Dynamic binding
- ▸ Ephemeral (no binding)

Static binding is the default method of port binding. vCenter assigns a dvPort to a virtual machine NIC (vNIC) when it is connected to the dvPortGroup for the first time. The assigned dvPort will remain reserved for the virtual machine until and unless the virtual machine is removed from the port group. Temporarily disconnecting the vNIC will not remove the reservation. This type of binding has several advantages over the other types of binding methods because it retains the port statistics, which is essential if you want to monitor a virtual machine's traffic.

Dynamic binding is a method that will not be included with the future versions of vSphere. It is deprecated as of vSphere 5. The way it works is when a virtual machine is powered-on, a dvPort is dynamically allocated to a vNIC of the virtual machine that is connected to the dvPortGroup. The dvPort allocated in this manner will not be reserved. The moment the vNIC is disconnected or if the virtual machine is vMotion'ed or powered off, the dvPort is unallocated and made available for any other virtual machine to procure.

Ephemeral binding, although categorized as a binding method, does no real binding. Ports are created and deleted on demand. A dvPort is created and allocated to a vNIC of a powered on virtual machine connected to the dvPortGroup. The dvPort is deleted if the vNIC is disconnected or if the VM is vMotion'ed or powered off. There is no reliance on vCenter for the port allocation.

Port allocation

The port allocation method determines how the pool of available dvPorts on a dvPortGroup is managed. There are two types of port allocation methods:

- ▶ Elastic
- ▶ Fixed

Elastic is the default port allocation method for a dvPortGroup. As with vSphere 5.5, elastic dvPortGroups have eight dvPorts by default. However, if there is a need for more dvPorts, let's say you connected more than eight vNICs to the dvPortGroup, then port allocation is expanded automatically by the number of ports needed. When the ports are no longer needed, the port allocation is reduced but not lowered than what was configured on the dvPortGroup.

Fixed allocation will configure the set value for the number of ports as the limit to the dvPortGroup. For instance, if you set the allocation method to fixed and set the number of ports as five, then you will not be able to connect more than five vNICs to the dvPortGroup.

Network resource pools

The network resource pool option available during the dvPortGroup creation wizard will allow you to select a user-defined network resource pool. If no user-defined resource pools are available, it will default to the system network resource pool "Virtual Machine Traffic", although this is not explicitly indicated in the user interface.

Adding hosts to a vSphere Distributed Switch

Once a VDS has been created, we now have to add the ESXi hosts to the VDS so that it's physical NIC can be mapped.

How to do it...

The following procedure explains how to attach ESXi hosts to a VDS:

1. Connect to the vCenter Server using the vSphere Web Client and use the keyboard shortcut *Ctrl + Alt + 6* to go to the **Network Inventory** view.

2. Right-click on the VDS to which you want to add the hosts to, and click on the **Add and Manage Hosts** menu item as demonstrated in the following screenshot:

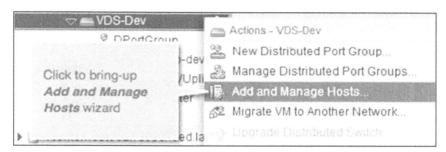

3. In the **Add and Manage Hosts** wizard, select **Add hosts** and click on **Next** to continue.

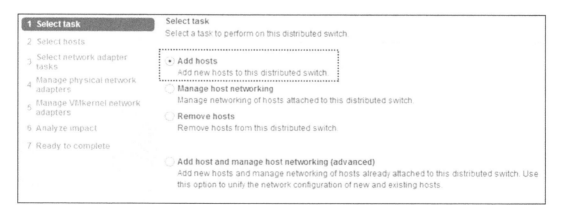

4. On the next screen, click on **New hosts** to bring up the **Select new hosts** window.

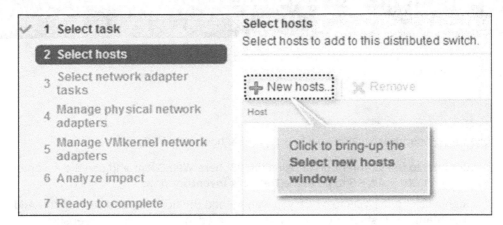

5. In the **Select new hosts** window, select the hosts that you want to add to the VDS and click on **OK**.

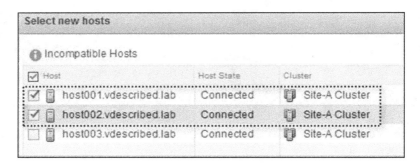

6. The **Select hosts** wizard should now show the added hosts. Click on **Next** to continue.

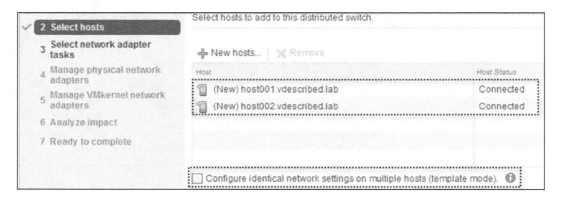

Use the **Configure identical network** settings on multiple hosts (template mode) if you want uniform networking configuration across hosts. For more information, read the section *Use a Host as a Template to Create a Uniform Networking Configuration on a vSphere Distributed Switch in the vSphere Web Client* of the *vSphere networking guide for vSphere 5.5* at `http://bit.ly/vsphere55_networking_guide`.

7. On the next **Select network adapter tasks** screen, choose whether to manage either physical or VMkernel adapters, or both. Both are selected by default as shown in the following screenshot. Since recovering from human errors during VMkernel port migrations would need more manual work, choosing only to manage physical adapters while adding hosts to a VDS is a common practice. You can also choose **Migrate virtual machine networking** and **Manage advanced host settings** as part of the same wizard. However, this is not a common practice as these can only be achieved once the hosts have been added to the VDS.

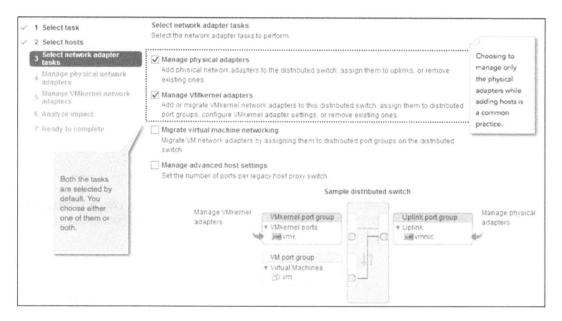

8. If you proceed with only **Manage physical adapters** selected, then on the next screen you will be presented with a list of available vmnics that can be mapped to the dvUplinks of this VDS. Select unused vmnic(s) from the list and click on **Assign uplink** to bring up the **Select an uplink** window.

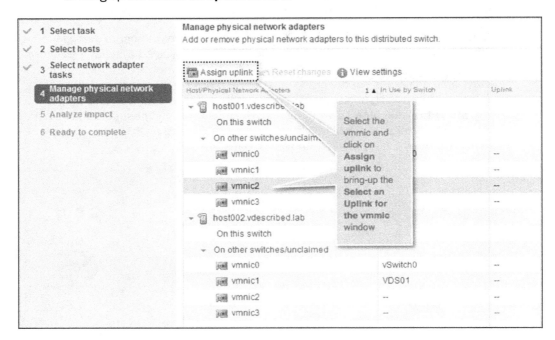

In the **Select an Uplink** window, select an unused dvUplink for the chosen vmnic and click on **OK** to return to the wizard screen, showing the uplink assignments. With the uplink assigned to the vmnics, click on **Next** to continue.

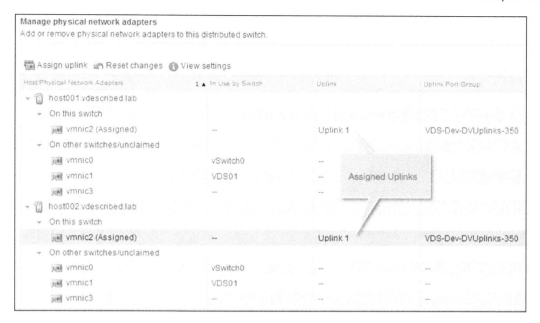

9. The **Analyze impact** screen will display the impact validation results on the network dependent services in use, for instance iSCSI. If there are no impacts, then proceed further by clicking on **Next** to continue. If there is an impact, then you will have to work on remediating the impact.

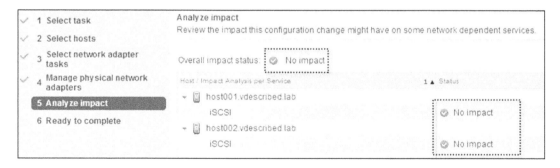

10. In the **Ready to complete** screen, review the summary of the settings and click on **Finish** to add the hosts to the VDS.

 The number of physical adapters that you choose from each host cannot exceed the number of dvUplinks.

Migrating a virtual machine network from a vSphere Standard Switch to a vSphere Distributed Switch

Once you have a VDS set up with ESXi hosts added to it, the next most common step is to migrate the virtual machine network on to the dvPortGroup on the VDS.

Getting ready

To ensure that the virtual machines do not lose network connectivity when they are migrated to a VDS, verify that at least one or more physical adapters backing the virtual machine network have already been mapped to an uplink on the VDS and is an active uplink on the destination dvPortGroup. Refer to the *Mapping a physical adapter (vmnic) to a dvUplink* recipe for instructions on how to do this.

Also make sure that the dvPortGroup is configured with the same VLAN, MTU, and link aggregation (if any) settings as well.

How to do it...

The following procedure will guide you through the steps required to migrate a virtual machine network from a standard vSwitch to a VDS:

1. Connect to the vCenter Server using the vSphere Web Client and use the keyboard shortcut *Ctrl + Alt + 6* to go to the **Network Inventory** view.

2. Right-click on the VDS to which you intend to migrate the virtual machine network and click on the menu item **Migrate VM to Another Network** to bring up the **Migrate Virtual Machine Networking** wizard, as shown in the following screenshot:

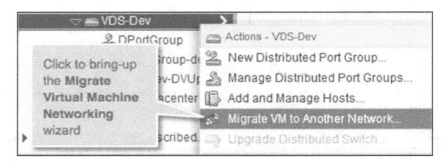

3. In the **Migrate Virtual Machine Networking** wizard, select a standard vSwitch port group to which the virtual machine is currently connected to as the source network and a dvPortGroup configured to connect to the virtual machine network as the destination network. Click on **Next** to continue.

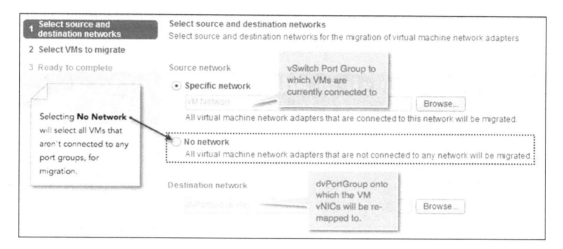

4. On the next screen, select the VMs that you intend to migrate and click on **Next** to continue.

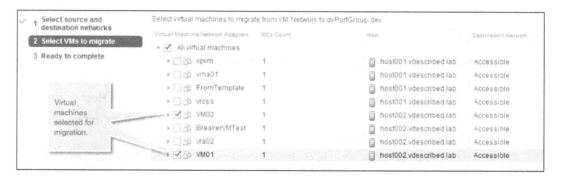

5. In the **Ready to complete** screen, review the chosen settings and click on **Finish** to reconfigure the virtual machines to join the dvPortGroup.

6. The **Recent Tasks** pane should show the progress of the task. You should also see the **Reconfigure virtual machines** task for each of the selected VMs completed successfully.

How it works...

When you migrate a virtual machine network from a vSphere Standard Switch to a vSphere Distributed Switch, it changes the network label (port group) mapping for the selected vNICs to match the dvPortGroup's name. As long as the destination dvPortGroup has uplinks that support the virtual machine network traffic (for example, it is on the same VLAN), the network connectivity for the VMs will remain unaffected.

Mapping a physical adapter (vmnic) to a dvUplink

Mapping a physical adapter to an existing dvUplink has to be done per host. Keep in mind that the physical adapter count cannot exceed the dvUplink count.

How to do it...

A physical adapter (vmnic) can be connected to a VDS either by using the vSphere Web Client GUI or by using the ESXi CLI.

Using the vSphere Web Client

The following procedure explains how to add an uplink to a VDS by using the vSphere Web Client:

1. Connect to the vCenter Server using the vSphere Web Client and use the keyboard shortcut *Ctrl + Alt + 6* to go to the **Network Inventory** view.

2. Right-click on the VDS you would like to map a physical adapter to and click on the menu item **Add and Manage Hosts** to bring up the **Add and Manage Hosts** wizard.

3. In the **Add and Manage Hosts** wizard, select the option **Manage host networking** and click on **Next** to continue.

4. In the next **Select hosts** screen, click on **Attached hosts** to bring up the **Select member hosts** window as shown in the following screenshot:

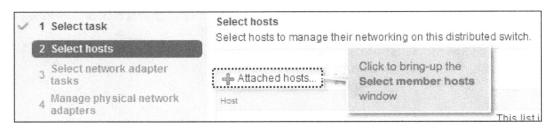

5. From the **Select member hosts** window, choose the ESXi host whose physical adapter has to be mapped to this VDS, and click on **OK** to return to the wizard screen.

6. The **Select hosts** screen will now show the chosen ESXi host(s). Click on **Next** to continue.

7. In the **Select network adapter tasks** screen, select only the **Manage physical adapters** option and click on **Next** to continue.

8. In the **Manage physical network adapters** screen, select the physical adapter (vmnic) you intend to map to this VDS, and click on **Assign Uplink** to bring up the **Select an Uplink** window.

9. From the **Select an Uplink** window, choose an unused dvUplink to map the vmnic to, and click on **OK** to return to the wizard screen.

10. The wizard screen will now show the vmnic mapped to an uplink. Click on **Next** to continue.

11. The **Analyze impact** screen will display the impacts that this configuration change will bring in, if any. If there are no impacts, then you are good to proceed with the wizard by clicking on **Next**, else you will have to find a way to remediate the impacts listed.

12. The **Ready to complete** screen reviews the changes listed. Click on **Finish** to initiate the configuration of the VDS.

Using esxcfg-vswitch

The following procedure explains how to map a physical NIC to a VDS:

1. SSH to the ESXi host as root, or use a direct console access method such as HP ILO or DRAC and log in as root.

2. List all the vSwitches on the ESXi server by issuing the following command, and identify the VDS to which the physical NICs need to be mapped:

```
esxcfg-vswitch -l
```

Output:

```
~ # esxcfg-vswitch -l
Switch Name       Num Ports   Used Ports   Configured Ports   MTU      Uplinks
vSwitch0          128         4            128                1500     vmnic0

   PortGroup Name            VLAN ID   Used Ports   Uplinks
   VM Network                0         0            vmnic0
   Management Network        0         1            vmnic0

Switch Name       Num Ports   Used Ports   Configured Ports   MTU      Uplinks
vSwitch1          128         6            128                1500     vmnic1,vmnic4

   PortGroup Name            VLAN ID   Used Ports   Uplinks
   NewKer                    0         1            vmnic1

DVS Name          Num Ports   Used Ports   Configured Ports   MTU      Uplinks
DSwitch01         512         7            512                1500     vmnic5,vmnic6,vmnic7

   DVPort ID                 In Use    Client
   24                        1         vmnic7
   25                        1         vmnic6          This is the DSwitch to which we
   26                        1         vmnic5          will be adding an physical NIC
   27                        0

~ #
```

3. Use the following command to map a physical NIC (vmnic) to a DVPort ID:

   Syntax:

   ```
   esxcfg-vswitch -P <physical  NIC> -V <DVPort ID>  <dvSwitch>
   ```

   Example:

   ```
   esxcfg-vswitch -P vmnic3 -V 27 VDS01DSwitch01
   ```

   Output:

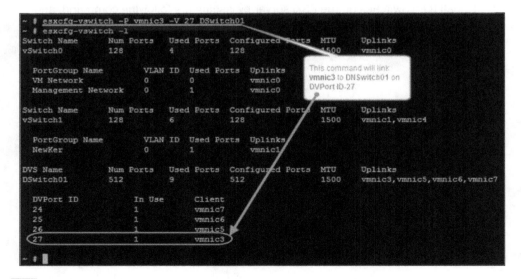

How it works...

As you have already seen in the previous sections, when you create a VDS, you choose the number of dvUplinks allowed. The number of dvUplinks dictates the maximum number of physical NICs that can be used from each of the ESXi servers.

Every dvUplink needs a port on the VDS; hence, it gets a port ID, referred to as the DVPort ID.

Unlike using the vSphere Web Client GUI, where you choose the dvUplink and then map a vmnic to it, the `esxcfg-vswitch` command requires you to specify the DVPort ID corresponding to the dvUplink. If you attempt to do this by using the port ID for another uplink, the `esxcfg-vswitch` command will fail with an error:

```
~ # esxcfg-vswitch -P vmnic4 -V 27 DSwitch01
Sysinfo error on operation returned status : Busy. Please see the VMkernel log for
detailed error information
~ #
```

There's more...

To unmap a physical network adapter from a VDS using the vSphere Web Client, follow these steps:

1. From the *Using the vSphere Web Client* section in this recipe, follow step 1 through step 7, and at step 8 select an uplink to remove and click on **Unassign adapter** to remove the mapped uplink, as demonstrated in the following screenshot:

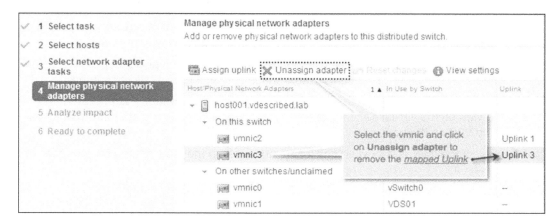

2. Once done, proceed to finish the wizard as usual to complete the configuration of the VDS.

To achieve the same using the ESXi CLI, issue the following command:

▶ Syntax:

```
# esxcfg-vswitch -Q <vmnic> -V <dvPort ID> <VDS>
```

▶ Example:

```
# esxcfg-vswitch -Q vmnic5 -V 26 VDS01DSwitch01.
```

Configuring security, traffic shaping, teaming and failover on a vSwitch and a VDS

The security, traffic shaping, teaming and failover settings function in the same manner for a standard vSwitch and a VDS, with a couple of exceptions regarding traffic shaping and load balancing methods. Unlike a standard vSwitch, a VDS can handle both ingress and egress traffic shaping. VDS also has a load balancing method called *Route based on physical NIC load*.

How to do it...

In this recipe, we will learn how to reach and locate these settings on a vSwitch and VDS.

On a standard vSwitch

The following procedure will guide you through the steps required to locate and edit the security, traffic shaping, teaming and failover settings on a standard vSwitch:

1. Connect to the vCenter Server using the vSphere Web Client and use the keyboard shortcut *Ctrl + Alt + 3* to switch to the **Hosts and Clusters** inventory view.

2. Select the ESXi host from the inventory that has the vSwitch port group on which you intend to configure the security, traffic shaping, teaming, and failover settings.

3. With the ESXi host selected, navigate to **Manage | Networking | Virtual Switches** to view all the virtual switches on the host. This will list both the standard vSwitches and VDS on the host.

4. Select the intended vSwitch and locate and click on the label of the port group to select it.

5. With the port group selected, click on the pencil icon to bring up the **Edit Settings** window for the port group, as shown in the following screenshot:

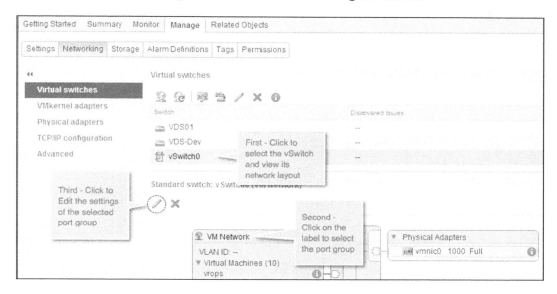

In the **Edit Settings** window, you will find the **Security**, **Traffic shaping**, and **Teaming and failover** properties on the left pane of the window. You can click on each of these items to view the current configuration or to modify it.

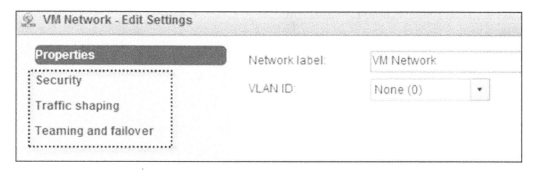

6. Click on **OK** to close the window, saving all the changes made, if any.

On a VDS

The following procedure will guide you through the steps required to locate and edit the security, traffic shaping, teaming and failover settings on a VDS:

1. Connect to the vCenter Server using the vSphere Web Client and use the keyboard shortcut *Ctrl + Alt + 6* to switch to the **Networking** inventory view.

2. Right-click on the dvPortGroup you would like to view or configure the security, traffic shaping, teaming and failover settings on, and click on **Edit Settings** as indicated in the following screenshot:

3. In the **Edit Settings** window, you will see the **Security**, **Traffic shaping**, and **Teaming and failover** properties on the left pane. You can click on each of the pane items to view the current configuration or to modify it.

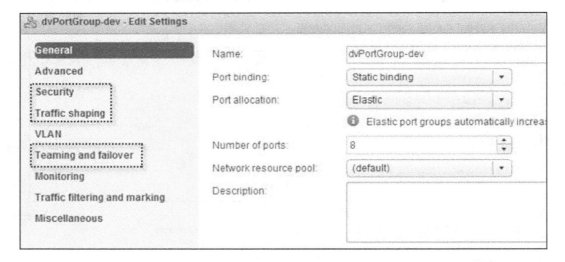

4. Click on **OK** to close the window, saving all the changes made, if any.

How it works...

In the *How to do it...* section, we learned how to get to the settings on both the vSwitch and the VDS. In this section, we will visit each of these settings categories and understand how they work. Before we begin, let's try to understand which settings are included under these categories on a vSwitch and VDS with the help of this table:

Category	vSwitch	VDS
Security	▸ Promiscuous mode ▸ MAC address changes ▸ Forged transmits	▸ Promiscuous mode ▸ MAC address changes ▸ Forged transmits
Traffic shaping	▸ Outbound (egress) traffic only ▸ Average bandwidth ▸ Burst size ▸ Peak bandwidth	▸ Both inbound (ingress) and outbound (egress) traffic ▸ Average bandwidth ▸ Burst size ▸ Peak bandwidth
Teaming and failover	▸ Load balancing ▸ Route based on originating virtual port ▸ Route based on IP hash ▸ Route based on source MAC hash ▸ Use explicit failover order ▸ Failover detection ▸ Failover order	▸ Load balancing ▸ Route based on originating virtual port ▸ Route based on IP hash ▸ Route based on source MAC hash ▸ Route based on physical NIC load ▸ Use explicit failover order ▸ Failover detection ▸ Failover order

Security

Let's try to understand the security policies first. The security policies behave the same on both the standard vSwitch and the VDS. However, they can be applied on both inbound and outbound traffic on a VDS and only on the outbound traffic on a standard vSwitch. It is important to understand what inbound and outbound traffic means. The inbound traffic (ingress) is the traffic leaving a virtual machine and entering a vSwitch or VDS and the outbound traffic (egress) is the traffic leaving a vSwitch or VDS and entering a virtual machine.

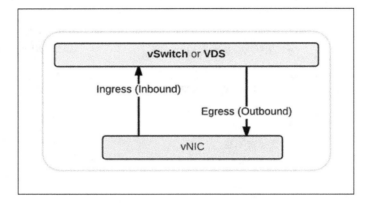

 There is a lot of misconception about ingress/egress traffic in various books and blogs. VMware have released a *KB - 2033534* article clarifying their actual meaning at `https://kb.vmware.com/kb/2033534`.

There are three policies that can be set to either accept or reject traffic:

- Promiscuous mode
- MAC address changes
- Forged transmits

Promiscuous mode, if configured to **Accept** on a port group, will allow all the virtual machine vNICs connected to that port group to see all the traffic on the vSwitch or VDS. Since this is not an advisable configuration, it is set to **Reject** by default. When set to **Reject**, the vNICs can only see traffic destined to their MAC address. This mode is usually enabled on a port group with one or more network monitoring VMs, so that they can analyze the traffic on the vSwitch or VDS. Such VMs are configured in a separate port group that sees traffic from a particular subnet it needs to monitor. By doing so, you are enabling promiscuousness on only those network monitoring VMs.

MAC address changes and **forged transmits** are security policies that allow or disallow virtual machine traffic if there is a MAC address mismatch. Every virtual machine has two MAC addresses by definition. The MAC address that is assigned to the vNIC of a virtual machine when the vNIC gets created is called the **initial MAC address**. The MAC address that a guest operating system configures for the network interface it detects is called the **effective MAC address**. The effective MAC address should generally match the initial MAC address (which is actual MAC on NIC). However, the guest operating systems do enable a service or a user to change the effective MAC address at the operating system level, if required. Also, keep in mind that every frame that leaves the virtual machine will have the effective MAC address in its header. MAC address changes affect the traffic leaving a virtual machine, in a way that if the effective MAC address does not match with the initial MAC address on the NIC, then the port/dvPort to which the vNIC was connected to is blocked until the effective MAC address is changed to match the initial MAC address. Forged transmits work in the same way but in the opposite direction. It affects the traffic entering a virtual machine.

Traffic shaping

Traffic shaping works by setting limits on how the physical adapter bandwidth is consumed by vNICs. The limit options are the same for both vSwitch and VDS, the only difference being that a vSwitch can apply shaping limits only on egress traffic, whereas a VDS can apply shaping limits on both ingress and egress traffic. There are three types of traffic shaping limits:

- ▸ **Average bandwidth**: This defines the average rate at which a vNIC can consume the physical adapter bandwidth. It is specified in **kilobits per second** (**kbps**).

- ▸ **Peak bandwidth**: This defines the peak bandwidth rate at which a vNIC can consume in. It is specified in **kilobits per second** (**kbps**).

- ▸ **Burst size**: This defines the amount of data in **kilobytes** (**KB**) that can be sent at peak bandwidth rate.

 Traffic shaping is rarely implemented and is only used as a last resort, as contention for network resources can be well handled by network teaming.

Teaming and failover

NIC teaming is the concept of using more than one physical adapter on an ESXi host to provide load balancing, redundancy, and bandwidth aggregation.

Load balancing

A standard vSwitch offers four load balancing methods, whereas a VDS offers an additional *Route based on Physical NIC load* mechanism:

Load balancing mechanism	Standard vSwitch	VDS
Route based on the originating virtual port	Yes	Yes
Route based on IP Hash	Yes	Yes
Route based on source MAC Hash	Yes	Yes
User explicit failover order	Yes	Yes
Route based on Physical NIC load	No	Yes

Route based on the originating virtual port: With this mechanism, every virtual port to which a vNIC connects to is associated with an uplink (vmnic) in a round-robin fashion. This means that, if there were only two physical uplinks—vmnic1/dvuplink1 and vmnic2/dvuplink2, and four virtual ports—port1, port2, port3, and port4, then port1, and port3 will be associated with vmnic1/dvuplink1 and port3, and port4 will be associated with vmnic2/dvuplink2. Once associated, the uplinks will be used for traffic unless there is an uplink failure, a VMotion, or a power-cycle of the VM. This is the default load balancing mechanism chosen for both vSwitch and VDS.

Route based on IP Hash: The hash of the source and destination IP addresses of a packet is used to determine the choice of the physical uplink. This load balancing mechanism is a requirement if you use link aggregation (EtherChannel).

Route based on source MAC Hash: The hash of the source MAC address of a frame is used to determine the physical uplink to be used for traffic. This mechanism is rarely used.

User explicit failover order: Although this is categorized as a load balancing mechanism, it does not perform any load balancing. With explicit failover configured, only one of the active uplinks will be used for the traffic. The other active uplinks will only be selected as per the failover order, in the event of an uplink failure.

Route based on Physical NIC load: This is only available with the VDS. With this load balancing mechanism, if a physical uplink sustains a saturation level of 75 percent for 30 seconds, then it will choose to move some of the virtual ports associated with that uplink to another active uplink in an effort to reduce the saturation level on the affected NIC.

Failover Detection and Failover Order

There are two other features categorized under **Teaming and failover**, and they are:

- ▶ Failover Detection
- ▶ Failover Order

Failover Detection is used to determine the liveliness of a physical uplink. There are two mechanisms that are used for this, and they are Link Status Only and beacon probing. Link Status Only is used to determine the connectivity status of the physical uplink, which could have encountered a NIC failure, or a cable disconnect, and so on. Beacon probing is used to determine upstream failure. For more information on beacon probing, read the *VMware KB article 1005577* at `http://kb.vmware.com/kb/1005577`.

Failover Order, as the name suggests, determines the failover of the physical uplinks. A physical uplink can be in three different states: Active, Standby, and Unused.

Active	Standby	Unused
Handles the network traffic	Becomes active only if all the Active adapters fail	Will never be used by the vSwitch or VDS

Migrating VMkernel interfaces between a standard vSwitch and VDS

Similar to the virtual machine network, the VMkernel interfaces can also be migrated to the VDS. There are different GUI locations from where this can be achieved. In this recipe, we will achieve this task by initiating a wizard from the networking inventory.

Getting ready

Before you begin migrating the VMkernel interfaces from a vSwitch to VDS, it is important to make sure you have a dvPortGroup configured with the necessary dvUplinks and ensure the other settings such as VLAN, MTU, and LACP (if required) are configured correctly.

How to do it...

The following procedure explains how to migrate the management network from vSwitch to VDS:

1. Connect to the vCenter Server using the vSphere Web Client and use the keyboard shortcut *Ctrl + Alt + 6* to go to the Network Inventory view.

2. Right-click on the VDS on which you want to migrate the VMkernel interfaces to and click on **Add and Manage Hosts**.

3. In the **Add and Manage Hosts** window, select the **Manage host networking** option and click on **Next** to continue.

4. On the next screen, select the hosts window and use the **Attached hosts** option to select ESXi hosts whose VMkernel interfaces need to be migrated. With the hosts selected, click on **Next** to continue.

5. On the **Select network adapter tasks** window, select only the option **Manage VMkernel adapters** and click on **Next** to continue, as indicated in the following screenshot:

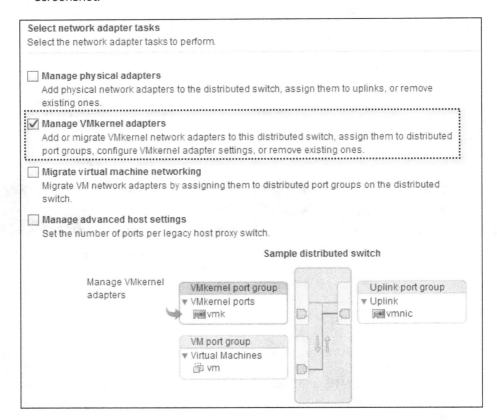

Select network adapter tasks
Select the network adapter tasks to perform.

☐ **Manage physical adapters**
Add physical network adapters to the distributed switch, assign them to uplinks, or remove existing ones.

☑ **Manage VMkernel adapters**
Add or migrate VMkernel network adapters to this distributed switch, assign them to distributed port groups, configure VMkernel adapter settings, or remove existing ones.

☐ **Migrate virtual machine networking**
Migrate VM network adapters by assigning them to distributed port groups on the distributed switch.

☐ **Manage advanced host settings**
Set the number of ports per legacy host proxy switch.

6. On the **Manage VMkernel network adapters** window, select the VMkernel adapter that you want to migrate and click on **Assign port group** to bring up the **Assign destination port group** window.

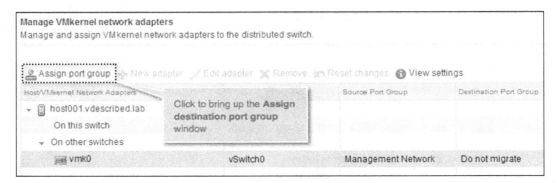

Manage VMkernel network adapters
Manage and assign VMkernel network adapters to the distributed switch.

7. In the **Assign destination port group** window, you will be provided with a list of all the available dvPortGroups on all the distributed switches. Select the one that was planned for the VMkernel adapter and click on **OK** to return to the wizard screen.

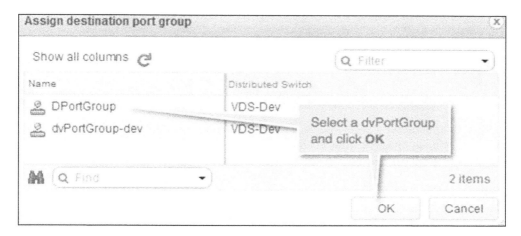

8. The wizard screen will now show the destination port group mapped. Click on **Next** to continue.

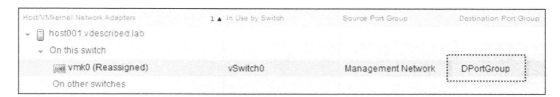

9. The **Analyze impact** screen will make you aware of any problems that this configuration change will cause. If there are no impacts, click on **Next** to continue. If there are possible impacts, find a way to remediate them before you proceed.

10. In the **Ready to complete** screen, review the settings and click on **Finish** to perform the configuration change.

How it works...

During the migration of the VMkernel interface, the communication over these resources will remain unaffected. However, if for any reason you end up migrating the management VMkernel interface to a dvPortGroup without the necessary configuration to support the traffic for the interfaces, then you will lose connectivity to the ESXi host. To recover from this, you will need to get to the console of the ESXi host via the host's IPMI console such as the DRAC, ILO, or KVM and use the DCUI to restore the standard vSwitch or use the CLI to modify the configuration of the dvPortGroup.

See also

> ▶ More information on migrating a VMkernel interface used for the management network between standard vSwitches (VMware Knowledge Base article 2037654) is available at http://kb.vmware.com/kb/2037654.

Creating additional VMkernel interfaces on a VDS

Apart from the default VMkernel interface for the Management network, a need might arise to create additional VMkernel interfaces on a VDS. For example, VMotion, iSCSI, or vSphere replication will need a VMkernel interface for communication.

Getting ready

Create a new dvPortGroup or configure an existing dvPortGroup with the necessary configuration such as VLAN, MTU, and LACP (if required) before you proceed with creating a VMkernel interface.

How to do it...

The following procedure will guide you through the steps required to create a VMkernel interface on a VDS:

1. Follow steps 1 through 6 from the previous recipe, *Migrating VMkernel interfaces between a standard vSwitch and VDS*.

2. On the **Manage VMkernel network adapters** window, select the ESXi host onto which you want to create a new VMkernel interface and click on **New Adapter** to bring up the **Add Networking** wizard.

3. On the **Add Networking** wizard, browse and select a dvPortGroup to place the VMkernel interface on and click on **Next** to continue.

4. On the **Port properties** window, set the IP settings and enable services if needed. Click on **Next** to continue.

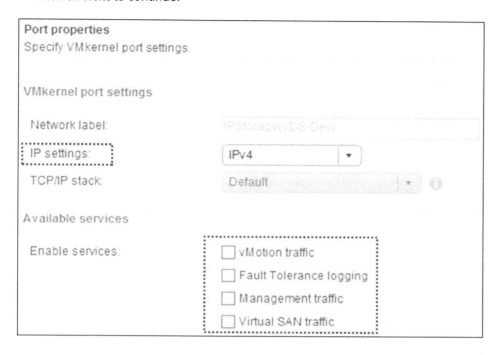

5. On the **IPv4 settings** window, choose the option **Use static IPv4 settings** to supply an IP address and a net mask. Click on **Next** to continue.

6. On the **Ready to complete** screen, review the settings and click on **Finish** to return to the **Add and Manage Hosts** wizard screen.

7. You should now see the new VMkernel interface listed for the ESXi host as seen in the following screenshot. Click on **Next** to continue.

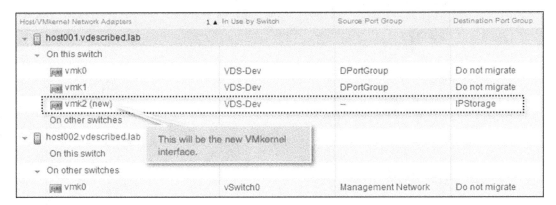

8. The **Analyze Impact** screen will make you aware of any problems that this configuration change will cause. If there are no impacts, click on **Next** to continue. If there are possible impacts, find a way to remediate them before you proceed.

9. On the **Ready to complete** screen for the **Add and Manage Hosts** wizard, click on **Finish** to create the VMkernel interface.

How it works...

You should now see the new VMkernel adapter created on the host as shown:

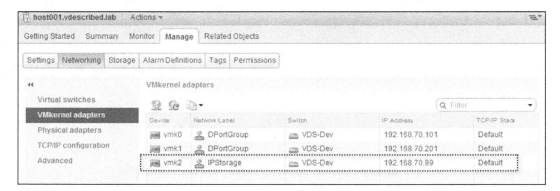

To verify whether the VMkernel interface has been configured correctly, make sure it can ping its gateway by issuing the following command:

▸ Syntax:

```
# vmkping -I <vmk adapter> <gateway IP>
```

▸ Example:

```
# vmkping -I vmk1 192.168.70.2
```

Creating a backup of a VDS

You can export the configuration of a vSphere Distributed Switch to maintain a backup.

How to do it...

The following procedure explains how to export the VDS configuration:

1. Right-click on the VDS and navigate to **All vCenter Actions | Export Configuration** to bring up the **Export Configuration** dialog box.

2. Select the configuration to export. You can choose between exporting **Distributed switch and all port groups** or **Distributed switch only**. Supply an optional description if needed and click on **OK** to export the configuration, as demonstrated in the following screenshot:

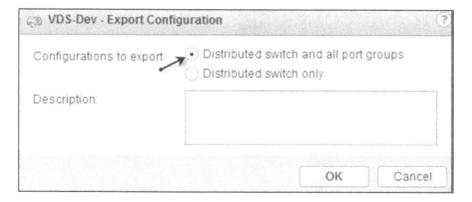

3. Click on **Yes** in the **Confirm Configuration Export** dialog box:

4. Select a location to save the exported configuration to and click on **Save** to create a backup `.zip` archive.

How it works...

The backup taken is a snapshot of the current VDS configuration. The ZIP archive created will contain the VDS data in binary format. However, it does include a `data.xml` file with the VDS metadata. This backup ZIP archive can be used to restore the VDS configuration or to create a VDS in a new data center.

See also

▶ The *Importing a VDS into the data center from a backup* recipe

Restoring a VDS configuration

The fact that we can create a backup of a VDS enables the ability to restore its configuration from a backup. The restore functionality is particularly useful when the changes made to a VDS have yielded undesired results.

Getting ready

Since the restore is done from an existing backup, make sure you have the VDS backup ZIP archive handy.

How to do it...

The following procedure explains how to restore the VDS configuration:

1. Right-click on the VDS and navigate to **All vCenter Actions | Restore Configuration** to bring up the **Restore switch configuration** wizard.

2. In the **Restore switch configuration** wizard, click on **Browse** to locate and select the VDS backup ZIP archive.

3. Choose between **Restore distributed switch and all port groups** or **Restore distributed switch only** and click on **Next** to continue, as shown in the following screenshot:

Restore switch configuration
Restore distributed switch from a file.

ⓘ Restoring a distributed switch backup will overwrite the settings of the switch and its port groups. Port groups that are not part of the backup will be retained.

Select a distributed switch backup file

Click to locate and select the backup ZIP archive.

Browse...

◉ Restore distributed switch and all port groups
○ Restore distributed switch only

Select a preferred option and click Next

4. Review the **Import Settings** section on the **Ready to complete** screen, and click on **Finish** to initiate the restore operation.

How it works...

If the restore operation completes successfully, the changes made to the VDS after the snapshot (backup or export operation) will be lost.

Importing a VDS into the data center from a backup

It is possible to import a VDS into a data center from a configuration backup. Unlike the restore operation which can only be done on a VDS, the import operation can be performed on a data center with or without the existing Distributed Switches in them. This functionality will come in handy if you want to create a similar VDS in a different data center. Refer to the *Creating a backup of a VDS* recipe to learn how to back up the VDS configuration.

How to do it...

The following procedure explains how to import a VDS into the data center:

1. Right-click on the data center to which you intend to import the VDS to, and navigate to **All vCenter Actions | Import Distributed Switch** to bring up the **Import Distributed Switch** wizard.

2. Click on **Browse** to locate and select the ZIP archive.

3. If applicable, choose **Preserve original distributed switch and port group identifiers** by selecting the checkbox next to this option. Click on **Next** to continue.

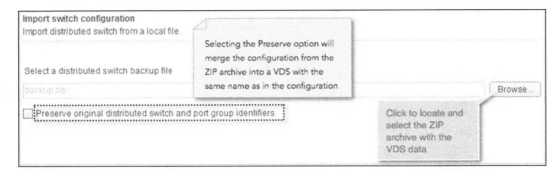

4. Review the **Import Settings** section on the **Ready to complete** screen, and click on **Finish** to initiate the import operation.

How it works...

If we select the **Preserve original distributed switch and port group identifiers** option and the data center to which the VDS is being imported to has a VDS with the same name, then that VDS or its port groups are not deleted. Instead, the information from the backup file is merged and updated with the existing VDS.

If we do not select the **Preserve original distributed switch and port group identifiers** option and the data center to which the VDS is being imported into has a VDS with the same name, then that VDS or its port groups are not deleted, but a new VDS with the configuration from the backup file is created. For example, if the data center had a VDS with the name VDS01DSwitch01, then the new VDS will be called VDS01DSwitch01 (1).

Creating Network Resource Pools on a VDS

Much like with the compute resources of an ESXi cluster, you can use resource pools on a VDS to configure Shares, Bandwidth Limitation, and **Quality of Service** (**QoS**) values. Such resource pools are referred to as **Network Resource Pools** (**NRP**). The vSphere feature that enables the use of Network Resource Pools is called Network I/O Control. There are two types of Network Pools, namely System Network Pools and User-defined Network Pools. In this recipe, we will learn how to create a User-defined Network Pool.

Getting ready

Network I/O Control is **Enabled** by default when you create a VDS. If you had chosen to disable it at the time of creation, then you should enable NIOC to make use of the Network Pools. NIOC can be enabled from the **Edit Settings** page of a VDS.

How to do it...

The following procedure will guide you through the steps required to create a User-defined Network Pool on a VDS:

1. Connect to the vCenter Server using the vSphere Web Client and use the keyboard shortcut *Ctrl + Alt + 6* to go to the Network Inventory view.

2. Select the VDS on which you want to create the Network Resource Pool and navigate to its **Manage | Resource Allocation** tab.

3. At the **Resource Allocation** tab, click on the green (+) icon to bring up the **New Network Resource Pool** window as shown in the following screenshot:

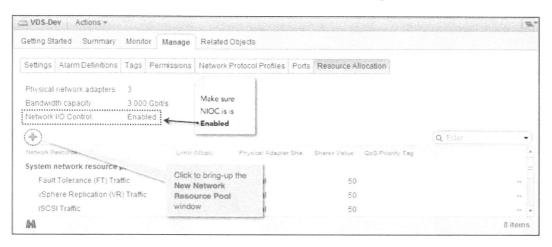

4. On the **New Network Resource Pool** window, supply a name and an optional description for the resource pool, and also configure the limit, physical adapter shares, and the QoS tag (0 to 7). Once done, click on **OK** to create the pool.

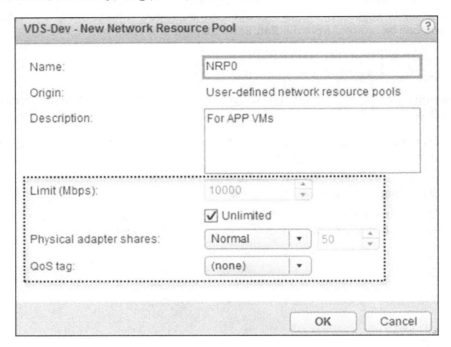

5. The newly created network pool should now be listed under the **User-defined network resource pools** category.

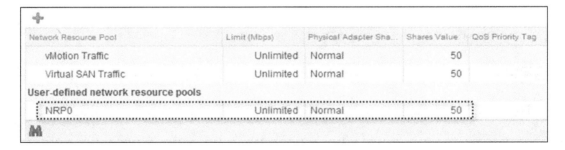

6. Once you have the user-defined network resource pools created, they can now be associated with dvPortGroups on the same VDS. This can be done from the **Edit Settings** window of a dvPortGroup, under the **General** tab, by using the **Network resource pool** drop-down box and selecting **User-defined network pool** from the list.

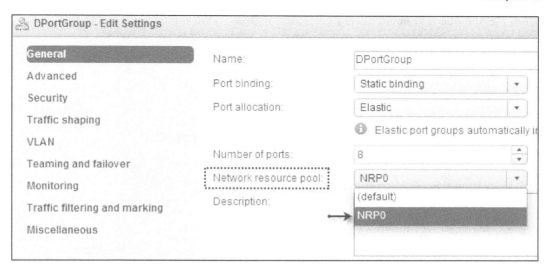

How it works...

Network I/O Control is used for bandwidth distribution to different traffic types in response to contention for bandwidth in a physical uplink. There are three criteria specific to each network resource pool that NIOC uses for bandwidth distribution:

- ▸ Limit (Mbps)
- ▸ Physical Adapter Shares
- ▸ Quality of Service (QoS) tag

Limit: This is measured in Mbps and is the maximum bandwidth a physical uplink can consume.

Physical Adapter Shares: These are ratio-based predefined share values that are used to manage the distribution of the total bandwidth available during contention. As the name suggests, the shares are applied at a physical adapter (dvUplink) level.

If an uplink is saturated, then shares of only those traffic types using the uplink at that point in time are considered. For instance, if dvUplink2 is saturated and if only VMotion and Management Traffic are hitting the uplink, then the shares configured on the Management Traffic NRP and vMotion Traffic NRP will be considered for bandwidth distribution.

Quality of Service (QoS) tag: This enables the use of IEEE 802.1p QoS tagging for the traffic corresponding to the NRP it is configured on. You can set priority values from zero (Lowest) to seven (Highest). Although this is set at NRP level, your physical switching environment handles the Quality of Service.

NIOC has the ability to automatically categorize ingress traffic into different traffic types. As indicated at the beginning of the recipe, there are two types of Network Pools:

- System network resource pools
- User-defined resource pools

System network resource pools

These are the eight default traffic classifications available with NIOC:

- Fault Tolerance Traffic
- vSphere Replication Traffic
- iSCSI Traffic
- Management Traffic
- NFS Traffic
- Virtual Machine Traffic
- VMotion Traffic
- Virtual SAN Traffic

By default, NIOC learns and categorizes traffic entering a VDS (ingress traffic) into these traffic types and applies the Limit and Shares on it. These pools cannot be manually assigned to a dvPortGroup.

User-defined network resource pools

These are custom resource pools for the Virtual Machine Traffic. These can be manually assigned to a dvPortGroup. Only the VMs that are connecting to such a port group are affected by the bandwidth distribution methods of that Network Resource Pool. The traffic from the other virtual machines is automatically classified under the System Network Pool Virtual Machine Traffic.

Enabling port mirroring on a VDS

Starting with vSphere Distributed Switch 5.0, you can enable port mirroring. Port mirroring is a functionality that allows the replication of network traffic on a port (source) to another port or uplink (destination) on the VDS. This is particularly useful when you have a packet analyzer or **Intrusion Detection System** (**IDS**) deployed on the network. Port mirroring can only be enabled on a vSphere Distributed Switch and not on a vSphere Standard Switch.

Getting ready

Identify the virtual machine on which you have the packet analyzer installed, as this information is needed when you configure port mirroring.

How to do it...

The following procedure explains how to enable port mirroring on a VDS:

1. Select the VDS on which you intend to enable port mirroring, and navigate to **Manage | Settings**.

2. Under the **Settings** tab, select **Port mirroring**.

3. Click on **New** to bring up the **Add Port Mirroring Session** wizard as shown in the following screenshot:

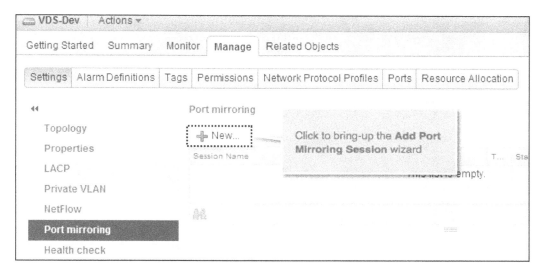

4. In the **Add Port Mirroring Session** wizard, select the desired session type and click on **Next** to continue. In this example, we have chosen the session type to be **Distributed Port Mirroring**:

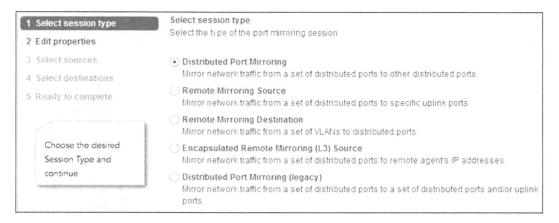

5. On the next screen, update the following details:

   1. Supply a name in the **Name** field.

   2. Change the **Status** property of the session to **Enabled**.

   3. Set **Normal I/O on destination ports** to **Allowed**, if you intend to allow other network traffic (such as RDP) on the destination ports that will be selected.

   4. You can also choose to configure the values for mirrored packet length and sampling rate if necessary.

   5. Click on **Next** to continue.

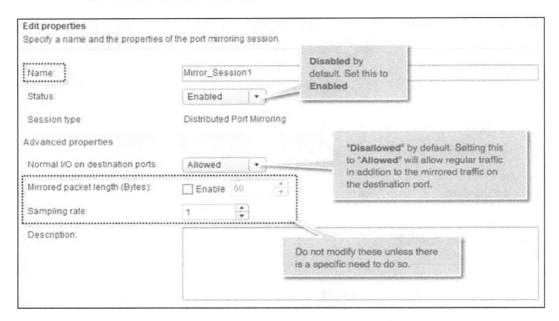

6. On the **Select sources** screen, click on the (+) icon to bring up the **Select Ports** window.

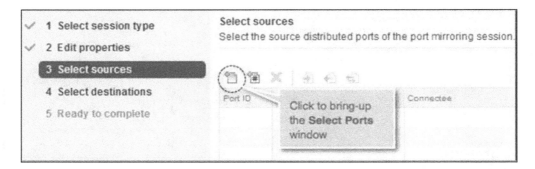

7. On the **Select Ports** window, select the port whose traffic should be mirrored and click on **OK** to return to the wizard.

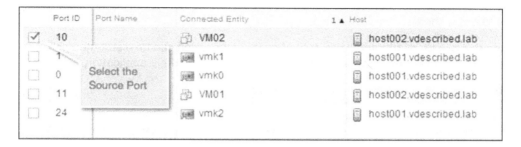

8. Once you are back to the wizard screen, you should see the source **Port ID** listed. Click on **Next** to continue.

9. On the **Select destinations** screen, click on the (+) icon again to bring up the **Select Ports** window.

10. On the **Select Ports** window, select the port to which the mirrored traffic should be sent to and click on **OK** to return to the wizard.

11. Back at the wizard screen, you should now see the destination **Port ID** listed. Click on **Next** to continue.

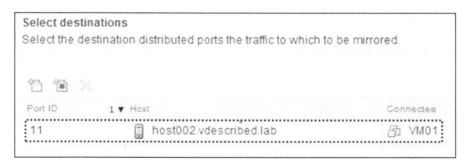

12. In the **Ready to complete** screen, review the settings and click on **Finish** to create and enable a port mirroring session.

How it works...

Once port mirroring is enabled, all the traffic that arrives at the chosen source is mirrored (replicated) to the desired destination.

The source can be distributed ports or VLANs. The destination can be distributed ports, uplinks, or IP addresses of machines running the traffic monitoring application.

There are five mirroring session types, as follows:

▶ **Distributed port mirroring**: This is used for replicating network traffic from one or more distributed ports to distributed port(s) to which the vNIC(s) of the VM(s) running the packet monitoring software are attached. This session type will work only if the source and destination VMs are on the same ESXi host.

▶ **Remote mirroring source**: This is used when the traffic analyzer is a machine connected to one of the ports on the physical switch. This would require a configuration change on the physical switch to mirror the traffic received on a physical port to another physical port on the same switch to which the packet analyzer machine is connected or to a port on a different switch (with the help of RSPAN VLAN).

▶ **Remote mirroring destination**: This is used when you want to monitor traffic in a particular VLAN by mirroring the traffic to a VM connected to a distributed port.

▶ **Encapsulated remote mirroring (L3) source**: This is used when the packet analyzer is on a machine on a different L3 subnet. In this case, the source will be the distributed ports and the destination will be the IP address of the packet analyzer machine.

▶ **Distributed port mirroring (legacy)**: This is used when we need uplinks and distributed ports as the destination.

You can also control the maximum packet size and the sampling rate of a mirroring session using the following:

▶ **Maximum packet length (bytes)**: This is the maximum size of a packet that will be allowed to be mirrored. The reminder of the packet will be truncated. The default size is 60 bytes.

▶ **Sampling Rate**: This determines the rate at which the packets are mirrored. The default value of **1** will allow you to capture every single packet. If you increase the value to **3**, then every third packet will be mirrored.

Enabling NetFlow on a VDS

NetFlow is an industry standard for network traffic monitoring. Although originally developed by Cisco, it has since become an industry standard. Once enabled, it can be used to capture IP traffic statistics on all the interfaces where NetFlow is enabled, and send them as records to the NetFlow collector software. Starting with vSphere Distributed Switch 5.0, we can enable NetFlow at the VDS or dvPortGroup level. From vSphere 5.1 onwards, VMware supports NetFlow version 10 (IPFIX).

How to do it...

The following procedure explains how to enable NetFlow on a VDS:

1. Select the VDS on which you intend to enable NetFlow, and navigate to **Manage | Settings**.

2. Under the **Settings** tab, select **NetFlow** and click on **Edit** to bring up the **Edit NetFlow Settings** window as demonstrated in the following screenshot:

3. On the **Edit NetFlow settings** window, supply the IP address and the UDP port of the NetFlow collector machine, and then specify the value for **Switch IP address**. The switch IP is a dummy IP and is only used as an identifier by the NetFlow collector. Also, modify the advanced settings if necessary, and click on **OK**.

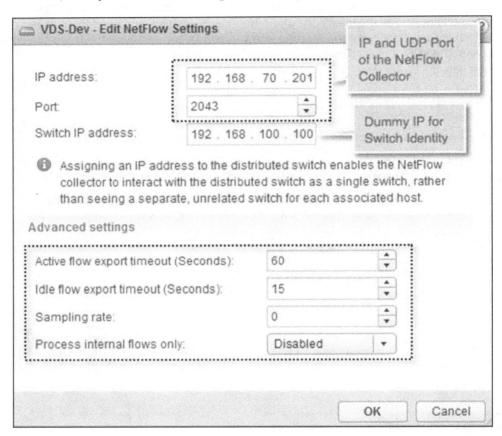

How it works...

NetFlow, once configured on the VDS, will allow the NetFlow collector software to capture and analyze statistics for the VDS. The VDS is identified by the NetFlow collector software using the IP address that we assigned to the VDS while configuring NetFlow on it. The IP assigned to the VDS doesn't give it a network identity. It is only used by the NetFlow collector to uniquely identify the VDS. If you do not specify an IP, then you will see a separate session for the ESXi host that is a member of the VDS.

Once NetFlow is enabled on the VDS, you can then configure it on each of the dvPortGroups on the same VDS. To enable NetFlow on a dvPortGroup, bring up its **Edit Settings** window and navigate to **Monitoring**. It is **Disabled** by default.

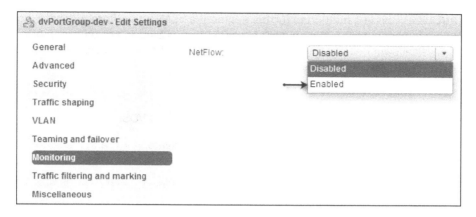

Although the NetFlow configuration is straightforward, there are a few advanced settings that you will need to understand. You generally wouldn't have to modify the advanced settings, but it is worth knowing what they are:

- **Active flow export timeout (Seconds)**: This is the amount of time the VDS will wait before it fragments the flow of traffic before it is sent to the NetFlow collector. The default timeout value is 60 seconds.

- **Idle flow export timeout (Seconds)**: This is the amount of time the VDS will wait to report an idle flow to the NetFlow collector. The default value is **15**.

- **Sampling rate**: This is the rate at which packets are sent to the NetFlow collector. The default value is **0**, which means every packet is to be sent. If you increase this value to **5** for instance, then it will send every fifth packet to the NetFlow collector.

- **Process internal flows only**: This is **Disabled** by default. If **Enabled**, then only the packets exchanged between the VMs running on the same ESXi host are sent to the NetFlow collector.

 The technical overview whitepaper from Cisco, available at http://bit.ly/cisco_netflow, will give you more insight into NetFlow's use cases.

Configuring private VLANs on a VDS

VLANs provide logical segmentation of a network into different broadcast domains. **Private VLANs** (**PVLANs**) provide a method to further segment a VLAN into different private groups. We can add and configure PVLANs on a vSphere Distributed Switch. For private VLANs to work, the physical switches backing your environment should be PVLAN aware.

How to do it...

The following procedure explains how to configure PVLANs on a VDS:

1. Select the VDS on which you intend to enable a private VLAN, and navigate to **Manage | Settings**.

2. Under the **Settings** tab, select **Private VLAN**, and click on **Edit** to bring up the **Edit Private VLAN Settings** window.

3. Click on **Add** under the **Primary VLAN ID** section to add a primary VLAN ID.

4. Click on **Add** under the **Secondary VLAN ID** section to add secondary VLANs of the type **Community** or **Isolated**, as shown in the following screenshot:

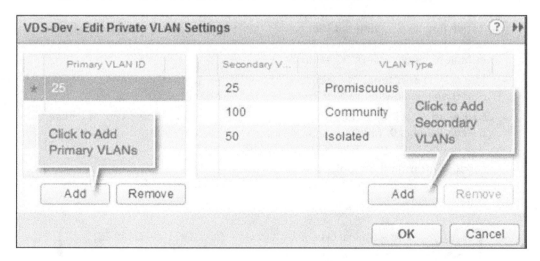

5. Click on **OK** to confirm the settings.

6. Private VLANs, once configured, can be used with port groups. The port groups can be configured to use any of the secondary PVLANs created. This is done in the **Edit Settings** window for a port group. The VLAN section will allow you to set **VLAN type** to **Private VLAN**, and let you choose the secondary PVLAN IDs.

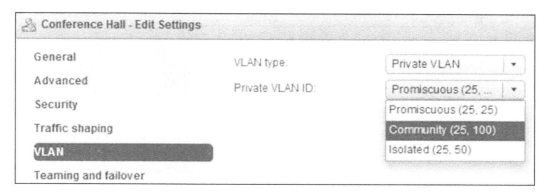

How it works...

Now that we have learned how to configure them, let's try and understand how they work. Private VLAN is not a VMware concept and is a switching concept that is in use in various environments. For Private VLANs to work, you will need to create the primary and secondary VLANs on the physical switch and associate them. So, what are primary and secondary VLANs? A primary VLAN is a VLAN that is configured as a primary private VLAN on the physical switch interface in **Promiscuous** mode. Secondary VLANs are VLANs that are associated to a primary VLAN. There are three types of secondary private VLANs, as follows:

- ▶ **Promiscuous PVLAN**: VMs in a promiscuous PVLAN can communicate with any VM belonging to any of its secondary PVLANs. The promiscuous PVLAN will act as a gateway for other secondary PVLANs.

- ▶ **Community PVLAN**: VMs in a community PVLAN can only talk among VMs in the same community PVLAN or the promiscuous PVLAN. It cannot communicate with VMs in any other secondary PVLAN.

> ▸ **Isolated PVLAN**: VMs in an isolated PVLAN are isolated from every other VM in the same isolated PVLAN. It can only communicate with the VMs in a promiscuous PVLAN. There can only be a single isolated PVLAN per primary PVLAN.

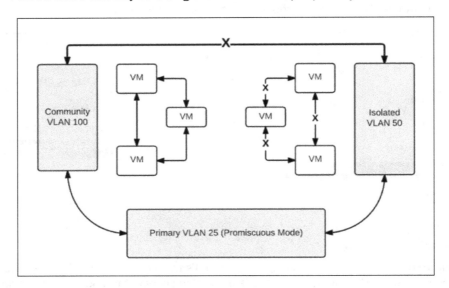

Here is an example of how it is configured on a physical switch. So we will configure a primary VLAN 25, a secondary VLAN 100 in community mode, and another secondary VLAN 50 in isolated mode.

```
vdescribed-labSW1(config)#vtp mode transparent
Device mode already VTP TRANSPARENT
vdescribed-labSW1(config-vlan)#vlan 25
vdescribed-labSW1(config-vlan)#private-vlan primary
vdescribed-labSW1(config-vlan)#private-vlan association 100,50
vdescribed-labSW1(config-vlan)#
vdescribed-labSW1(config-vlan)#
vdescribed-labSW1(config-vlan)#vlan 100
vdescribed-labSW1(config-vlan)#private-vlan community
vdescribed-labSW1(config-vlan)#
vdescribed-labSW1(config-vlan)#vlan 50
vdescribed-labSW1(config-vlan)#private-vlan isolated
vdescribed-labSW1(config-vlan)#
vdescribed-labSW1(config-vlan)#
vdescribed-labSW1(config-vlan)#int fa 0/1
vdescribed-labSW1(config-if)#switchport mode private-vlan promiscuous
vdescribed-labSW1(config-if)#switchport private-vlan mapping 25 100,50
vdescribed-labSW1(config-if)#
vdescribed-labSW1(config-if)#
vdescribed-labSW1(config-if)#int fa0/4
vdescribed-labSW1(config-if)#switchport mode private-vlan host
vdescribed-labSW1(config-if)#switchport private-vlan mapping 25 100
vdescribed-labSW1(config-if)#
vdescribed-labSW1(config-if)#
vdescribed-labSW1(config-if)#int fa0/6
vdescribed-labSW1(config-if)#switchport mode private-vlan host
vdescribed-labSW1(config-if)#switchport private-vlan mapping 25 50
vdescribed-labSW1c(config-if)#
```

Callout boxes:

- VLAN 25 being configured as Primary. 100 and 50 being associated as Secondary VLANs.
- VLAN 100 being configured as **Community** and VLAN 50 as **Isolated**
- **Port 0/1** - Promiscuous ; Mapped Primary and Secondary VLANs to the port
- **Port 0/4** - host mode ; Mapped Secondary VLAN 100 to the port
- **Port 0/6** - host mode ; Mapped Secondary VLAN 50 to the port

7
Creating and Managing VMFS Datastores

In this chapter, we will cover the following recipes:

- ▶ Viewing the LUNs presented to an ESXi host
- ▶ Viewing the datastores seen by the ESXi hosts
- ▶ Viewing and changing the multipathing of a LUN
- ▶ Creating a VMFS datastore
- ▶ Expanding/growing a VMFS datastore
- ▶ Extending a VMFS datastore
- ▶ Unmounting a VMFS datastore
- ▶ Mounting a VMFS datastore
- ▶ Deleting a VMFS datastore
- ▶ Upgrading from VMFS3 to VMFS5
- ▶ Mounting VMFS from a snapshot LUN
- ▶ Resignaturing VMFS on a snapshot LUN
- ▶ Masking paths to a LUN
- ▶ Unmasking paths to a LUN
- ▶ Creating a datastore cluster
- ▶ Enabling Storage DRS

Introduction

Storage is an integral part of any infrastructure. It is used to store the files backing your virtual machines. There are different types of storage that can be incorporated into a virtual infrastructure, and these types are determined based on a variety of factors, such as the type of disks used, the type of storage protocol used, and the type of connectivity used. The most common way to refer to a type of storage presented to a VMware environment is based on the protocol used and the connection type.

VMware supports the following types of storage based on the protocol and connection type in use:

▶ **Fiber Channel (FC) storage**: This connects over the FC SAN fabric network. It uses the FC protocol to encapsulate the SCSI commands. Hosts connect to the FC network using an **FC Host Bus Adapter** (**FC-HBA**). The core of the FC network are the fabric switches that enable connecting the hosts and storage arrays to the network.

▶ **FC over Ethernet (FCoE)**: This connects over an FCoE-converged network. Hosts connect using a **Converged Network Adapter** (**CNA**). FC frames are encapsulated in ethernet frames requiring a larger MTU of 2,500 bytes. This would mean that the IP network infrastructure devices should be configured to support this. FCoE is gaining prominence in most modern data centers implementing a converged infrastructure.

▶ **Network Attached Storage (NAS)**: This connects over the IP network and hence is easier to implement in an existing infrastructure. Unlike FC and FCoE, this is not a lossless implementation. As the SCSI commands are sent over the TCP/IP network, they are prone to experience packet loss due to various reasons. Although this behavior does not break anything, it will have an impact on the performance when compared to FC or FCoE.

    ❑ **iSCSI**: Internet SCSI allows you to send SCSI commands over an IP network to a storage system that supports the use of this protocol.

    ❑ **NFS**: Network File System is a distributed filesystem protocol that allows you to share access to files over the IP network. Unlike iSCSI, FC, FCoE, or DAS, this is not block storage protocol. VMware supports NFS Version 3.

▶ **Direct Attached Storage (DAS)**: This is used for local storage.

 To best use your vSphere environment, your ESXi hosts need access to shared storage.

Keep in mind that FC, FCoE, and iSCSI are used to present block storage devices to ESXi, whereas NFS presents file storage. The key difference here is that the block storage can be presented in raw format with no filesystem on it; file storage is nothing but a network folder mount on an already existing filesystem.

There are four other common terms that we use when dealing with storage in a VMware environment, namely LUN, datastore, VMFS, and NFS. The following points will introduce you to these terms and what they represent in a VMware environment:

▶ **LUN**: When storage is presented to an ESXi host, the space for it is carved from a pool in the storage array. Each of the carved-up containers of disk blocks are called logical units and are uniquely represented by a **Logical Unit Number** (**LUN**). The concept of LUN is used when you present block storage. It is on this LUN that you create a filesystem, such as VMFS.

▶ **Datastore**: This is the vSphere term used to refer to a storage volume presented to an ESXi. The volume can be a VMFS volume on a LUN or an NFS mount. All files that make up a virtual machine are stored in a datastore. With the datastore being a managed object, most common file operations such as create, delete, upload, and download are possible. Keep in mind that you can't edit a configuration directly from the datastore browser as it doesn't integrate with a text editor. The configuration file—for instance, the .vmx file—must be downloaded, edited, and re-uploaded to modify the file.

▶ **VMFS volume**: A block LUN presented from an FC/iSCSI/DAS array can be formatted using the VMware's proprietary filesystem called **VMFS**. VMFS stands for Virtual Machine File System.

The current version of VMFS is Version 5. VMFS will let more than one host have simultaneous read/write access to the volume. To make sure that a VM or its files are not simultaneously accessed by more than one ESXi host, VMFS uses an on-disk locking mechanism called **distributed locking**.

VMFS Version 5 supports the following:

- ❏ A maximum volume size of 64 TB
- ❏ A uniform block size of 1 MB
- ❏ Smaller subblocks of 8 KB

To place a lock on a VMFS volume, vSphere will either have to use an SCSI-2 reservation or if the array supports VAAI, it can use an **Atomic Test and Set** (**ATS**) primitive.

The VMware KB 2003813 *vSphere 5.x FAQ for VMFS-5* should be a good read. It is available at http://kb.vmware.com/kb/2003813.

▶ **NFS volume**: Unlike a VMFS volume, an NFS volume is not created by formatting a raw LUN with VMFS. NFS volumes are just mounts created to access the shared folders on an NFS server. The filesystems on these volumes are dependent on the type of NFS server.

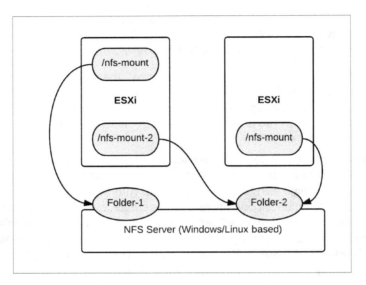

Viewing the LUNs presented to an ESXi host

In this recipe, we learn how to view the LUNs presented to an ESXi host.

During the initial phase of adding shared storage to an ESXi host, LUN devices are presented to the ESXi host. The presentation is achieved at the storage and fabric levels. We will not get into the details of how a LUN is presented using the storage or fabric management software as that is beyond the scope of this book.

Once the LUNs are made available to the ESXi hosts, you can then format them with VMFS to host the virtual machine files. The LUNs can also be presented as RAW volumes to the virtual machines, in which case they are called **Raw Device Mappings** (**RDM**). For more information on RDMs, refer to the recipe *Attaching RDM to a virtual machine* in *Chapter 10, Creating and Managing Virtual Machines*.

In this recipe, we will learn how to view the LUNs that are already presented to an ESXi host.

Getting ready

You need administrator access to the vCenter or root access to an ESXi server. Connect to a vCenter using the vSphere Web Client and to a single ESXi host using either the ESXi interface or SSH (if enabled). Also, once the LUNs have been presented, rescan all the HBAs to make sure that the ESXi finds the newly presented LUNs.

How to do it...

All the LUNs presented to the ESXi host can be viewed in three ways:

- ▶ Using the vSphere Web Client to view the LUNs
- ▶ Using the ESXi CLI to view the LUN information
- ▶ Using the vSphere Web Client

> We will not be discussing the vSphere client method for any of the tasks in this chapter or the book, unless it is necessary.

Using the vSphere Web Client to view the LUNs

The following procedure will help you view the LUN information using the vSphere Web Client:

1. Use the vSphere Web Client to connect to vCenter Server.
2. Navigate to **Home** | **Hosts and Clusters** | **Cluster** | **Hosts**.
3. Click on the ESXi host to view its page.
4. Go to the **Manage** tab and then click on **Storage**. This will show you all the LUNs seen by that ESXi host:

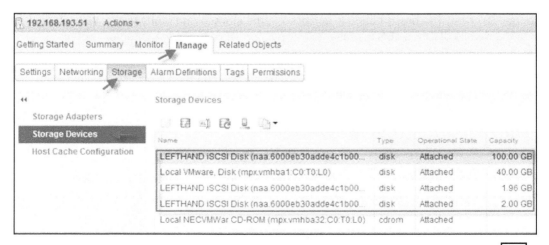

Using the ESXi CLI to view the LUN information

The following procedure will help you view the LUN information using the ESXi CLI. This method is especially helpful if vCenter is not available:

1. Connect to the ESXi console using console access methods such as ILO (HP) or DRAC (Dell). You could also SSH to the ESXi host using tools such as PuTTy or SecureCRT. Have a look at the *There's more...* section of this recipe to see how to enable and use SSH.

   ❑ You can download Putty from `http://www.chiark.greenend.org.uk/~sgtatham/putty/download.html`.

   ❑ You can download SecureCRT at `http://www.vandyke.com/download/securecrt/download.html`.

2. At the ESXi console, log in as root by issuing the following command:

   `esxcfg-scsidevs -u`

   The command will list all the devices seen by the ESXi host along with their NAA and VML IDs, as shown in the following screenshot:

```
~ # esxcfg-scsidevs -u          Command to
Primary UID                     be executed    Other UID
mpx.vmhba1:C0:T0:L0                            vml.0000000000766d686261313a303a30
mpx.vmhba32:C0:T0:L0                           vml.0005000000766d68626133323a303a30
naa.6000eb30adde4c1b000000000000000c           vml.02000000006000eb30adde4c1b000000000000000c695343534944
naa.6000eb30adde4c1b000000000000001e           vml.02000000006000eb30adde4c1b000000000000001e695343534944
naa.6000eb30adde4c1b0000000000000020           vml.02000000006000eb30adde4c1b0000000000000020695343534944
naa.6000eb30adde4c1b000000000000007e           vml.02000000006000eb30adde4c1b000000000000007e695343534944
naa.6000eb30adde4c1b0000000000000083           vml.02000000006000eb30adde4c1b0000000000000083695343534944
~ #
```

How it works...

During the initial phase of adding shared storage to an ESXi host, LUN devices are presented to the ESXi host. The presentation is achieved at the storage and fabric levels. We won't get into the details of how a LUN is presented using storage or fabric management software because that is beyond the scope of this book.

Once the LUNs are made available to the ESXi hosts, you can then form VMFS volumes on them to host the virtual machine file. The LUNs can also be presented as RAW volumes to the virtual machines.

There's more...

For SSH to work, SSH should be enabled on the ESXi host. For instructions on how to enable SSH on the ESXi host, refer to VMware KB 2004746 at `http://kb.vmware.com/kb/2004746`.

Viewing the datastores seen by the ESXi hosts

Storage LUNs formatted with the VMFS or NFS mounts are generally referred to as datastores. All the datastores seen by an ESXi host can be viewed separately in the vCenter Web Client GUI or by using a CLI command. Even a direct connection to the ESXi host using the vSphere client will let you manage or interact with the datastore object.

How to do it...

You could use the vSphere Web Client, the vSphere Client, or the ESXi CLI to view the datastores presented to an ESXI host. In this section, I will cover the use of the vSphere Web Client and the ESXi CLI to achieve the objective. Hence, this section has been further divided into two subsections:

▸ Using the vSphere Web Client to view the datastores

▸ Using the ESXi CLI to view the datastores

Using the vSphere Web Client to view the datastores

The following steps will help you view the datastores from the vSphere Web Client GUI:

1. Use the vSphere Web Client to connect to the vCenter host.

2. Navigate to **Home | Hosts and Clusters**. Click on the **Cluster** and then click on **Hosts**.

3. Click on the ESXi host to view its page.

4. Click on the **Related Objects** tab and then on the **Datastores** subtab to view all the datastores.

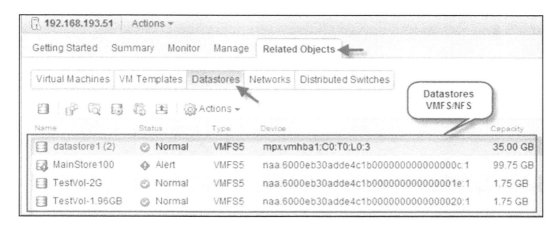

Using the ESXi CLI to view the datastores

The following steps will help you list the datastores seen by the ESXi host.

1. Connect to the ESXi console using ILO (HP) or DRAC (Dell), or using SSH to the ESXi server with tools such as PuTTy or SecureCRT.

2. At the ESXi console, log in as root.

3. Issue the following command to list the datastores:

   ```
   esxcli storage filesystem list
   ```

   The output is as follows:

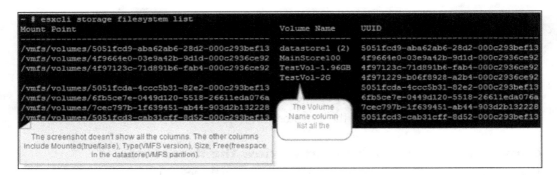

Viewing and changing the multipathing of a LUN

Storage LUNs presented to the ESXi hosts preferably need to be made highly available. This is achieved by enabling multiple connectivity paths between the ESXi hosts and the SAN storage. Once configured correctly, these paths can then be used either to failover or load balance the I/O activity.

In this section, we will learn how to view the current multipathing configuration for a particular LUN.

How to do it...

Information regarding the multipathing for a LUN can be viewed either from the vSphere Web Client GUI or using ESXi CLI. In this recipe, I will cover both these methods.

Using the vSphere Web Client GUI

The following steps will help you view the multipathing information using the vSphere Web Client:

1. Use the vSphere Web Client to connect to vCenter Server.

2. Navigate to **Home** | **Storage**:

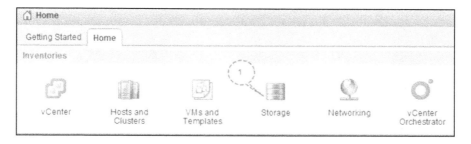

3. From the Inventory list, click on the datastore whose multipathing needs to be verified.

4. Navigate to **Manage** | **Settings** | **Connectivity and Multipathing** to view all the ESXi servers that have access to the datastore:

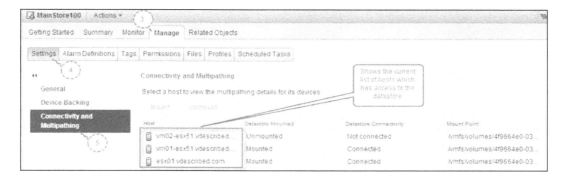

5. Highlight the host you would like to verify and click on **Edit Multipathing....**

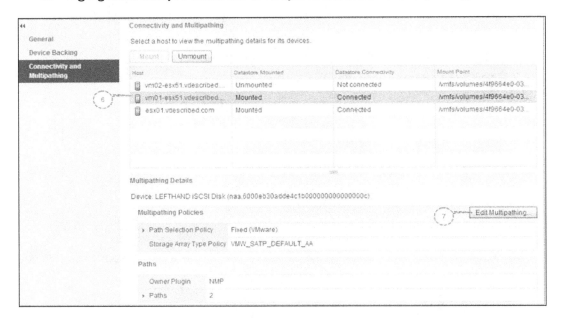

6. Once you click on the **Edit Multipathing...** button, it should bring up a separate window showing the multipathing details of the LUN on that host.

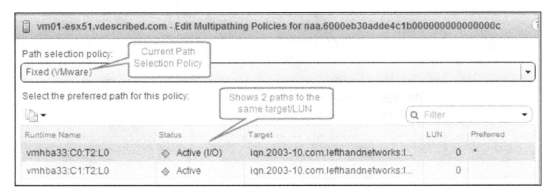

7. You could also choose to change the current **Path selection policy** by selecting a different one from the drop-down menu.

Using ESXi CLI

The `esxcfg-mpath` command available at the ESXi's command-line interface can be used to view the multipathing information corresponding to the LUN.

The following procedure will guide you through the steps required to use the CLI to do this:

1. Connect to the ESXi console using console access methods such as **ILO (HP)** or **DRAC (Dell)**. You could also **SSH** to the ESXi host using tools such as PuTTy or SecureCRT.

2. Log in as root to perform the task.

3. Issue the following command to view the multipathing information:

   ```
   esxcfg-mpath -L -d <NAA ID of the LUN>
   ```

   Example:

   ```
   esxcfg-mpath -L -d naa.6001438005dec70f0000900001000000
   ```

   Output:

```
~ # esxcfg-mpath -L -d naa.6001438005dec70f0000900001000000  <-----
vmhba4:C0:T0:L1 state:active naa.6001438005dec70f0000900001000000 vmhba4 0 0 1 NMP active san
 fc.2000b499baaa8af3:1000b499baaa8af3 fc.50001fe1501add40:50001fe1501add48
vmhba3:C0:T1:L1 state:active naa.6001438005dec70f0000900001000000 vmhba3 0 1 1 NMP active san
 fc.2000b499baaa8aef:1000b499baaa8aef fc.50001fe1501add40:50001fe1501add4d
vmhba3:C0:T0:L1 state:active naa.6001438005dec70f0000900001000000 vmhba3 0 0 1 NMP active san
 fc.2000b499baaa8aef:1000b499baaa8aef fc.50001fe1501add40:50001fe1501add49
vmhba4:C0:T3:L1 state:active naa.6001438005dec70f0000900001000000 vmhba4 0 3 1 NMP active san
 fc.2000b499baaa8af3:1000b499baaa8af3 fc.50001fe1501add40:50001fe1501add4a
vmhba4:C0:T2:L1 state:active naa.6001438005dec70f0000900001000000 vmhba4 0 2 1 NMP active san
 fc.2000b499baaa8af3:1000b499baaa8af3 fc.50001fe1501add40:50001fe1501add4e
vmhba4:C0:T1:L1 state:active naa.6001438005dec70f0000900001000000 vmhba4 0 1 1 NMP active san
 fc.2000b499baaa8af3:1000b499baaa8af3 fc.50001fe1501add40:50001fe1501add4c
~ #
```

   You could also use the `esxcli` command to get the multipathing information. Here is the syntax:

   ```
   esxcli storage core path list -d <NAA ID of the LUN>
   ```

   Example:

   ```
   esxcli storage nmp device list -d naa.6001438005dec7
   0f0000900001000000
   ```

4. You could also choose to change the PSP corresponding to the LUN by issuing the following command:

   ```
   esxcli storage nmp device set -d <NAA ID of the LUN> --psp=<PSP to
   be used>
   ```

   Example:

   ```
   esxcli storage nmp device set -d naa.6001438005dec7
   0f0000900001000000 --psp=VMW_PSP_MRU
   ```

5. If you change the PSP, it is important to make sure that the change was successful. This is done by issuing the following command:

```
esxcli storage nmp device list -d <NAA ID of the LUN> | grep PSP
```

Example:

```
esxcli storage nmp device list -d naa.6001438005dec7
0f0000900001000000 | grep PSP
```

How it works...

A path to a LUN includes the Host Bus Adapter (HBA)/initiator, the fabric/network switches, and the storage controllers in the array. The availability of a path will be affected if any of these hardware components along the path fail or stop functioning. Multipathing is a method to configure and maintain multiple paths between the host and the storage array. Although redundant fabric switches will be used to achieve this, the multipathing information available at ESXi will not show the switches involved.

Storage multipathing on an ESXi host is achieved with the help of a framework of APIs called **Pluggable Storage Architecture** (**PSA**). The APIs can be used by the storage vendors to write their own **Multipathing Plugins** (**MPP**), thus enabling a closer integration of their storage devices. Some examples for available third-party MPPs available are as follows:

► EMC PowerPath.

► Dell EqualLogic MEM for iSCSI Multipathing.

► VERITAS Dynamic Multipathing for VMware.

► The default multipathing plugin on an ESXi host is called **Native Multipathing Plugin** (**NMP**). The NMP adds support for all the supported storage arrays in the VMware Compatibility List.

The NMP has two sub plugins known as **Storage Array Type Plugin** (**SATP**) and **Path Selection Plugin** (**PSP**). VMware includes the SATP and PSP associations for all tested and supported storage arrays in the form of claim rules.

Storage Array Type Plugin (**SATP**) detects the path state and handles path failover, whereas **Path Selection Plugin** (**PSP**) determines which available physical path should be used to send the I/O.

VMware supports the following path selection plugins:

► **Most Recently Used (MRU)**: In the event of a path failover, this would continue to use the path even if the original path becomes accessible again. Its initial path selection happens during the boot up of ESXi, where it selects the first-discovered parch as the active path. MRU is the preferred PSP for active/passive arrays and ALUA-based arrays.

- ▸ **Fixed**: One of the multiple paths available is marked as the preferred path. So, in the event of a preferred path becoming accessible again, it will failback to the preferred path. This is most commonly used with active/active and ALUA-based arrays.

- ▸ **Round Robin (RR)**: This distributes I/O to all the active paths. By default, it distributes 1000 IOs on an active path before it sends the next 1000 IOs down the next active path.

We discussed choosing a PSP depending on the array type, so it is important to understand different array types from the multipathing perspective. The array type is determined by the mode in which it operates. There are three such types from a multipathing perspective:

- ▸ **Active/active array**: This supports the simultaneous ownership of a LUN by more than one storage processor.

- ▸ **Active/passive array**: This has a set of storage processors (controllers) that act as active controllers and the remaining are on standby and will only be used in the event of a failover.

- ▸ **Asymmetric Logical Unit Access (ALUA) based array**: This uses the concept of optimized and nonoptimized paths. Here, a nonoptimized path is a data path to the LUN via the interconnecting controller.

There's more...

You could also use the following `esxcli` command to view the multipathing information of a LUN. Here is the syntax:

```
# esxcli storage core path list –d <NAA ID of the LUN>
```

Creating a VMFS datastore

Once we have presented RAW LUNs to an ESXi host for it to be used as a storage container for virtual machine data, it needs to be formatted using VMFS. Creating a VMFS datastore is the process of formatting a LUN by creating a VMFS partition on it.

A datastore (VMFS volume) can be created either by using the vSphere Web Clients' New Datastore wizard or by using ESXi's command-line interface.

Getting ready

Make sure you have the NAA ID, LUN ID, and the size of the LUN, which you have presented to the ESXi host. This is to make sure that you don't end up using an unintended LUN. Do a rescan on the HBAs for the ESXi to detect the presented LUN.

How to do it...

As mentioned before, we can create an VMFS datastore using the following two methods:

- ▶ Using the New Datastore wizard
- ▶ Using the ESXi CLI to create a new VMFS volume

Using the New Datastore wizard

The New Datastore wizard is available from the vSphere Web Clients' GUI. The following procedure will guide you through the steps required in achieving this:

1. Use the vSphere Web Client to connect to vCenter Server.
2. Navigate to **Home** | **Storage**.
3. With the data center object selected, navigate to **Related Objects** | **Datastores**:

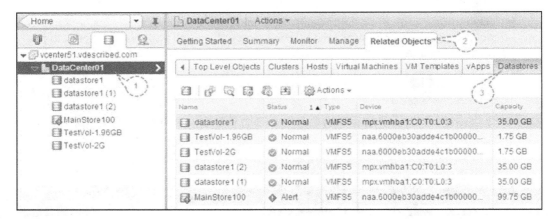

4. Click on the **New Datastore** icon:

5. In the **New Datastore** wizard, type a datastore name and click on **Next**.

6. Choose the filesystem type as **VMFS** and click on **Next**.

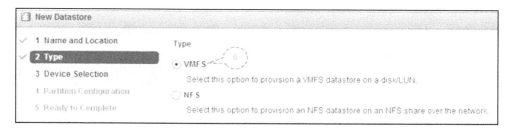

7. Select a host from the list to which the LUN was presented. This will show all the RAW LUNs seen by the selected ESXi host:

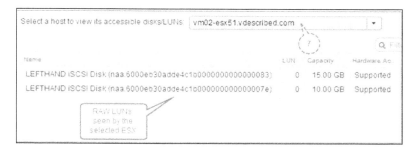

8. Identify and select the RAW LUN you intend to create the VMFS volume on and click on **Next**:

9. Choose the VMFS version and click on **Next**:

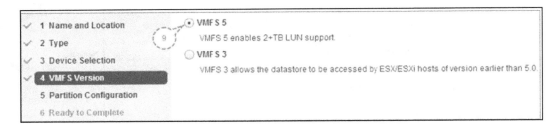

 We have chosen **VMFS 5** as the LUN is presented only to ESXi hosts of Version 5 and above.

10. On the partition configuration screen, choose **Use all available partitions** and click on **Next**.

    The datastore size slider can be used to adjust the size of the VMFS partition that will be created on the LUN. In this example, we have slid the size to 10 GB:

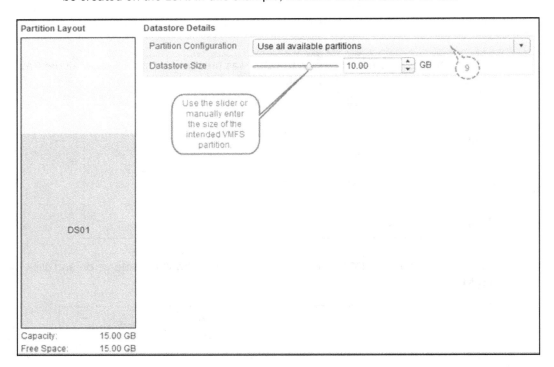

11. On the **Ready to Complete** screen, review the information and click on **Finish**:

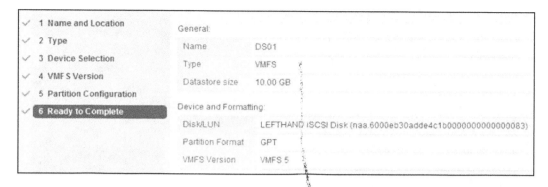

Using ESXi CLI to create a VMFS volume

Keep the NAA ID, LUN ID, and the size of the LUN handy. This is to make sure that you don't end up using an unintended LUN. The command procedures can sometimes be confusing and hard to remember, so I have devised a flowchart that will provide you with an overview of the procedure:

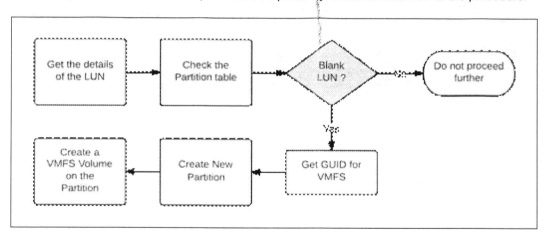

For this example, the NAA ID of the LUN is `naa.6000eb30adde4c1b0000000000000083`.

1. Fetch the details of the device corresponding to the NAA ID using the following command and make a note of the Devfs path:

   Syntax:

   ```
   esxcli storage core device list -d <NAA ID of the device>
   ```

   Command:

   ```
   esxcli storage core device list -d naa.6006048cea95042c3e14f1524e7
   0e300
   ```

Output:

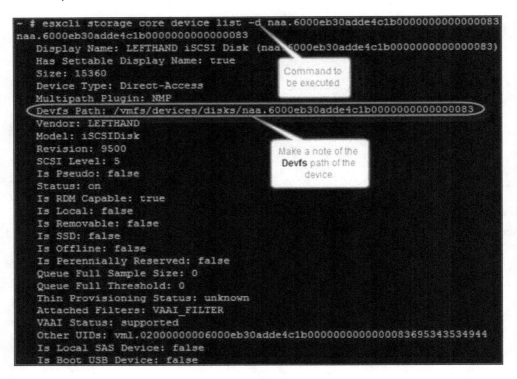

 Note that DevFs is nothing but the console device path of the LUN.

2. Verify the partition table of the device using the following command:

Syntax:

partedUtil getptbl "Devfs Path of the device"

Command:

**partedUtil getptbl /vmfs/devices/disks/ naa.6000eb30adde4c
1b0000000000000083**

Output:

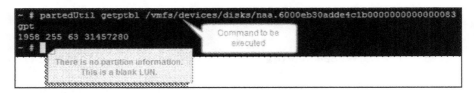

From the output, this is a blank LUN with a CHS value of 394 cylinders, 255 heads, 63 sectors per track, and 6340608 sectors.

1. Get the GUID value for VMFS by issuing the following command:

   ```
   partedUtil showGuids
   ```

   Output:

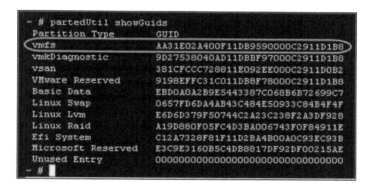

2. Create a new partition on the device using the following command:

   Syntax:

   ```
   partedUtil setptbl "Devfs path of the device" DiskLabel ["partNum
   startSector endSector type/guid attribute"]
   ```

   Syntax with the type/GUID attributes values:

   ```
   partedUtil setptbl "Devfs path of the device" DiskLabel ["partNum
   startSector endSector AA31E02A400F11DB9590000C2911D1B8 0"]
   ```

3. From the second step we know that the number of sectors available is 31457280, but as the start sector is set to 128, the end sector value will be 31457280 - 128, which is 31457152.

   Command:

   ```
   partedUtil setptbl "/vmfs/devices/disks/ naa.6000eb30adde4c
   1b0000000000000083" gpt "1 128 31457152 AA31E02A400F11DB9590000C29
   11D1B8 0"
   ```

   Output:

4. Create a VMFS volume on the device partition using the following command:

Syntax:

```
vmkfstools --createfs vmfs5 --blocksize 1M --setfsname datastore
name Devfs path of the device:Partition Number
```

Output:

```
vmkfstools -C --createfs [vmfs3|vmfs5]
            -b --blocksize #[mMkK]
            -S --setfsname fsName
        -Z --spanfs span-partition
        -G --growfs grown-partition
    deviceName

        -P --queryfs -h --humanreadable
        -T --upgradevmfs
    vmfsPath
```

Command:

```
vmkfstools --createfs vmfs5 --blocksize 1M --setfsname NewDS /
vmfs/devices/disks/ naa.6000eb30adde4c1b0000000000000083:1
```

```
~ # vmkfstools --createfs vmfs5 --blocksize 1M --setfsname DS01 /vmfs/devices
/disks/naa.6000eb30adde4c1b0000000000000083:1
create fs deviceName:'/vmfs/devices/disks/naa.6000eb30adde4c1b00000000000000083
:1', fsShortName:'vmfs5', fsName:'DS01'
deviceFullPath:/dev/disks/naa.6000eb30adde4c1b0000000000000083:1 deviceFile:na
a.6000eb30adde4c1b0000000000000083:1
Checking if remote hosts are using this device as a valid file system. This ma
y take a few seconds...
Creating vmfs5 file system on "naa.6000eb30adde4c1b0000000000000083:1" with bl
ockSize 1048576 and volume label "DS01".
Successfully created new volume: 5080368b-6ec44f54-5d45-000c293bef13
~ #
```

> Command to be executed

> Indicates successful creation of the filesystem

There's more...

AA31E02A400F11DB9590000C2911D1B8 is the GUID type value for a VMFS partition. The decimal type is 251 and the hexadecimal type is 0xFB.

The start sector value for a VMFS partition can also be set to 2048. I have used 128 for demonstration purposes only. In fact, when you create a datastore using the Add Storage wizard, it sets the start sector to 2048 by default. The default start sector for VMFS3 is 128, and this works with VMFS5 as well.

Expanding/growing a VMFS datastore

It is likely that you would run out of free space on a VMFS volume over time as you end up deploying more and more VMs on it, especially in a growing environment. Fortunately, accommodating additional free space on a VMFS volume is possible. However, this requires that the LUN either has free space left on it or it has been expanded/resized in the storage array.

The procedure to resize/expand the LUN in the storage array differs from vendor to vendor, and as this is beyond the scope of this book, we assume that the LUN either has free space on it or has already been expanded.

The following flowchart provides a high-level overview of the procedure:

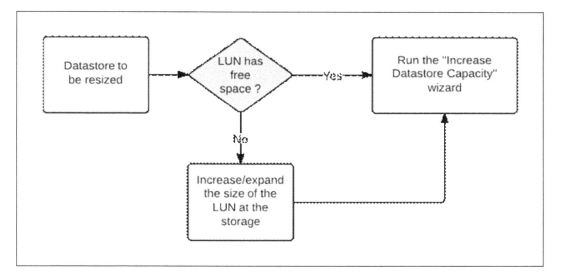

How to do it...

We can expand a VMFS datastore using two methods:

- Using the Increase Datastore Capacity wizard
- Using the ESXi CLI tool vmkfstools

Before attempting to grow the VMFS datastore, issue a rescan on the HBAs to ensure that the ESXi sees the increased size of the LUN.

Also, make note of the NAA ID, LUN number, and the size of the LUN backing the VMFS datastore that you are trying to expand/grow.

Using the Increase Datastore Capacity wizard

We will go through the following process to expand an existing VMFS datastore using the vSphere Web Client's GUI.

1. Use the vSphere Web Client to connect to vCenter Server.

2. Navigate to **Home | Storage**.

3. With the data center object selected, navigate to **Related Objects | Datastores**:

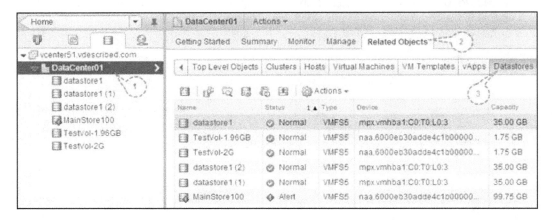

4. Right-click on the datastore you intend to expand and click on **Increase Datastore Capacity...**:

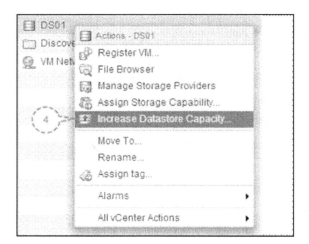

5. Select the LUN backing the datastore and click on **Next**:

6. Use the **Partition Configuration** drop-down menu to select the free space left in DSO1 to expand the datastore:

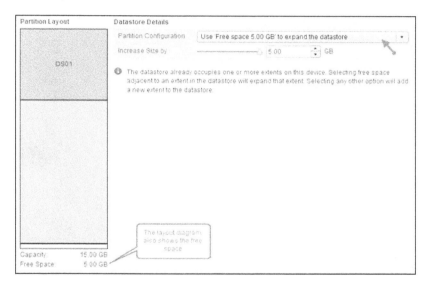

7. On the **Ready to Complete** screen, review the information and click on **Finish** to expand the datastore:

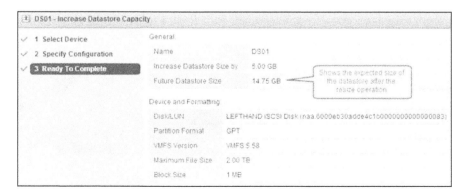

Using the ESXi CLI tool vmkfstools

A VMFS volume can also be expanded using the vmkfstools tool. As with the use of any command-line tool, it can sometimes become difficult to remember the process if you are not doing it often enough to know it like the back of your hand.

Hence, I have devised the following flowchart to provide an overview of the command-line steps that needs to be taken to expand a VMFS volume:

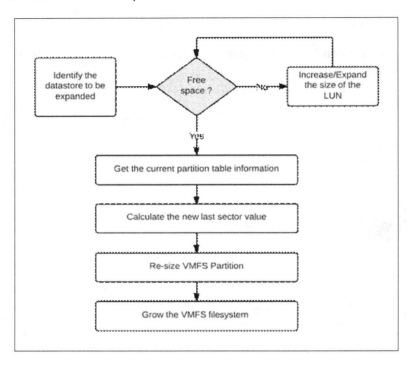

Now that we know what the order of the steps would be from the flowchart, let's delve right into the procedure:

1. Identify the datastore you want to expand using the following command, and make a note of the corresponding NAA ID:

```
esxcli storage vmfs extent list
```

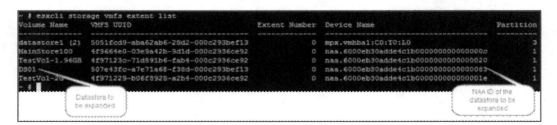

Here, the NAA ID corresponding to the DSO1 datastore is `naa.6000eb30adde4c 1b0000000000000083`.

2. Verify if the ESXi sees the new size of the LUN backing the datastore by issuing the following command:

```
esxcli storage core device list -d naa.6000eb30adde4c
1b0000000000000083
```

3. Get the current partition table information using the following command:

Syntax:

```
partedUtil getptbl "Devfs Path of the device"
```

Command:

```
partedUtil getptbl /vmfs/devices/disks/ naa.6000eb30adde4c
1b0000000000000083
```

4. Calculate the new last sector value. Moving the last sector value closer to the total sector value is necessary in order to use additional space.

The formula to calculate the last sector value is as follows:

(Total number of sectors) – (Start sector value) = Last sector value

So, the last sector value to be used is as follows:

(31457280 – 2048) = 31455232

5. Resize the VMFS partition by issuing the following command:

    Syntax:

    ```
    partedUtil resize "Devfs Path" PartitionNumber NewStartingSector
    NewEndingSector
    ```

    Command:

    ```
    partedUtil resize /vmfs/devices/disks/ naa.6000eb30adde4c
    1b0000000000000083 1 2048 31455232
    ```

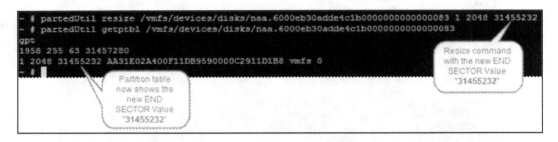

6. Issue the following command to grow the VMFS filesystem:

    Command syntax:

    ```
    vmkfstools --growfs <Devfs Path: Partition Number> <Same Devfs
    Path: Partition Number>
    ```

    Command:

    ```
    vmkfstools --growfs /vmfs/devices/disks/ naa.6000eb30adde4c
    1b0000000000000083:1 /vmfs/devices/disks/ naa.6000eb30adde4c
    1b0000000000000083:1
    ```

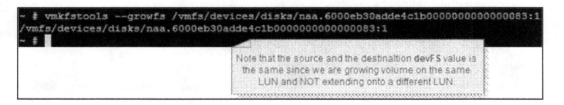

Once the command is executed successfully, it will take you back to the root prompt. There is
no on-screen output for this command.

How it works...

Expanding a VMFS datastore refers to the act of increasing its size within its own extent. This
is possible only if there is free space available immediately after the extent. The maximum
size of a LUN is 64 TB, so the maximum size of a VMFS volume is also 64 TB.

The virtual machines hosted on this VMFS datastore can continue to be in the power-on state while this task is being accomplished.

Extending a VMFS datastore

In the recipe *Expanding/growing a VMFS datastore*, we discussed the procedure involved in increasing the size of a datastore on the same LUN backing the VMFS volume, and that was possible only if the LUN has unused free space on it or was expanded.

You can run into a situation where there is no unused space on the LUN backing the VMFS volume, but your datastore runs out of space. Fortunately, vSphere supports the spanning of a VMFS volume onto multiple LUNs. This means you can span the VMFS volume onto a new LUN so that it can use the free space on it. This process of spanning a VMFS volume onto another LUN is called extending a VMFS datastore.

Getting ready

The VMs running on the volume can still remain powered on while this task is being accomplished. The following flowchart provides a very high-level overview of the procedure:

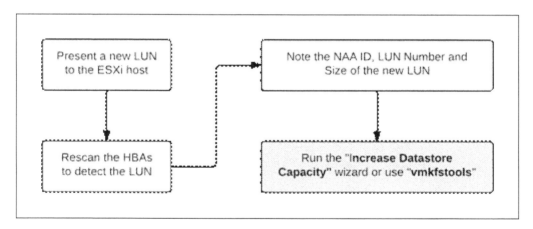

How to do it...

We can extend the size of a VMFS datastore by using either of the following methods:

▶ Using the **Increase Datastore Capacity** wizard
▶ Using the ESXi CLI tool vmkfstools

Using the Increase Datastore Capacity wizard

The following procedure will guide you through the steps required to extend a VMFS datastore using the Increase Datastore Capacity wizard:

1. Use the vSphere Web Client to connect to vCenter Server.

2. Navigate to **Home** | **Storage**.

3. With the data center object selected, navigate to **Related Objects** | **Datastores**.

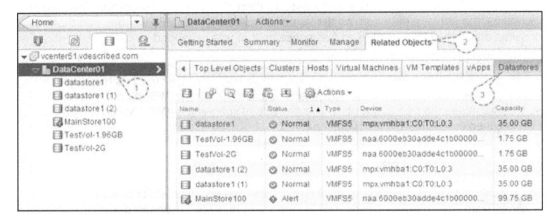

4. Right-click on the datastore you intend to expand and click on **Increase Datastore Capacity....**

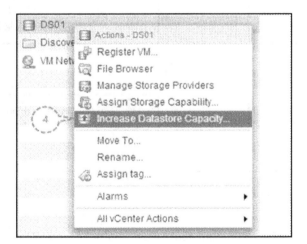

5. Select the RAW LUN available to extend the datastore onto it.

6. Select **Use all available partitions** from the partition configuration drop-down box, choose a size to use, and click on **Next**.

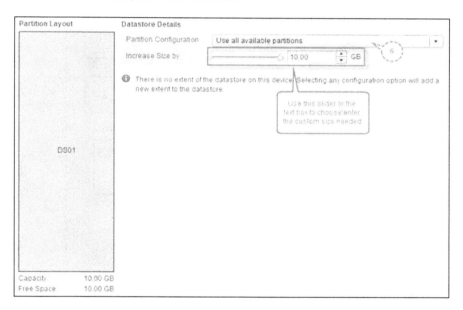

7. Review the details in the **Ready to Complete** screen and click on **Finish**:

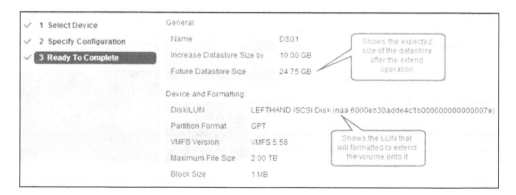

Using vmkfstools

In this section, we will learn how to use the CLI tool vmkfstools to extend the VMFS volume. This flowchart provides an overview of the command-line procedure:

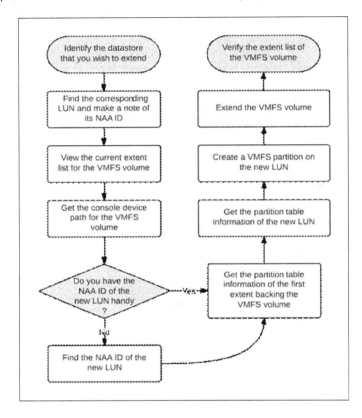

The following procedure will guide you through the steps required to extend a VMFS volume using CLI. To demonstrate, we have presented a 5 GB blank LUN to the ESXi hosts.

1. Identify the datastore you want to expand using the following command and make a note of the corresponding NAA ID:

```
esxcli storage vmfs extent list
```

2. Verify the list of extents used currently by the volume using the following command:

   `Vmkfstools -P /vmfs/volumes/DS01`

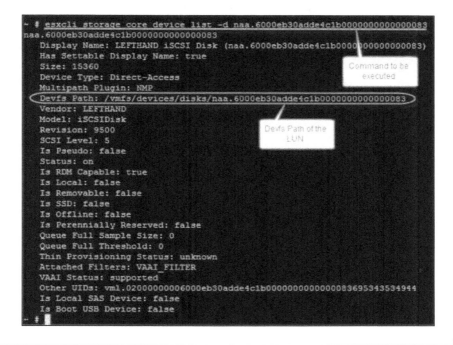

3. Get the `Devfs/Console device` path of the VMFS datastore and the LUN that will be used as an extent for the datastore.

   Syntax:

   `esxcli storage core device list -d <NAA ID of the device>`

   From step 2, we know that the NAA ID of "DS01" is `naa.6000eb30adde4c 1b0000000000000083`.

   Command:

   `esxcli storage core device list -d naa.6000eb30adde4c 1b0000000000000083`

4. If you don't have the NAA ID of the new blank LUN handy, we can look up the LUN info using the size by executing the following command:

```
esxcfg-scsidevs -l | grep "Size: 5" -B 3 -A 3
```

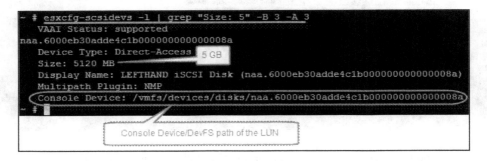

Console Device/DevFS path of the LUN

5. Get the partition table information of the first extent (LUN) backing the datastore DS01 and the new 5-GB blank LUN.

The commands to be executed are as follows:

```
partedUtil getptbl /vmfs/devices/disks/naa.6000eb30adde4c
1b0000000000000083
```

```
partedUtil getptbl /vmfs/devices/disks/naa.6000eb30adde4c1b0000000
00000008a
```

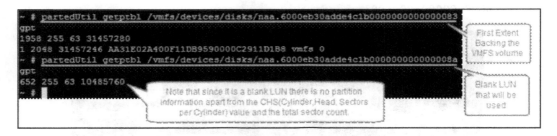

First Extent Backing the VMFS volume

Note that since it is a blank LUN there is no partition information apart from the CHS(Cylinder,Head, Sectors per Cylinder) value and the total sector count.

Blank LUN that will be used

6. Create a partition of the type VMFS on the new extent LUN (blank LUN being used to add an extent to the datastore DS01).

The formula to find the end sector value is as follows:

Total number of sectors - start sector value = Last sector value

10485760 (total sectors) - 2048(start sector) = 10483712 (end sector value)

Command:

```
partedUtil setptbl " /vmfs/devices/disks/naa.6000eb30adde4c1b00000
0000000008a" gpt "1 2048 10483712 AA31E02A400F11DB9590000C2911D1B8
0 "
```

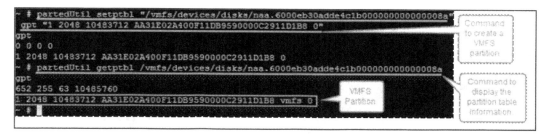

7. Extend the VMFS volume onto the new partition on the extent LUN by issuing the following command.

Syntax:

```
vmkfstools --spanfs <partition on the extent-LUN> <partition on
the VMFS volume LUN>
```

Here, the partitions are specified by using the following format:

```
<Devfs Path>:< Partition Number>
```

Command:

```
vmkfstools --spanfs /vmfs/devices/disks/naa.6006048c00e2cfeec4f4df
7b671fd574:1 /vmfs/devices/disks/naa.6006048c99a9f599493c52669bb2
ea63:1
```

Enter 0 for _yes when prompted to confirm the action:

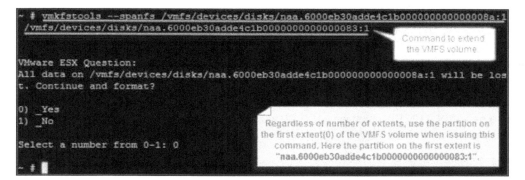

 Regardless of the number of extents, use the partition on the first extent (0) of the VMFS volume when issuing this command. Here, the partition on the first extent is naa.6000eb30adde4c 1b0000000000000083:1, and the first argument to the command is the partition on the LUN onto which VMFS will be extended.

8. Issue the command vmkfstools -P to check if the volume now spans more than one extent. In this case, it should span across three extents in total:

```
~ # vmkfstools -P /vmfs/volumes/DS01/
VMFS-5.58 file system spanning 3 partitions.
File system label (if any): DS01
Mode: public
Capacity 31406948352 (29952 file blocks * 1048576), 30402412544 (28994 blocks) avail
UUID: 50806bf8-f720ef8c-3456-000c293bef13
Partitions spanned (on "lvm"):
        naa.6000eb30adde4c1b0000000000000083:1
        naa.6000eb30adde4c1b000000000000007e:1      Now shows
        naa.6000eb30adde4c1b000000000000008a:1      three extents
Is Native Snapshot Capable: YES
~ #
```

How it works...

Unlike expanding/growing a VMFS volume, extending a volume will make the volume span across multiple LUNs, and this is done by adding further extents to the VMFS volume.

When I say "adding further extents", the contextual meaning refers to the primary partition on the new LUN, which will be used to extend the VMFS volume onto it.

A VMFS datastore can span across a maximum of 32 LUN extents.

The size of the extent can now be greater than 2 TB, the limit being the maximum VMFS volume size of 64 TB.

The first extent on the VMFS volume contains the metadata for the entire set of extents. If the LUN with the first extent was lost, then you would end up losing data on all the other dependent extents.

Here is what an extended VMFS volume would look like. The volume was initially 300 GB in size and was backed by LUN-A, which was of the same size. The volume was then extended onto a new LUN (LUN-B), which was 100 GB in size, thus increasing the effective size on the VMFS volume to 400 GB:

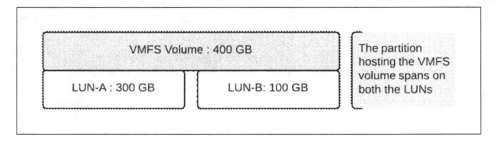

A common misconception is that if either of these LUNs (LUN-A or LUN-B) goes offline or is inaccessible, the VMFS volume (datastore) will become inaccessible as well. This is not true. When you add extents to a datastore, the very first LUN that originally backed the datastore will become the head extent because it holds all the information regarding the other extents. If for any reason you lose the head extent, then that would make the entire VMFS datastore go offline. However, if you lose an extent that is not a head extent, then the datastore will still remain accessible, but only the virtual machines whose VMDKs depend on the lost extent will become inaccessible.

Unmounting a VMFS datastore

Unmounting a datastore is a way of telling the ESXi host that the LUN will no longer be available for any I/O operation, until it is re-mounted. It is recommended to unmount a VMFS datastore before the LUN backing it is unpresented from an ESXi host.

It is advised that you take care of the following before you proceed with the unmount operation:

 ▶ All the VMs should be migrated off to a different datastore
 ▶ The datastore should be removed from a datastore cluster
 ▶ The datastore should remain unmanaged by Storage DRS (SDRS)
 ▶ Storage I/O Control (SIOC) should be disabled for the datastore
 ▶ Should not be in use as a vSphere HA heartbeat datastore

How to do it...

A VMFS volume can be unmounted from the vSphere Web Client GUI or using the tools available in the ESXi's CLI. In the *How to do it...* section of this recipe, we will cover both of these methods.

Using the vSphere Web Client GUI to unmount a datastore

The vSphere Web Client can be used to unmount a datastore. It is particularly useful when you have to unmount the datastore from multiple ESXi hosts. This is because it has a vCenter-level vantage point. The following steps will guide you through the process of unmounting a VMFS datastore using the vSphere Web Client:

1. Use the vSphere Web Client to connect to vCenter Server.

2. Navigate to **Home** | **Storage**.

3. With the data center object selected, navigate to **Related Objects | Datastores**.

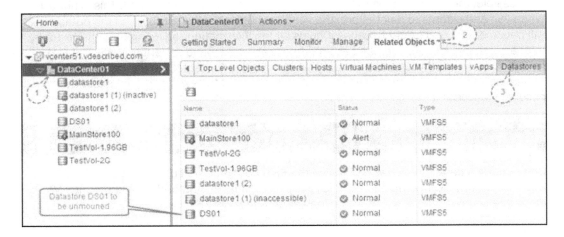

4. Right-click on the datastore you wish to unmount and navigate to **All vCenter Actions | Unmount Datastore**:

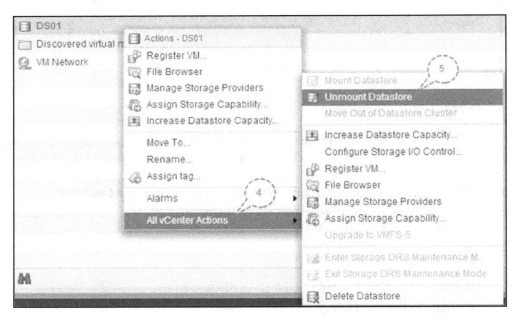

5. Select the ESXi host you wish to unmount the volume from and click on **OK**:

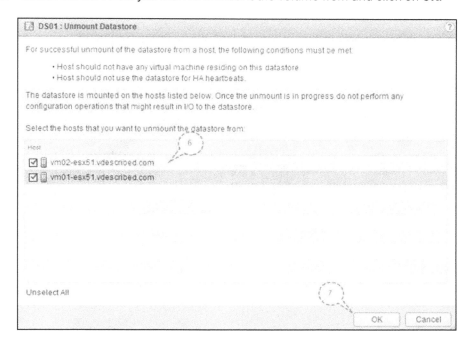

6. Verify the **Recent Tasks** pane to make sure that the volume unmount operation has completed successfully on the selected ESXi hosts.

Using the ESXi CLI tool "unmount"

The vSphere esxcli can be used to unmount the VMFS datastore, but keep in mind that as it is a command line, it is done at a per host level. If you need to unmount the datastore this way on more than one ESXi host, then you will have to SSH/console into each of those ESXi hosts and issue the unmount command.

The following procedure will guide you through the steps required to unmount a VMFS volume using the ESXi CLI:

1. View all the volumes available by executing the following command:

```
esxcli storage filesystem list
```

2. Unmount the datastore by issuing the following command:

   Syntax:

```
esxcli storage filesystem unmount --volume-label <name of the
datastore>
```

   Command:

```
esxcli storage filesystem unmount --volume-label DS01
```

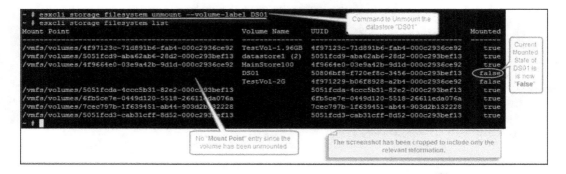

 Note that in the preceding screenshot, we have executed a second command to list the volumes.

Mounting a VMFS datastore

A previously unmounted VMFS datastore can be re-mounted to the ESXi host. Doing so will make the datastore available for I/O operations.

How to do it...

The mount operation can be performed from the vSphere Web Client GUI or using the ESXi CLI. This section will cover both the methods.

Using the vSphere Web Client UI to mount

The following procedure will guide you through the steps required to mount a VMFS volume using the vSphere Web Client.

1. Use the vSphere Web Client to connect to vCenter Server.

2. Navigate to **Home** | **Storage**.

3. With the data center object selected, navigate to **Related Objects** | **Datastores** and find the datastore in the **Unmounted** state:

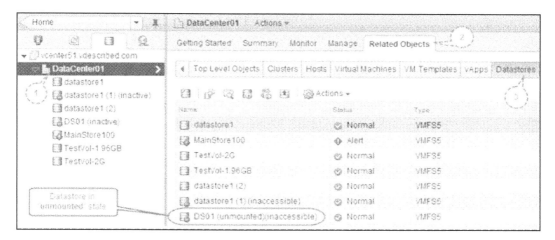

4. Right-click on the unmounted datastore and navigate to **All vCenter Actions |
Mount Datastore**:

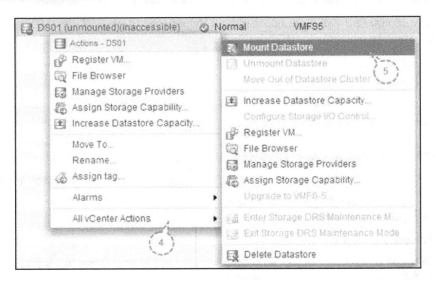

5. Select the ESXi host to which the volume should be mounted and click on **OK** to
initiate the mount operation:

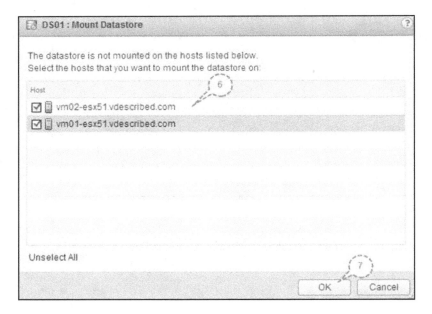

6. Verify the **Recent Tasks** pane to ensure that the mount operations have successfully completed on all the ESXi hosts that were selected.

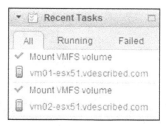

Using esxcli to mount an unmounted volume

vSphere esxcli can also be used to mount an unmounted volume. The CLI operation can only be performed on a per-host basis. As with the unmount operation, if a volume needs to be mounted this way to multiple ESXi hosts, then you will have to SSH/console into each of those hosts and issue the mount command.

The following procedure will help you mount an unmounted VMFS datastore:

1. View all the volumes available on the host, which should also list the volumes in the unmounted state.

   Command:

   ```
   esxcli storage filesystem list
   ```

2. Issue the following command to mount the volume.

   Syntax:

   ```
   esxcli storage filesystem mount --volume-label <name of the datastore>
   ```

Command:

```
esxcli storage filesystem mount --volume-label DS01
```

Deleting a VMFS datastore

Unlike the unmount operation, a delete operation will destroy all the data on the datastore. Once done, you cannot revert this operation. Hence, ensure that you move all the virtual machine data that is currently on the datastore to another datastore.

How to do it...

The following procedure will guide you to delete a datastore from the vSphere Web Client:

1. Use the vSphere Web Client to connect to the vCenter Server.

2. Navigate to **Home** | **Storage**.

3. With the data center object selected, navigate to **Related Objects** | **Datastores** and identify the VMFS datastore to be deleted:

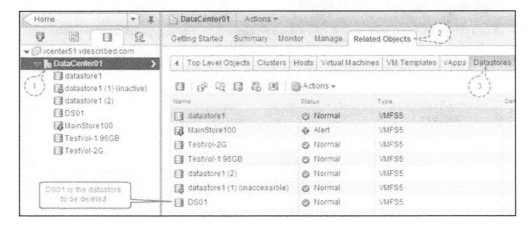

4. Right-click on the datastore to be deleted and navigate to **All vCenter Actions** | **Delete Datastore**.

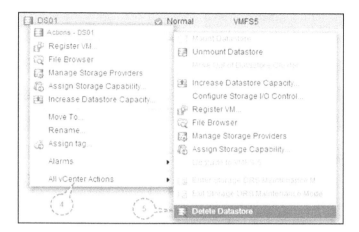

5. Click on **Yes** in the **Confirm Delete Datastore** dialog box:

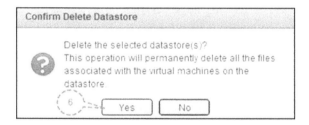

6. Verify the **Recent Tasks** pane, which should show that **Remove datastore** completed successfully.

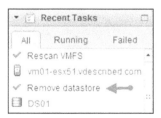

Upgrading from VMFS3 to VMFS5

There are several enhancements added to version 5 of VMFS. Knowing these enhancements will definitely motivate you to upgrade to this version. Nevertheless, the upgrade process is nondisruptive.

Although this is an in-place upgrade, you should take the following precautions before upgrading:

▶ Back up the virtual machines on the volume, or migrate them off to a different datastore

▶ Ensure that there are no ESX 3.x or ESX 4.x servers in the environment accessing the same datastore

The VMware® vSphere® VMFS-5 Upgrade Considerations whitepaper explains more about VMFS-5 enhancement and the upgrade considerations. You can access the paper at `http://www.vmware.com/files/pdf/techpaper/VMFS-5_Upgrade_Considerations.pdf`.

How to do it...

The VMFS upgrade can be done in two ways:

▶ By using the vSphere Web Client GUI

▶ By using the ESXi CLI tool vmkfstools

Upgrading the VMFS using the vSphere Web Client GUI

The following procedure will guide you through the steps required to upgrade a VMFS datastore:

1. Use the vSphere Web Client to connect to vCenter Server.

2. Navigate to **Home | Storage**.

3. With the data center object selected, navigate to **Related Objects | Datastores** and identify the VMFS datastore to be upgraded.

4. Right-click on the VMFS-3 datastore and navigate to **All vCenter Actions | Upgrade to VMFS-5**:

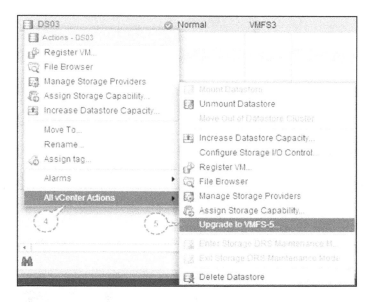

5. Select the datastore from the list and click on **OK**:

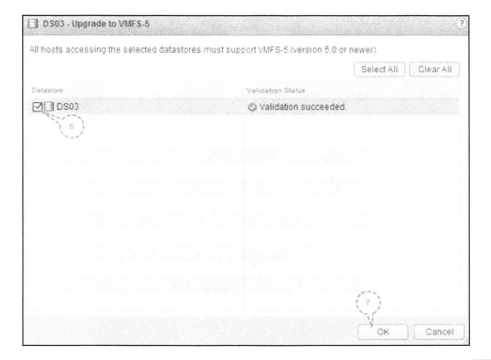

6. Verify the **Recent Tasks** pane to make sure that the **Upgrade VMFS** tasks have been successfully completed:

Upgrading using the ESXi CLI tool vmkfstools

A VMFS3 volume can also be upgraded from the ESXi CLI. The tool that can be used for this purpose is known as **vmkfstools**. The following procedure will guide you through the use of the tool to accomplish the upgrade from VMFS-3 to VMFS-5.

1. Identify the VMFS3 volume to be upgraded by issuing the following command:

   ```
   esxcli storage filesystem list
   ```

2. Query the filesystem details for reference. (This step is not mandatory.)

   ```
   vmkfstools -Ph -v10 /vmfs/volumes/DS03
   ```

3. Issue the following command to perform the upgrade:

    `vmkfstools --upgradevmfs /vmfs/volumes/DS03/`

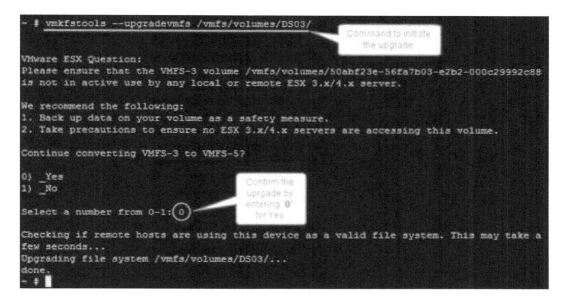

4. Verify that the upgrade is complete by querying the filesystem again:

    `vmkfstools -Ph -v10 /vmfs/volumes/DS03`

How it works...

The upgrade process, regardless of the method, is now in place. The VMFS5 data structures are appended to the existing VMFS3 data structures making the process seamless.

A few things don't change after an upgrade from VMFS3 to VMFS5:

▶ The uniform 1 MB block size is not implemented during the upgrade. The upgrade will retain VMFS3's block size value. Use StorageMotion to move VM from an old VMFS to the new version 5 (to improve the block size).

▶ The subblock size will also remain unchanged at 64 KB.

▶ It will retain VMFS3's limit on the maximum number of files per datastore.

▶ It will retain the MBR partition type until the volume grows beyond 2 TB.

▶ The VMFS partition's start sector value is also retained at 128.

▶ The VAAI ATS flag cannot be enabled on a VMFS volume upgraded from VMFS3 to VMFS5.

 To fully utilize VMFS5's features, you can create a new VMFS5 volume, migrate the VMs from the VMFS3 volume to the VMFS5 volume, and then destroy the VMFS3 volume.

Mounting VMFS from a snapshot LUN

Some environments maintain copies of the production LUNs as a backup, by replicating them. These replicas are exact copies of the LUNs that were already presented to the ESXi hosts. If for any reason a replicated LUN is presented to an ESXi host, then the host will not mount the VMFS volume on the LUN. This is a precaution to prevent data corruption.

You can, however, force mount such a volume, but you need to make sure that the original LUN is unpresented.

How to do it...

The act of mounting a snapshot volume can be done in two ways:

▶ Using the vSphere Web Client's New Datastore wizard

▶ Using the ESXi CLI

Using the New Datastore wizard

The following procedure will guide you through the steps required to mount a VMFS volume on a replica LUN or a LUN detected as a snapshot:

1. Use the vSphere Web Client to connect to vCenter Server.

2. Navigate to **Home | Storage**.

3. With the data center object selected, navigate to **Related Objects | Datastores** and click on the **New Datastore** icon:

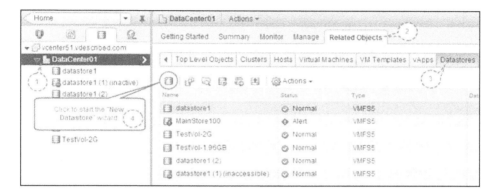

4. In the **New Datastore** wizard, there is no need to supply a new name as it will not be used. Leave it at its default value and click on **Next**:

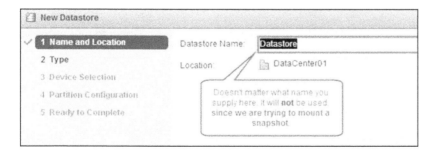

5. Select the filesystem as **VMFS** and click on **Next**:

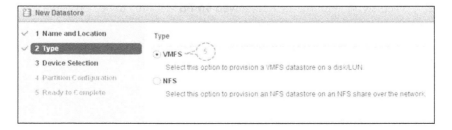

6. Select an ESXi host from the list shown in the following screenshot to populate the LUN devices seen by it, select the LUN marked as **Snapshot Volume**, and click on **Next**:

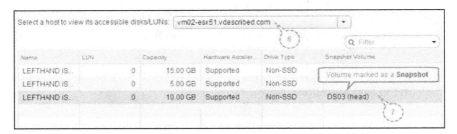

7. Choose the option **Keep existing signature** and click on **Next**.

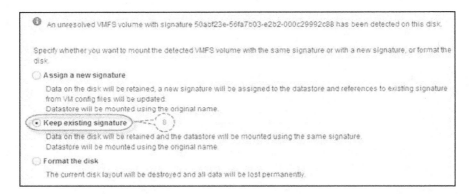

8. Review the **Ready to Complete** screen and click on **Finish** to mount the volume:

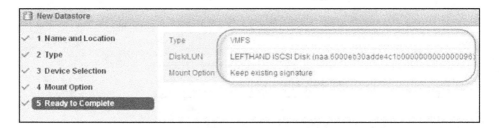

9. Verify the task pane for the task **Resolved VMFS volumes** to be completed successfully:

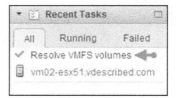

Using ESXi CLI

A volume on a snapshot LUN can also be mounted using the ESXi CLI commands.

The following procedure will guide you through the steps required to mount such a volume:

1. List all the volumes detected as snapshots by the ESXi host by executing the following command:

    `esxcli storage vmfs snapshot list`

2. Issue the command to mount the snapshot volume.

    Syntax:

    `esxcli storage vmfs snapshot mount -n -l "Volume_Label"`

    Command:

    `esxcli storage vmfs snapshot mount -n -l "DS03"`

> The `-n` option in the preceding command will do a nonpersistent mount of the volume, which means you will not find the LUN mounted after a host reboot. Issuing the command without the `-n` switch will do a persistent mount of the volume, which means the LUN will remain mounted even after a reboot.

How it works...

Every VMFS volume, when created, gets assigned a **UUID** that is unique. When a LUN is replicated, it will still have the same UUID because the UUID is stored in the VMFS' **superblock**. When an ESXi host detects that a different LUN has the same UUID, it marks the volume on that LUN as a snapshot and by default will not mount it. The decision to mount the VMFS is left to the administrator.

If the administrator decides to mount the snapshot volume to an ESXi host, which already has the original volume presented to it, then they will have to unpresent the original volume and then mount the snapshot volume. Otherwise, they will end up corrupting both the LUNs.

Resignaturing VMFS on a snapshot LUN

Resignaturing is done when you know that the LUN that has been detected as a snapshot is indeed a snapshot and you intend to use it going forward. For example, if the LUN is presented at a DR site, and if you do not want to retain the same UUID, then you can choose to resignature the VMFS volume.

How to do it...

Resignaturing can be done in two ways:

- ▶ Using the vSphere Web Client's New Datastore wizard
- ▶ Using ESXi CLI

Using the datastore wizard

Much like mounting a VMFS volume residing on a snapshot LUN, which we discussed in the previous section, you can follow the same new storage wizard to resignature the snapshot LUN.

The following procedure will guide you through the steps required to mount a VMFS volume on a replica LUN or a LUN detected as snapshot:

1. Use the vSphere Web Client to connect to vCenter Server.
2. Navigate to **Home | Storage**.
3. With the data center object selected, navigate to **Related Objects | Datastores** and click on the **New Datastore** icon.
4. In the **New Datastore** wizard, there is no need to supply a new name, as it will not be used. Leave it at its default name and click on **Next**.
5. Select the filesystem as **VMFS** and click on **Next**.
6. Select an ESXi host from the list to populate the LUN devices seen by it and select the LUN marked as **Snapshot Volume** and click on **Next**.

 For screenshots until the sixth step, refer to the previous recipe **Mounting VMFS from a snapshot LUN**. Screenshots were not included in this section because they are exactly the same.

7. Choose the option **Assign a new signature** and click on **Next**:

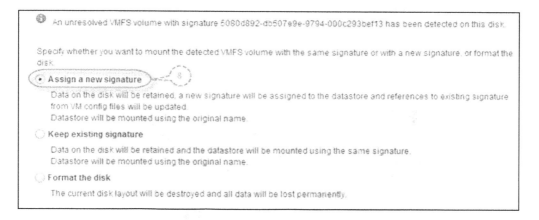

8. Review the **Ready to Complete** screen and click on **Finish**.

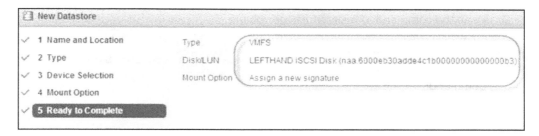

9. Verify the **Recent Tasks** pane to make sure that the task **Resignature unresolved VMFS volume** has been completed successfully:

Using ESXi CLI

The VMFS volume can also be resignatured using CLI commands. The following procedure will guide you through the commands to be executed to resignature a snapshot volume:

1. List all the VMFS volumes detected as snapshots by executing the following command:

   ```
   esxcli storage vmfs snapshot list
   ```

   ```
   ~ # esxcli storage vmfs snapshot list
   50ac2480-34aab91d-fb4b-000c29992c88
      Volume Name: DS-15G
      VMFS UUID: 50ac2480-34aab91d-fb4b-000c29992c88
      Can mount: true
      Reason for un-mountability:
      Can resignature: true
      Reason for non-resignaturability:
      Unresolved Extent Count: 1
   ~ #
   ```

2. Issue the command to resignature the volume.

   Syntax:

   ```
   esxcli storage vmfs snapshot resignature -l <volume_Label>
   ```

   Command:

   ```
   esxcli storage vmfs snapshot resignature -l "DS-15G"
   ```

How it works...

The resignature operation will update the VMFS super block with a new UUID. The datastore aliases are prepended with snap-.

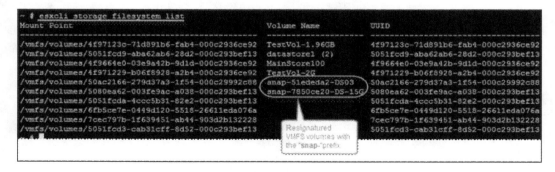

The following screenshot shows the vSphere Web Client GUI listing the resignatured volumes, prepended with the text **snap-**:

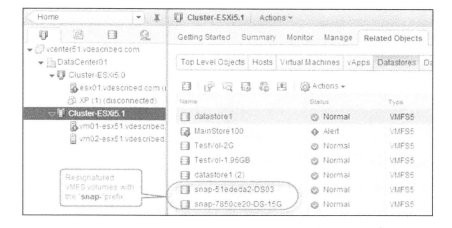

You will have to power off the running virtual machines and rename the datastores as needed and then re-register the VMs as the inventory registrations use the absolute path (with the UUID) to the VMX file.

Masking paths to a LUN

You can remove access to a LUN by masking all of its paths to the ESXi host. This can be used when troubleshooting storage issues. This is achieved by using the `MASK_PATH` PSA plugin to claim the paths corresponding to the intended LUN.

The following flowchart provides an overview of the procedure:

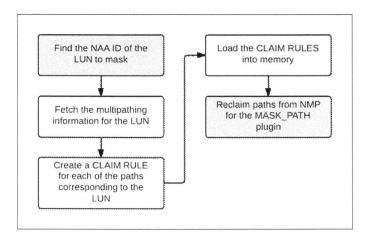

How to do it...

The following procedure will help you mask paths to a LUN:

1. Get the NAA ID of the LUN, which needs to be masked, by issuing the following command. The following command will list all the NAA IDs seen by the ESXi:

    ```
    esxcfg-scsidevs -u
    ```

2. Get the multipathing information of the LUN by issuing the following command.

    Syntax:

    ```
    esxcfg-mpath -l -d <naa-id of the LUN>
    ```

    Example:

    ```
    esxcfg-mpath -l -d naa.6000eb30adde4c1b0000000000000112
    ```

3. Create a claim rule for each of the paths to the LUN by issuing the following command.

    Syntax:

    ```
    esxcli storage core claimrule add -r <rule number> -t location -A
    <hba> -C <channel number> -L <LUN Number> -P MASK_PATH
    ```

    Example:

    ```
    esxcli storage core claimrule add -r 120 -t location -A vmhba33 -C
    1 -L 0 -P MASK_PATH
    ```

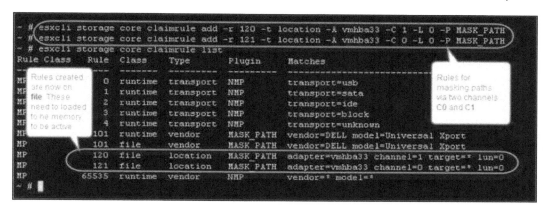

4. Load the rules on the file into the memory by issuing the following command:

```
esxcli storage core claimrule load
```

5. Reclaim the paths for MASK_PATH from NMP by issuing the following command:

```
esxcli storage core claiming reclaim -d <NAA ID of the LUN>
```

Example:

```
esxcli storage core claiming reclaim -d naa.6000eb30adde4c
1b0000000000000112
```

Unmasking paths to a LUN

It is possible to unmask paths to a LUN. Deleting the claim rules, which were created to assign the ownership of the paths to the `MASK_PATH` plugin, and unclaiming the paths from the plugin, does this. Understanding how the paths to a LUN are masked will be a good starting point for this task. Read the recipe *Masking paths to a LUN* before you begin. The following flowchart provides an overview of the unmasking procedure:

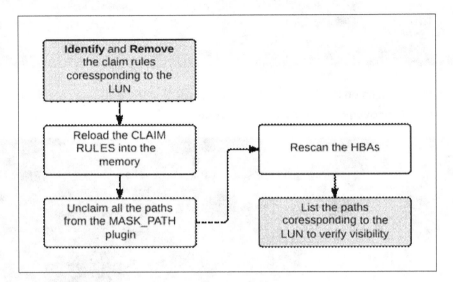

How to do it...

The following procedure will help you mask paths to a LUN:

1. Identify the claim rules corresponding to the LUN and remove them.

   Syntax:

   ```
   esxcli storage claimrule remove -r <rule ID>
   ```

   We know that the rule IDs are 120 and 121 from the recipe *Masking paths to a LUN*.

   Example:

   ```
   esxcli storage core claimrule remove -r 120
   esxcli storage core claimrule remove -r 121
   ```

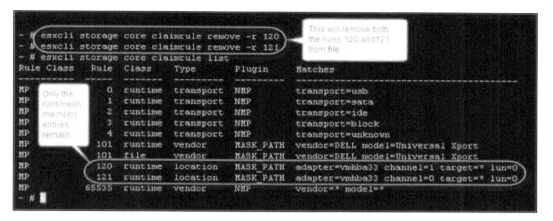

2. Now that the rules have been deleted from the file, reload the claim rules to the memory to remove the runtime entries. Issue the following command to load the rules in the memory:

```
esxcli storage core claimrule load
```

The runtime entries for 120 and 121 will be removed from the memory because they don't have a corresponding file entry.

3. Unclaim all the paths for the LUN from the MASK_PATH plugin by issuing the following command:

Syntax:

```
esxcli storage core claiming unclaim -t location -A <HBA> -C
<Channel> -L <LUN ID> -P MASK_PATH
```

Example:

```
esxcli storage core claiming unclaim -t location -A vmhba33 -C 0
-L 0 -P MASK_PATH
```

```
esxcli storage core claiming unclaim -t location -A vmhba33 -C 1
-L 0 -P MASK_PATH
```

4. Issue a rescan on the HBAs.

Syntax:

```
esxcfg-rescan <HBA>
```

Example:

```
esxcfg-rescan vmhba33
```

5. Verify the LUN's visibility by listing all the paths corresponding to it.

    Syntax:

    ```
    esxscfg-mpath -l -d <naa-id of the LUN>
    ```

    Example:

    ```
    esxcfg-mapth -l -d naa.6000eb30adde4c1b0000000000000112
    ```

Creating a datastore cluster

Datastores presented to the ESXi servers can be grouped together into a single I/O and capacity pool known as the datastore cluster. The main purpose of creating a datastore cluster is to leverage Storage DRS's functionality to load balance the datastore's space utilization and I/O capacity.

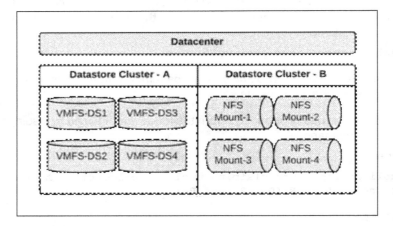

For datastores to be in a datastore cluster, they should meet the following requirements:

▶ The datastores in a datastore cluster should only be accessible to ESXi hosts from a single data center

▶ A single datastore cluster cannot contain both VMFS and NFS volumes

▶ All the ESXi hosts accessing the datastores should be of Version ESXi 5.0 or higher

There are a few more requirements documented in the *Datastore Cluster Requirements* section of the *vSphere Resource Management* guide at http://bit.ly/vsphere55_ Resource_Management_Guide.

How to do it...

The following procedure will guide you through the steps required to create a datastore cluster:

1. Use the vSphere Web Client to connect to the vCenter Server.
2. Navigate to **Home** | **Storage**:

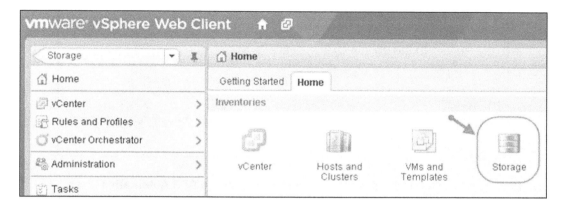

3. Right-click on the data center in which you intend to create the datastore cluster and click on **New Datastore Cluster...** to bring up the New Datastore Cluster wizard.

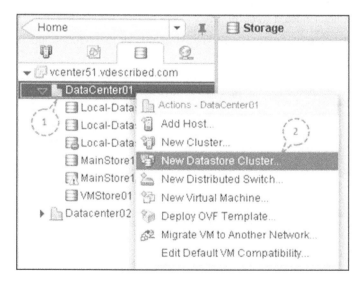

4. In the New Datastore Cluster wizard, specify a datastore cluster name. By default, the wizard will enable SDRS on the New Datastore Cluster. You will notice that the checkbox **Turn ON Storage DRS** is preselected. As we are *not* enabling Storage DRS now, uncheck the box **Turn on Storage DRS** and click on **Next** to continue:

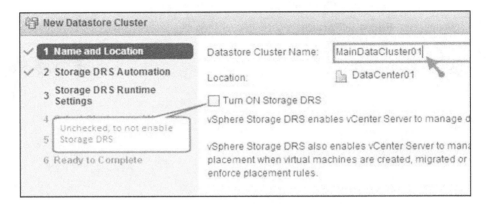

5. The next screen will prompt you to select the **Storage DRS Automation** levels. As we have chosen *not* to enable Storage DRS, we do not have to modify any of these settings. Click on **Next** to continue.

6. The next screen will prompt you to select **Storage DRS Runtime Settings**. As we have chosen not to enable Storage DRS, do not modify any of the runtime settings. Click on **Next** to continue.

7. On the next screen, select the ESXi host cluster or individual hosts and click on **Next** to continue.

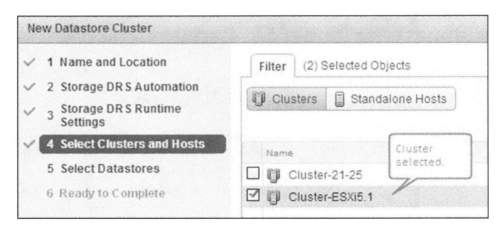

8. The next screen will, by default, list only the datastores connected to all the selected ESXi hosts. In this case, we selected a cluster, so the datastore connected to all the ESXi hosts in the cluster will be listed for selection. Select the datastores and click on **Next** to continue.

9. On the **Ready to Complete** screen, review the configuration and hit **Finish** to create the datastore cluster.

10. The **Recent Tasks** pane should show the **Move datastores into a datastore cluster** task as completed successfully:

How it works...

A datastore cluster created without enabling Storage DRS is just a container for the selected datastores. Although Storage DRS is not enabled, the statistics will be collected, but there will be no load balancing.

The New Datastore Cluster wizard will, by default, list only those datastores that are connected to all the selected ESXi hosts. This is because SDRS won't be able to migrate the VM storage to datastores inaccessible to the ESXi hosts.

When you choose datastores to be part of a datastore cluster, it is best practice to choose similar datastores. The similarities include RAID level, VAAI, storage protocols (FC, iSCSI, NFS), and storage type (SSDs, SATA, and so on). It is also considered best practice to choose datastores of similar sizes.

There's more...

Read the VMware vSphere® Storage DRS Interoperability Guide at `http://www.vmware.com/files/pdf/techpaper/vsphere-storage-drs-interoperability.pdf`.

Enabling Storage DRS

Storage DRS is a mechanism to balance space utilization and the I/O load on datastores in a datastore cluster by migrating (Storage vMotion) the VMs. Storage DRS can only be enabled on a datastore cluster. To learn how to create a datastore cluster, read the recipe *Creating a datastore cluster*.

It also influences the initial placement of the VMs on the datastores. For the Storage DRS' I/O load balancing to work, all the hosts accessing the datastores should be of Version ESXi 5.0 or above. Also, the cluster should not contain replicated and nonreplicated datastores. In this recipe, we will learn how to enable Storage DRS.

How to do it...

The following procedure will guide you through the steps required to enable SDRS on a datastore cluster:

1. Use the vSphere Web Client to connect to vCenter Server.

2. Navigate to **Home** | **Storage**.

3. Select the datastore cluster from the left pane and navigate to the **Manage** tab and then to the **Settings** subtab:

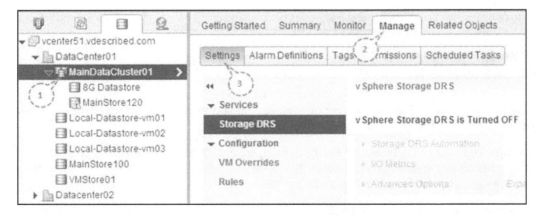

4. Click on **Storage DRS** and then click on **Edit** to bring up the **Edit Storage DRS Settings** window:

5. In the **Edit Storage DRS Settings** windows, select the checkbox **Turn ON vSphere Storage DRS**:

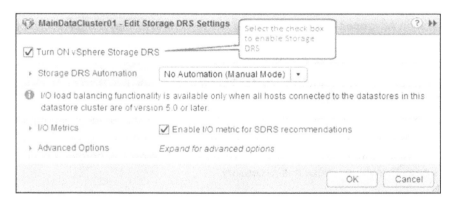

6. Click on **Storage DRS Automation** to expand the automation settings; choose an automation level and the space utilization threshold. By default, the automation level is set to **No Automation (Manual Mode)**. You can also select **Fully Automated**. The space utilization threshold percentage is set to **80** by default. Do not change the slider position unless it is necessary.

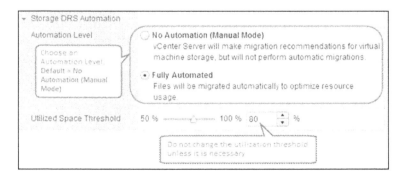

7. Click on **I/O Metrics** to expand the I/O metrics settings. Choose to enable/disable the I/O load balancing for Storage DRS by selecting/deselecting the checkbox **Enable I/O metric for SDRS recommendations**. It is enabled by default. Also choose **I/O Latency Threshold**. The default value is 15 ms (milliseconds).

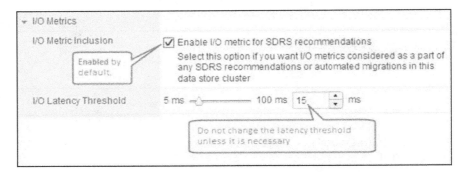

8. Click on **Advanced Options** to expand the window to display the advanced options.

9. Choose to enable/disable the **Default VM affinity** rule by selecting/deselecting the checkbox **Keep VMDKs together by default**.

10. Choose the periodicity of the **cluster imbalance check**. It is 8 hours by default. Do not change this unless it is necessary.

11. Choose **I/O Imbalance Threshold**. Leave the slider at its default position, unless a change is necessary.

12. Choose **Minimum Space Utilization Difference**. The default percentage is **5**. Do not change this value unless it is necessary.

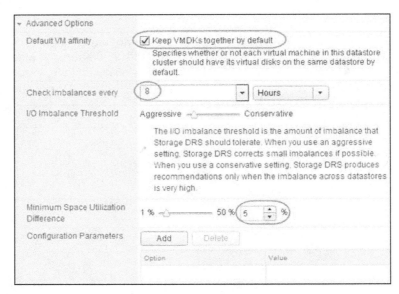

13. Click on **OK** to confirm the settings and enable Storage DRS.

14. The **Recent Tasks** pane should show a **Configure Storage DRS** task as completed successfully.

How it works...

Once Storage DRS is enabled on a datastore cluster, it generates Storage vMotion recommendations based on the space usage and the latency threshold as follows:

- ▶ Default space utilization threshold = 80 percent
- ▶ Default I/O latency = 15 milliseconds

Load balancing based on space utilization cannot be disabled, but load balancing based on the I/O load can be disabled.

Initial placement

When you deploy a VM onto a datastore cluster with SDRS enabled, SDRS will provide placement recommendations based on the space utilization and the I/O load on the datastores. This reduces the complexity in decision making when you have a large number of datastores in the environment, and of course, they should be part of a datastore cluster for this to work. SDRS provides placement recommendations and chooses one of the recommended datastores. However, the user can opt to select another recommended datastore. Although I/O load balancing can be disabled, the SDRS will still have access to the I/O statistics of the datastores. If SDRS finds more than one datastore suitable to place the virtual machine, then it will choose the datastore with the lowest I/O load.

Balancing space utilization

With Storage DRS not enabled, it is quite possible that over time, when you deploy more and more virtual machines, you end up saturating the free space on a set of datastores, while leaving a few other datastores underutilized. This could eventually cause "out-of-space" conditions, affecting the running VMs, but with Storage DRS enabled in a datastore cluster, the space utilization on the datastores and the growth rate of the VMDKs (if thin provisioned) is monitored. The default threshold for space utilization is 80 percent. Storage DRS will start generating Storage VMotion recommendations when the threshold is exceeded.

Balancing I/O load

The I/O load on a datastore is measured based on the current I/O latency, as seen by the virtual machines running on them. The default threshold for the latency is 15 milliseconds (15000 microseconds). If I/O load balancing is enabled, then the I/O latency statistics are evaluated every 8 hours. SDRS uses 16 hours worth of data to generate Storage vMotion recommendations. The migrations based on I/O load imbalance occur only once a day.

See also

▸ There is much more that you need to know about SDRS. Read *Chapter 12, Creating a Datastore Cluster*, and *Chapter 13, Using Datastore Clusters to Manage Storage Resources*, in the *vSphere Resource Management guide* available at `http://pubs.vmware.com/vsphere-55/topic/com.vmware.ICbase/PDF/vsphere-esxi-vcenter-server-55-resource-management-guide.pdf`.

8
Managing iSCSI and NFS Datastores

In this chapter, we will cover the following recipes:

- ▶ Adding the software iSCSI adapter
- ▶ Preparing the vSphere network for iSCSI multipathing
- ▶ Binding VMkernel interfaces to the software iSCSI adapter
- ▶ Adding an iSCSI target server to the software iSCSI adapter
- ▶ Creating an NFS Datastore

Introduction

Both iSCSI and NFS are storage solutions that can leverage the existing TCP/IP network infrastructure. Hence, they are referred to as IP-based storage. Before we start learning how to configure them, let's delve into some iSCSI and NFS fundamentals.

iSCSI fundamentals

Internet Small Computer System Interface (**iSCSI**) is a protocol used to transport SCSI command over a TCP/IP network. In an iSCSI environment, the server or the host uses iSCSI initiators (hardware/software) to connect to iSCSI targets on an iSCSI storage system. This is detailed in the following list:

- ▶ **iSCSI initiator**: An iSCSI initiator can be either a software or hardware iSCSI adapter that connects to an iSCSI target. The hardware iSCSI adapter can further be dependent or independent. Dependent hardware iSCSI will reply on ESXi for network configuration and management. However, independent will handle both the network configuration and management and the packet processing. The initiator or Host Bus Adapter (HBA) resides on the ESXi server.

- ▶ **iSCSI target**: An iSCSI target is a term used to refer to either a network interface on the array, or the LUN itself. Some arrays, such as Dell EqualLogic and HP LeftHand Networks, present each LUN as a target to the iSCSI initiator.

- ▶ **iSCSI session**: An iSCSI session is established between an iSCSI initiator and an iSCSI target. Each session can have one or more connections to the target. With software iSCSI configured, a session is established between each bound VMkernel interface (vmk) and an iSCSI target. For example, if there are two vmk interfaces bound to the iSCSI initiator, then the initiator will establish two separate sessions for each target it sees.

- ▶ **iSCSI connection**: Each iSCSI session can have multiple connections to the target portal.

- ▶ **iSCSI portal**: An iSCSI portal at the target is a combination of the target server's IP and the default listening port 3260. An iSCSI portal at the initiator is the IP address of the initiator/VMkernel interface.

- ▶ **CHAP**: The Challenge-Handshake Authentication Protocol is used by iSCSI to make sure that the initiator and target trust each other.

- ▶ **Dynamic discovery**: Dynamic discovery is one of the common methods of target discovery implementation. This is particularly useful when the iSCSI server has made a larger number of LUNs/targets available via its interface.

- ▶ **Static discovery**: Static discovery is primarily used in scenarios where the iSCSI array has presented fewer targets/LUNs. It is also used to provide restrictive access to the initiator; that is, it can be used to configure the initiator in such a manner that it only sees specified targets.

NFS fundamentals

Network File System (**NFS**) is a protocol used to provide access to shared filesystem level location, such as a folder over a TCP/IP network. VMware currently supports NFS version 3. In its early days, NFS was commonly used to store ISOs, templates, and so on in a VMware environment. However, it has gained prominence over the years. It has seen several performance enhancements and is now a strong candidate for hosting your enterprise workloads.

- ▶ **NFS Datastore**: An NFS mount that connects to a folder residing on a filesystem in the NFS Storage System. This way the NFS Storage System allows the ESXi host to access its filesystem, but the access is restricted to the shared folder.

- ▶ **NFS export**: An NFS server or Storage System creates shares on its local filesystem to be used by the NFS clients; in our case an ESXi host. These shares are referred to as exports.

Adding the software iSCSI adapter

The software iSCSI adapter is not created by default. It has to be manually created and enabled. In this recipe, we will learn how to enable the software iSCSI adapter. There can only be one software iSCSI adapter per ESXi server.

Getting ready

The software iSCSI adapter will use the VMkernel network stack to establish sessions with the iSCSI targets. Hence, by default it will use the management network's VMkernel interface (vmk0). It is recommended that you create a different VMkernel interface for iSCSI or NFS. This will become essential when the management network is in a different subnet than the IP Storage network. For instructions on how to create a VMkernel interface, read the recipes *Creating a VMkernel interface on a standard vSwitch* and *Creating additional VMkernel interfaces on a VDS* in *Chapter 6, Configuring vSphere Networking*. Also, when you create the ports you do not have to select a traffic type, because there isn't one specifically for IP storage. Hence, all you need is a VMkernel interface.

How to do it...

The following steps will help you to create and enable the software iSCSI adapter:

1. Connect to vCenter using the vSphere Web Client, and at the inventory **Home**, click on **Hosts and Clusters** as shown in the following screenshot:

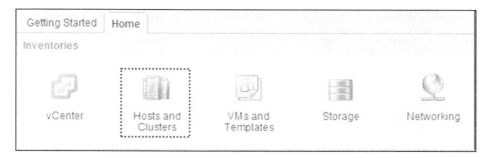

2. Highlight an ESX server and navigate to **Manage | Storage | Storage Adapters**. Click on the **+** icon and select **Software iSCSI adapter** as demonstrated in the following screenshot:

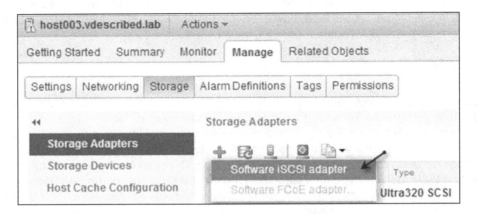

3. Click on **OK** to confirm the addition of a software iSCSI adapter:

4. You should see the following two tasks completed in the **Recent Tasks** pane:

   ❑ **Open firewall ports**

   ❑ **Change Software Internet SCSI Status**

   Once done, the software iSCSI adapter will be listed under **Storage Adapters** as **Enabled** by default as explained in the following screenshot:

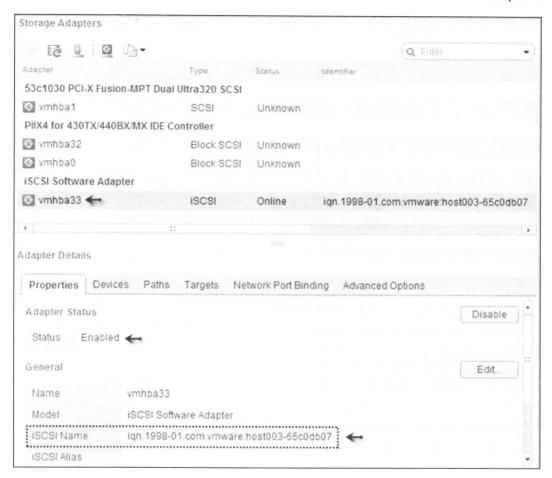

How it works...

During the creation of the software iSCSI adapter, all it does is enable the software iSCSI plugin and open all outgoing connections for the TCP port 3260 in the ESXi server's firewall.

The following is a screenshot from the **Security Profile** page showing the firewall configuration for the software iSCSI client:

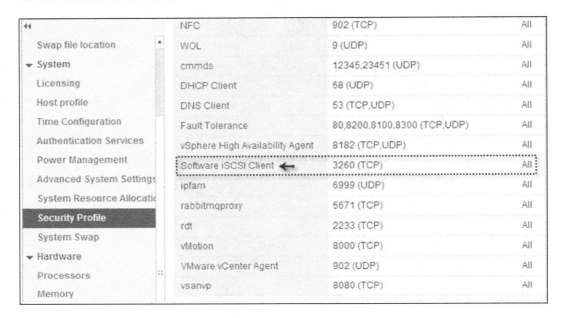

There's more...

Enabling Jumbo Frames can significantly increase the iSCSI throughput. We will not discuss the procedure to enable Jumbo Frames in this recipe, because it has been well documented in the VMware Knowledgebase article 1007654 available at `http://kb.vmware.com/kb/1007654`.

For Jumbo Frames to work on all the TCP/IP networks, components between the source and the destination should have support for Jumbo Frames enabled.

For information regarding the configuration of hardware iSCSI adapters, refer to the sections *Setting up Independent Hardware iSCSI Adapters* and *Configuring Dependent Hardware iSCSI Adapters* in the vSphere Storage Guide (`http://bit.ly/vsphere55_Storage_Guide`).

Preparing the vSphere network for iSCSI multipathing

iSCSI multipathing will depend on the type of storage and the network topology in use. There are two methods:

▸ **Multipathing for iSCSI using port binding**: This is achieved by having two VMkernel interfaces configured with an active adapter each, but no standby adapters. Once done, these VMkernel (vmk) interfaces should be bound to the software iSCSI adapter. Read the recipe *Binding VMkernel interfaces to the software iSCSI adapter* for more details.

▸ **Multipathing for iSCSI without port binding**: Read the *When not to use port binding* section in the VMware KB: 2038869 for more details (`http://kb.vmware.com/kb/2038869`).

In this recipe, we will learn how to prepare the vSphere network for iSCSI multipathing by creating multiple VMkernel interfaces by using the same set of physical NICs in alternating active/unused pairs. This method is used to achieve iSCSI multipathing using the port binding method.

How to do it...

The following procedure will guide you through the steps required to create and configure port groups to aid in iSCSI multipathing:

1. Create an additional VMkernel interface using the Add Networking wizard, with an obvious exception of using the same vSwitch, a new port group, and a different static IP configuration, similar to the one shown in the following table:

Port group name	IP address	Subnet mask
iSCSI-PG2	192.168.193.57	255.255.255.0

For instructions on how to create a VMkernel interface, read the recipes *Creating a VMkernel interface on a standard vSwitch* and *Creating additional VMkernel interfaces on a VDS* in *Chapter 6, Configuring vSphere Networking*.

2. Once done, you should see two port groups connected to the same vSwitch as demonstrated in the following screenshot:

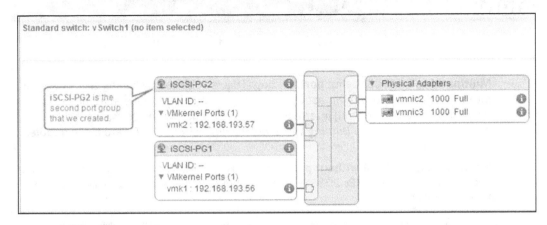

3. Select the port group by clicking on its name which is nothing but a hyperlink. With the port group selected, click on the pencil icon to bring up the **Edit Settings** window, so that the failover order can be modified in such a manner that a port group uses only one active vmnic and no standby vmnic.

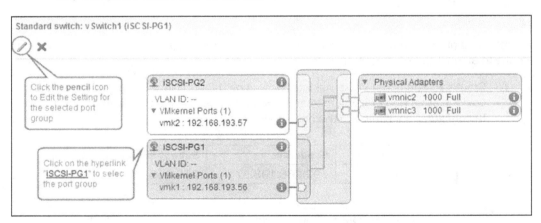

4. On the **Edit Settings** windows, go to **Teaming and failover** and select the checkbox **Override** under the **Failover order** section as shown in the following screenshot:

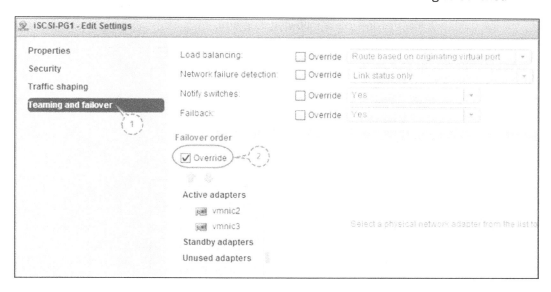

5. Select one of the adapters (vmnic), move it to the **Unused adapters** section, and click on **OK**:

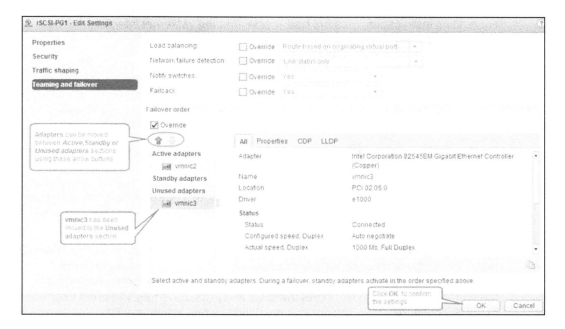

6. Follow the same GUI method on the second port group as well. The only difference being that the second port group **vmnic3** becomes the **Active adapter** and **vmnic2** the **Standby adapter**. Once done, the vmnic allocation to the iSCSI port groups should look like the one in the following diagram:

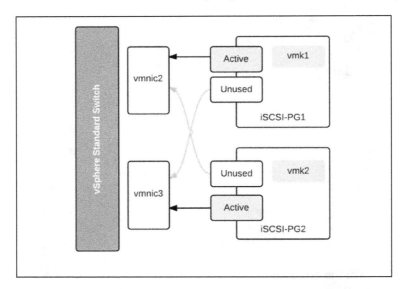

7. Now the two VMkernel interfaces should be bound to the software iSCSI adapter. For binding instructions, read the next recipe, *Binding VMkernel interfaces to the software iSCSI adapter*.

How it works...

The number of paths that can be enabled to an iSCSI array will depend on the type of array in use. For instance, there are single and multiportal storage arrays, which are described as follows:

▶ **Single-portal storage** arrays such as Dell EqualLogic and HP StoreVirtual (formerly LeftHand Networks) advertise only a single storage port for the clients/initiators to connect to. Hence, the number of paths to such an array will depend on the number of VMkernel interfaces you configure for use with iSCSI. For example, if you configure four VMkernel interfaces for use with the iSCSI adapter, then you get four paths to the storage.

▶ **Multi-portal storage** arrays such as EMC CLARiiON advertise more than one storage port. Hence, the number of number of paths to such an array is multiple of the number of VMkernel interfaces for iSCSI and number of storage ports. For example, if the storage makes two target ports available and if you have four VMkernel interfaces for iSCSI configured, then you get four multiplied by two, which is eight possible paths to the storage.

As per the vSphere Storage guide, a virtual machine's I/O might be delayed for up to 60 seconds while path failover takes place. Such a delay will allow the SAN to stabilize its configuration after the topology changes. In general, the I/O delays might be longer on active-passive arrays and shorter on active-active arrays.

Binding VMkernel interfaces to the software iSCSI adapter

Binding is the final stage of configuration to be done at the ESXi server to enable iSCSI multipathing. It refers to the process of associating existing VMkernel (vmk) interfaces to the software iSCSI adapter, thereby letting NMP manage multiple paths to the iSCSI targets.

 Keep in mind that the iSCSI initiator and the iSCSI target should be in the same subnet. iSCSI port binding does not support routing.

The VMkernel interfaces should be first prepared with only one active and no standby adapters. This is discussed in detail in the *Preparing the vSphere network for iSCSI multipathing* recipe.

Once the VMkernel interfaces have been prepared, you could use the instructions in this recipe to bind the interfaces to the software iSCSI adapter.

How to do it...

The following instructions will guide you through the process of binding the VMkernel interfaces to the software iSCSI adapter:

1. On the ESXi server, navigate to **Manage | Storage | Storage Adapters** and select the iSCSI software adapter.

2. Navigate to the **Network Port Binding** tab for the iSCSI software adapter and click on the green **+** icon to bring up the **Bind vmhba3x with VMkernel Adapter** window as shown in the following screenshot:

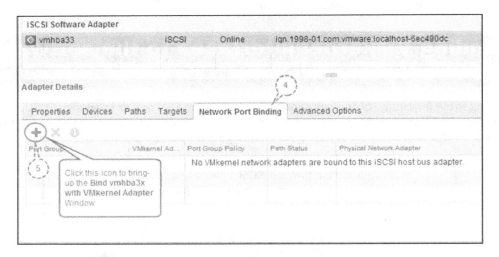

3. On the **Bind vmhba3X with VMkernel Adapter** window, select the port group associated with the VMkernel interfaces and click on **OK** to bind them:

4. Once the adapters are bound, you will see them listed under the **Network Port Binding** tab as indicated in the following screenshot:

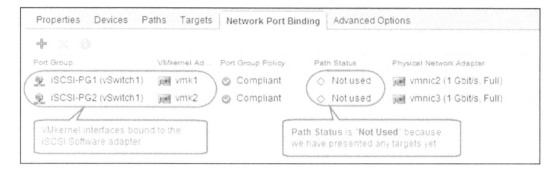

There's more...

Port binding is not always required for iSCSI multipathing. Read VMware KB#2038869 for more details (`http://kb.vmware.com/kb/2038869`).

Adding an iSCSI target server to the software iSCSI adapter

For the ESXi server to be able to see iSCSI targets/LUNs, the iSCSI adapter needs to be configured with the details of the iSCSI target server. The target server is nothing but an iSCSI array. Here the term "target" can refer to the network interfaces on the iSCSI array or individual LUNs. The definition changes depending on the type of array being used. For example, a Dell EqualLogic array will present its LUNs as targets.

In this recipe, we will learn how to provide the iSCSI array details to the iSCSI software adapter.

How to do it...

The following procedure will guide you through the steps required to add an iSCSI target server:

1. On the ESXi server, navigate to **Manage | Storage | Storage Adapters** and select the iSCSI software adapter of your choice.

2. With the adapter selected, go to the **Targets** tab and then under **Dynamic Discovery** click on **Add** to bring up the **Add Send Target Server** window as explained in the following screenshot:

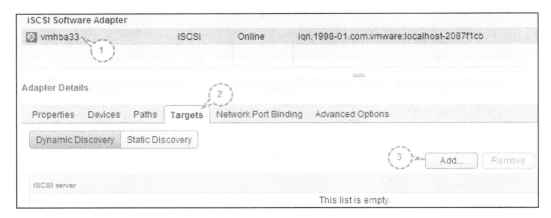

3. In the **Add Send Target Server** window, supply the IP address/FQDN of the iSCSI server and click on **OK**.

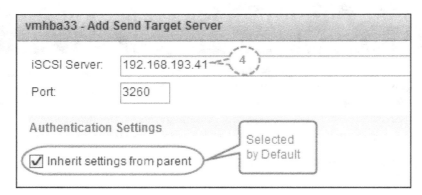

4. The **Recent Tasks** pane should show the following two tasks completed successfully:

    ❏   **Add Internet SCSI send targets**

    ❏   **Update Internet SCSI authentication properties**

5. Issue a rescan on the software iSCSI adapter to find the presented LUN devices.

6. Once the rescan is complete, the **Devices** tab should show all the detected LUNs as shown in the following screenshot:

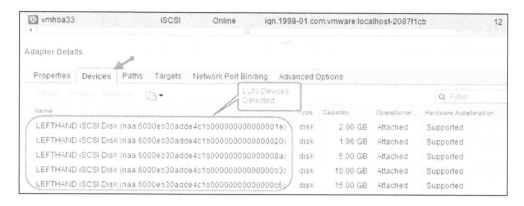

How it works...

Once the iSCSI target information has been added to the iSCSI software initiator, it will appear as an iSCSI server entry under the **Dynamic Discovery** tab.

A `SEND TARGETS` command is sent from each vmk interface to the target portal; in response, the array will send a list of all available targets presented to the initiator. The target list received from the array will appear in the **Static Discovery** tab as depicted in the following screenshot:

Since we have two VMkernel interfaces bound to the iSCSI software initiator, we will have two sessions for each LUN seen by the initiator, as depicted in the following diagram:

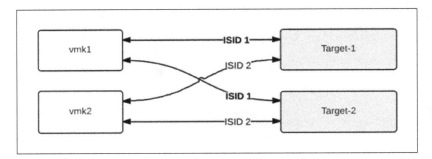

The following screenshot shows the session from each vmk interface to a LUN on a LeftHand iSCSI. Each session will have an **iSCSI Session ID** (**ISID**) associated with it. Keep in mind that LeftHand is a single portal storage.

Now, if you review the multipathing information for a LUN, you should see two paths:

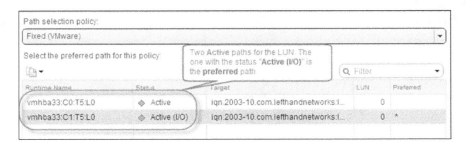

You might have noticed that one of the paths has been marked as **Active (I/O)**. This is the path to the target that can issue the commands to the LUN.

Creating an NFS Datastore

For an ESXi host to access a share available on an NFS server or storage system, it would need to mount the share and make it available as a datastore to use it. This recipe will walk you through the steps required to do this.

Getting ready

You will need the FQDN/IP address of the NFS server and the folder path (export) information handy before you proceed. Your storage admin can provide you with this information. NFS will also require a VMkernel interface to connect to the storage. Hence, make sure one is already created for this purpose. For instructions on how to create a VMkernel interface, read the recipes *Creating a VMkernel interface on a standard vSwitch* and *Creating additional VMkernel interfaces on a VDS* in *Chapter 6, Configuring vSphere Networking*.

How to do it...

The following procedure will guide you through the steps required to mount an NFS share as a datastore to the ESXi server.

1. With the ESXi host selected, navigate to **All vCenter Actions | New Datastore** to start the **New Datastore** wizard.

2. In **New Datastore**, as you initiated the wizard from a host, it will show the host selected. Click on **Next** to continue.

3. Select the datastore type as **NFS** and click on **Next** to continue.

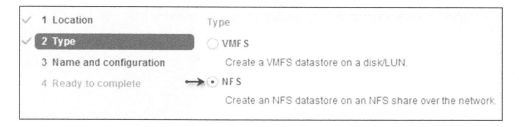

4. Supply a name in the **Datastore name** field, FQDN or IP of the NFS **Server** and the **Folder** path to the export created on the NFS server as shown in the following screenshot:

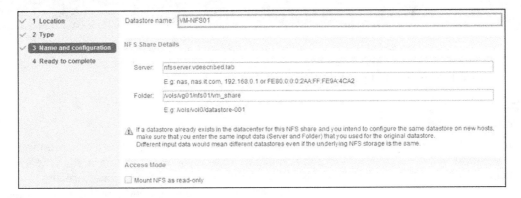

5. Review the **Ready to Complete** screen and click on **Finish**:
6. The **Recent Tasks** pane should show a **Create NAS datastore** task completed successfully:

How it works...

By default, you can only create eight NFS mounts per ESXi server. Although this limit can be increased up to 256 by using the advanced setting **NFS.MaxVolumes**, increasing this limit would generally require an increase in the minimum amount of VMkernel TCP/IP heap memory. The minimum heap memory value can be specified using the advanced setting **Net. TcpipHeapSize**. You can also set the maximum amount of heap size using the advanced setting **Net.TcpipHeapMax**. Most vendor documentation will have guidelines regarding the configuration of these parameters. Make sure you refer to them before you modify the defaults.

For more information regarding these parameters, refer to the VMware Knowledge Base article 2239 at `http://kb.vmware.com/kb/2239`.

There is no limit on the size of an NFS Datastore. If there is any such limit, then it is imposed by the NFS server and not by the ESXi server.

9
vSphere Storage Policies and Storage I/O Control

In this chapter, we will cover the following recipes:

- ► Adding a storage provider
- ► Creating user-defined capability tags for datastores
- ► Creating VM storage policies
- ► Assigning VM storage policies to virtual machine disks
- ► Enabling Storage I/O Control
- ► Modifying disk shares on a VM

Introduction

As our virtual data centers continue to host diverse VM workloads, it becomes important to segregate, isolate, and allocate storage resources in a manner to optimize performance and reliability. To achieve this, the VMs should be placed on the datastores with the characteristics that would aid in smooth functioning of these workloads. Unfortunately, most VMware administrators wouldn't necessarily have the visibility to the underlying storage characteristics, largely due to the fact that in most organizations, a different team manages the storage. A VMware administrator would generally request for a LUN of a particular size, the storage administrator carves a LUN from an available storage pool and presents it to the ESXi host. This would mean that the administrator would only be able to distribute the workloads across multiple datastores based on space utilization.

So, how can the administrator get around this problem? There are two ways:

▶ Use a worksheet or any form of record keeping methods to maintain a list of all the LUNs presented to the ESXi hosts and its storage characteristics. The storage characteristics information has to be collected from the storage team.

▶ If the array is capable of VMware **vStorage API for Storage Awareness** (**VASA**), then a VASA provider from the storage vendor can be deployed and configured to fetch the storage characteristics.

In vSphere 5.5, storage profiles are now called *VM Storage Policies*. You now do not have an option to create the user-defined Storage capabilities. Instead, you create and use tags, and then associate them with a datastore. Storage policies dictate the placement of the VMs onto datastores that meet the performance characteristics need of the VMs.

In VM Storage Policies, every storage characteristic will have an impact on either the performance or reliability a LUN can offer. Before we proceed further, it is important to know what some of these storage characteristics could be and what role do they play in the decision making regarding the placement of the VMs. Here is a common list of the storage characteristics and their impact on the performance and reliability.

	Impact	
Characteristic	Performance	Reliability
Raid level	Yes	Yes
Underlying disk technology	Yes	Yes
Spindle speed	Yes	No
Capacity	No	No
Storage protocol	Depends on how the array and the access to the array is configured	

In vSphere terms, these characteristics are referred to as *Storage Capabilities*, which like we discussed earlier can be either be system learned (via VASA) or user defined. Regardless of whether they are learned or defined, there should be a way to associate VMs to the datastores with the desired capability. Such an association is created using storage policies. Once the policies are defined, the VM disks can then be associated to these policies. This will allow vSphere to make the VM placement decisions.

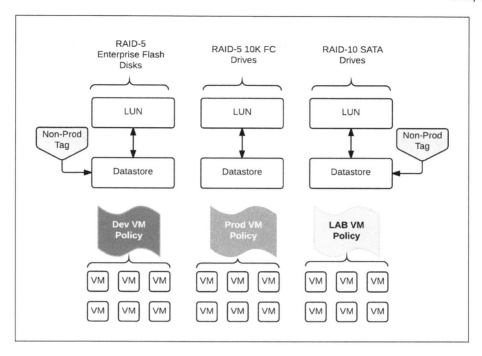

Storage policies will allow an administrator to group datastores under policies based on the datastore's capability. These capabilities can be related to the capacity, performance, or redundancy characteristics. The capabilities can either be learned via VASA if the storage array supports the API or via user-defined capability tags. Storage profiles will require an **Enterprise plus License**.

In **Storage I/O Control** (**SIOC**), as with sharing computing resources among the running VMs, you can share the I/O bandwidth to a LUN among the VMs. Based on the shares set on the virtual disks residing on the SIOC-enabled datastores, SIOC will throttle the VMkernel LUN queue depth during contention.

In this chapter, we will learn how to use the storage profiles to ensure that the VMs are placed in appropriate datastores, and how to use the Storage I/O Control to manage queue bandwidth between VMs. Before we begin with the configuration tasks, it will be beneficial to understand the concepts.

Adding a storage provider

If you have a VASA capable array, then you can add a VASA provider to the vCenter Server so that it can generate array capabilities for each LUN or datastore. A capability generated by the provider is called a **system storage capability**.

To check whether the array used in your environment is VASA capable, use the *VMware Compatibility Guide* available at `http://www.vmware.com/resources/compatibility/search.php?deviceCategory=vasa`.

The HP StoreVirtual VSA used in the lab for this book is VASA capable. In this recipe, you will about how to add a storage provider corresponding to the array to the vCenter Server.

Getting ready

Since we are using a HP StoreVirtual VSA, you will need a storage provider server configured with HP OneView for the storage installed. Since the installation instructions are beyond the scope of this book, we assume that the insight control for storage is installed and configured correctly. For instructions specific to the storage provider, refer to the vendor documentation.

How to do it...

The following instructions explain how to add a storage provider to the vCenter Server:

1. Connect to the vCenter Server using vSphere Web Client
2. Use the keyboard shortcut *Ctrl + Alt + 5* to bring up the storage tree in the vCenter Inventory.
3. Select the vCenter Server that was registered to the storage provider and navigate to **Manage | Storage Providers**.

4. In the **Storage Providers** tab, click on the green + icon to bring up the **New Storage Provider** window.

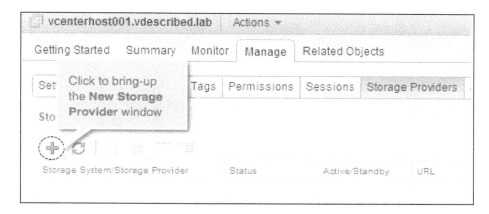

5. In the **New Storage Provider** window, supply a name, the provider URL, and the credentials to connect to the storage provider server, and click on **OK**.

6. You should now be prompted with a security alert for the certificate of the provider server. Click on **Yes** to trust the certificate to add the storage provider.

How it works...

Once the storage provider is added, it should be listed online under the **Storage Providers** tab:

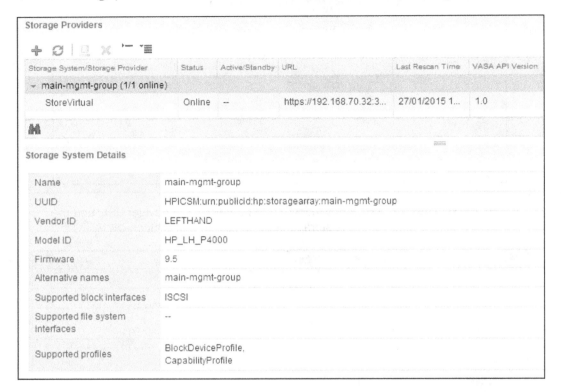

The datastores corresponding to the LUNs on the array will show the VASA-propagated system storage capabilities. None of the capabilities have to be manually assigned. VASA will auto-propagate the capability of the underlying LUN to its corresponding datastore.

For example, the following is a screenshot showing the system-generated capability of one of the datastores:

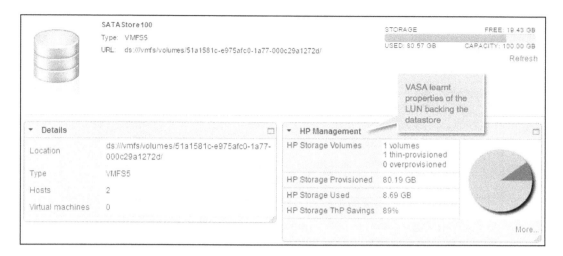

See also

For more information on using storage providers, read the *Using Storage Providers* section in the *vSphere Storage guide* at `http://bit.ly/vsphere55_storage_guide`.

Creating user-defined capability tags for datastores

Unlike with vSphere 5.1 where you had an option to create user-defined storage capability, with vSphere 5.5, you will use the vCenter's tagging mechanism to create and associate tags to datastores. The tags are user defined and can have any name and category that the user would define. The tags can then be included in a storage policy to aid in the placement of VMs on them.

How to do it...

The following procedure will guide you through the steps required in creating user-defined tags for the datastore:

1. Connect to the vCenter Server using vSphere Web Client.

2. Use the keyboard shortcut *Ctrl + Alt + 5* to bring up the storage tree in the vCenter Inventory.

3. Select the datastore from the Inventory to create a tag and navigate to **Manage | Tags** and click on the tag icon with a + on it to bring up the **New Tag** window.

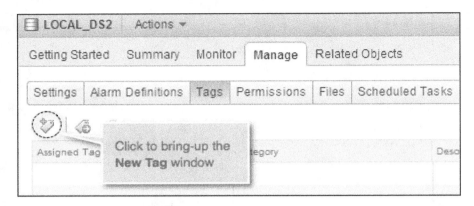

4. In the **New Tag** window, supply a name for the tag. Make sure you supply a meaningful name matching the capability/property of the datastore that you intend to tag. Choose an existing category or create a new category. Click on **OK** to create and assign the tag to the datastore.

How it works...

Tags can also be created from the various levels of the vCenter Inventory. If you were to create a tag for a level other than the intended datastore, then you will have to manually assign the tag to a datastore. To manually assign a tag to a datastore, right-click on the intended datastore, and click on **Assign Tag** to select a tag and associate it with the datastore.

Creating VM storage policies

Once you have the VASA provider added or the user-defined datastore tags created, you can create storage policies to define VM placement guidelines. For example, LUNs thin provisioned, wherein **Thin Provisioned Volume**, being a capability, can be categorized so that VMs running applications that do not demand first-write performance can be placed on these datastores. The first-write performance could be impacted on a thin provisioned volume because the volume should be increased in size before the data is first written to it.

Getting ready

VM storage policies are enabled, by default, but it is important to verify the same. Navigate to the vCenter Inventory home and click on **VMware Storage Polices**. Click on the Enable VMware Storage Policies icon ( ) to view the status of the VMware storage policies. It could be either **Enabled**, **Disabled**, or **Unknown**. Its status can be changed at the Cluster or Host level.

How to do it...

The following procedure will guide you through the steps required to create the storage policies:

1. Connect to the vCenter Server using vSphere Web Client.
2. Use the keyboard shortcut *Ctrl + Alt + 1* to bring up the vCenter Web Client home.
3. At the Inventory home, click on **VM Storage Policies** to bring up the **VMware Storage Policies** window.
4. At the **VM Storage Policies** window, click on the new storage policy icon to bring up the **Create New VM Storage Policy** wizard.

5. In the **Create New VM Storage Policy** wizard, supply a name and an optional description for the policy and click on **Next** to continue.

6. On the next **Rule-Sets** wizard screen, click on **Next** to continue.

7. If you have a VASA provider added, use the drop-down box listed against **Rules** based on vendor-specific capabilities and select the vendor provider. In this case, it is **HP Insight Control Storage Manager** (**HPICSM**).

8. With the VASA provider selected, click on **Add Capability** and choose **SystemLabel** as the capability.

9. With **SystemLabel** selected, use the drop-down box to select the capability from the list available from the storage provider. In this case, we have selected **HP P4000 Thin Provisioned Volume**. We could also add a tag to this ruleset in case the placement decision has been made based on more than one category. To add a tag-based rule, click on the button **Add tag-based rule**. Once you have prepared the ruleset, click on **Next** to continue.

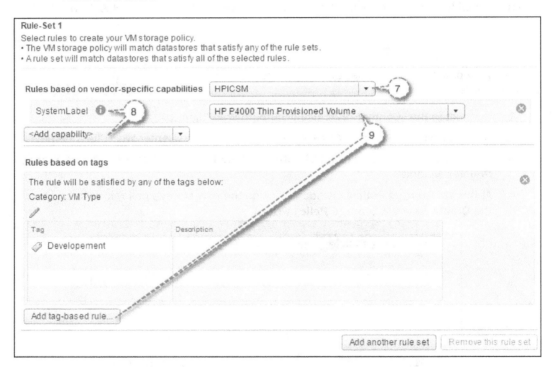

10. On the next screen, only the datastores matching the ruleset will be displayed. For instance, if you select **Thin Provisioned Volume** as the vendor capability and a tag as **Development**, then only the datastores that have the vendor capability chosen and the **Development** tag assigned to them will be listed. Make sure you see all the datastores that you intended to be included in the policy and click on **Next** to continue.

Matching resources
As defined, this VM storage policy matches the following storage:

Name	Datacenter	Type	Free	Capacity
SATAStore100	Datacenter1	VMFS 5	19.43 GB	100.00 GB

11. In the **Ready to Complete** screen, review the settings and click on **Finish**.

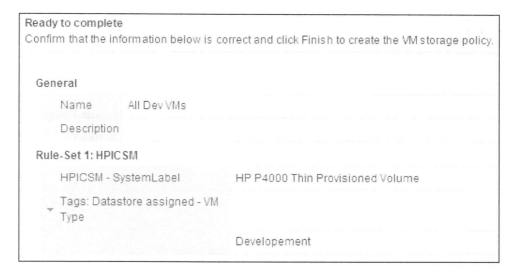

Ready to complete
Confirm that the information below is correct and click Finish to create the VM storage policy.

General
     Name   All Dev VMs
     Description
Rule-Set 1: HPICSM
     HPICSM - SystemLabel   HP P4000 Thin Provisioned Volume
     Tags: Datastore assigned - VM Type
        Developement

12. Once done, you should see the new storage policy created and listed.

VM Storage Policies

Objects

Actions

Name	Description	VC
Tier-1		vcenterhost001.vdescribed.lab
All Dev VMs		vcenterhost001.vdescribed.lab

Assigning VM storage policies to virtual machine disks

With VM storage polices created, the job is half done, unless you assign the policies to virtual machine disks.

Getting ready

You need to have VM storage policies created before it can be assigned. Read the recipe *Creating VM storage policies* for instructions on how to create them.

How to do it...

The following procedure will guide you through the steps required in assigning VM storage policies to VM disks:

1. Connect to the vCenter using vSphere Web Client.

2. Use the keyboard shortcut *Ctrl + Alt + 4* to bring up the VMs and templates tree in the vCenter Inventory.

3. Select a VM from the inventory and navigate to **Manage | VM Storage Policies**.

4. While in the **VM Storage Policies** tab, click on the **Manage VM Storage Policies** button.

5. In the **Manage VM Storage Policies** window, select **Home VM storage policy** and click on **Apply to disks** to set the same policy to every disk attached to the VM. You can also set the VM Storage Policy individually on those virtual disks. Once done, click on **OK** to save the settings.

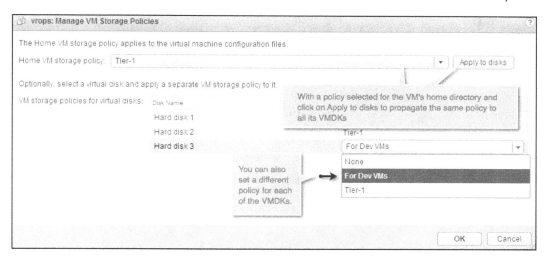

6. You should now see the policies assigned to the VM's home directory and the VMDKs listed under **VM Storage Policy assignments**.

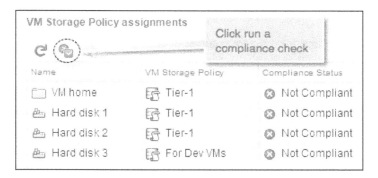

How it works...

Once VM Storage policies are assigned to a VM and its VMDKs, its profile compliance status will remain *Non-Compliant* unless they are moved to a datastore matching the VM storage policy. The VM can be moved using the migration wizard. In the migration wizard, the intended VM storage policy can be selected to list the compliant datastores so that the VM and its files can be moved to one of them.

Enabling Storage I/O Control

SIOC is used to throttle the VMkernel device queue depth of a LUN, based on the shares set on the virtual machine disks contending for I/O bandwidth. SIOC can only be enabled on datastores (FC/ISCSI/NFS) and not on RDMs. It cannot be enabled on datastores with multiple extents. In this recipe, you will learn how to enable SIOC on a datastore.

Getting ready

Enterprise Plus Licensing is required for SIOC.

How to do it...

SIOC has to be enabled on each datastore. The following procedure explains how to achieve the same:

1. Connect to the vCenter Server using vSphere Web Client.

2. Use the keyboard shortcut *Ctrl + Alt + 5* to bring up the storage tree in the vCenter Inventory.

3. Select a datastore from the inventory, navigate to **Manage | Settings**, and edit the datastore capabilities:

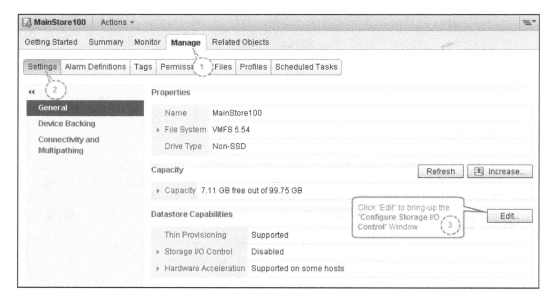

4. In the **Configure Storage I/O Control** window, select the **Enable Storage I/O Control** checkbox. Unless you want to modify the **Congestion Threshold** criteria and its value, you can leave the **Percentage of peak throughput** value at its default of **90%**. You can also set **Congestion Threshold** to be the latency. By default, the latency threshold value is **30ms**.

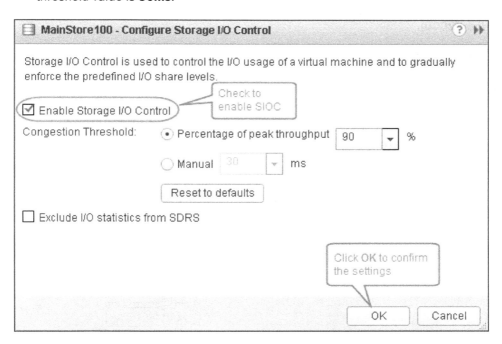

How it works...

Once Storage IO Control has been enabled, the datastore will be monitored for bandwidth congestion. If congestion is detected, it checks the peak throughput or latency values against the value configured when SIOC was enabled. Based on the level of congestion, the VMkernel device queue depth is throttled accordingly.

 vSphere 5.1 onwards, SIOC is enabled by default, but only in the Stats Only mode. While in this mode, the SIOC will not throttle the queue depth, but only collect I/O statistics. This behavior remains unchanged with vSphere 5.5 as well.

See also

▶ For more information on SIOC, read the *vSphere 5.5 Resource Management* guide available at `http://bit.ly/vsphere55_storage_management_guide`.

Modifying disk shares on a VM

Setting custom disk shares is particularly useful when you want to make sure that a VM receives a larger chunk of the disk bandwidth during contention. By default, the disk share is set to **Normal (1000)**. The other presets available to set custom shares are **Low (500)** and **High (2000)**.

In this recipe, you will learn how to set custom disk shares.

How to do it...

The following procedure explains how to set customize disk share values on a VM:

1. Go to **Edit Settings** for the VM that you are concerned with.

2. Expand the hard disk entry, select a planned shares value, and click on **OK** to confirm your settings. You can also set a **Limit - IOPs** value if necessary.

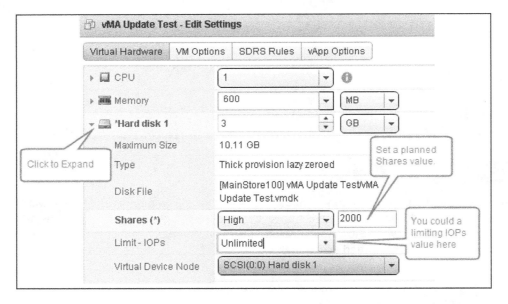

SIOC will take into account the custom share value when throttling the VMkernel device queue.

How it works...

Disk shares are applied at the **virtual machine disk** (**VMDK**) level. The shares will come into effect only when there is contention for the disk bandwidth. The shares are relative to the shares set for the other VMDKs on the same ESXi host. SIOC will take into account the custom share value when throttling the VMkernel device queue.

10
Creating and Managing Virtual Machines

In this chapter, we will cover the following recipes:

- ▶ Creating a virtual machine
- ▶ Creating a new hard disk for a virtual machine
- ▶ Adding an existing hard disk to a virtual machine
- ▶ Attaching RDM to a virtual machine
- ▶ Mapping a virtual machine's vNIC to a different port group
- ▶ Adding a new virtual network adapter to a virtual machine
- ▶ Creating a virtual machine snapshot
- ▶ Deleting a virtual machine snapshot
- ▶ Reverting to a current virtual machine snapshot
- ▶ Switching to an arbitrary virtual machine snapshot
- ▶ Consolidating snapshots
- ▶ Exporting a virtual machine

Introduction

A virtual machine emulates a physical machine with well-known hardware on which traditional operating systems such as Microsoft Windows and Linux can be installed and operated. It is based on the Intel 440BX chipset with Phoenix BIOS Version 6. This can change with a new release. It also emulates other hardware such as the VGA controller, SCSI controllers, network cards, and various other devices.

The virtual machine components

A virtual machine will have the following default virtual hardware components:

- Memory, CPUs, a SCSI controller, hard disks, and network adapters
- Video card, VMCI device, CD/DVD drive, and floppy drive

Additional components can be added using the **Add Hardware** wizard. The hardware wizard presents the following components:

- Network adapter
- Hard disk (new/existing/RDM)
- Serial port, parallel port, host USB device, USB controller, and SCSI controller
- SCSI device, PCI device
- Floppy drive CD/DVD drive

Files that back a virtual machine

Every virtual machine is backed by a set of files. The virtual machine configuration file with the extension `.vmx` holds all the virtual machine's configuration information. For files associated with a virtual machine, refer to the following table:

Configuration file	File extension
The virtual machine configuration file	`*.vmx`
The virtual disk descriptor file	`*.vmdk`
The virtual disk data file	`*-flat.vmdk`
The RDM mapping file (physical compatibility mode)	`*-rdmp.vmdk`
The RDM mapping file (virtual compatibility mode)	`*-rdm.vmdk`
The virtual machine snapshot database	`*.vmsd`
The virtual machine snapshot state file	`*.vmsn`
The virtual machine snapshot delta file	`*-delta.vmdk`
The virtual machine team information file	`*.vmxf`
The virtual machine swap file	`*.vswp`
The virtual machine BIOS file	`*.nvram`

The virtual machine configuration file

The **virtual machine configuration** (**VMX**) file holds all the configuration information for the virtual machine, which includes:

- The CPU and memory configuration
- The virtual disk drives used

- ▸ The virtual network card information
- ▸ The guest OS information
- ▸ The BIOS UUID of the virtual machine
- ▸ The vCenter Server assigned UUID of the virtual machine

The following are a few of the entries that appear in the VMX file:

- ▸ **numvcpus**: This entry indicates the number of processors (sockets).
- ▸ **cpuid.coresPerSocket**: This entry indicates the number of cores per processor.
- ▸ **scsiX.virtualDev**: This entry indicates the type of SCSI controller used.
- ▸ **ethernetX.virtualDev**: This entry indicates the type of Ethernet adapter used.
- ▸ **ethernetX.generatedAddress**: This entry indicates the Mac address generated by the ESXi server for that particular virtual network adapter.
- ▸ **guestOS**: This entry indicates the guest operating type set for the virtual machine.
- ▸ **uuid.bios**: This entry indicates the UUID of the virtual machine.
- ▸ **vc.uuid**: This is the UUID that is generated when a VM is added to the inventory using vCenter. This is not the vCenter's instance UUID.

The virtual machine BIOS file

The virtual machine BIOS (NVRAM) file holds the virtual BIOS (Phoenix BIOS) for a virtual machine. It can be accessed by pressing the function key *F2* during the VM boot up. This file is created when the virtual machine is powered on for the first time. All of the BIOS changes are saved to this file. If the file is manually deleted, you will lose the previous BIOS configuration, but the file is regenerated with the defaults during the next power on. For instance, if you were to forget the BIOS password, then a neat way to reset is to turn off the VM, delete the NVRAM file, and power on the VM to regenerate a new NVRAM file with a fresh BIOS.

Virtual machine enhancements available with vSphere 5.5

The following are some of the virtual machine enhancements available with VMware vSphere 5.5:

- ▸ New virtual hardware Version 10
- ▸ New **Advanced Host Controller Interface** (**AHCI**)
- ▸ New virtual-SATA controller with support for both VMDKs and CD-ROM devices
- ▸ vSGA now supports both NVIDIA and AD GPUs

To learn more about what's new, refer to the *What's New in VMware vSphere® 5.5 Platform* whitepaper at `http://www.vmware.com/files/pdf/vsphere/VMware-vSphere-Platform-Whats-New.pdf`.

Also, for a feature comparison between different virtual hardware versions, refer to table 5-2 on page 75 in *vSphere Virtual Machine Administration Guide* for vSphere 5.5 at `http://bit.ly/VMAdminGuide55`.

Creating a virtual machine

A virtual machine can be created by either using the vSphere Web Client interface, or by using the vSphere Client interface connected directly to the ESXi server. In this recipe, we will learn how to create virtual machine by using the vSphere Web Client interface.

How to do it...

To create a virtual machine, we will use the **New Virtual Machine** wizard. There are many GUI locations from where the wizard can be started. However, in this recipe, we will use the virtual machine inventory as a starting place.

The following procedure explains how to create a virtual machine by using the vSphere Web Client:

1. Connect to the vCenter Server as an administrator by using the vSphere Web Client.

2. Navigate to the **VMs and Templates** view from the inventory **Home** as shown in the following screenshot:

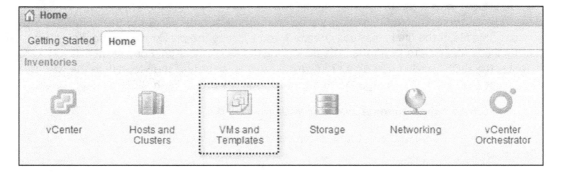

3. Navigate to and right-click on **Datacenter**, and then click on the **New Virtual Machine...** menu item, as shown in this screenshot, to bring-up the **New Virtual Machine...** wizard:

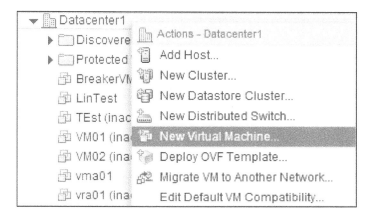

4. On the **New Virtual Machine** wizard, select the **Create a new virtual machine** option and click on **Next** as indicated in the following screenshot:

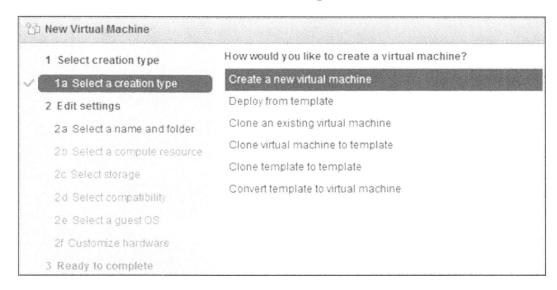

5. Provide a name for the virtual machine, choose an inventory location (data center), and then click on **Next**, as demonstrated in the following screenshot:

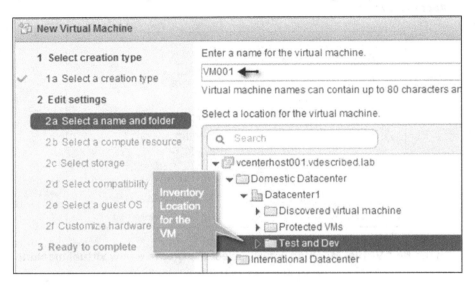

 Only folders of the type VM and template will be listed in the New Virtual Machine wizard.

6. Navigate to **Select a compute resource** (a cluster or an ESXi server) for the virtual machine, and then click on **Next** as shown in the following screenshot:

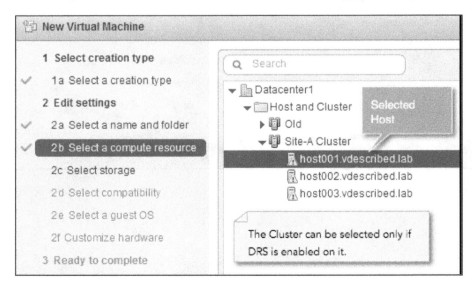

7. Choose a datastore for the virtual machine files, and then click on **Next**. On this screen we can also use **VM Storage Profile** to filter the datastores, as shown in the following screenshot:

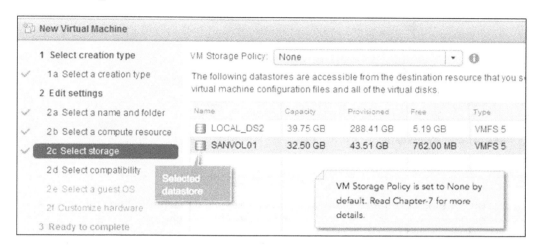

 By default, the **VM Storage Policy** option is set to **None**.

Learn more about VM storage policies in *Chapter 9, vSphere Storage Policies and Storage I/O Control*.

8. Select a virtual machine compatibility mode by clicking on **Select compatibility**:

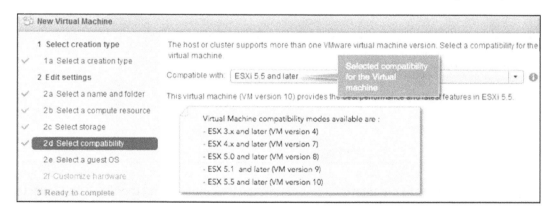

9. Select the **Guest OS Family** and **Guest OS Version** details, and then click on **Next**:

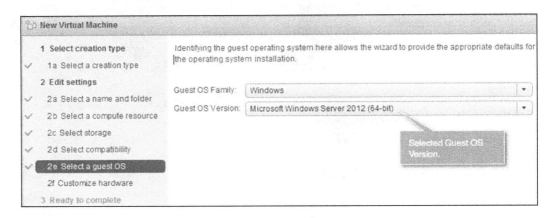

10. On the next **Customize hardware** screen, the virtual machine's hardware can be modified if necessary. Once done, click on **Next** to continue:

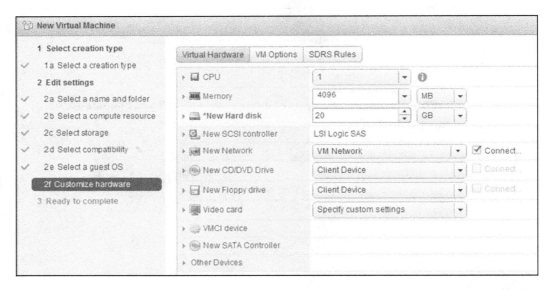

11. On the **Ready to complete** screen, review the information, and then click on **Finish** to create the virtual machine.

Creating a new hard disk for a virtual machine

The need to add an additional hard drive is driven by the guest OS or the VM design requirements. The virtual machine can be in a powered on state while we add the hard disk.

How to do it...

You can add a new virtual hard disk to a VM by editing the settings for the VM.

The following procedure explains how to add a new hard disk to a virtual machine:

1. Navigate to the **VM and Templates** inventory view, select and right-click on the VM to which you intend to add a hard disk, and then click on **Edit Settings**, as shown in the following screenshot:

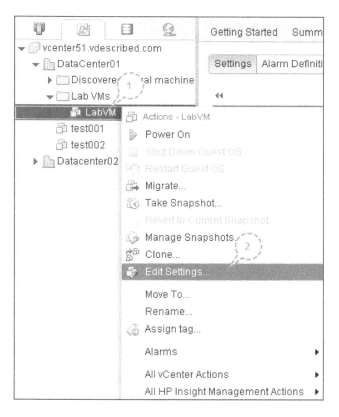

2. Use the **New device** option available in the **Edit Settings** window, select **New Hard Disk** as the device option, and then click on **Add** as indicated in the following screenshot:

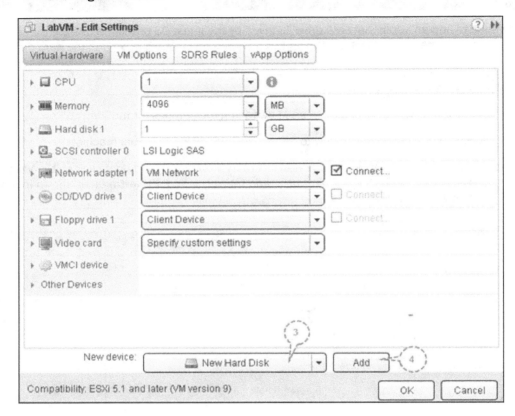

3. Once this is done, a **New Hard disk** device entry will be added to the **Edit Settings** window as demonstrated in this screenshot:

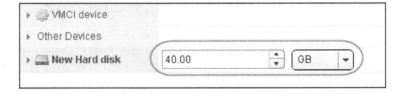

4. Click on the **New Hard disk** device entry to expand it, and reveal all the advanced settings for that hard drive entry.

5. Select **Maximum Size**, **Location**, **Disk Provisioning**, **Virtual Device Node**, and **Disk Mode**.

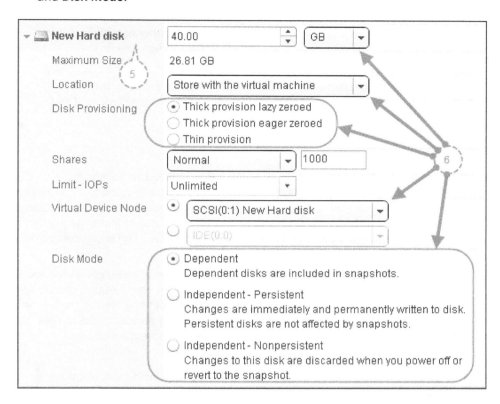

6. By default, the **Location** option selected is **Store with the virtual machine**. This is the recommended setting in most environments, for easier file management. For a traditional virtual machine, you would not need to modify these options.

7. Click on **OK** to confirm the settings. You should see the **Reconfigure virtual machine** task completing successfully in the **Recent Tasks** pane, as displayed in the following screenshot:

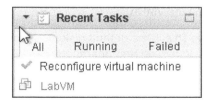

How it works...

The **virtual machine disk** (**VMDK**) can be provisioned using two different methods: thick provisioning and thin provisioning. Thick provisioning can be further categorized into lazy zeroed thick provisioning and eager zeroed thick provisioning.

 Zeroing is a process of writing zeroes to the disk blocks corresponding to a VMDK, to make sure that the existing data in those blocks, if any, is not exposed via the new VMDK.

The thick provisioning methods are as follows:

▶ **Eager zeroed thick provisioning**: An eager zeroed thick disk, when created, will get all the space allocation it needs, and all the disk blocks allocated to it are zeroed out. The creation time of an eager zeroed disk is longer compared to a lazy zeroed or thin-provisioned disk. An eager zeroed thick disk offers better first write performance. This is due to the fact that the disk blocks corresponding to an eager zeroed disk are already zeroed out during its creation.

▶ **Lazy zeroed thick provisioning**: A lazy zeroed thick disk will also get all the space allocation it needs at the time of creation, but unlike an eager zeroed disk, it does not zero out all the disk blocks. Each disk block is zeroed out only during the first write. Although it doesn't offer the first write performance like an eager zeroed disk, all the subsequent writes to the zeroed blocks will have the same performance.

 First write occurs when a disk block corresponding to a VMDK is accessed for the first time to store data.

▶ A thin-provisioned disk will not use all the disk space assigned to it during creation. It will only consume the disk space needed by the data on the disk. For instance, if you create a thin VMDK of 10 GB, then the initial size of the VMDK will not be 10 GB. When data gets added to it, the VMDK will grow in size to store the added data. If a 100 MB file is added to the VMDK, then the VMDK will grow by 100 MB.

A virtual machine disk can also be in two different disk modes. These modes determine what operations can be performed on the VMDK:

▶ **Dependent disk mode**: This is the default disk mode for all the virtual machine disks that you create. All the VMDK related operations can be performed while it is in dependent mode.

▸ **Independent disk mode**: When a virtual disk is in independent mode, no snapshot operations are allowed on it. These types of virtual disks are particularly useful for use with virtual machines in testing and development environments, when you would need to make changes and test the results, and also want to revert to a standard base line after the tests. It is also useful when you are using virtual machines to perform tests that can yield unpredictable results. These kinds of VMs are generally not backed up. An independent disk can have two fundamental behavioral modes:

  ❑ **Persistent mode**: In this mode, all changes made to the files on disk are written to the disk. Because these changes are immediately written to the disk, they are retained across reboots. In a test/development environment, this mode is used to save changes to the test base line.

  ❑ **Nonpersistent mode**: In this mode, changes made are not immediately written to the disk and are lost when you reboot or shutdown the virtual machine. This mode is generally used in test environments, where changes can yield unpredictable results.

Adding an existing hard disk to a virtual machine

You can add an existing hard disk (VMDK) to a virtual machine. This is again done from the **Edit Settings** window of the virtual machine. The virtual machine can be in the powered on state while you add the hard disk.

How to do it...

The following procedure explains how to add an existing virtual hard disk (VMDK) to the VM:

1. Navigate to the **VM and Templates** inventory view, select and right-click on the VM to which you intend to add an existing virtual hard disk (VMDK), and then click on **Edit Settings**.

2. Use the **New device** option available in the **Edit Settings** window, select **Existing Hard Disk** as the device option, and then click on **Add** as shown in the following screenshot:

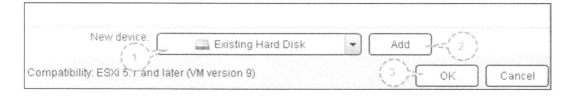

3. Navigate to the location of the VMDK, select the VMDK file, and then click on **OK** to confirm the selection.

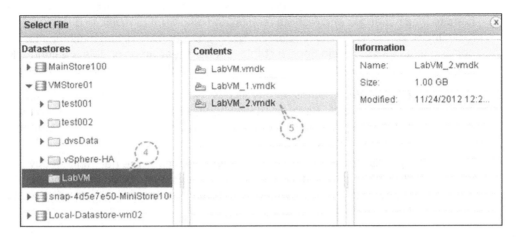

4. A **New Hard disk** entry should now be visible on the **Settings** page. Click on it to expand the advanced/additional settings for the virtual hard disk. Change **Virtual Device Node** or **Disk Mode** only if necessary:

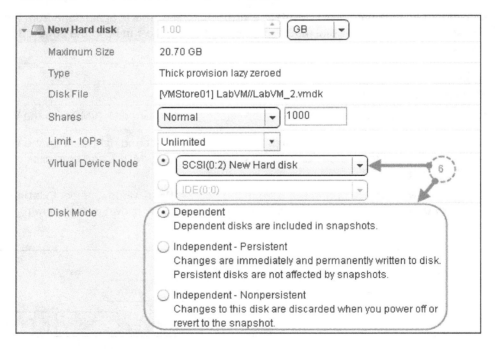

5. Click on **OK** to confirm the settings and reconfigure the virtual machine.

How it works...

Typical situations when this is done.

Attaching RDM to a virtual machine

In many environments, there will be requirements or special cases that warrant the use of **Raw Device Mappings** (**RDM**). The use of RDMs allows the guest operating system running in a VM to create its native filesystem on a LUN device.

Getting ready

Present a LUN to the ESXi hosts. You might need to contact your storage administrator for the same. Once the LUN is presented, rescan the HBAs to make sure that the LUN is visible to the ESXi hosts. Keep in mind that only a LUN with no VMFS on it can be presented as an RDM. The benefits of using raw device mappings have been outlined in the *vSphere 5.5 Storage* guide on page 156 at `http://bit.ly/vsphere55_Storage_Guide`.

How to do it...

The following procedure explains how to attach an RDM to a virtual machine:

1. Navigate to the **VM and Templates** inventory view, select and right-click on the VM to which you intend to add/map an RDM LUN, and then click on **Edit Settings**.

2. Use the **New device** option available in the **Edit Settings** window, select **RDM Disk** as the device option, and then click on **Add** as indicated in the following screenshot:

3. In the **Select Target LUN** window, select the LUN that has to be added in RDM, and then click on **OK**:

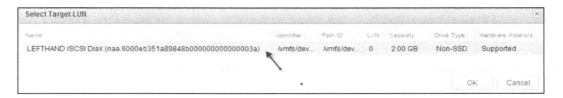

4. A **New Hard disk** entry for the RDM should now be visible on the settings page. Click on it to expand the advanced/additional settings for the hard disk. Change **Location**, **Virtual Device Node**, and RDM **Compatibility Mode** as needed. Click on **OK** to confirm the settings and attach the RDM.

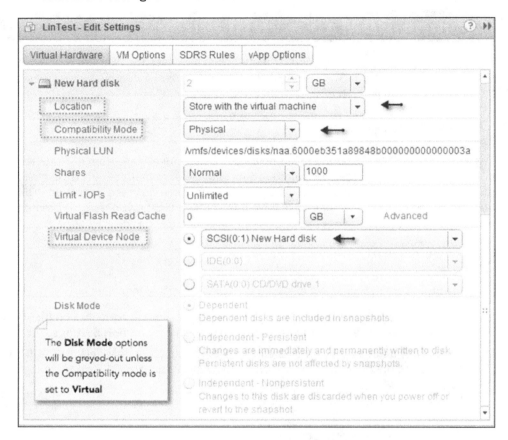

5. Click on **OK** to confirm the settings and attach the RDM.

How it works...

RDMs can be presented to a VM in two compatibility modes:

▶ **Physical compatibility**: In this mode, all the SCSI commands except the **REPORT LUNs** command is sent to the device directly. Therefore, this mode is also referred to as a pass-through mode.

▶ **Virtual compatibility**: In this mode, only the READ and WRITE commands are sent to the device. In this mode, the RDM will be compatible with most of the tasks that can be performed on a traditional VMDK.

The following table provides a reference to understand the compatibility between the RDM modes and the vSphere Functionalities such as VMotion, Virtual Machine Snapshots, Storage VMotion, and MSCS (Microsoft Clustering Service):

RDM mode	vMotion	Storage vMotion	Virtual Machine Snapshots	MSCS—clustering across ESXi hosts	MSCS—clustering within an ESXi host	MSCS—clustering between a virtual machine and a physical server
Physical	Yes	Yes	No	Yes	No	Yes
Virtual	Yes	Yes	Yes	Yes (Windows 2003 only)	Yes	No

There's more...

When configuring RDMs for MSCS, you will have to create and use a new SCSI controller for the RDM and the SCSI controller should be in either of the following **SCSI Bus Sharing** modes depending on the type of clustering configuration:

▶ **Virtual**: The SCSI controller should be in this mode if you are implementing an MSCS Cluster within an ESXi host.

▶ **Physical**: The SCSI controller should be in this mode if you are implementing an MSCS Cluster across ESXi Hosts or an MSCS Cluster between a virtual machine and a physical server. The following screenshot explains this:

Mapping a virtual machine's vNIC to a different port group

A virtual machine connects to the network via its virtual network adapter. The **virtual network adapter** of a VM is referred to as a **vNIC**. The vNIC connects to a port group on a vSwitch (standard/distributed). A vNIC cannot be directly connected to a vSwitch; it can only be mapped to any of the port groups present on the vSwitch. A port group is a set of ports on a vSwitch grouped together under a common configuration, for example, a VLAN.

If there is a need, we can reconfigure the vNIC to connect to another existing port group, or to a newly created port group. To learn more about creating and managing port groups, read *Chapter 6, Configuring vSphere Networking*.

In this recipe, we will learn how to reconfigure a virtual machine to map its vNIC to different port groups.

How to do it...

The following procedure guides you through the steps required to map a VM's vNIC to different port groups:

1. Navigate to the **VM and Templates** inventory view, select and right-click on the VM, and then click on **Edit Settings**.

2. Use the drop-down box next to the **Network adapter** entry to select the port group to which the vNIC should be connected, and then click on **OK** to confirm the settings as shown in the following screenshot:

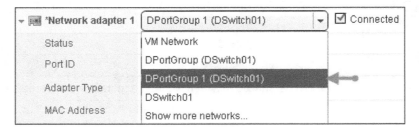

3. Click on **OK** to confirm the changes.

How it works...

Once the virtual machine's vNIC has been reconfigured to connect to a different port group, all the network I/O via vNIC will be affected by the configuration on the port group. That is, if the port group has a VLAN ID set on it, then the VM will have access to the subnet corresponding to that VLAN. The vNIC to port group mapping can be changed while the virtual machine is running.

Adding a new virtual network adapter to a virtual machine

You can add an additional virtual network adapter to a virtual machine. Such a need is dictated by the purpose of the virtual machine. In this recipe, we will learn how to add a new virtual network adapter to a VM.

How to do it...

The following procedure explains how to add a new virtual network adapter to a VM:

1. Navigate to the **VM and Templates** inventory view, select and right-click on the VM to which you intend to add a virtual network adapter (vNIC), and then click on **Edit Settings**.

2. Use the **New device** option available in the **Edit Settings** window, select **Network** as the device option, and then click on **Add** as demonstrated in the following screenshot:

3. A **New Network** entry for the adapter will be made available on the settings page. Use the drop-down box next to **New Network** to select a port group.

4. Select the network **Adapter Type** and a port group to connect the network adapter:

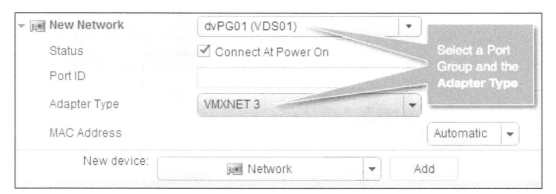

5. Click on **OK** to confirm the settings and exit the **Edit Settings** window.

Creating a virtual machine snapshot

There are times when you need to save the current state of an application's or operating system's configuration before you experiment with a change. A real-life example would be during a system development life cycle where changes are inevitable, and you need the ability to undo a change. vSphere allows you to save the state of a virtual machine regardless of its power state.

A virtual machine snapshot can capture the following data:

▶ The contents of the virtual machine's memory

▶ The virtual machine's settings

▶ The state of the virtual disks

For you to perform snapshot operations on a virtual machine, you need to be connected to the vCenter Server either by using vSphere Web Client or vSphere Client, or by using the vSphere Client to the ESXi server hosting the virtual machine.

> Snapshots cannot be created on virtual disks (VMDK) in independent mode and on RDMs in physical compatibility mode.

How to do it...

The following procedure guides you through the steps required to create a snapshot on a virtual machine:

1. Navigate to the **VM and Templates** inventory view, select and right-click on the VM for which you intend to create a snapshot, and then click on **Take Snapshot...** as shown in the following screenshot:

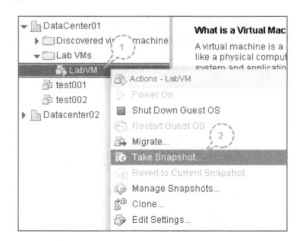

2. Provide a **Name** for the snapshot and an optional **Description**. The **Quiesce the guest file system (Needs VMware tool installed)** option requires VMware tools to be installed, and the **Snapshot the virtual machine's memory** option is selected by default for a powered on virtual machine. Click on **OK**.

3. The progress of the task can be tracked in the **Recent Tasks** pane:

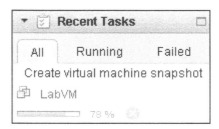

4. Once the tasks complete successfully, right-click on the VM again, and then click on **Manage Snapshots**:

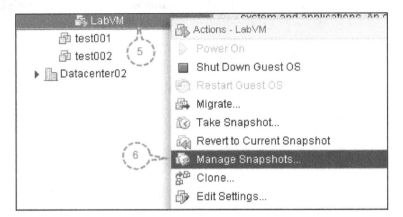

5. The Snapshot Manager for the virtual machine should show the newly created snapshot and its details, including the creation date and its disk usage. Take a look at the following screenshot:

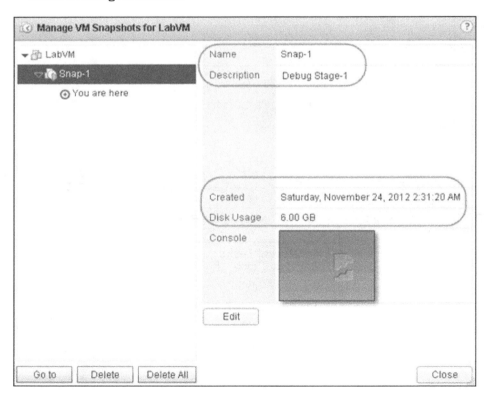

How it works...

When you create a snapshot, you have options to snapshot the virtual machine's memory and to quiesce the guest filesystem. Quiescing the filesystem would mean bringing the data that is on disk to a state that would enable backups. It would even flush the buffers on to the disk or pause the running applications. For quiescing to work, you will need VMware Tools installed.

If the memory was chosen to be included in the snapshot, then the ESXi server will flush all the virtual machine's memory contents to disk. The flushed memory contents are stored in the virtual machine state file (*vmsn). While this is taking place, the virtual machine will temporarily remain frozen or unresponsive.

 The VMSN will hold the memory, VMX, and the BIOS state information.

The amount of time for which the virtual machine will continue to be in the unresponsive state depends on the amount of time that is needed to dump the memory to disk. The amount of memory that needs to be flushed and the disk performance are also contributing factors.

Once the memory is dumped to disk, the subsequent disk I/O will be redirected to a snapshot difference file called the delta file. The delta file is also a virtual disk data file, and is referenced by using a virtual disk descriptor file.

```
/vmfs/volumes/508278d5-d383bbda-bfaa-000c293bef13/LabVM # ls -lh *vmdk
-rw-------    1 root     root        4.0K Nov 23 21:01 LabVM-000001-delta.vmdk
-rw-------    1 root     root         312 Nov 23 21:   LabVM-000001.vmdk
-rw-------    1 root     root        1.    Snapshot    7:56 LabVM-flat.vmdk
-rw-------    1 root     root        4    deltas       7:56 LabVM.vmdk
-rw-------    1 root     root        4.     :0  LabVM_1-000001-delta.vmdk
-rw-------    1 root     root         316 Nov 23 21:0  LabVM_1-000001.vmdk
-rw-------    1 root     root        1.0G Nov 23 18:44 LabVM_1-flat.vmdk
-rw-------    1 root     root         466 Nov 23 18:44 LabVM_1.vmdk
-rw-------    1 root     root        1.0G Nov 23 18:51 LabVM_2-flat.vmdk
-rw-------    1 root     root         466 Nov 23 18:51 LabVM_2.vmdk
-rw-------    1 root     root        5.0G Nov 23 19:57 LabVM_3-rdmp.vmdk
-rw-------    1 root     root         493 Nov 23 19:57 LabVM_3.vmdk
/vmfs/volumes/508278d5-d383bbda-bfaa-000c293bef13/LabVM #
```

The delta file will continue to hold all the disk I/O changes, from the time at which the snapshot was taken. For the server to do the I/O to the delta file, the virtual machine should be configured to access the delta files instead of the base virtual disk. This happens automatically when you create a snapshot.

 The delta disk cannot grow beyond the size of the original base disk.

The **virtual machine snapshot database** (**VMSD**) is also updated. The **Snapshot Manager** GUI will refer to VMSD file for displaying the snapshot information. The snapshot chain is also updated by modifying the descriptors of the child disks. The effect on the virtual machine is the same for all the snapshot operations (`createSnapshot`/`RemoveSnapshot`/ `RemoveAllSnapshots`/`RevertToSnapshot`/`Consolidate`).

There's more...

If left unattended, snapshots can double a VM's disk foot print on the datastore. This is because a snapshot can grow as large as the base-original disk. It can also affect the performance of the VM since every write would need ESXi to allocate disk blocks and grow the delta file. It is important to periodically monitor the VMs for left over snapshots and deleting them.

For best practices on creating virtual machine snapshots, read the VMware Knowledge Base article 1025279. It is available at:

`http://kb.vmware.com/kb/1025279`

Also, the Knowledge Base article 1009402, *Working with snapshot*, should be a good read. It is available at the following link:

`http://kb.vmware.com/kb/1009402`

Deleting a virtual machine snapshot

To delete a virtual machine snapshot, you should use the virtual machine Snapshot Manager.

You can perform two types of delete operations:

- **Delete operation**: This operation will let you choose a snapshot to be deleted. When this is done, the data held by its VMSN, the changes recorded by the VMX, and the delta file are committed (written) to its immediate parent.
- **Delete all operation**: When this operation is performed, only the contents of the current snapshot and its delta file are committed to the base disk. The rest will be discarded; the VMSN and the delta files will be deleted as well.

How to do it...

The following procedure explains how to delete a virtual machine snapshot using
Snapshot Manager:

1. Right-click on the VM and click on **Manage Snapshots...**:

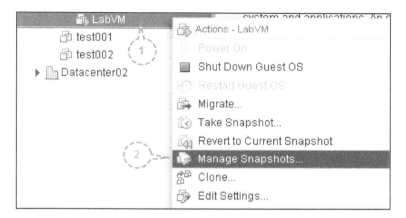

2. Select the snapshot to be deleted, and then click on **Delete** as indicated in the
following screenshot:

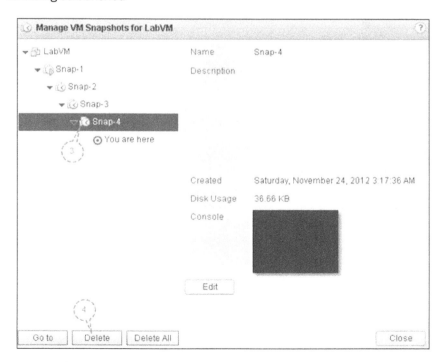

3. Click on **Yes** in the pop-up window that appears to confirm the delete operation:

How it works...

To explain how the delete operation works, let's use the following table for reference:

	File at the GOS	Snapshot file	Snapshot delta file
Base disk(No snapshots)	Test		Ubuntu-flat.vmdk
Snap-1	Test	Ubuntu-Snapshot1.vmsn	Ubuntu-000001-delta.vmdk
When a new file Test1 is created, Ubuntu-000001-delta.vmdk will hold the file Test1.			
Snap-2	Test, Test1	Ubuntu-Snapshot2.vmsn	Ubuntu-000002-delta.vmdk
When a new file Test2 is created, Ubuntu-000002-delta.vmdk will hold the file Test2.			
Snap-3	Test, Test1, Test2	Ubuntu-Snapshot3.vmsn	Ubuntu-000003-delta.vmdk
When a new file Test3 is created, Ubuntu-000003-delta.vmdk will hold the file Test3.			
Snap-4	Test, Test1, Test2, Test3	Ubuntu-Snapshot4.vmsn	Ubuntu-000004-delta.vmdk
When a new file Test4 is created, Ubuntu-000004-delta.vmdk will hold the file Test4.			

If **Snap-4** in the preceding table is deleted, then the contents of the snapshot, **Snap-4** (Test, Test1, Test2, and Test3) and the contents of the delta file Ubuntu-000004-delta.vmdk (Test4) are committed to delta of the immediate parent snapshot, **Snap-3**. So the delta Ubuntu-000003-delta.vmdk file will now hold the Test, Test1, Test2, Test3, and Test4 files.

However, when a delete all operation is issued, the contents of current snapshot and its delta are committed to the base disk. The rest will be discarded; the VMSN and the delta files will be deleted as well. If the current snapshot is **Snap-4,** then after a delete all operation, the base disk will have the Test, Test1, Test2, Test3, and Test4 files.

During the remove operations, the snapshot manager will remove the entry corresponding to the chosen snapshot from the snapshot database. This is done prior to updating the child VMDK's descriptor file with the new parent disk's Content ID (CID) value.

See also

▶ Refer to the *Unable to delete the virtual machine snapshot due to locked files* VMware Knowledge Base article 2017072 at `http://kb.vmware.com/kb/2017072`

Reverting to a current virtual machine snapshot

The whole idea behind taking a snapshot is to save the current state of the virtual machine so that it will remain unaffected by the changes you intend to make. In a situation where you would want to discard the changes you made and return to the saved state of the virtual machine, the **Revert to Current Snapshot** operation is performed.

 You will not need the snapshot manager to perform the revert operation.

How to do it...

The following procedure guides you through the steps required to revert to the current snapshot:

1. Right-click on the VM and click on **Revert to Current Snapshot**:

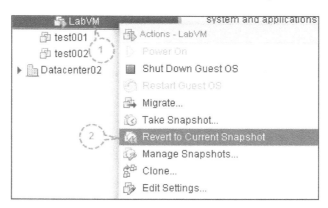

2. Click on **Yes** to confirm the revert operation:

How it works...

Reverting to a current snapshot will discard its delta contents. The contents of the delta file are permanently lost unless it is saved in a subsequent snapshot. That is, if the current snapshot isn't parenting a child snapshot, then its delta data is lost forever.

In our example (refer to the table from the previous recipe), the current snapshot was **Snap-4**, and its delta was saved to the Test4 file. After the **Revert to Current Snapshot** operation, the contents of its delta file Ubuntu-000004-delta.vmdk are discarded and **Snap-4** will only have the Test, Test1, Test2, and Test3 files.

Switching to an arbitrary virtual machine snapshot

The **Go to** option lets you revert to a selected snapshot. This is particularly useful if you want to discard all the changes that you have made to the virtual machine and return to an older than most recent snapshot state of the virtual machine.

This process does require using the **Snapshot Manager** for the virtual machine.

How to do it...

The following procedure explains how to perform a selective revert operation on an older snapshot in the chain:

1. Right-click on the VM and click on **Manage Snapshots...**.

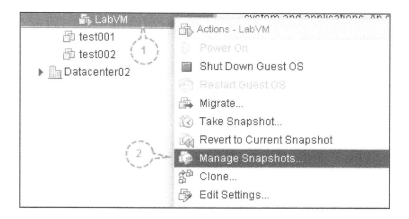

2. Select the snapshot to which you want to revert, and then click on **Go to** to perform a selective revert operation as demonstrated in the following screenshot:

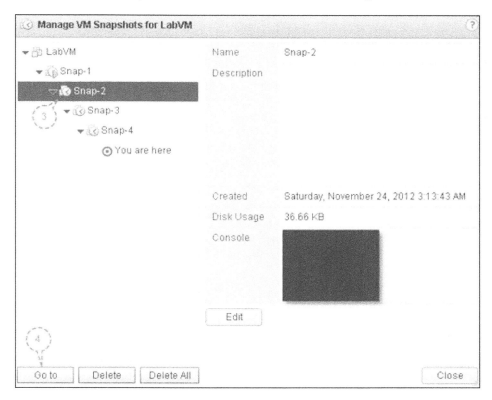

3. Click on **Yes** to confirm the Go to operation.

How it works...

When you revert to a particular snapshot, the process will discard all the contents of its difference file (delta) and all the subsequent snapshots. Reverting to a snapshot will result in the selected snapshot's state minus the contents of its delta being restored.

For example, while the VM is currently running on the delta of **Snap-4**, if we revert to **Snap-2**, this will discard the contents of the delta file Ubuntu-000002-delta.vmdk (which holds the Test2 file) and the contents of all the other snapshots that were subsequently created. So after reverting to **Snap-2**, the OS will only have the Test and Test1 files.

Even though it discards the contents of its delta, it does not delete the delta file, because the snapshots that were taken subsequent to that depend on the delta of its parent. That is, **Snap-3** depends on the delta of **Snap-2**. Therefore, **Snap-3** will have the state that **Snap-2** has and the changes recorded in **Snap-2**'s delta. So after reverting to **Snap-2**, if we go back to **Snap-3**, you will see the Test, Test1, and Test2 files in there. If we go back to **Snap-4**, you will see the Test, Test1, Test2, and Test3 files.

There is a caveat that you should keep in mind when you choose to revert to snapshots. When you revert from a snapshot to an older one, the delta of the current snapshot (if it is the last snapshot in the chain) will be lost. That is, if **Snap-4** is the last snapshot in the chain, then if you revert from **Snap-4** to an older snapshot up the chain, this will result in the loss of the contents of the delta file Ubuntu-000004-delta.vmdk, which contains the Test4 file.

> If we revert to a virtual machine snapshot that doesn't have the memory captured, it will result in the virtual machine being powered off.

Consolidating snapshots

Snapshot consolidation is a process of merging the content of all the snapshots to the base disk. We have seen snapshot consolidations fail for various reasons. For instance, a backup appliance that hot adds the VMDK to its proxy server to back up its content should ideally remove the hot-added VMDK and issue a delete operation on the snapshot it created. If for some reason, it fails to remove the hot-added VMDK, then all subsequent snapshot delete operations that it issues will also fail. This is because the file is in use. If this goes undetected, then you will be left with a lot of snapshot delta files, eventually using up a lot/all the free space on the datastore. Things get worse when the snapshot manager does not show all the left-over snapshots, leaving the user/administrator with no GUI control over the situation.

Fortunately, starting with vSphere 5, you have a GUI option to consolidate the left-over snapshot files. In this recipe, we will learn how to use this new feature.

How to do it...

The following procedure explains how to perform a snapshot consolidation operation:

1. Right-click on the VM and navigate to **All vCenter Actions | Snapshots**, and then click on **Consolidate**.
2. Click on **Yes** to confirm the consolidate operation.

How it works...

The consolidate operation is performed when a snapshot delete/delete all operation fails, but it also removes the snapshot information from **Snapshot Manager**. If this happens, the VM's folder will still have the snapshot files (deltas) and the virtual machine will also be running on the snapshot disk.

Prior to the addition of the **Consolidate** option, the administrator could use several methods to consolidate snapshots. They could go through the tedious task of verifying the snapshot chain to make sure it is not broken, and then issue `vmkfstools -i` on the current snapshot (most recent) to clone and consolidate the delta.

See also

► Refer to the *Consolidating snapshots in vSphere 5.x* (VMware Knowledge Base article 2003638) at `http://kb.vmware.com/kb/2003638`

Exporting a virtual machine

A virtual machine can be packaged for transport. vSphere provides a method to do so, by exporting a virtual machine in an **open virtual machine format** (**OVF**), which is an open standard developed by the **Distributed Management Task Force** (**DMTF**) with cooperation from VMware, Citrix, IBM, Microsoft, Sun, and other companies.

There are two formats to package a virtual machine and its files:

▶ Open Virtualization Format (OVF)

▶ Open Virtualization Archive (OVA)

Read the *How it works...* section of the following recipe to understand the difference between the two formats.

How to do it...

The following procedure explains how to export a virtual machine to OVA or OVF format:

1. Right-click on the VM and navigate to **All vCenter Actions | Export OVF Template...**:

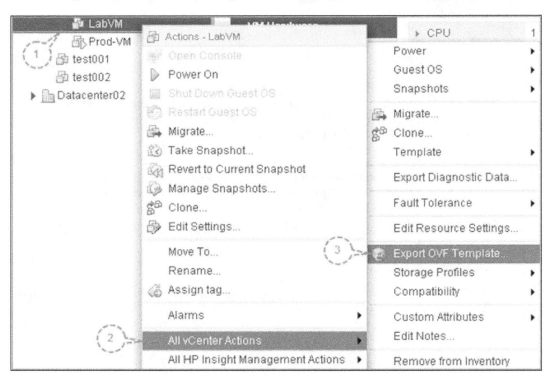

2. In the **Export OVF Template** window, provide a name for the template, choose an export folder and export format, and then click on **OK** to initiate the export as shown in the following screenshot:

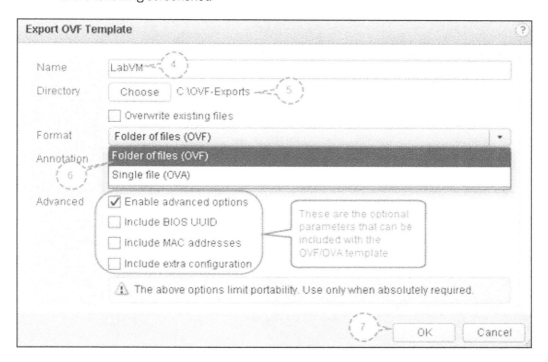

How it works...

The OVF will package all the virtual machine files into a single folder. It will have an OVF descriptor file that will have an extension .ovf, a manifest (.mf) file, the virtual disks, and certificates, if any:

Name ▲	Date modified	Type	Size
LabVM.mf	12/10/2012 6:11 AM	MF File	1 KB
LabVM.ovf	12/10/2012 6:11 AM	OVF File	10 KB
LabVM-disk1.vmdk	12/10/2012 6:10 AM	VMDK File	67 KB
LabVM-disk2.vmdk	12/10/2012 6:11 AM	VMDK File	67 KB

The manifest file contains the SHA1 digest of all files in the package. The OVA is simply a TAR file with the OVF folder packaged inside it. The .ova extension can even be changed to TAR and have its content extracted by a unarchiver such as 7—Zip.

11
Configuring vSphere HA

In this chapter, we will cover the following recipes:

- ▶ Enabling vSphere HA on a cluster
- ▶ Configuring vSphere HA Admission Control
- ▶ Setting the host isolation response for an HA cluster
- ▶ Setting the VM restart priority for an HA cluster
- ▶ Configuring VM monitoring
- ▶ Configuring datastore heartbeating
- ▶ Configuring a VM to override host monitoring and VM monitoring settings
- ▶ Disabling host monitoring

Introduction

VMware vSphere HA (High Availability) is a functionality that is used to configure a cluster of ESXi hosts to respond to an unplanned downtime event and ensure the availability of the virtual machines that were running on them, with very minimal downtime possible. Although that was a very simple definition, there is more to what vSphere HA can do in terms of providing high availability to the virtual machines running on the HA protected hosts. It can monitor the guest operating systems and the applications running inside of a virtual machine and then decide to restart the affected virtual machine in an effort to reduce the downtime of a service due to an affected guest operating system hosting the service or a nonresponsive application corresponding to the service. Having said all that, it is important to understand that even though HA is configured on a cluster of ESXi hosts, it only provides high availability for the virtual machines and not for the hosts. It cannot start up or restart an affected ESXi host.

In this chapter, we will learn how to enable and configure vSphere HA, but before we begin, let's go over what is new with vSphere HA with the release of vSphere 5.5:

- Making HA VM anti-affinity rule aware: With vSphere 5.5, you can now make vSphere HA aware of the VM anti-affinity rule, by just configuring an advanced setting. Both vSphere 5.5 HA and the previous versions ignore the anti-affinity rules by default, but with Version 5.5, the advanced setting can override the default behavior. Here is the advanced parameter and value that needs to be configured to achieve it:

  ```
  das.respectVmVmAntiAffinityRules = "true"
  ```

- vSphere App HA replaces the application monitoring feature available with the previous versions of HA. It leverages vFabric Hyperic to monitor supported applications.

Enabling vSphere HA on a cluster

vSphere HA is not enabled by default on a host cluster. It has to be manually enabled. In this recipe, we will understand the requirements of a HA cluster, how it is enabled, and how it works.

Getting ready

Since vSphere HA is enabled at the cluster level, you will need access to a vCenter Server using vSphere Web Client or the vSphere Client to accomplish the configuration. Although there is nothing more you would need to enable HA, it is important to make sure that the ESXi hosts participating in a HA cluster:

- Have access to the same shared storage
- Have access to the same virtual machine networks
- Have CPUs from the same family and feature set

 For more information, refer to the vSphere HA checklist on page 25 in the *vSphere Availability Guide* for vSphere 5.5.

If any of the preceding factors are not considered when designing an HA cluster, then it could either leave HA nonfunctional, increase the unplanned downtime, or even affect the performance of the guest operating system and the applications running inside the virtual machines.

How to do it...

The following steps will walk you through the procedure of enabling HA on an ESXi cluster:

1. From vCenter's **Home** inventory, navigate to the **Hosts and Clusters** view.

2. Select the cluster and navigate to **Manage | Settings | vSphere HA**, and click on **Edit**.

3. On the **Edit Cluster Settings** window, select the **Turn ON vSphere HA** checkbox, and click on **OK** to enable HA.

How it works...

Starting with vSphere 5.0, HA has been completely recoded. It is now referred to as the **Fault Domain Manager**. It no longer uses Legato's AAM. The earlier concept of primary and secondary master has been relinquished as well. With FDM, only one among all the ESXi hosts in the cluster can become the master. The remaining hosts are slaves.

When you enable HA on a cluster, the FDM agents available on the vCenter Server are transferred and installed on the ESXi hosts in the cluster. Then one of the ESXi hosts is elected as a master and the remaining hosts become the slave hosts. Although vCenter is used for enabling and configuring HA, HA can continue to function without vCenter being available.

 On a cluster of auto-deployed ESXi hosts, it is important to package the vSphere HA VIB (vmware-fdm) into the image profile.

For now, let's assume that everything went well with the configuration of HA on a cluster, and we now have a single master and several slave nodes. So how does HA choose which host becomes the master? How does HA monitor and manage the cluster for unplanned outages?

The first question to answer is how does HA elect a master node? During the election process, a host with access to the largest number of datastores will be chosen as the master and the remaining hosts are marked as slaves. Every set of slave nodes will have a master. If there is a network partition in the HA cluster, meaning if a group of hosts can't communicate with another group of hosts in the same cluster but can communicate amongst the hosts within the groups, then a network partition between the two groups is said to exist. In such a scenario, there would be an election for a master within those groups.

The second question to answer is how does HA monitor and manage the cluster for unplanned outages? We now know for a fact that every HA cluster will have a master and a set of slaves. One of the roles of the master is to monitor the slaves for their liveliness. This is done using network heartbeats that are exchanged between the master and the slaves over their management network. Network heartbeats are only sent over the VMkernel ports that are configured to handle ESXi management traffic. Since all the heartbeat traffic is over the management network, it is important to build network resiliency for the management network. The network heartbeats are exchanged every second. If the any of the slave hosts stop receiving heartbeats from the master, then it will begin determining whether it is network isolated with the master. This entire process can take up to a minute before it decides to execute the isolation response.

Fault Domain Manager (FDM) also introduced the concept of **datastore heartbeating**, which is again used to check the liveliness of a slave when the master is not able to communicate with it over the network. More about datastore heartbeating will be discussed in the *Configuring datastore heartbeating* recipe in this chapter. If the master is unable to receive network heartbeats from the slave and if the slave is also not heartbeating the datastore, then the master will try to restart the virtual machines on that slave. Keep in mind that the number of attempts that a master will perform to restart a virtual machines is five, and all these attempts are spread over a period of 30 minutes.

vSphere HA once enabled and configured correctly, in the event of a host failure or a network isolation, the virtual machines that were running on the failed host can be restarted on another ESXi host from the same cluster. Keep in mind that the manner in which HA reacts to a network isolation depends on how it is configured to react to such occurrences.

There is lot more to how HA functions and also those that is not covered in this *How it works...* section. There are several reference materials on vSphere HA. I have included a few reference materials in the *See also* section of this recipe.

See also

- Read the *How vSphere HA Works* section on page 11 in the *vSphere Availability Guide* for vSphere 5.5 (`http://bit.ly/HA55Guide`)
- Duncan Epping's HA Deep Dive on his blog site `http://yellow-bricks.com` is also a very good read

Configuring vSphere HA Admission Control

A well-configured HA cluster will have enough free resources to restart all the business-critical VMs running on the hosts, in the event of host failures. This amount of free resources is referred to as the **failover capacity**.

Failover capacity determines the number of the ESXi hosts that can fail in an HA cluster, and still leave enough resources to support all the powered-on VMs. We can use admission control to control and monitor the failover capacity.

There are three admission control methods (policies):

▸ Define the failover capacity by reserving a static number of hosts

▸ Define the failover capacity by reserving a percentage of the cluster resources

▸ Specify dedicated failover hosts

 Note that admission control can be disabled by selecting the **Do not reserve failover capacity** option or by just unchecking the admission control checkbox.

Any operation that violates the resource constraints imposed by the admission control policy will not be permitted. Some of these operations include a VM power-on operation, a vMotion operation, and a change in the CPU/memory reservation of the VM.

How to do it...

We can define the failover capacity of the HA cluster by:

▸ Specifying a static number of hosts that will be available for failover

▸ Reserving a percentage of the cluster resources for failover

▸ Specifying dedicated failover hosts

The following procedure explains how to specify a static number of hosts for failover:

1. From the vCenter's **Home** inventory, navigate to the **Hosts and Clusters** view.

2. Select the cluster and navigate to **Manage | Settings | vSphere HA**, and click on **Edit**.

3. In the **Edit Cluster Settings** window, click on **Admission Control** to expand and view its additional settings.

4. To define a reserved failover capacity in terms of the number of hosts that will be available to failover VMs, select the **Define failover capacity by static number of hosts** option.

5. Also, choose a **Slot size policy** value for the VMs. The policy can either calculate slot size based on the powered-on VMs, or you can specify a custom (fixed) slot size. Here we have selected the **Cover all powered-on virtual machines** option, as shown in the following screenshot:

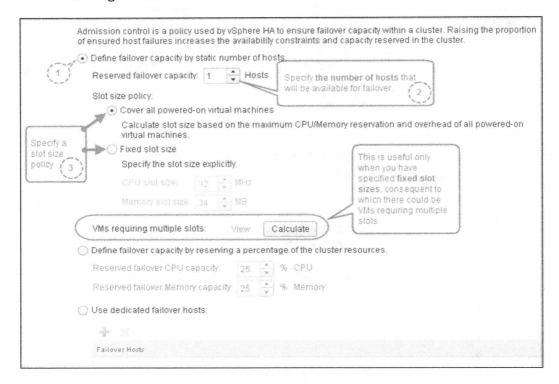

6. Click on **OK** to confirm the settings and reconfigure the cluster.

The following procedure explains how to reserve a percentage of the cluster resources (CPU and memory resources) for failover:

1. From the vCenter's **Home** inventory, navigate to the **Hosts and Clusters** view.

2. Select the cluster and navigate to **Manage | Settings | vSphere HA**, and click on **Edit**.

3. In the **Edit Cluster Settings** window, click on **Admission Control** to expand and view its additional settings.

4. Specify a failover capacity by reserving a percentage of CPU and memory resources from the cluster as demonstrated in the following screenshot:

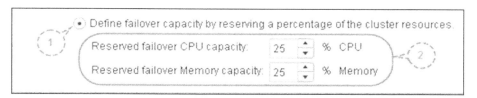

5. Click on **OK** to confirm the settings and reconfigure the cluster.

The following procedure explains how to specify the hosts that will be used as failover hosts:

1. From the vCenter's **Home** inventory, navigate to the **Hosts and Clusters** view.

2. Select the cluster and navigate to **Manage | Settings | vSphere HA**, and click on **Edit**.

3. In the **Edit Cluster Settings** window, click on **Admission Control** to expand and view its additional settings.

4. Select the **Use dedicated failover hosts** option, and click on the green **+** icon to bring up the **Add Failover Hosts** window:

5. On the **Add Failover Host** window, select the host(s) to be added as failover host(s), and then click on **OK** as shown in the following screenshot:

6. The **Settings** screen should now list the selected host as a failover host:

7. Click on **OK** to confirm the settings and reconfigure the cluster.

How it works...

The vSphere HA admission control is used to make sure that no operation will lower the failover capacity of the cluster, thereby preserving enough resources in the HA cluster to run VMs that are restarted in the event of a host(s) failure. This is done using the following three admission control policies:

- **Failover capacity by static number of hosts**: Any operation that would cause the failover capacity (consequent to the number of powered-on VMs and its CPU/memory reservations) to be lower than the configured failover capacity, will not be permitted.

- **Failover capacity by reserving a percentage of the cluster resources**: Any operation that would cause the current (calculated) CPU/memory failover capacity to be lower than the configured failover capacity will not be permitted.

- **Dedicated failover hosts**: By selecting dedicated failover hosts, vSphere HA admission control will not allow any operations to be performed on those hosts.

See also

- The admission control and slot calculation has been well explained in Duncan Epping's *HA Deepdive* blog. This is a good read and is available at `http://www.yellow-bricks.com/vmware-high-availability-deepdiv/`.

Setting the host isolation response for an HA cluster

The **host isolation response** setting is used by the ESXi host, which detects itself as being isolated (management-network-isolated) from the network, to decide whether to change the power state of the virtual machines running on it or to leave it unchanged.

There are three host isolation responses, as follows:

- **Leave powered on**: This setting will not modify the power state of the running virtual machines

- **Power off then failover**: This setting will hard power off the running virtual machines

- **Shut down then failover**: This setting will issue a graceful shutdown of the virtual machines

In this recipe, we learn how to set the host isolation response on the cluster.

How to do it...

The following procedure explains how to set/modify the host isolation response settings on the cluster:

1. From the vCenter's **Home** inventory, navigate to the **Hosts and Clusters** view.

2. Select the cluster and navigate to **Manage | Settings | vSphere HA**, and click on **Edit**.

3. In the **Edit Cluster Settings** window, click on **Host Monitoring** to expand and view its additional settings.

4. Click on the **Host isolation response** drop-down box to select the required isolation response.

5. With a planned isolation response selected, click on **OK** to confirm the changes.

See also

▶ The *vSphere HA Advanced Attributes* section on page 31 of the *vSphere Availability* guide for vSphere 5.5 should be a good read. The guide is available via the `http://bit.ly/HA55Guide`.

Setting the VM restart priority for an HA cluster

Setting restart priorities for individual VMs will help VMware HA to determine which VM should be restarted when an ESXi host fails. In this recipe, we learn how to configure the VM restart priority for an HA cluster.

How to do it...

The following procedure explains how to set/modify VM restart priority settings for an HA cluster:

1. From the vCenter's **Home** inventory, navigate to the **Hosts and Clusters** view.

2. Select the cluster and navigate to **Manage | Settings | vSphere HA** and click on **Edit**.

3. In the **Edit Cluster Settings** window, click on **Host Monitoring** to expand and view its additional settings.

4. Use the **VM restart priority** drop-down menu to choose the **Disabled**, **Low**, **Medium**, or **High** priority setting.

5. With the planned **VM restart priority** option selected, click on **OK** to confirm the changes.

How it works...

The restart priorities set are relative. HA will restart VMs with the highest priority first. If the priority is set to **Disabled** for a VM, then in the event of a host failure, that particular VM will not be restarted. The priorities set are only for HA to determine the restart order; they don't affect the VM monitoring.

So when does setting priorities come-in handy? The very simple example is to set the highest restart priority to the virtual machine hosting the database server so that other virtual machines running services that depend on a connection to the database server won't have any issues when they start up.

The previous example was indeed a very simple one, but there is a greater purpose for the VM restart priorities. In the *Configuring vSphere HA Admission Control* recipe, we learned how to set the failover capacity for an HA cluster. Now, let's assume that we have set the Failover capacity to 2 ESXi hosts. With that configuration in place, if more than 2 ESXi hosts fail then you would want to make sure that even though your cluster capacity is reduced than for what you were prepared for, the high priority VMs are started first. This can be achieved by setting VM restart priorities. It is a common practice to leave the cluster's restart priority at **Medium** and set the high priorities needed for virtual machines.

Configuring VM monitoring

vSphere HA can be configured to monitor virtual machines, so that unresponsive VMs can be restarted (*reset*). This is achieved by enabling VM monitoring on the HA cluster.

You can also enable application monitoring. This will restart a VM if the VMware Tools application heartbeats are not received within a predefined timeout value.

How to do it...

The following procedure describes how to configure VM monitoring on an HA cluster:

1. From the vCenter's **Home** inventory, navigate to the **Hosts and Clusters** view.
2. Select the cluster and navigate to **Manage | Settings | vSphere HA**, and click on **Edit**.
3. In the **Edit Cluster Settings** window, click on **VM Monitoring** to expand and view its additional settings.
4. To enable VM monitoring, you can choose between the **Disabled**, **VM Monitoring only**, and **VM and Application Monitoring** options.

5. With the monitoring type selected, set a planned **Monitoring Sensitivity** value, and click on **OK** as shown in the following screenshot:

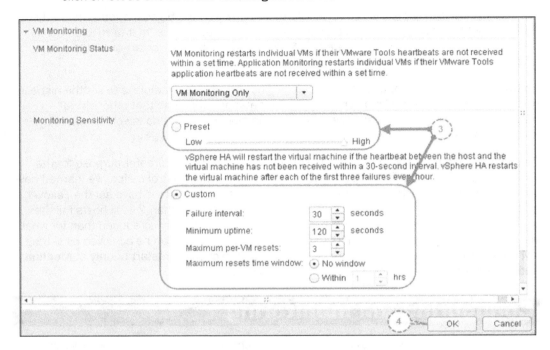

How it works...

VM monitoring is very handy when you have VMs hosting services for which you can't afford longer downtime.

Once enabled, VM monitoring, with the help of VMware Tools installed in the VMs, will monitor for heartbeats from the VMs. Failure detection happens at different intervals of non-receipt of the VM's heartbeat. The intervals are governed by the monitoring sensitivity configured for the VM.

The default monitoring sensitivity is **High**, in which case the VM monitoring expects a heartbeat from the VM every 30 seconds. If the heartbeat is not received, then VM monitoring will look for any storage or network I/O activity in the past 120 seconds (this is the default das. iostatsInterval value). If there are *none,* then the VM is *reset,* and more importantly it is reset only three times during an hour's reset-time window.

 Note that a screenshot of the virtual machine's console will be taken prior to a reset operation.

Configuring datastore heartbeating

vSphere HA uses datastore heartbeating to check the liveliness of a host if it can't be reached on the management network. This is enabled by default, but we are allowed to choose the datastore that we want to use for heartbeating.

How to do it...

The following procedure explains how to select a datastore for heartbeating:

1. From the vCenter's **Home** inventory, navigate to the **Hosts and Clusters** view.
2. Select the cluster and navigate to **Manage | Settings | vSphere HA**, and click on **Edit**.
3. On the **Edit Cluster Settings** window, click on **Datastore Heartbeating** to expand and view its additional settings:

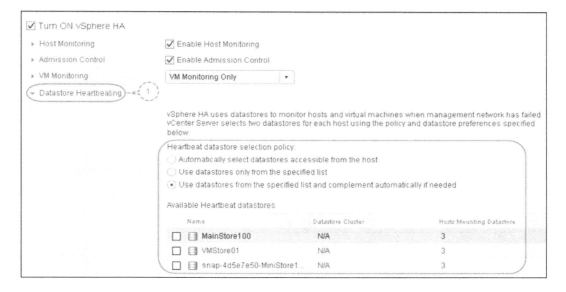

4. Choose between the **Automatically select datastores accessible from the host**, **Use datastores only from the specified list**, and **Use datastores from the specified list and complement automatically if needed** options as demonstrated in the following screenshot. In this example, let's choose the third option and manually select the datastores. Click on **OK** to confirm the selection:

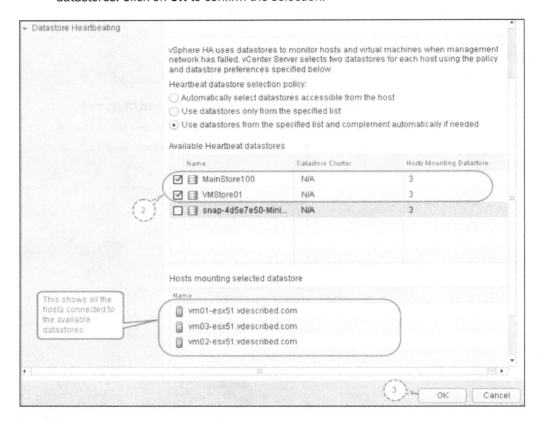

How it works...

Datastore heartbeating is enabled by default when you enable HA on an ESXi cluster. With heartbeating enabled, the master host in the HA cluster can check the liveliness of a slave host if it can't be reached over the management network.

HA, by default, chooses two heartbeat datastores per host. It does so by making sure that it selects two datastores that are not backed by the same NFS server or storage array and are mapped to at least two ESXi hosts. This value can be modified by adding the advanced parameter das.heartbeatDsPerHost. The maximum value is **5**. To do that, click on **Datastore Heartbeating** to expand and view its additional settings in the **Edit Cluster Settings** window. Click on **Advanced Options** to expand it, and click on the **Add** button to add the parameter as shown in the following screenshot:

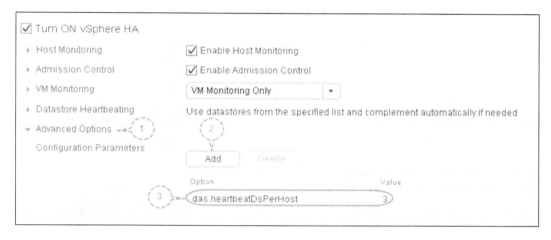

HA creates heartbeat files (-hb) in a directory called .vSphere-HA at the root of a heartbeat datastore. These files help HA to verify whether the slave host is still alive. The -poweron files have a list of powered on VMs on the host.

The following screenshot depicts the contents of the directory:

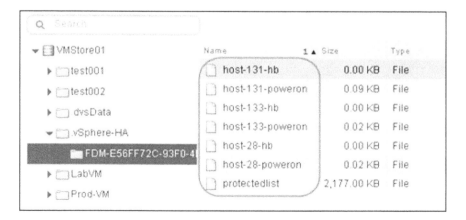

Configuring a VM to override host monitoring and VM monitoring settings

It is possible to configure a virtual machine to override the host monitoring and VM monitoring settings. The settings are overridden by creating **VM overrides**.

The settings that can be overridden are as follows:

▸ VM restart priority

▸ Host isolation response

▸ VM monitoring and monitoring sensitivity

How to do it...

The following procedure explains how to configure VM(s) to override HA cluster settings:

1. From the vCenter's **Home** inventory, navigate to the **Hosts and Clusters** view.

2. Select the cluster and navigate to **Manage | Settings | VM Overrides**.

3. On the **VM Overrides** page, click on the **Add** button to bring up the **Add VM Overrides** window as demonstrated in the following screenshot:

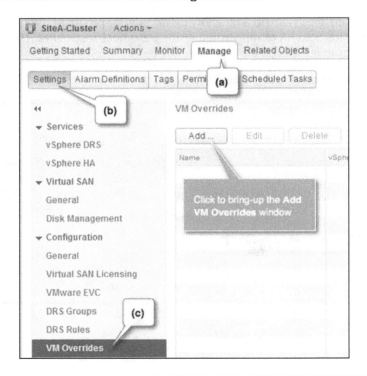

4. In the **Add VM Overrides** window, click on the green **+** icon to bring up the **Select a VM** window:

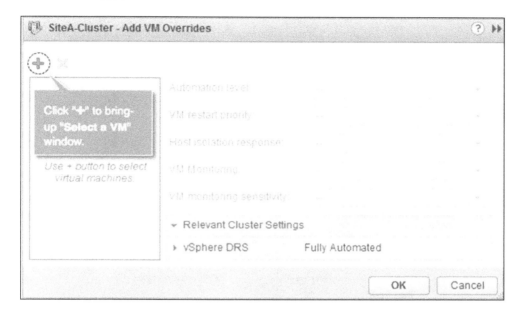

5. In the **Select a VM** window, select a virtual machine and click on **OK**:

6. With the VM now added to the **Add VM Overrides** window, modify the settings for the selected VM, and click on **OK**:

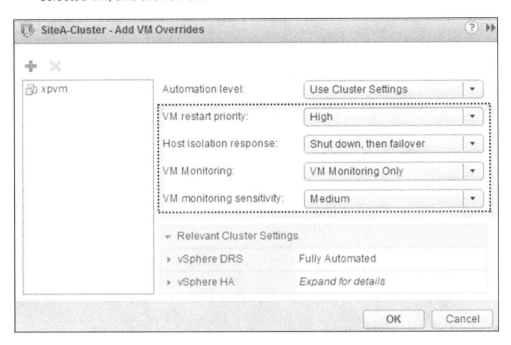

How it works...

The **Host Monitoring** or **VM Monitoring** settings that you configure at a per-virtual machine level will override the cluster-wide settings. The choice to do so will depend on the design of your environment. As we discussed earlier, setting cluster-wide VM restart priority to **Medium** and then setting the appropriate restart priorities for individual virtual machines is a common practice. This is achieved by configuring VM overrides for those virtual machines.

Disabling host monitoring

Host monitoring is generally disabled during network maintenance activities that would affect the host's management network connectivity. This is done to prevent unnecessary triggering of the host isolation response configured for the HA cluster. Host monitoring can be disabled by editing the cluster settings.

How to do it...

The following procedure explains how to disable host monitoring:

1. From the vCenter's **Home** inventory, navigate to the **Hosts and Clusters** view.
2. Select the cluster and navigate to **Manage** | **Settings** | **vSphere HA**, and click on **Edit**.
3. Deselect the **Enable Host Monitoring** checkbox and click on **OK**:

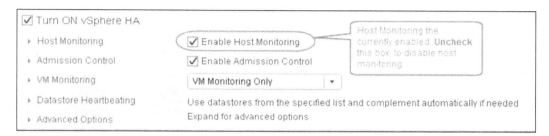

4. The runtime information for HA should now show the **Host Monitoring** value as **Disabled**:

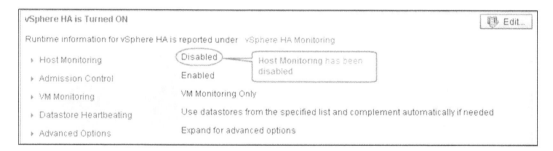

How it works...

Disabling **Host Monitoring** will not remove the HA agents from the ESXi host, hence HA will still be able to detect a host failure, but it will not restart the VMs from the failed host.

12
Configuring vSphere DRS, DPM, and VMware EVC

In this chapter, we will cover the following recipes:

- ▸ Enabling vSphere DRS on a cluster
- ▸ Configuring VMware EVC
- ▸ Choosing a DRS automation level
- ▸ Overriding the cluster automation level for a VM
- ▸ Setting a migration threshold
- ▸ Creating DRS host groups
- ▸ Creating DRS VM groups
- ▸ Creating VMs to host affinity rules
- ▸ Creating VM affinity/anti-affinity rules
- ▸ Configuring vSphere Distributed Power Management
- ▸ Enabling power management on a per-host level

Introduction

VMware vSphere **Distributed Resource Scheduler** (**DRS**) is a series of algorithms devised to manage an aggregated pool of computing resources and distribute virtual machines among the ESXi hosts in a cluster in an effort to reduce any resource imbalance in the cluster. DRS can only be enabled on an ESXi host cluster via vCenter Server. Balancing the computing resources will ensure that a **virtual machine** (**VM**) gets the resources it needs, thereby increasing the service levels.

DRS monitors resource utilization on the ESXi hosts, does an intelligent allocation of resources, balances the computing capacity, and also helps in reducing the power consumption in the data center using DRS's power management feature known as **Distributed Power Management** (**DPM**). VMware DPM can help reduce the energy consumption of a data center by vacating VMs from an underutilized host and leaving that host in a power-off state.

Apart from a few advanced options, there is no real functionality change in vSphere 5.5. The advanced options include the following:

 ▶ **LimitVMsPerESXHostPercent**: This controls the number of VMs a host in the DRS cluster can run. LimitVMsPerESXHost is a similar parameter on vSphere 5.5, which is less dynamic as it places a limit that has to be modified if the cluster host configuration changes. This advanced parameter is not used to correct the current cluster state, but it is used to manage further deployment of VMs.

 For instance, you have a three-host cluster and currently have 40 VMs running on them. However, you plan to deploy another 20 VMs into the cluster, and this will increase the total number of VMs in the cluster to 60. As per the new parameter, the VMs per host limit number is calculated as follows:

 Mean of the total expected number of virtual machines: 60/3 = 20 VMs

 LimitVMsPerHostPercent value = 50%

 Syntax:

 The new VMs/host limit = Mean + (LimitVMsPerHostPercent * Mean)

 Example:

 VMs/host limit = 20 + (50% * 20) = 30 VMs per host

 DRS can now be made aware of latency-sensitive VMs by setting the **Latency Sensitivity** option of a VM to **Low**, **Normal** (default), **Medium**, or **High**. This is available under the **VM Options** tab in the **Edit Settings** window of a virtual machine. While generating migration recommendations, DRS will presume such VMs to have a soft affinity with the hosts they are currently running on and will not be migrated unless the migration is absolutely necessary to reduce the resource imbalance in the DRS cluster.

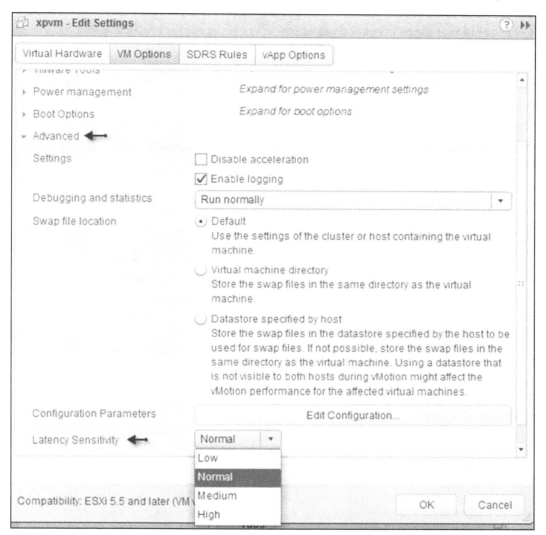

► **Better management of CPU ready time and memory demand**: There are more details on the earlier mentioned features in VMworld 2013's *Session VSVC5280 – DRS: New Features, Best Practices and Future Directions* available at http://www.vmworld.com/community/sessions/2013/.

In this chapter, we will discuss how to enable and configure DRS and its features.

Enabling vSphere DRS on a cluster

vSphere DRS should be enabled on an ESXi host cluster manually and this can only be done from vCenter Server.

Getting ready

Make sure VMotion is enabled and working on all the ESXi hosts in the cluster. Also, you will need access to the vCenter Server.

How to do it...

The following procedure explains how to enable DRS on a cluster:

1. From the vCenter's inventory home, navigate to the **Hosts and Clusters** view.
2. Select the cluster, navigate to **Manage** | **Settings** | **vSphere DRS**, and click on **Edit**.
3. In the **Edit Cluster Settings** window, select the **Turn ON vSphere DRS** checkbox. Leave **DRS Automation**, **Power Management**, and **Advanced Options** at their default settings for now and click on **OK** to enable DRS.
4. The cluster's settings page should now show DRS as enabled. It should read **vSphere DRS is Turned ON**.

How it works...

So how does DRS really work? DRS, once enabled, will aggregate the resources from the participating ESXi hosts as cluster resources. Its job is to load balance the DRS cluster for better utilization of the cluster resources. It does so by migrating or generating migration recommendations for VMs whenever needed. It also provides initial placement for the VMs. Migration recommendations will be generated by vSphere DRS only when it identifies a resource imbalance in the cluster. Resource imbalance is determined on a per-ESXi-host basis. It does so by considering the resource reservations for all of the VMs on the ESXi host, comparing these against the total capacity of the host, and then checking whether the host can or cannot meet the cumulative resource reservations of the VMs.

The result will become a deviation metric, which is then compared against the migration threshold set on the cluster. DRS does this imbalance check on every ESXi host in the DRS cluster every 5 minutes. After DRS detects a cluster imbalance, it will check the migration threshold value set on the cluster. If the deviation calculated is more than the migration threshold, then DRS will generate a migration recommendation.

DRS generates a migration recommendation by simulating the migration of each VM on the ESXi host in order to recalculate the cluster imbalance metric. It will then choose a VM that would best serve in reducing the resource crunch on the host.

Configuring VMware EVC

In a heterogeneous vSphere environment, you might end up having hosts in a cluster with same make CPUs but with uncommon feature sets. For vMotion to work, the underlying CPU features on the cluster hosts should be identical. With EVC, you can now present a common CPU feature set across the hosts to the VMs.

Getting ready

EVC enables a common baseline across a heterogeneous set of hosts, so it is quite possible that most of the already running VMs are using CPU feature sets that might become unavailable after setting the EVC baseline. Hence, it is recommended to either power off the VMs or evacuate the cluster (by migrating (VMotion) the VMs to another cluster or a set of standby hosts), though you will have to power off the VMs before they are moved back into the EVC cluster running a lower baseline. If you don't have enough hosts in your environment to move the VMs out temporarily, create a new EVC cluster with the required baseline and then start moving empty hosts from the old cluster to the new cluster; then, power off the VMs and start migrating them into the new cluster.

How to do it...

The following procedure will help you configure EVC on an ESXi cluster:

1. Connect to vCenter Server and migrate all the VMs to another host that is not in the cluster or power them off.

2. From the vCenter's inventory home, navigate to the **Hosts and Clusters** view.

3. Select the cluster and navigate to **Manage | Settings | VMware EVC** and click on **Edit** to bring up the **Change EVC Mode** window.

4. In the **Change EVC Mode** window, select an **EVC** mode. You get to choose from the following two options:

   - **Enable EVC for AMD Hosts**
   - **Enable EVC for Intel Hosts**

5. Click on **OK** if the validation succeeds.

6. Power off the migrated VMs (if not done already), move them back to the EVC cluster, and power them back **ON**.

How it works...

All that EVC does is present a common baseline (CPU feature set) to the VMs running on the ESXi hosts in the EVC-enabled cluster. We have more than one baseline available to choose from, both AMD and Intel processors. Setting a baseline that has more CPU features than the current CPU features doesn't require the running VM to be evacuated, but keep in mind that the VM needs to be power cycled to see the new features.

If you are downgrading to a lower baseline (a lower feature set compared to the current baseline), then you will need to power off the VMs.

See also

The following Knowledge Base articles are good reads:

- *EVC and CPU Compatibility FAQ* (Knowledge Base article 1005764) at `http://kb.vmware.com/kb/1005764`
- *Enhanced vMotion Compatibility (EVC) processor support* (Knowledge Base article 1003212) at `http://kb.vmware.com/kb/1003212`

Choosing a DRS automation level

By default, DRS works at the **Fully Automated** automation level. You can, however, choose to set it to **Manual** or **Partially Automated**. Although the names of the automation levels are self-explanatory, there are a few additional differences:

- **Fully Automated**: This automatically carries out VM initial placements and migrations
- **Partially Automated**: This does VM initial placements automatically, but migration recommendations are displayed to the administrator and are not performed until the administrator applies them
- **Manual**: This displays both the initial placement and the migration recommendations to the administrator; it requires the administrator's approval to be applied

Getting ready

This is done on a DRS-enabled cluster, so make sure you have access to the vCenter managing the intended ESXi cluster.

How to do it...

The following procedure will help you modify the DRS automation level:

1. From the vCenter's inventory home, navigate to the **Hosts and Clusters** view.
2. Select the cluster and navigate to **Manage** | **Settings** | **vSphere DRS** and click on **Edit**.
3. On the **Edit Cluster Settings** page, click on **DRS Automation** to expand it and view the options. Choose any one of the three automation levels available for selection.
4. Click on **OK** to confirm the settings and reconfigure the cluster.

How it works...

The DRS automation level defines how DRS will react to cluster resource imbalances and whether it requires little or no manual intervention.

DRS can choose to apply the generated migrations/placement recommendations or present them to the administrator to choose from. If there is more than one migration recommendation, then the administrator is provided with a prioritized list of recommendations to choose from. Initial placement refers to the process of choosing an ESXi host from a DRS cluster to power on or resume a VM. DRS generates these recommendations by choosing an ESXi host that has enough resources to run the VM being powered on or resumed.

The following table depicts how migration recommendations and initial placements are dealt with, based on the DRS automation level configured on the cluster:

Automation level	Virtual machine migrations (VMotion)	Virtual machine initial placement
Fully Automated	VMs are automatically migrated.	VM is powered on or resumed on a suitable ESXi host automatically.
Partially Automated	Migration recommendations are displayed to the administrator. The administrator has to manually apply one of the migration recommendations.	VM is powered on or resumed on a suitable ESXi host automatically.
Manual	Migration recommendations are displayed to the administrator. The administrator has to manually apply one of the migration recommendations.	Initial placement recommendations are displayed to the administrator. The administrator has to manually apply one of the placement recommendations.

Overriding the cluster automation level for a VM

In the previous recipe, we learned how to set the cluster-wide automation levels. In this section, we will learn how to set an automation level that is different from the DRS cluster automation level on a per-VM basis. The cluster settings are overridden by creating VM Overrides.

Getting ready

This is done on a DRS-enabled ESXi cluster, so make sure you have access to the vCenter managing the intended DRS cluster.

How to do it...

The following procedure will help you configure a VM to override the cluster automation level:

1. From the vCenter's inventory home, navigate to the **Hosts and Clusters** view.
2. Select a cluster and navigate to **Manage | Settings | VM Overrides**.
3. On the VM Overrides page, click on the **Add** button to bring up the **Add VM Overrides** window.
4. In the **Add VM Overrides** window, click on the + icon to bring up **the Select a VM** window.
5. In the **Select a VM** window, select the VM whose settings need to be overridden and click on **OK**. This should take you back to the **Add VM Overrides** window.
6. In the **Add VM Overrides** window, you should now see the added VM. With the VM selected, choose the required **Automation level** and click on **OK**.

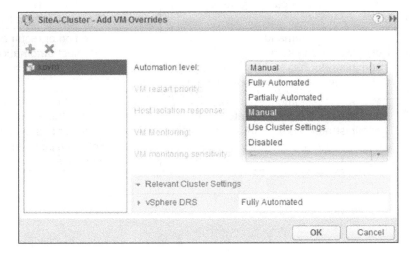

How it works...

An override (VM Override) created for a VM will allow that VM to have an automation level different from the cluster level settings. For instance, if the cluster's DRS automation level is Automatic, then you can set an override for a particular VM with a different automation level. This is particularly used for special-case VMs.

Let's say you need more control and awareness over the initial placement and migration activities corresponding to a specific VM running a business-critical service or application. You can create an override for the VM and set its DRS automation level to Manual. From then on, all placement and migration recommendations specific to that VM will be displayed for the administrator's approval.

Setting a migration threshold

You can control the migration recommendations that vSphere DRS can generate or apply. Each migration recommendation generated by DRS will have a priority level associated with it based on the level of load imbalance in the cluster.

The migration threshold will determine which priority recommendations are to be displayed or applied. The threshold can be modified on the cluster settings page.

Getting ready

This is done on a DRS enabled ESXi cluster. So make sure you have access to the vCenter managing the intended DRS cluster.

How to do it...

The following procedure will guide you through the steps required to set a migration threshold:

1. From the vCenter's inventory home, navigate to the **Hosts and Clusters** view.
2. Select the cluster, navigate to **Manage | Settings | vSphere DRS**, and click on **Edit**.

3. On the **Edit Cluster Settings** page, click on **DRS Automation** to expand it and view the available options. Use the **Migration Threshold** slider to adjust the threshold level.

Conservative ———————————△——————————— Aggressive

Apply priority 1, priority 2, and priority 3 recommendations.
vCenter Server will apply recommendations that promise at least good improvements to the cluster's load balance.

4. Click on **OK** to apply the changes and reconfigure the cluster.

How it works...

Setting a migration threshold will not stop DRS from generating recommendations. Recommendations are generated, but before they are "displayed" (if manual/partially automated) or "applied" (if fully automated), the priority level associated with the recommendations will be compared against the migration threshold set for the cluster. If the migration threshold doesn't cover the priority of the recommendation, then it is ignored; otherwise it is displayed or applied.

The following are the available threshold levels:

▶ **Conservative Level**: This will display/apply only priority 1 recommendations

▶ **Conservative Level +1**: This will display/apply only priority 1 and priority 2 recommendations

▶ **Mid-level (default)**: This will display/apply priority 1, priority 2, and priority 3 recommendations

▶ **Aggressive Level -1**: This will display/apply priority 1, priority 2, priority 3, and priority 4 recommendations

▶ **Aggressive Level**: This will apply all recommendations

Creating DRS host groups

DRS provides an option to segregate VMs and ESXi hosts into their own groups. The groups are used with VM-Host affinity rules. These rules do not address individual VMs/hosts. These groups are created using the DRS Groups Manager.

The creation of DRS hosts/VMs groups is a prerequisite for the creation of affinity rules. This recipe covers how to create DRS host groups.

Getting ready

This is done on a DRS-enabled ESXi cluster, so make sure that you have access to a vCenter managing the intended DRS cluster.

How to do it...

The following procedure will help you create DRS host groups:

1. From the vCenter's inventory home, navigate to the **Hosts and Clusters** view.
2. Select a cluster, navigate to **Manage | Settings | DRS Groups**, and click on **Add** to bring up the **Create DRS Group** window.
3. In the **Create DRS Group** window, supply a name for the group, choose the type as **Host DRS Group**, and click on the **Add** button to bring up the **Add DRS Group Member** window.
4. In the **Add DRS Group Member** window, select the hosts that should be added to the group and click on **OK**.
5. The **Create DRS Group** window should now list all of the hosts added as the to-be members of the group. Click on **OK** to create the group.

Creating DRS VM groups

Just like DRS host groups, you will also need to create DRS VM groups so that they can be used to create VM-Host affinity rules.

How to do it...

The following procedure will help you create host/VM DRS groups:

1. From the vCenter's inventory home, navigate to the **Hosts and Clusters** view.
2. Select a cluster, navigate to **Manage | Settings | DRS Groups**, and click on **Add** to bring up the **Create DRS Group** window.
3. In the **Create DRS Group** window, supply a name for the group, choose the type as **VM DRS Group**, and click on the **Add** button to bring up the **Add DRS Group Member** window.
4. In the **Add DRS Group Member** window, select the VMs that should be added to the group and click on **OK**.
5. The **Create DRS Group** window should now list the VMs that have been added to the members of the group. Click on **OK** to create the group.

Creating VMs to the host affinity rules

We can create rules that will determine the VM Host DRS placement rules. This is done by creating VMs to the host's affinity rules. The rules determine if a group of VMs can run on a group of chosen ESXi hosts. For instance, VMs in the VMs Group - B can not only be configured to have a placement affinity (must run or should run) with Host Group B, but also have an anti-affinity towards Host Group A. This scenario has been depicted in the following diagram:

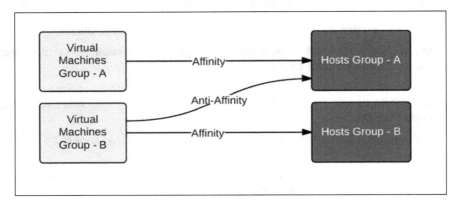

Getting ready

The creation of VMs to hosts' affinity rules requires DRS hosts/VMs groups to be created. The DRS groups should list both the Host and VM groups that have been created.

For instructions on how to create DRS Hosts and VM groups, read the recipes *Creating DRS host groups* and *Creating DRS VM groups* in this chapter.

How to do it...

The following procedure will help you create a VMs-to-hosts affinity rule:

1. From the vCenter's inventory home, navigate to the **Hosts and Clusters** view.

2. Select the cluster and navigate to **Manage | Settings | DRS Rules** and click on **Add** to bring up the **Create DRS Rule** window.

3. On the **Create DRS Rule** window, supply a name for the rule and choose the rule type as **Virtual machines to Hosts**. Select a VM Group, a rule, and a host group; then click on **OK** to create the rule.

How it works...

A DRS rule can indicate either a requirement or a preference.

The "must" rules dictate a requirement and the "should" rules specify a preference. The must rules are as follows:

  ▸ **Must run on hosts in a group**
  ▸ **Must not run on hosts in a group**

The "should" rules are as follows:

- **Should run on hosts in a group**
- **Should not run on hosts in a group**

The "must" rules should be mandatorily met, while the "should" rules just state the preference (the VMs can run on other hosts).

The VM-Host affinity rules are generally used to meet the specific requirements for the VMs. The requirements could be of any nature, such as licensing or hardware.

Keep in mind that vSphere HA, DRS, and DPM will not violate the "must" rules. Hence, the "must" rules should be defined cautiously as they could even prevent vSphere HA from restarting VMs, thus affecting the availability SLA of these VMs.

Creating VM affinity/anti-affinity rules

Unlike the VM-Host affinity rules, the inter-virtual machine (VM-VM) affinity rules can work between individual VMs.

Getting ready

These rules are created for VMs that are in a DRS-enabled ESXi cluster, so make sure you have access to a vCenter managing the cluster.

How to do it...

The following procedure will help you create an inter-VM affinity/anti-affinity rule:

1. From the vCenter's inventory home, navigate to the **Hosts and Clusters** view.
2. Select the cluster, navigate to **Manage | Settings | DRS Rules**, and click on **Add** to bring up the **Create DRS Rule** window.
3. In the **Create DRS Rule** window, supply a name for the rule and choose the rule type. In this example, we have selected the rule **Separate Virtual Machines**. If you intend to keep the VMs together, then select the rule **Keep Virtual Machines Together**.

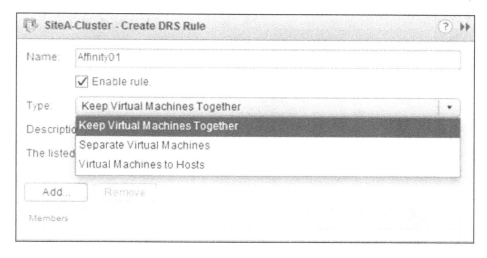

4. With the rule selected, click on the **Add** button to bring up the **Add Rule Member** window.

5. In the **Add Rule Member** window, select the VMs to be added and click on **OK**.

6. The **Create DRS Rule** window should now list the VMs added as to-be members that would participate in the rule. Click on **OK** to create the rule.

How it works...

An inter-VM rule determines whether the VMs participating in the rule should or should not run on the same ESXi hosts. The following diagram depicts the affinity and anti-affinity behaviors:

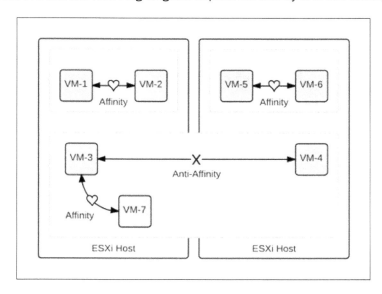

Now let's review both the rules:

- **Keep virtual machines together**: When this rule is set, the DRS will try to keep the participating VMs on the same ESXi host.

- **Separate virtual machines**: When this rule is set, the DRS will try to make sure that none of the participating VMs run on the same host as the other participating VMs.

 When there is a conflict between rules, the oldest rule takes preference and the others will be disabled by DRS.

The examples are as follows: anti-affinity—2 AD servers, affinity—DB, and app server (better communication as not needed outside of ESXi).

Configuring vSphere Distributed Power Management

A DRS cluster can be configured to change the power state of the selected hosts in order to reduce the power consumption by the cluster. This feature is called vSphere Distributed Power Management and is configurable only if the cluster is DRS-enabled.

 DPM is disabled by default. You will need to edit the DRS cluster settings to enable DPM.

Getting ready

vSphere DPM uses IPMI for power management. Hence, for the ESXi hosts to be managed by DPM, they have to be configured with their corresponding IPMI settings. This has to be done at a per-ESXi host level under **Manage | Settings | Power Management**.

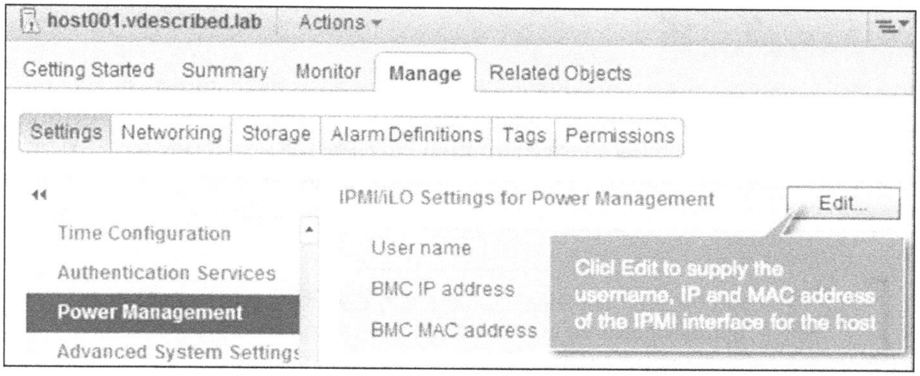

How to do it...

The following procedure will help you enable and configure DPM on a DRS-enabled cluster:

1. From the vCenter's inventory home, navigate to the **Hosts and Clusters** view.
2. Select the cluster, navigate to **Manage** | **Settings** | **vSphere DRS**, and click on **Edit**.
3. On the **Edit Cluster Settings** page, click on **Power Management** to expand it and view the subsettings. Note that the default setting is **Off**. Select either the **Manual** or **Automatic** automation level. Modify the **DPM Threshold** if necessary and click on **OK**.

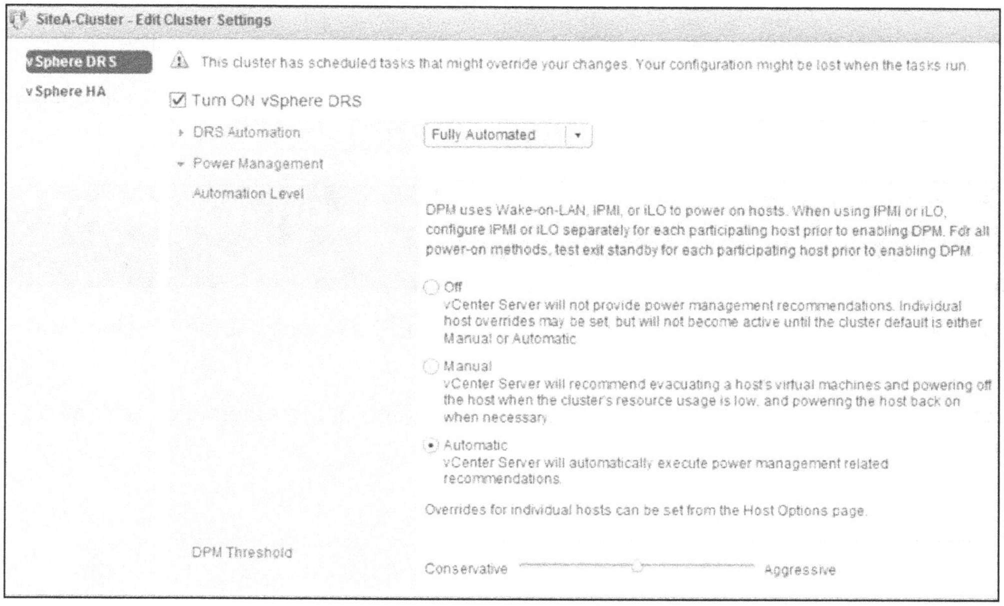

4. Click on **OK** to acknowledge the warning and enable power management.

How it works...

Once enabled, power management (vSphere DPM) will analyze the cumulative resource requirement (current usage and reservations), verify the HA requirements, and determine the number of hosts required to meet them. From then on, DPM will selectively put ESXi host/hosts into standby mode. Prior to putting an ESXi into standby mode, DPM will leverage DRS' ability to distribute the VMs running on the selected ESXi host to the other ESXi hosts in the cluster.

 Although a host is said to be put in standby mode by DPM, it is actually powered off. Standby mode is kind of a misnomer.

DPM requires hardware support for power management and can use the following protocols:

- **Intelligent Platform Management Interface** (**IPMI**)
- **Hewlett-Packard Integrated Lights-Out** (**HP iLO**)
- **Wake-On-LAN** (**WOL**)

DPM can operate in three modes:

- **Off**: In this mode, DPM is disabled
- **Manual**: In this mode, the DPM recommendations are displayed for the administrator to choose and confirm
- **Automatic**: In this mode, the DPM recommendations are automatically executed

The DPM threshold, much like DRS's migration threshold, will display/apply recommendations based on the priority assigned to the recommendation.

Enabling power management on a per-host level

Power management can be modified on a per-host level. The settings at the host level will override the cluster-level DPM settings.

Power management is set at the host level by modifying the DPM's automation level on each host.

Getting ready

This is done to override the DPM's cluster level settings, so make sure that you have access to the vCenter managing the intended host cluster with DPM enabled.

How to do it...

The following procedure will help you set the DPM automation level on a host:

1. From the vCenter's inventory home, navigate to the **Hosts and Clusters** view.
2. Select the cluster and navigate to **Manage | Settings | Host Options**.
3. Select a host and click on **Edit** to bring up the **Edit Host Options** window.
4. In the **Edit Host Options** window, change the DPM power mode to the desired automation level and click on **OK**. You can choose to ignore the BMC fields as they are not mandatory to set the host-level DPM automation. However, they are essential for DPM to function. Read the *Getting ready* section of the *Configuring vSphere Distributed Power Management* in this chapter for more information.
5. The **Host Options** page should now show the configured **Power Management** for the host.

13
Upgrading and Patching Using vSphere Update Manager

In this chapter, we will cover the following recipes:

- ▶ Preparing database connectivity for VUM
- ▶ Installing vSphere Update Manager
- ▶ Installing the vSphere Update Manager plugin
- ▶ Adding a download source
- ▶ Creating a baseline
- ▶ Importing ESXi Images
- ▶ Creating a host baseline group
- ▶ Creating a VM and VA baseline group
- ▶ Remediating a host or a cluster
- ▶ Remediating a VM or a VA
- ▶ Staging patches
- ▶ Installing the Update Manager Download Service
- ▶ Configuring UMDS and downloading data
- ▶ Creating a shared repository
- ▶ Using a shared repository

Introduction

Updating and patching your vSphere environment is part of a periodic maintenance routine. Although the update/upgrade/patching can be done manually, it becomes a tedious process when dealing with a large environment. **vSphere Update Manager** (**VUM**) provides a method to manage patching and the upgrade process with ease. It can not only be used to upgrade/patch your ESXi host, but also third-party products such as the Cisco Nexus 1000v.

In this chapter, we will learn how to install and configure VUM and also how to use it to perform patching and upgrading tasks.

Preparing database connectivity for VUM

Before you install VUM, you need to decide whether to use an existing or separate database server or use the installer-packaged SQL Express. The installer-packaged SQL Express is only recommended for nonproduction environments. Most environments will already have a DB server hosting other databases. You could either choose to host the VUM database on the existing DB server or install and configure a new DB server.

For a list of compatible databases with vSphere Update Manager, you can use the **VMware Product Interoperability Matrixes**.

 For more details, visit `http://www.vmware.com/resources/compatibility/sim/interop_matrix.php`.
Select **Solution/Database Interoperability**. In step 1, select the product as **VMware vCenter Update Manager**, **Version** as **5.5**, and in step 2, which is the **Add Database** step, add any database as needed.

In this recipe, we will learn how to create and configure access to a new DB created on a separate DB server. The installation of SQL Server is beyond the scope of this book. It is recommended to contact your DBA for information regarding this.

The following flow chart depicts a high-level overview of the procedure:

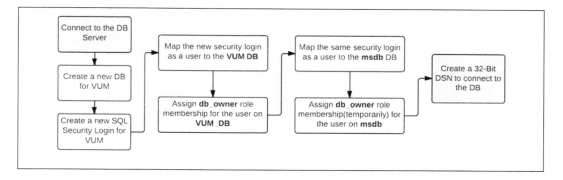

How to do it...

The following instructions will help you create a new database, configure permissions, and create a 32-bit DSN for the VUM installation:

1. Connect to **Microsoft SQL Server Management Studio** as a database server administrator.

2. Right-click on the **Databases** folder and click on **New Database**:

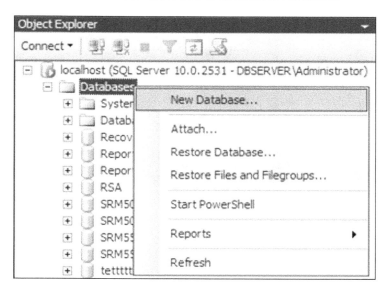

3. In the **New Database** window, supply a **Database name** and click on **OK** with the defaults unmodified, as shown in the following screenshot:

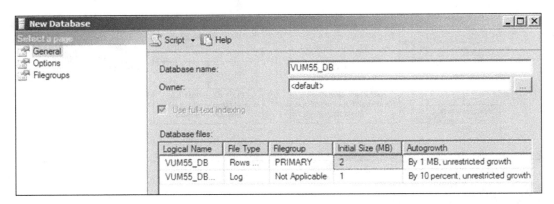

4. Expand the **Security** folder for the DB server, right-click on **Logins**, and click on **New Login...**:

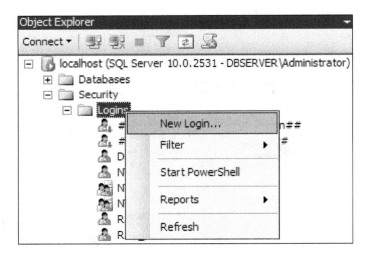

5. In the **Login – New** window, supply a **Login name**, select **SQL Server authentication**, and supply a password and the **Default database** name to the VUM database:

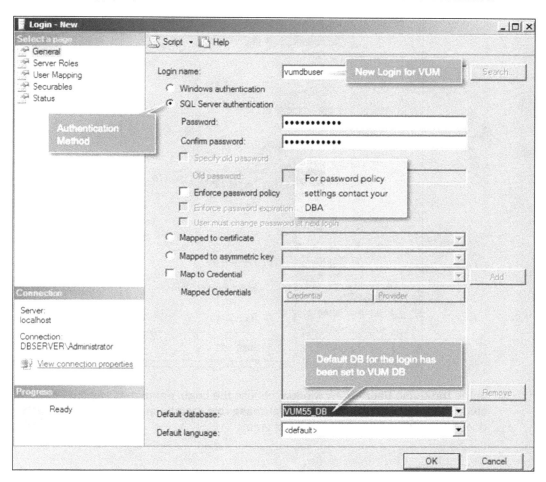

6. Expand the **Security** folder under the **VUM55_DB** folder. Right-click on **Users** and click on **New User...**:

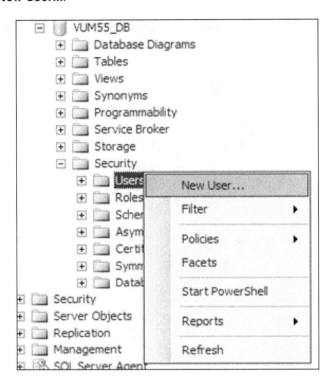

7. In the **Database User – New** window, choose the **Login name** that was created in step 5 and supply a username. Set **Database role membership** to **db_owner**. It doesn't have to own the **db_owner** schema:

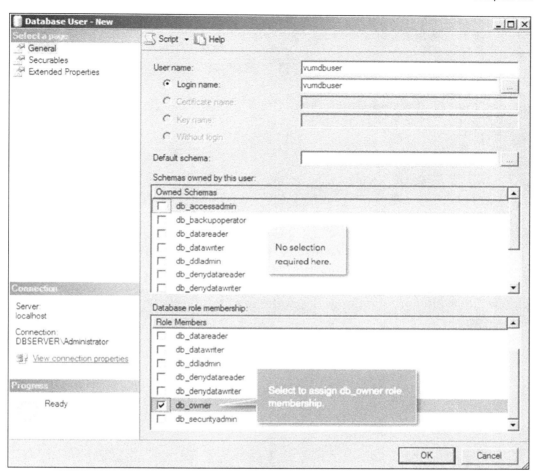

 The username used here is only an alias to the login name. A login name can be presented for different databases with different aliases.

8. Repeat step 6 and step 7 on the **msdb** database. The **msdb** database is located under the **System Databases** folder:

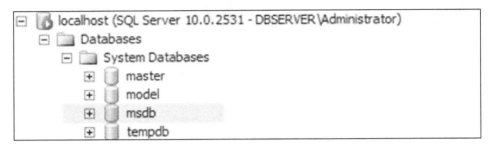

9. Now, log in to the machines where you intend to install VUM to create a 32-bit DSN for VUM database connectivity and VUM installation.

10. Navigate to **Start | Run** and execute the `.exe` file located at `C:\Windows\SysWOW64\odbcad32.exe`:

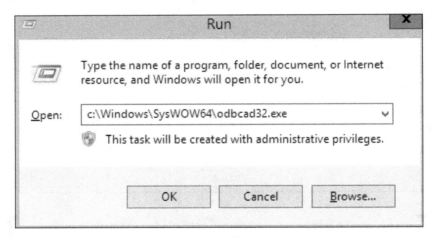

11. In the **ODBC Data Source Administrator (32-bit)** window, navigate to the **System DSN** tab and click on **Add...** to bring up the **Create New Datasource** window for the DSN:

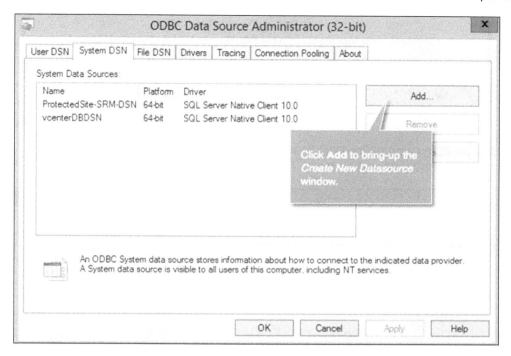

12. In the **Create New Data Source** window, scroll down to the end of the list and select the **SQL Server Native Client 10.0** item from the list. You might need a different version of Native Client if you are connecting to SQL Server 2012:

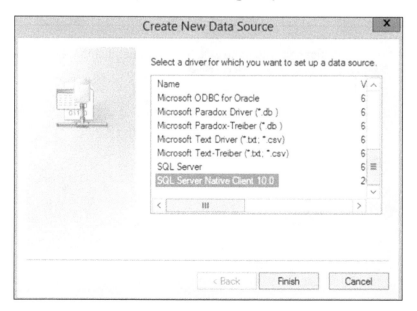

Some systems might not have SQL Server Native Client installed.
If that is the case, then you can download and install the client from Microsoft's website. It is available at the following URLs:

- ▶ http://bit.ly/SQLServer2K8_FeaturePack
- ▶ http://bit.ly/SQL2K12_FeaturePack

13. Supply a name for the DSN, choose the SQL Server instance you would like to connect to, and click on **Next**:

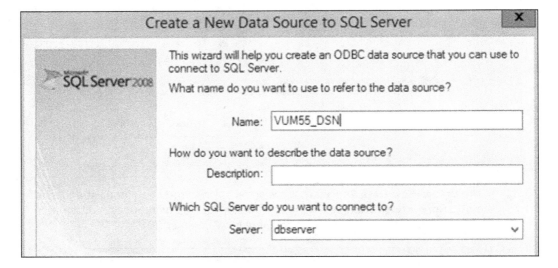

14. Select the authentication type to be SQL Server authentication, supply the database login ID and credentials, and click on **Next**:

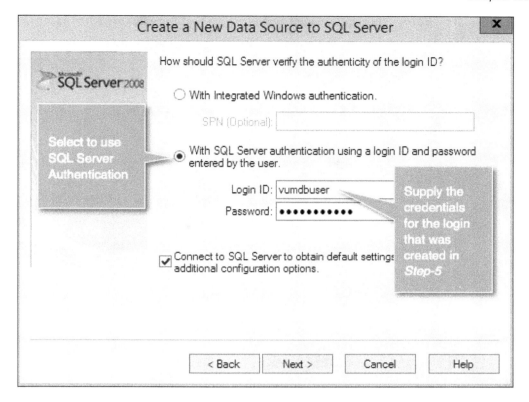

15. Change the default database to the one we created for VUM in step 2 and click on **Next**:

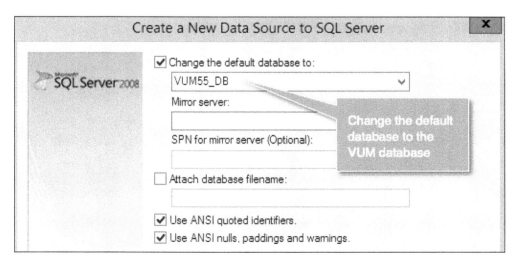

16. On the next screen, click on **Finish**, then click on **Test Data Source** and click on **OK** to create the DSN:

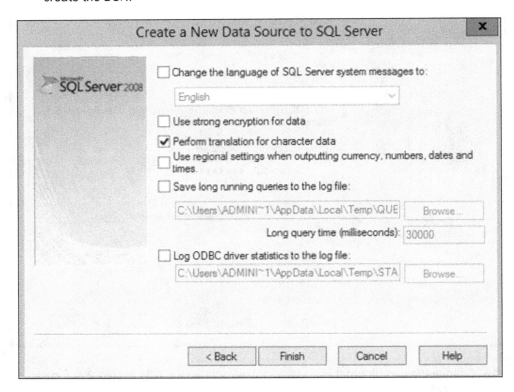

17. You should now see the new DSN created in the **ODBC Data Source Administrator (32-bit)** window, as shown in the following screenshot:

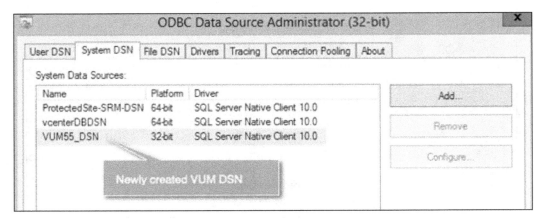

18. You are now all set to begin the VUM installation process. Refer to the recipe *Installing vSphere Update Manager* for installation guidelines.

How it works...

Even though VUM can only be installed on a 64-bit machine, it is a 32-bit application, and hence it needs a 32-bit DSN for database connectivity.

VUM can use the vCenter Server's database for its tables, but it is always best practice to have a separate database per component. The Update Manager installer can install a SQL Express database for smaller deployments not exceeding five hosts and 50 virtual machines. For a larger environment, you will need a separate SQL Server or Oracle DB Server.

See also

Use the **Sizing Estimator** for vSphere Update Manager 5.5 to determine the minimum amount of free space per month for database sizing estimates.

The Sizing Estimator is available at the vSphere Update Manager documentation site (`http://www.vmware.com/support/pubs/vum_pubs.html`).

Installing vSphere Update Manager

vSphere Update Manager (VUM) is used to patch both the ESXi hosts and **VM Guest Operating Systems**. Starting with vSphere Update Manager Version 5.x, patching VM Guest Operating Systems is no longer supported. vSphere Update Manager can be installed on the same machine running vCenter Server, however it is recommended to install it on a separate machine.

 vSphere Update Manager 5.5 can only be installed on a 64-bit machine.

Here are the compatible operating systems:

- Windows Server 2008 Service Pack 2
- Windows Server 2008 R2
- Windows Server 2008 R2 Service Pack 1
- Windows Server 2012
- Windows Server 2012 R2 (VUM 5.5 Update 1 onwards)

VMware might add/remove compatible operating systems for a new release/update. It is advised that you use the online VMware Compatibility Guide to verify the host OS compatibility available at `http://www.vmware.com/resources/compatibility/`.

Once you are at the compatibility guide page, choose **Host OS** as the main criteria, set the **Product Name** as **vCenter Update Manager**, **Product Release Version** as **vSphere Update Manager 5.5 Update1** or the latest, set the **OS Family Name** to **All**, and click on **Update and View Results**:

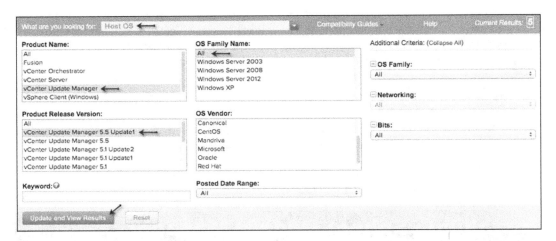

Getting ready

You need the following information handy in order to install vSphere Update Manager:

- ▶ Your vCenter Server IP address or FQDN
- ▶ Your vCenter Server administrator username and password

You also need to make the following decisions before you begin the installation:

- ▶ Choose between using an existing DB server or the installer-packaged SQL Express. For DB configuration guidelines, read the section *Preparing database connectivity for VUM*.
- ▶ Ports and proxy settings if needed (not recommended).
- ▶ Location for the patch store. Recommended size is 120 GB.
- ▶ Choose between using the VUM server for downloading patches or using UMDS.
- ▶ A compatible Windows version, if you are installing this on a different physical machine than vCenter Server.

How to do it...

The following instructions will guide you through the installation of vSphere Update Manager:

1. On the **vSphere 5.5 Installer** welcome window, select **VMware vSphere® Update Manager** and click on **Install** to start the installation wizard.

2. Click through the initial wizard screens, accept the license agreement, and click on **Next**.

3. You could instruct the installer to download the updates from the default upgrade/ patch sources immediately after the installation. In this example, we will choose not to download the updates by deselecting the checkbox **Download updates from default sources immediately after installation**. Click on **Next** to continue:

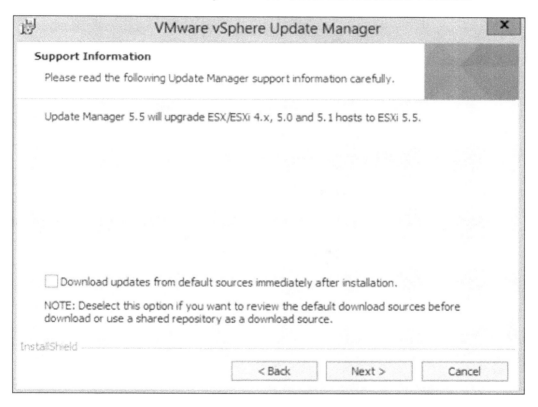

4. Supply the **vCenter Server Information** and click on **Next** to continue:

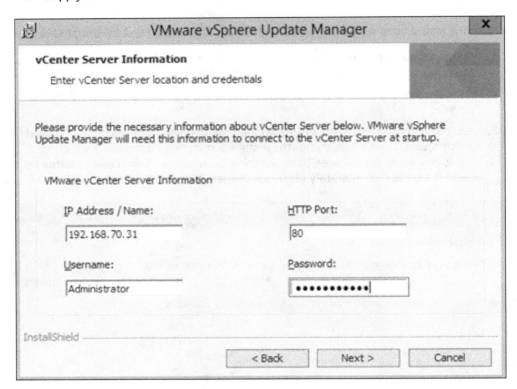

5. You can choose to install SQL Express, but since we already have a database created, select the option **Use an existing supported database** and choose the 32-bit DSN that we created for the vSphere Update Manager database and click on **Next**:

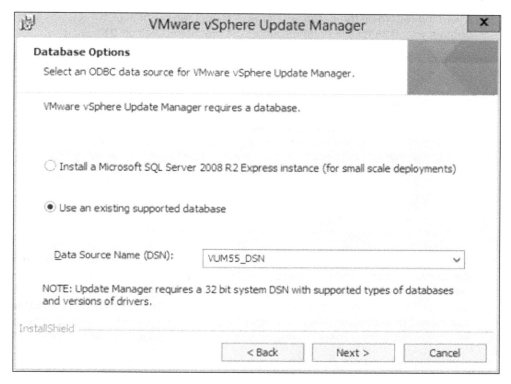

6. Supply the database login credentials and click on **Next**:

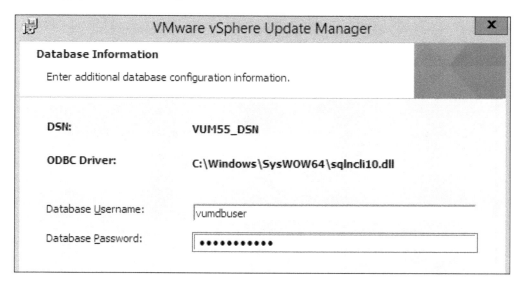

7. A warning regarding the database recovery model will be displayed if it is set to full. Contact your DBA for the organization's best practices. Click on **OK**:

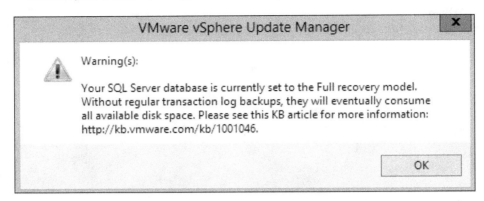

8. Choose how vSphere Update Manager will be identified on the network. This can be done by using either the IP address or FQDN of the machine it is installed on. If the server requires proxy information to get to the Internet, then you can configure the proxy on the wizard screen by selecting the option **Yes, I have Internet connection and I want to configure proxy settings now.**. We have *deselected* the option because we will be configuring UMDS to download the patches. Click on **Next** to continue:

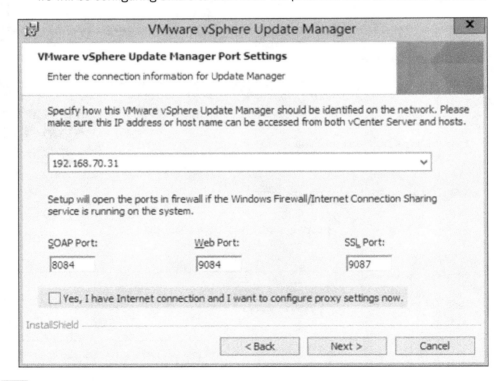

9. Modify the vSphere Update Manager install location and patch store location, if needed, and click on **Next**:

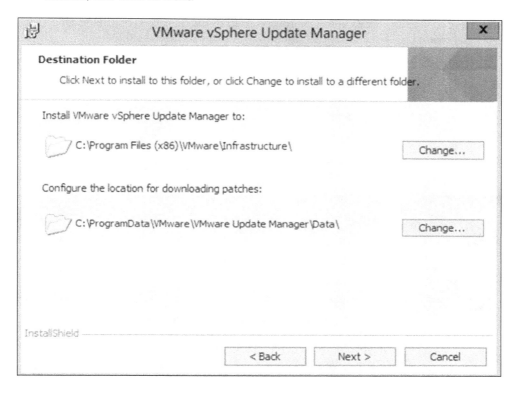

Although the default patch store location is the system drive (C:), it is recommended to have the patch store on a different drive to reduce the chances of using up all the free space in the system drive. If there enough free space, it would throw a warning informing you of this, as shown in the following screenshot:

Click on **OK** to close the warning.

10. On the **Ready to Install** screen, click on **Install** to initiate the installation.

11. Once the installation is complete, click on **Finish** to exit the installer.

12. Revoke the **db_owner** permissions assigned to the SQL login on the **msdb** database. The **msdb** database is located under the **System Databases** folder:

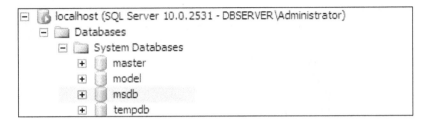

Installing the vSphere Update Manager plugin

For you to be able to manage and configure vSphere Update Manager, you need to install a plugin for use with vCenter Server and enable it.

 The vSphere Update Manage plugin has very limited support with vSphere 5.5 Web Client. All you can do is attach and scan hosts. This might change in the future releases, but for now, we need to use vSphere Windows Client for most of the tasks.

How to do it...

The following procedure will help you install and enable the vSphere Update Manager plugin for the vSphere Client:

1. Connect to vCenter Server and navigate to **Plug-ins | Manage Plug-ins...**.

2. On the **Plug-in Manager** window, you will see **VMware vSphere Update Manager Extension** under **Available Plug-ins**. Click on **Download and Install...** to install the plugin.

3. Run through the wizard to finish the plugin installation.

4. If the installation completes successfully, you should see the plugin listed with a status of **Enabled** under **Installed Plug-ins**:

5. vCenter's home inventory should list **Update Manager** under **Solutions and Applications**:

Adding a download source

vSphere Update Manager downloads patch definitions and notifications from online download sources.

By default, there are three download sources, namely ESXi updates, Cisco, and virtual appliances. You can also add a custom download source. This becomes necessary if your hardware vendor has system-specific updates.

How to do it...

The following procedure explains how to add a download source:

1. Connect to vCenter Server as an administrator using the vSphere Client.

2. Go to **Home | Update Manager**.

3. Navigate to the **Configuration** tab and then to **Download Settings** on the left pane.

4. Click on **Add Download Source...**:

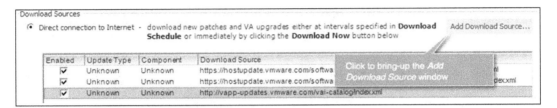

5. In the **Add Download Source** window, enter the URL in the **Source URL** field and click on **Validate URL**. If the validation completes successfully, then it will show as **Connected**. Click on **OK**:

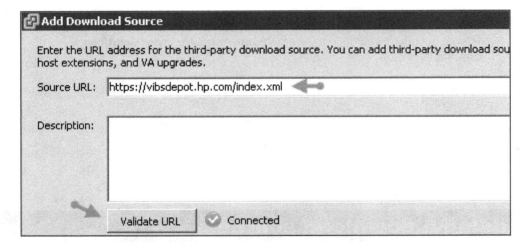

6. Once the custom source has been added to the list, click on **Apply** to save this configuration.

How it works...

vSphere Update Manager will periodically download the update/patch definitions based on the configured **Download Schedule**. However, you also have the option to initiate a download manually at any point in time. This can be done on the **Download Settings** page by clicking on the **Download Now** button.

By default, the download frequency is **Daily**, at a specified start time. This can be modified by clicking on the **Edit Download Schedule** link on the **Download Schedule** screen:

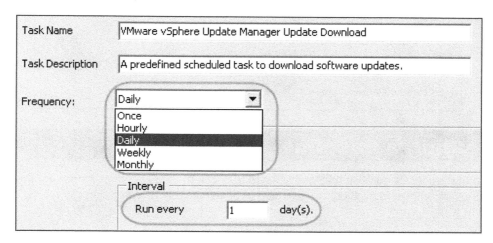

You can also choose the interval and the start time on the same screen.

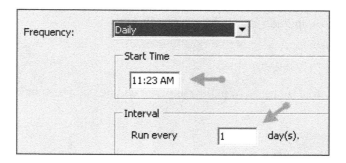

The notifications are also checked periodically. By default, the frequency is **hourly**. The schedule can be modified on the **Notification Check Schedule** screen, which can be reached from the left pane on the **Configuration** tab.

For both path definitions and notifications, a scheduled download can be disabled by unchecking the **Enable scheduled download** option on their respective screens:

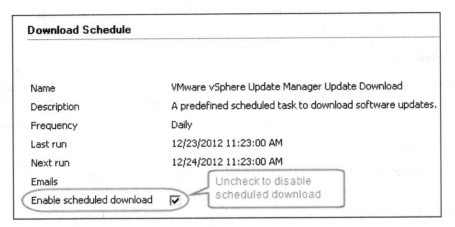

Creating a baseline

A **baseline** is a list of patches that can be used to check the ESXi hosts or **virtual appliances** for compliance. By default, there are two sets of baselines that are predefined:

- ► Critical host patches (dynamic)
- ► Non-critical host patches (dynamic)

The other baselines are:

- ► VMware tools upgrade to match host (dynamic)
- ► VM hardware upgrade to match host (dynamic)
- ► VA upgrade to latest (dynamic)

You can manually create a new custom baseline that can be used to check the ESXi hosts for compliance.

How to do it...

The following procedure will guide you through the steps required to create a baseline:

1. Connect to vCenter Server as an administrator using the vSphere Client.
2. Go to **Home | Update Manager**.

3. Navigate to the **Baselines and Groups** tab, select the **Hosts** view, and click on **Create..**, as shown in the following screenshot:

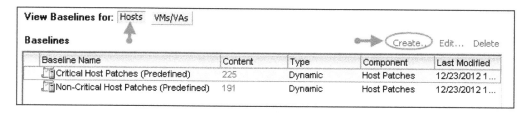

4. Enter a name for the baseline and select the baseline type. The selections available are:

   ❑ **Host Patch, Host Extension, and Host Upgrade**

   ❑ **VA Upgrade**

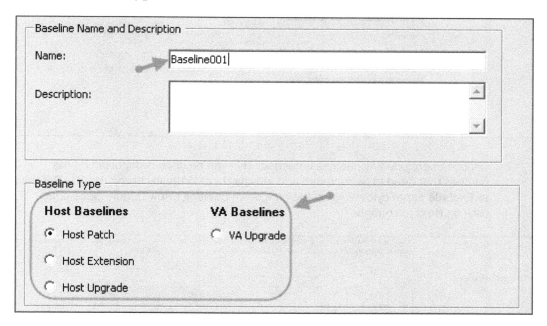

5. Select the baseline type as either **Fixed** or **Dynamic** and click on **Next**.

6. Specify a criterion by choosing the **Patch Vendor**, **Product**, **Severity**, and **Category** options and click on **Next**. By default, the **Severity** and **Category** options are set to **Any**:

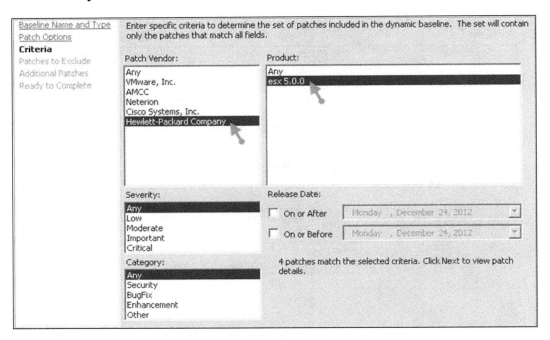

7. Choose to exclude any patches if needed. This can be done by highlighting the patches that need to be excluded and moving them to the exclusion list (the **Patches to Exclude** pane) by clicking on the blue down-pointing arrow button. Once done, click on **Next** to continue:

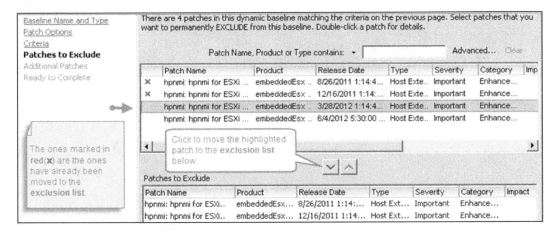

8. The next screen will list the patches that don't meet the criteria. You can choose to include any of these patches by highlighting and moving them to the inclusion list (the **Fixed Patches to Add** pane) as shown in the following screenshot:

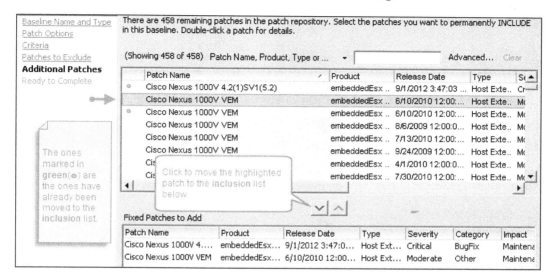

9. The **Ready to Complete** screen will summarize the options selected. Click on **Finish** to create the baseline.

How it works...

Creating a baseline is a method of creating a reference container for a set of patches that you would like to have installed on a host or a group of hosts.

There are four different types of baselines:

- **Host Patch**: This will include security patches, bug fixes, enhancements, and other general patches.
- **Host Upgrade**: This will only include ESXi images, which will be used to upgrade the ESXi host to a new updated version.
- **Host Extension**: This refers to the software updates pushed by the hardware vendor, which include hardware driver updates, updates that enable additional features, CIM providers, updates that enable supportability, and updates that improve performance.
- **VA Upgrade**: This refers to the upgrades available for the virtual appliances.

 Unlike other baseline types, a **Host Patch** baseline can be either **Fixed** or **Dynamic**.

A **Fixed** baseline type will not poll the patch repository for updates. You will have to manually modify the patch list.

A **Dynamic** baseline type will get updated when new patches meeting the criterion arrive at the patch repository.

> All predefined host patches are **Dynamic** in type. The new baseline wizard also defaults to **Dynamic** when creating a host patch baseline.

Importing ESXi Images

For you to be able to create a **Host Upgrade** baseline or a baseline group, you need to have ESXi Images imported to the vSphere Update Manager server's repository.

How to do it...

The following procedure will help you import an ESXi Image into vSphere Update Manager's repository:

1. Connect to vCenter Server as an administrator using the vSphere Client.
2. Go to **Home | Update Manager**.
3. Navigate to the **ESXi Images** tab and click on **Import ESXi Image** to bring up the **Import ESXi Image** wizard.
4. In the **Import ESXi Image** wizard, browse to add an ESXi Image and click on **Next**.
5. It will upload and import the image, as shown in the following screenshot:

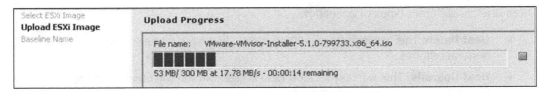

6. Once the upload is complete, the wizard will display the image details.
7. Subsequently, the wizard will prompt you to create an upgrade baseline. Enter a baseline name and click on **Finish**. On this screen, you can choose not to create a baseline by unchecking the **Create a Baseline using the ESXi Image** checkbox.

How it works...

When you import an ESXi Image by using the **Import ESXi Image** wizard, the wizard actually copies the ESXi Image contents to a folder at the following location:

```
C:\ProgramData\VMware\VMware Update Manager\Data\host_upgrade_
packages
```

The folder will contain the contents of the ISO image.

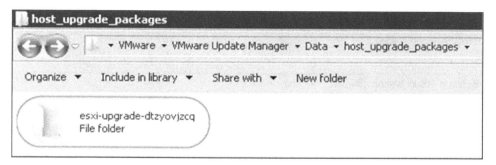

Creating a host baseline group

Host baseline groups are useful when you have to perform an upgrade. Also, post upgrade, you may need to install patches that were released at a later date than the host upgrade or an extension (for example, a driver upgrade) that will make the server hardware compatible with the newer upgrade.

It is a requirement that you already have the required ESXi Image imported. Read the recipe *Importing ESXi Images* for instructions.

How to do it...

The following procedure will help you create a host baseline group:

1. Connect to vCenter Server as an administrator using the vSphere Client.
2. Go to **Home | Update Manager**.
3. Navigate to the **Baselines and Groups** tab and click on the **Create** link corresponding to the baseline groups.

4. In the **New Baseline Group** wizard, select the baseline group type as **Host Baseline Group**, supply a name for the baseline group, and click on **Next** to continue, as shown in the following screenshot:

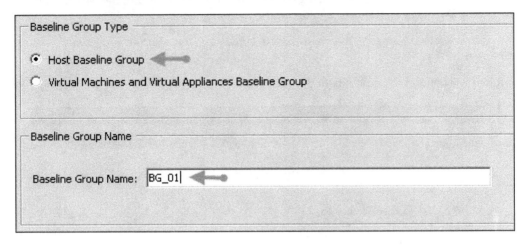

5. Choose an existing host upgrade baseline with the correct image or choose to **Create a new Host Upgrade Baseline** from this screen. With the required baseline selected, click on **Next** to continue:

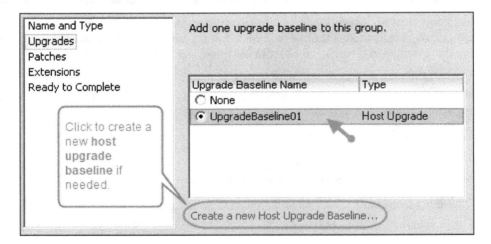

6. Select an existing host patch baseline or create a new one with the required criteria, and click on **Next**:

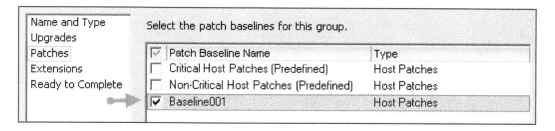

7. The **Ready to Complete** screen will summarize the options selected. Review the information provided and click on **Finish** to create the baseline group.

Creating a VM and VA baseline group

VM and VA baseline groups are useful when upgrading a **virtual appliance** (**VA**) and its dependent VMs. It uses the predefined upgrade baselines for a virtual machine (VM).

 Note that you cannot create a custom VM upgrade baseline.

How to do it...

The following procedure will help you create VM and VA baseline groups:

1. Connect to vCenter Server as an administrator using the vSphere Client.
2. Go to **Home** | **Update Manager**.
3. Navigate to the **Baselines and Groups** tab and click on the **Create** link corresponding to the baseline groups.

4. In the **New Baseline Group** wizard, select the **Baseline Group Type** as **Virtual Machines and Virtual Appliances Baseline Group**. Enter a group name and click on **Next** to continue:

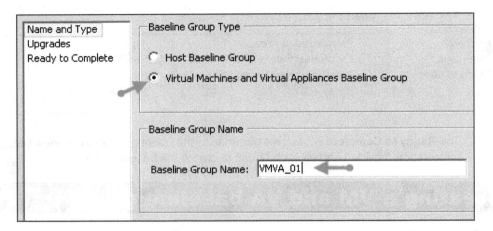

5. Select a **VA Upgrades** baseline, a **VM Hardware Upgrades** baseline, and a **VMware Tools Upgrades** baseline, and click on **Next** to continue:

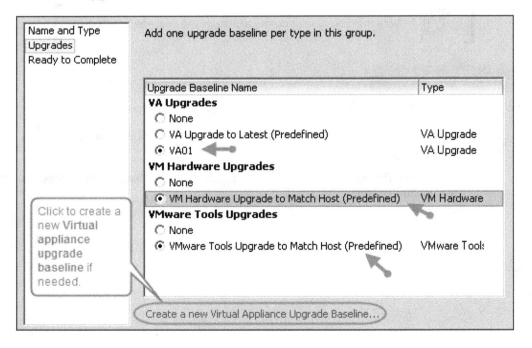

6. The **Ready to Complete** screen will summarize the options selected. Review the information provided and click on **Finish** to create the baseline group.

Remediating a host or a cluster

We learned how to create baselines and baseline groups. The purpose of creating these is to remediate an ESXi server. In this recipe, we will learn how to remediate an ESXi server or a cluster of ESXi hosts. **Remediation** refers to the process of installing the chosen patches or upgrades on the ESXi server.

How to do it...

The following procedure will guide you through the steps required to remediate an ESXi server:

1. Select an ESXi server or ESXi cluster from the inventory and navigate to the **Update Manager** tab and click on **Attach...** to bring up the **Attach Baseline or Baseline Group** window:

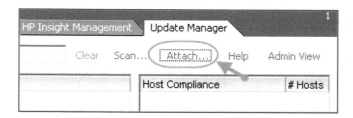

2. On the **Attach Baseline or Baseline Group** window, select a baseline or baseline group and click on **Attach** to tag it to the ESXi server as demonstrated in the following screenshot:

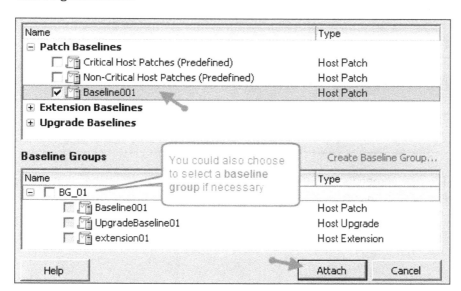

3. Once a baseline has been attached, click on **Scan** to scan for compliance.

4. The scan completes and displays the noncompliance details, if any.

5. Click on **Remediate...** to bring up the **Remediate** wizard.

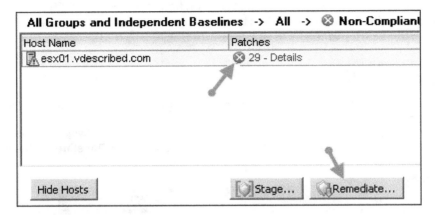

6. On the **Remediate** wizard screen, you will be shown the baselines selected. If multiple baselines are attached to the host, then you can choose to deselect individual baselines as well. Click on **Next** to continue:

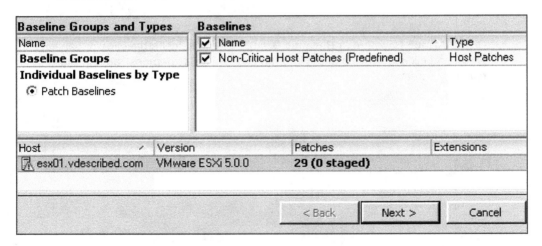

7. The next screen lists all the applicable patches. Deselect patches that you do not intend to install on the ESXi server, and click on **Next** to continue.

8. You could either run the remediation **Immediately** or schedule it to run at a specified time. Click on **Next** to continue:

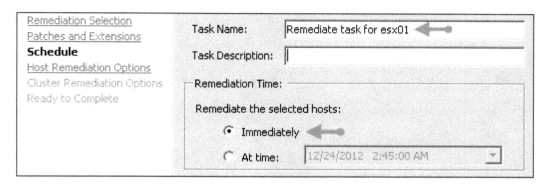

9. Set the host **Maintenance Mode Options**. Make sure that you disable any removable media. This is important because when a host tries to enter maintenance mode, the VMs on it are migrated (vMotion) to the other hosts in the cluster. VMs with removable media attached to them cannot be migrated using vMotion, hence preventing the host from entering maintenance mode.

10. Select the **Disable any removable media devices connected to the virtual machines on the host.** checkbox and click on **Next** to continue:

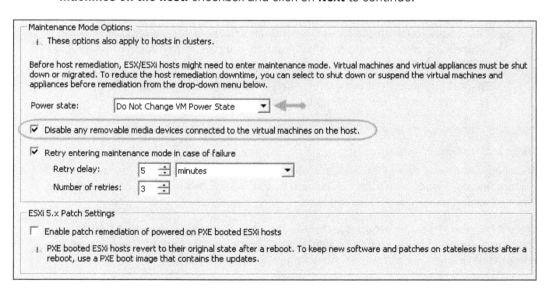

11. Set the **Cluster Remediation** options. You can disable High Availability admission control and Fault Tolerance (FT) to increase the chances of the host entering maintenance mode without any issues. You can also generate a report to see the recommendations:

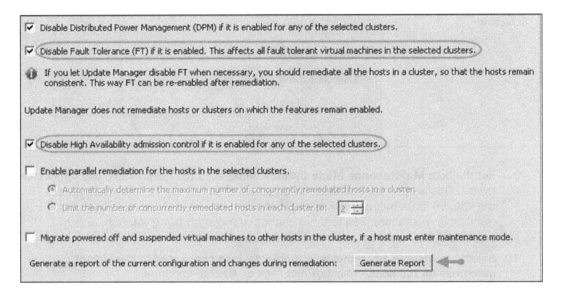

12. The **Ready to Complete** screen summarizes the selected options. Review the information provided and click on **Finish** to start the remediation or create the remediation schedule.

13. Once the remediation completes, scan the host for compliance again. It should then show the host/cluster as compliant to the baseline.

How it works...

Attaching a baseline to an ESXi host or a cluster of ESXi hosts is a way to inform vSphere Update Manager about the patches that you would like to have installed on the selected hosts/cluster.

Once a baseline/baseline group is attached to an entity, the entity needs to be scanned for compliance with the attached baseline. When you select a cluster to be scanned for compliance, it will scan all the ESXi hosts in the cluster.

Noncompliant hosts/clusters can be remediated. The remediation process will put the host in maintenance mode. By default, the VMs on the host will be migrated. If a cluster is chosen for remediation, then hosts in that cluster are remediated sequentially.

Here is what happens in a five-host cluster:

1. The first host in the cluster is put into maintenance mode. The VMs on it will be migrated to the remaining ESXi hosts with the help of DRS.

2. The first host is remediated.

3. Once the remediation completes, the host exits maintenance mode.

4. Once the first host is available in the cluster for hosting VMs again, the second host is put into maintenance mode for remediation.

5. This process continues until all five hosts are remediated.

What happens to the VMs on the host being put into maintenance mode by vSphere Update Manager can be controlled by using the **ESXi Host/Cluster Settings** under the Update Manager's **Configuration** tab. You can choose the option **Power Off virtual machines** or **Suspend virtual machines** as well:

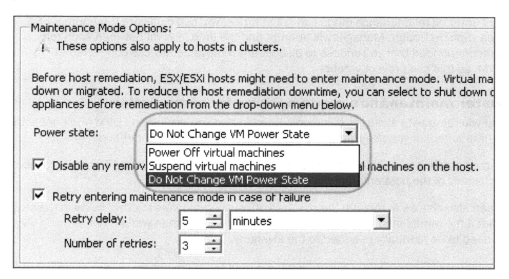

You can also choose to enable parallel remediation of the hosts in the cluster. This can be done by using the **ESXi Host/Cluster Settings** under the Update Manager's **Configuration** tab or through the remediation wizard.

☑ Enable parallel remediation for the hosts in the selected clusters.

   ⦿ Automatically determine the maximum number of concurrently remediated hosts in a cluster.

   ◯ Limit the number of concurrently remediated hosts in each cluster to: 2

There's more...

There is more to it. We have two maintenance mode options for remediation, which are as follows:

- ▶ Host maintenance mode options for remediation
- ▶ Cluster maintenance mode options for remediation

Host maintenance mode options for remediation

The host maintenance mode options can help you to reduce the downtime required to remediate an ESXi host, by either choosing to power off or suspend the VMs running on it. Choosing to power off / suspend the VMs will cut down the time otherwise required to vMotion the VMs off that host. However, keep in mind that we are gaining time at the expense of virtual machine downtime.

A host entering maintenance mode can fail at times. You can configure the number of retries vSphere Update Manager will attempt and the time interval between each retry. It is recommended that you choose to disable any removable devices connected to the VM, as this can prevent vMotion.

Cluster maintenance mode options for remediation

When you remediate a cluster, it is recommended that you disable the DPM and enable the EVC (if required). If you generate a report, it will post the same recommendations.

It is best practice to disable the high availability admission control and FT in order to increase the chances of the host entering maintenance mode successfully.

You can also choose to migrate the powered off/suspended VMs to other hosts in the cluster, so that if the remediated host fails to boot for some reason, then you are not left with VMs that need to be manually re-added to the inventory.

Enabling parallel remediation will reduce the amount of time needed to remediate the entire cluster, as it would concurrently remediate more than one host. Unless you want to limit the concurrency, leave it as automatic.

Remediating a VM or a VA

Virtual machines can be remediated by using one of the following two predefined baselines:

- ▶ VMware tools upgrade to match host
- ▶ VM hardware upgrade to match host

A virtual appliance (VA) can be remediated by either using the predefined baseline **VA Upgrade to Latest** or by using a custom baseline.

 Remediating a VM or a virtual appliance can't be done from the host and clusters inventory view. Make sure you change the view to **VMs and Templates**.

How to do it...

The following procedure will help you remediate a VM or a virtual appliance:

1. On vCenter Server, change the inventory view to **VMs and Templates**.
2. Select the VM to be remediated and navigate to its **Update Manger** tab.
3. Click on **Attach** to bring up the **Attach Baseline or Group** window.
4. On the **Attach Baseline or Group** window, select the VM upgrade baselines or a baseline group and click on **Attach**.

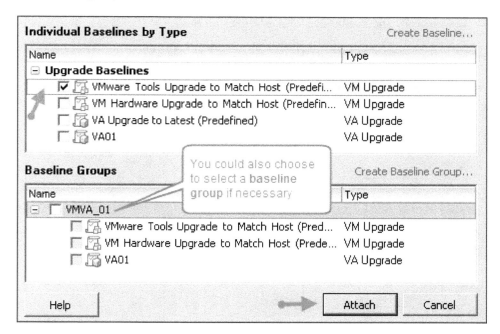

5. Scan the VM for compliance with the baseline.
6. Click on **Remediate** if the VM is noncompliant.

7. On the **Remediate** wizard screen, you can see the baselines selected. If multiple baselines are selected, then you can choose to deselect individual baselines as well:

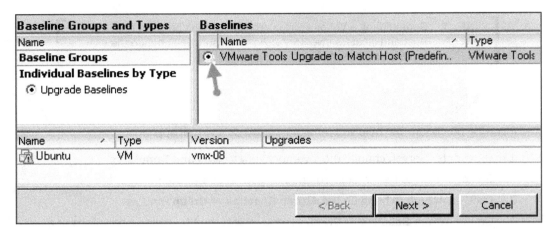

8. Enter a task name and schedule the upgrade at a specific time for powered on, powered off, and suspended VMs, and click on **Next**:

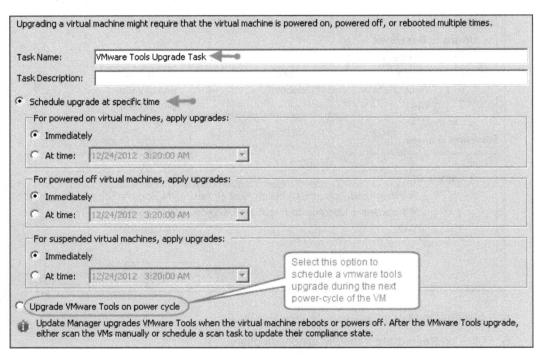

9. Choose the rollback options for the VM. This is achieved with the help of virtual machine snapshots. Select **Take a snapshot of the virtual machines before remediation to enable rollback.**. You can optionally specify a snapshot name and also choose to snapshot the virtual machine memory:

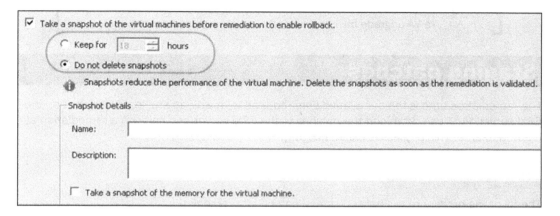

10. The **Ready to Complete** screen summarizes the settings. Review the settings and click on **Finish** to start remediating at the scheduled time.

How it works...

When you remediate Windows VMs, your system requires some a downtime during the reboot after the VMware tools upgrade, but there is no downtime for the virtual hardware upgrade.

Starting with vSphere 5.1, the downtime (reboot) required for a VMware tools upgrade has been reduced. Read the section *Reduced downtime upgrade for VMware tools* in the *What's New in VMware vSphere 5.1* whitepaper (`http://www.vmware.com/files/pdf/products/vsphere/vmware-what-is-new-vsphere51.pdf`).
The same applies for vSphere 5.5.

For Linux, Netware, and Solaris VMs, you will not need downtime for a tools upgrade, but you will need downtime for a virtual hardware upgrade.

Keep in mind that the VMs need to be in the powered on state for remediation. Powered off/suspended VMs will be powered on/resumed for remediation.

It is best practice to take snapshots of the VMs that will be remediated. Once the VMs are validated for proper functioning after remediating, delete the snapshots.

 Note that the steps involved in remediating a VA are exactly the same as VMs, the only difference being that you will be attaching a VA upgrade baseline instead of a VM upgrade baseline.

Staging patches

The remediation time is the *cumulative time* required to download and install patches on the ESXi server. VUM can download the patches to the ESXi server and perform a remediation at a later date/time. This process is called **staging**.

How to do it...

The following procedure will help you stage patches for remediation:

1. Attach a baseline to a host/cluster, and then click on **Scan** to scan for compliance.

2. If the scan reports noncompliance, then click on the **Stage** button to bring up the **Stage** wizard.

3. In the **Stage** wizard, make sure that the correct baseline is selected and click on **Next**:

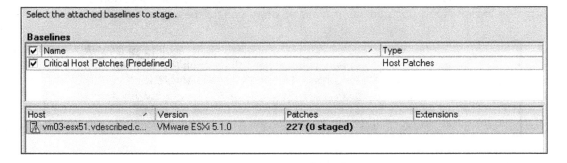

4. The next screen shows all the patches that will be staged. You can exclude patches by deselecting them, if needed.

5. On the **Ready to complete** screen, review the options and click on **Finish** to stage the patches.

How it works...

The staging process copies the patches to be installed onto the ESXi host. It is not required for the host to be in maintenance mode while the patches are being staged, hence saving a considerable amount of downtime for the ESXi server. The VMs can still continue to run while the patches are being staged.

Unlike remediation, staging cannot be scheduled. Once staging completes, remediation can be scheduled.

Installing the Update Manager Download Service

The **Update Manager Download Service** (**UMDS**) comes in handy when the Update Manger server doesn't have access to the Internet to download patches.

In this section, we will learn how to install Update Manager Download Service.

UMDS 5.5 should be installed on a 64-bit machine only. It cannot be installed on the same machine running vSphere Update Manager and it is only compatible with Update Manager 5.5.

If UMDS 5.5 is being installed on a machine running an older version of UMDS (UMDS 4.x or UMDS 5.x), then the older version should be uninstalled before installing UMDS 5.5.

How to do it...

The following procedure will help you install Update Manager Download Service:

1. Create a new database for UMDS as we did for VUM. Refer to the *Preparing database connectivity for VUM* section for guidelines. The procedure will remain the same except for the database name.

```
[-] 🗌 UMDS55_DB
    [+] 📁 Database Diagrams
    [+] 📁 Tables
    [+] 📁 Views
    [+] 📁 Synonyms
    [+] 📁 Programmability
    [+] 📁 Service Broker
    [+] 📁 Storage
    [+] 📁 Security
```

2. Create a 32-bit DSN as we did for VUM. If you are using the same DB login then make sure to change the default database to the UMDS's database:

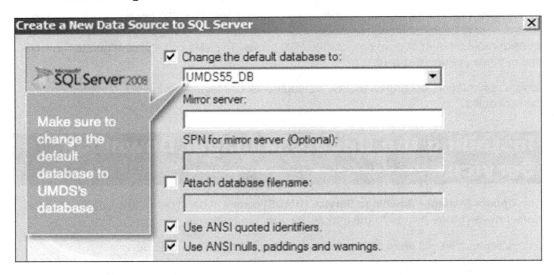

3. The UMDS's installer is located on the vCenter Server Installation DVD. Here is the location for the file:

```
DVD Drive:\VMware VIM\umds\VMware-UMDS.exe
```

Double-click on the VMware-UMDS.exe file to start the installation:

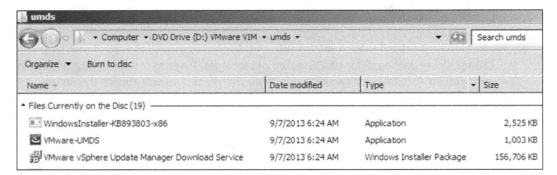

4. Go through the installation wizard and make sure that you select the DSN for UMDS:

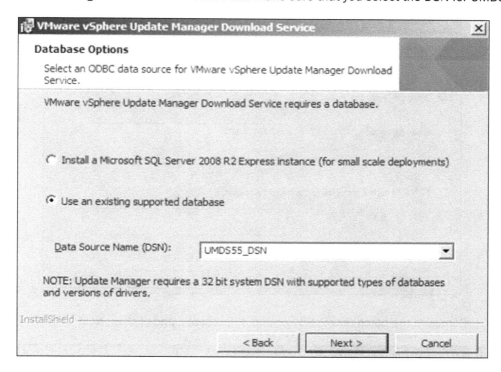

5. Supply the credentials for the DB login and click on **Next** to continue.

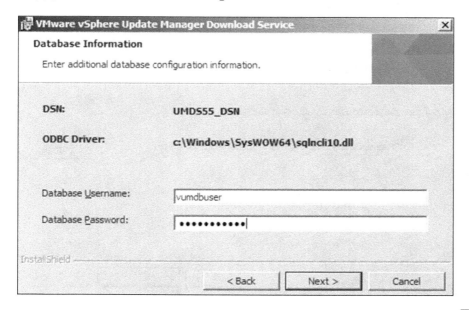

6. Configure the proxy settings if necessary, and click on **Next** to continue:

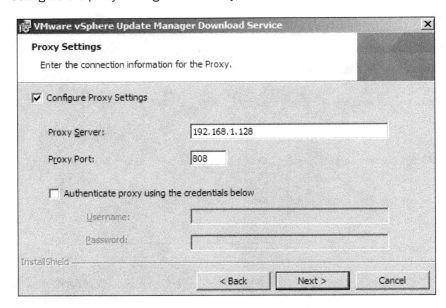

7. Configure the patch download location if necessary, and click on **Next**:

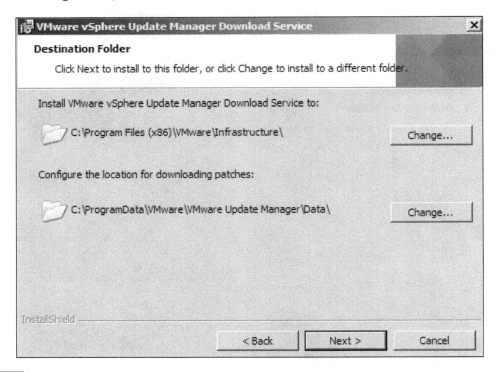

8. On the **Ready to Install** screen, click on **Install** to start the installation.

9. Once the installation is complete, click on **Finish** to exit the installer.

Configuring UMDS and downloading data

UMDS can be configured to download and export patches to a shared repository. The entire configuration is done via the Windows command line.

How to do it...

The following procedure will help you configure UMDS and download data:

1. Locate the `vm-umds.exe` file under the following directory:

   `C:\Program Files (x86)\VMware\Infrastructure\Update Manager`

2. By default, the UMDS will only download patches and notifications for hosts. To configure it to download the VA upgrades, you should run the following command:

   `vmware-umds -S --enable-host --enable-va`

```
c:\Program Files (x86)\VMware\Infrastructure\Update Manager>
  vmware-umds.exe -S enable-host --enable-va
[2014-08-20 15:51:32:695 '' 872 ALERT]  [logUtil, 265] Product = VMware Update M
anager, Version = 5.5.0, Build = 1302474
Setting up UMDS configuration
Virtual appliance upgrade downloads: Enabled

c:\Program Files (x86)\VMware\Infrastructure\Update Manager>
```

3. If you need to change the patch repository location (optional), then issue the following command:

   Syntax:

   `vmware-umds -S --patch-store your_new_patchstore_folder`

   Example:

   `vmware-umds -S --patch-store C:\DATA_LOC`

```
c:\Program Files (x86)\VMware\Infrastructure\Update Manager>
  vmware-umds -S --patch-store C:\DATA_LOC
[2014-08-20 16:10:22:827 '' 588 ALERT]  [logUtil, 265] Product = VMwar
e Update Manager, Version = 5.5.0, Build = 1302474
Setting up UMDS configuration
Directory for storing downloaded updates: C:\DATA_LOC
Directory C:\ProgramData\VMware\VMware Update Manager\Data\ is no long
er used as the patch store. You may want to delete its contents or mov
e it to the new location C:\DATA_LOC

c:\Program Files (x86)\VMware\Infrastructure\Update Manager>_
```

4. You can add a patch download source by using the following command:

   Syntax:

   ```
   vmware-umds -S --add-url https://host_URL/index.xml --url-type
   HOST
   ```

   Example:

   ```
   vmware-umds -S --add-url http://vibsdepot.hp.com/index.xml --url-
   type HOST
   ```

```
c:\Program Files (x86)\VMware\Infrastructure\Update Manager>
 vmware-umds -S --add-url http://vibsdepot.hp.com/hpq/jul2014/index-dr
v.xml --url-type HOST
[2014-08-20 16:14:02:072 '' 2696 ALERT] [logUtil, 265] Product = VMwa
re Update Manager, Version = 5.5.0, Build = 1302474
Setting up UMDS configuration
[2014-08-20 16:14:02:082 'DownloadMgr' 2696 DEBUG] [downloadMgr, 325]
 Maximum concurrent download limit: 2
[2014-08-20 16:14:02:086 'DownloadMgr' 2696 DEBUG] [downloadMgr, 326]
 Download recv timeout: -1
[2014-08-20 16:14:02:090 'DownloadMgr' 2696 DEBUG] [downloadMgr, 545]
 Url: http://vibsdepot.hp.com/hpq/jul2014/index-drv.xml, Download dest
ination: C:\Users\ADMINI~1\AppData\Local\Temp\2\vcimlpeupms.tmp
[2014-08-20 16:14:02:098 'DownloadMgr' 2696 DEBUG] [downloadMgr, 396]

            :                     :                     :
            :                     :                     :
            :                     :                     :

[2014-08-20 16:14:02:736 'DownloadMgr' 2696 DEBUG] [downloadMgr, 464]
 Download job <47951208> finished
[2014-08-20 16:14:02:742 'DownloadMgr' 2696 DEBUG] [downloadMgr, 477]
 Removing download job <47951208> in queue
[2014-08-20 16:14:02:748 'DownloadMgr' 2696 DEBUG] [downloadMgr, 496]
 Current download count: 0
[2014-08-20 16:14:02:761 'HostUpdateDepotManager' 2696 INFO] [vendorI
ndexParser, 36] vendor index contains 1 vendors.
Added HOST URL http://vibsdepot.hp.com/hpq/jul2014/index-drv.xml

c:\Program Files (x86)\VMware\Infrastructure\Update Manager>
```

5. To initiate a download from the patch download sources, issue the following command:

   ```
   vmware-umds -D
   ```

Creating a shared repository

We can export downloaded patch data from the repository used by the UMDS to a shared location so that the Update Manager server can be configured to use this shared location.

How to do it...

1. To export the downloaded patch data to a shared repository, issue the following command:

   Syntax:

   ```
   vmware-umds -E --export-store repository_path
   ```

   Example:

   ```
   vmware-umds -E --export-store C:\PatchRepo
   vmware-umds -E --export-store \\vcenterhost001\atvc
   ```

How it works...

The command copies the data from the patch store to the shared repository. You have to periodically export the patch data to keep the shared repository up to date. The shared repository folder should have read permissions over the network.

Using a shared repository

In scenarios where the Update Manager server cannot be provided with access to the Internet, you can configure the Update Manager server to access a shared repository containing patch data. For instructions on how to create a shared repository, read the recipe *Creating a shared repository*.

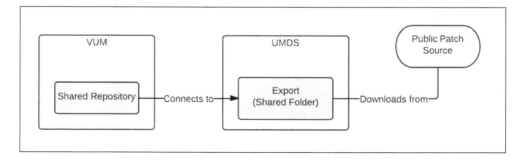

How to do it...

The following procedure will help you to configure access to a shared repository:

1. On the UMDS server, set the shared repository folder as the "export store". Read the *Creating a shared repository* section for instructions.

2. Once a shared repository has been created, connect to the vCenter Server by using the vSphere Client and navigate to **Home | Update Manager.** Navigate to the **Configuration** tab and then to **Download Settings**. Select the **Use a shared repository** option to specify a shared repository and click on **Validate URL**. If the validation is successful, it will show the status as **Connected**. Once the URL is validated, click on **Apply** to save the download settings.

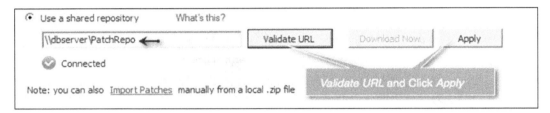

3. Now, you can click on **Download Now** to download patches from the shared repository:

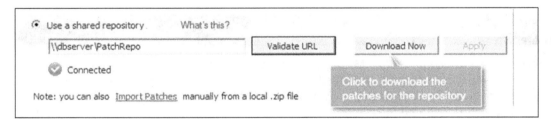

4. You should see a dialog box indicating that a new download task has been added to the **Recent Tasks** pane:

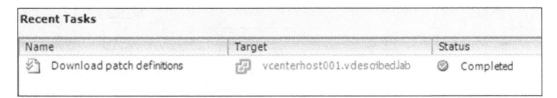

14
Using vSphere Management Assistant

In this chapter, we will cover the following recipes:

- ▶ Deploying the vMA appliance
- ▶ Preparing VMware vMA for first use
- ▶ Configuring VMware vMA to join an existing domain
- ▶ Adding vCenter to vMA with AD authentication
- ▶ Adding vCenter to vMA with fastpass (fpauth) authentication
- ▶ Adding an ESXi host to vMA
- ▶ Reconfiguring an added target server
- ▶ Running CLI commands on target servers
- ▶ Updating the vMA

Introduction

vSphere Management Assistant (**vMA**) is a Linux appliance that enables remote management of your vSphere environment via its command-line interface. The tool does not offer a graphical user interface. It was originally developed to replace the service console to run scripts or agents that are programmed to interact with the vSphere hosts. It comes packaged with the vSphere CLI (command-line interface) and the Perl SDK. vSphere CLI shouldn't be confused with vSphere Power CLI. While vSphere CLI is a bundle of Linux commands that can interact with the vSphere hosts, the latter is a Windows PowerShell plugin and executes PowerShell **cmdlets**.

vMA 5.5 is a virtual machine running SUSE Linux Enterprise Server 11 and it requires no separate licensing. It has the following components:

- ▶ vSphere CLI
- ▶ vSphere Software Development Kit for Perl
- ▶ Java Runtime Engine (JRE) Version 1.6
- ▶ An authentication component called the "vi-fastpass"

In this chapter, we will learn how to deploy and configure the appliance for use with vSphere environments.

Deploying the vMA appliance

The vMA appliance will be deployed as an appliance on an ESXi server. It is a single virtual machine appliance. The ZIP bundle containing the OVF and the related files can be downloaded from the **Download VMware vSphere** available at `http://bit.ly/download_vsphere`.

It will be listed as download under the **Drivers & Tools** category:

Product Downloads	Drivers & Tools	Open Source	Custom ISOs

Driver / Tool		Release Date	
> Driver CDs			
> VMware vCenter Support Assistant			
> Automation Tools and SDKs			
> vCenter Orchestrator Plug-ins			
∨ VMware vSphere Management Assistant			
VMware vSphere Management Assistant 5.5.0.1 (vMA	2014-04-04	Go to Downloads
VMware vSphere Management Assistant 5.5 (vMA)	2013-10-31	Go to Downloads

Getting ready

Once you have downloaded the ZIP bundle, extract it before the OVF in it can be used to deploy the appliance. The following screenshot shows the contents of the extracted folder:

Name	Date modified	Type	Size
vMA-5.5.0.1-1663088_OVF10.cert	3/11/2014 1:24 AM	CERT File	2 KB
vMA-5.5.0.1-1663088_OVF10.mf	3/11/2014 1:23 AM	MF File	1 KB
vMA-5.5.0.1-1663088_OVF10	3/11/2014 1:23 AM	Open Virtualization Format Package	30 KB
vMA-5.5.0.1-1663088-system	3/11/2014 1:23 AM	VMware virtual disk file	569,862 KB

The vMA appliance can be deployed onto an ESXi host by using a direct vSphere client connection to the host or by connecting to the vCenter Server.

Here is a table showing supported host and target vSphere versions:

Hosts	Targets
vSphere 5.0 or later	vSphere 5.0 or later
vSphere 5.1 or later	vSphere 5.1 or later
vSphere 5.5 or later	vSphere 5.5 or later

How to do it...

The following procedure will help you deploy the vMA appliance using the **vSphere Web Client interface**. The same can be achieved using the vSphere Client as well:

1. At the vSphere Web Client interface's inventory home, navigate to **Hosts and Clusters**.
2. Right-click on the ESXi cluster and then click on **Deploy OVF Template**.
3. In the **Deploy OVF Template** wizard, select the **Local File** option and then click on the **Browse...** button.
4. Select the OVF file from the extracted location and then click on **Next** to continue with the wizard.

5. Review the details of the OVF file and then click on **Next** to continue:

Product	vSphere Management Assistant (vMA)
Version	5.5.0.1
Vendor	VMware, Inc.
Publisher	⊘ VMware, Inc. (Trusted certificate)
Download size	556.5 MB
Size on disk	1.6 GB (thin provisioned) 3.0 GB (thick provisioned)
Description	The vSphere Management Assistant (vMA) allows administrators and developers to run scripts and agents to manage ESX/ESXi and vCenter Server systems.

6. Accept the license agreement and then click on **Next**.

7. Choose an inventory location for the appliance VM and then click on **Next**.

8. Choose a datastore for the VM and then click on **Next**.

9. Choose a port group to which the vNIC will be mapped. Set the **IP allocation** policy and **Protocol Settings** and then click on **Next**. Leave this at DHCP as none of these settings are pushed to the SLES VM during the deployment.

10. Review the **Ready to complete** screen and then click on **Finish** to deploy the appliance.

Note that it doesn't matter what IP allocation policy you choose or what IP address you specify; you will need to choose between a DHCP and a static configuration when you configure the appliance after the first boot.

Preparing VMware vMA for first use

After vMA is deployed, it will need to go through a few initial configuration steps before you can begin using it. The configuration is done at the appliance's guest operating system level.

The vMA appliance runs **SUSE Linux Enterprise Linux (SLES)** 11 SP1 as the guest operating system.

How to do it...

The following procedure will help you prepare the vMA VM for first use:

1. Power on the vMA VM and wait for the VM to boot up and display the network configuration main menu as shown in the following screenshot:

```
vma01
Starting D-Bus daemon                                                    done
Starting syslog services                                                 done
Initializing random number generator                                     done
    VMware vmci driver:                                                   done
    Starting VMware Tools guest operating system daemon:                  done
Starting vmware-vifpd:                                                    done

Starting vmware-vma:
Verifying vMA UUID ...
Verifying vMA UUID in firstboot ...

Updating sysctl configuration ...

Starting network configuration ...

 Main Menu

0)       Show Current Configuration (scroll with Shift-PgUp/PgDown)
1)       Exit this program
2)       Default Gateway
3)       Hostname
4)       DNS
5)       Proxy Server
6)       IP Address Allocation for eth0
Enter a menu number [0]: _
```

2. Enter 0 to check the current configuration:

```
vma01
 Network Configuration for eth0
 IPv4 Address:
 Netmask:
 IPv6 Address:
 Prefix:                                   Note that all the network
                                           settings are blank.
 Global Configuration
 IPv4 Gateway:
 IPv6 Gateway:
 Hostname:          localhost
 DNS Servers:
 Proxy Server:
```

3. Note that the IP configuration is blank. This stands true regardless of your choice between DHCP/Manual during the deployment wizard.

4. Enter 6 to select **IP Address Allocation for eth0** and supply the static configuration and then enter y to confirm the configuration as shown in the following screenshot:

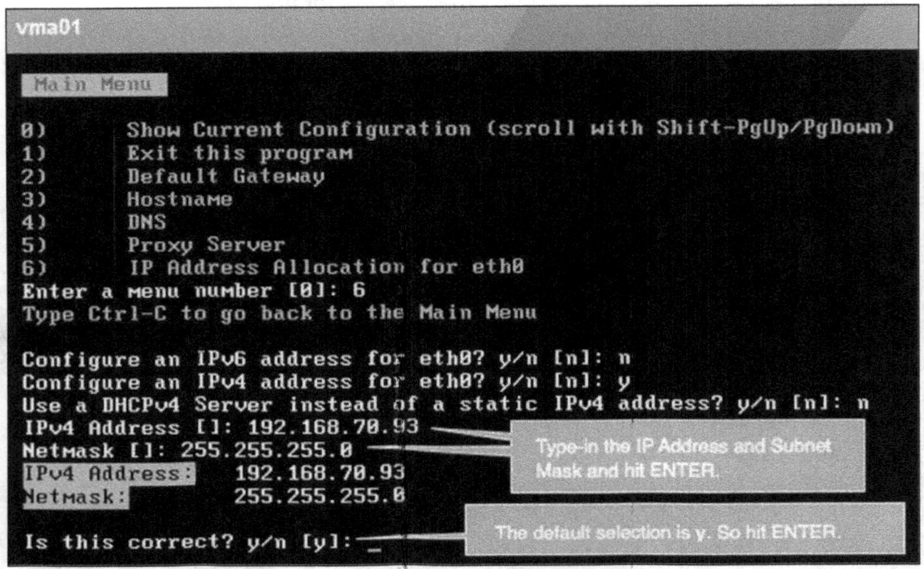

```
vma01

Main Menu

0)        Show Current Configuration (scroll with Shift-PgUp/PgDown)
1)        Exit this program
2)        Default Gateway
3)        Hostname
4)        DNS
5)        Proxy Server
6)        IP Address Allocation for eth0
Enter a menu number [0]: 6
Type Ctrl-C to go back to the Main Menu

Configure an IPv6 address for eth0? y/n [n]: n
Configure an IPv4 address for eth0? y/n [n]: y
Use a DHCPv4 Server instead of a static IPv4 address? y/n [n]: n
IPv4 Address []: 192.168.70.93
Netmask []: 255.255.255.0
IPv4 Address:   192.168.70.93          Type-in the IP Address and Subnet
Netmask:        255.255.255.0          Mask and hit ENTER.

Is this correct? y/n [y]: ___         The default selection is y. So hit ENTER.
```

5. Enter 2 to set the **Default Gateway**. Although, I have supplied an IPv4 address in this example, you can supply an IPv6 address instead. This step is completely dependent on your network infrastructure:

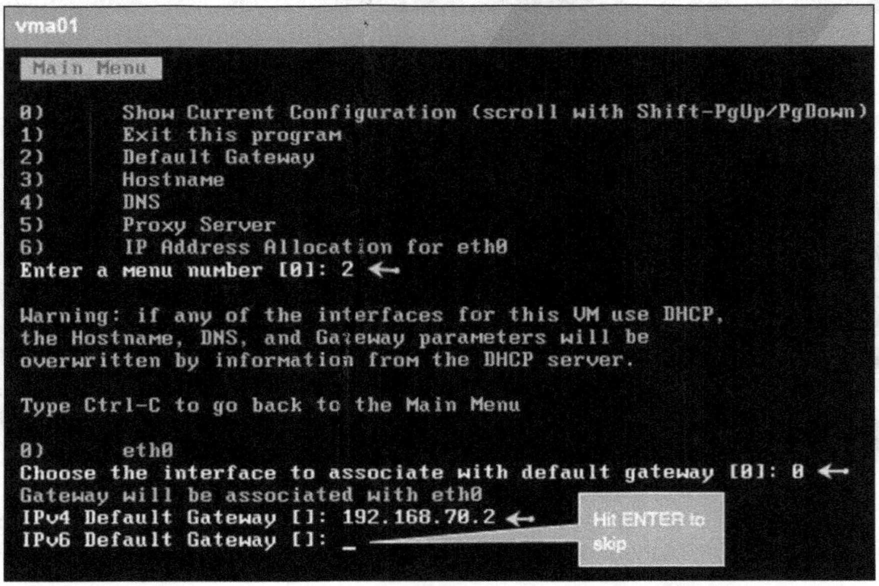

```
vma01

Main Menu

0)        Show Current Configuration (scroll with Shift-PgUp/PgDown)
1)        Exit this program
2)        Default Gateway
3)        Hostname
4)        DNS
5)        Proxy Server
6)        IP Address Allocation for eth0
Enter a menu number [0]: 2 ←

Warning: if any of the interfaces for this VM use DHCP,
the Hostname, DNS, and Gateway parameters will be
overwritten by information from the DHCP server.

Type Ctrl-C to go back to the Main Menu

0)        eth0
Choose the interface to associate with default gateway [0]: 0 ←
Gateway will be associated with eth0
IPv4 Default Gateway []: 192.168.70.2 ←       Hit ENTER to
IPv6 Default Gateway []: _                    skip
```

6. Enter 4 and supply the DNS Server details and hit *Enter*. Although I have supplied a single DNS sever address in this example, most environments will have a secondary DNS server:

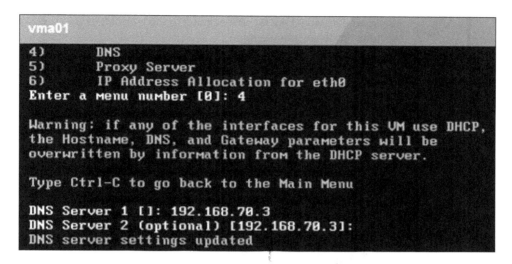

7. Enter 3 and supply a hostname and hit *Enter*:

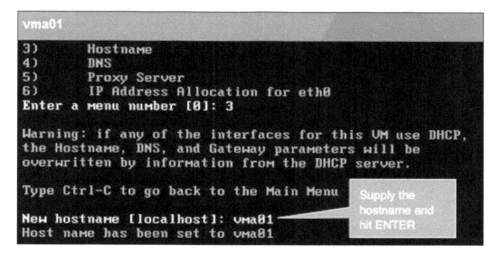

Enter 5:

 Supplying the proxy information is not a mandatory step. Most environments would not let vMA connect to the Internet, as a security hardening measure.

8. Enter 0 to verify that the newly supplied IP configuration has been applied:

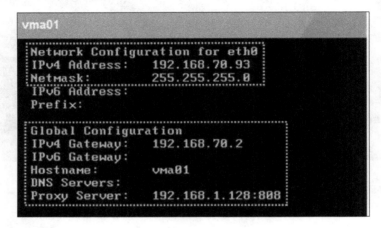

9. Enter 1 to exit the network configuration program and start the password configuration program:

```
vma01

Main Menu

0)      Show Current Configuration (scroll with Shift-PgUp/PgDown)
1)      Exit this program
2)      Default Gateway
3)      Hostname
4)      DNS
5)      Proxy Server
6)      IP Address Allocation for eth0
Enter a menu number [0]: 1 ←

Starting password configuration ...
The root account is disabled in this vMA virtual machine, which means no one can
  log in as root. The administrator account for vMA is called "vi-admin". In orde
r to log in to vMA, you need to log in as this user. This user has been pre-crea
ted in the vMA, and its password needs to be set now. Please enter a secure pass
word for the account now.

Please provide a password for the vi-admin user. If you are prompted for an old
password for this user, enter vmware.
Old Password: _ ←
```

10. Enter `vmware` as the password in the old password prompt as shown in the next
    screenshot, and then enter a new password. The new password must at least contain
    nine characters, including one uppercase, one lowercase, one numerical character,
    and one printable ASCII symbol:

```
Please provide a password for the vi-admin user. If you are prompted for an old
password for this user, enter vmware.
Old Password: ←
New password: ←
Retype new password: ←

Password for "vi-admin" is configured.


Starting certificate installation ...
Password changed.
```

11. The appliance will continue loading the guest OS of the appliance, and will eventually display its main screen, as demonstrated in the following screenshot:

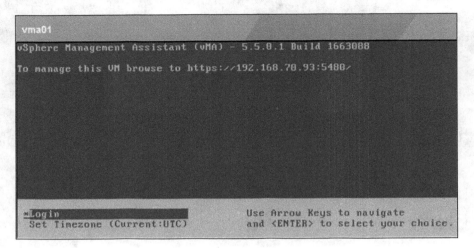

How it works...

Once the appliance has been configured for first use, you can perform various operations from the console of the appliance and its management home page. When you log in using the vi-admin user at the vMA appliance's management home page, you get options to reconfigure the network, the time zone, and to look for appliance updates.

The following tasks can be performed:

- From the console, you can perform the following tasks:
  - ❑ Add vCenter Servers or ESXi servers to vMA
  - ❑ Issue commands from the vMA console against the added servers
  - ❑ Configure the vMA's network and proxy settings
  - ❑ Configure the time zone settings

- From the web UI, you can perform the following tasks:
  - ❑ Configure the vMA's network and proxy settings
  - ❑ Configure the time zone settings
  - ❑ Update vMA

 The root user account on the appliance is not enabled. For tasks requiring root privileges, use the vi-admin user and sudo to get privileges.

Configuring VMware vMA to join an existing domain

VMware vMA can be configured to join an Active Directory domain and subsequently use an AD user to log in to the appliance and run the remote commands against the targets.

 The `vi-user` account cannot be used to run commands against AD targets. To be able to run commands on an AD target, you should either use the `vi-admin` account, or log in to the vMA appliance using an AD user.

How to do it...

The following procedure will guide you through the steps required to configure vMA to join an existing Active Directory domain:

1. Log in to the vMA console or SSH to it as the `vi-admin` user.

2. Issue the following command to add the vMA appliance to the domain:

   Syntax:

   ```
   sudo domainjoin-cli join <domain-name> <domain-admin-user>
   ```

   Example:

   ```
   sudo domainjoin-cli join vdescribed.com domuser
   ```

   Output:

```
vma01
vi-admin@vma01:~> sudo domainjoin-cli join vdescribed.lab domuser

We trust you have received the usual lecture from the local System
Administrator. It usually boils down to these three things:

    #1) Respect the privacy of others.
    #2) Think before you type.
    #3) With great power comes great responsibility.

vi-admin's password:
Joining to AD Domain:   vdescribed.lab
With Computer DNS Name: vma01

domuser@VDESCRIBED.LAB's password:
Warning: System restart required
Your system has been configured to authenticate to Active Directory for the
first time.  It is recommended that you restart your system to ensure that all
applications recognize the new settings.

SUCCESS
vi-admin@vma01:~> _
```

An AD user with the rights to join a machine to the domain.

Indicative of the fact that the domain-join was successful

3. Reboot the vMA appliance by issuing the `sudo reboot` command.

4. Check whether the domain login was successful by issuing the following command:

    `sudo domainjoin-cli query`

```
vma01
vi-admin@vma01:~> sudo domainjoin-cli query
vi-admin's password:
Name = vma01
Domain = VDESCRIBED.LAB
Distinguished Name = CN=VMA01,CN=Computers,DC=vdescribed,DC=lab
vi-admin@vma01:~> _
```

You should see a Distinguished Name (DN) generated for the AD object corresponding to the vMA VM as shown in the previous screenshot.

Adding vCenter to vMA with AD authentication

You can add vCenter Servers to vMA with AD authentication. This is considered to be more secure than the default fastpass authentication, which maintains a local cache of the credentials.

Getting ready

The domain user or its AD group should be assigned at least a read only role at the target vCenter Server.

How to do it...

The following procedure explains how to add the vCenter Server to the vMA by using AD authentication:

1. Log in to the vMA console or SSH as `vi-admin`.

2. Issue the following command:

    `vifp addserver <vCenter>  --authpolicy adauth --username <domain>\\<domain admin>`

    or

    `vifp addserver <vCenter>  --authpolicy adauth --username <domainuser>@<domain>`

Examples:

```
vifp addserver vcenterhost001.vdescribed.lab  --authpolicy adauth
--username vdescribed\\vcenteruser001
```

```
vifp addserver vcenter5x.vdescibed.com  --authpolicy adauth
--username vcenteruser001@vdescribed.lab
```

3. Issue the command `vifp listservers` to verify that the server has been added, as demonstrated in the following screenshot:

```
vma01
vi-admin@vma01:~> vifp addserver vcenterhost001.vdescribed.lab --authpolicy adau
th --username testuser001@vdescribed.lab
vi-admin@vma01:~>
vi-admin@vma01:~>
vi-admin@vma01:~> vifp listservers -l
vcenterhost001.vdescribed.lab    vCenter adauth
vi-admin@vma01:~> _
```

vCenter added with AD authentication

How it works...

Once configured correctly, you can issue vSphere CLI command on ESXi hosts managed by the added vCenter without prompting for the credentials of the ESXi hosts. However, it does prompt for the vCenter credentials.

> The <DOMAIN_USER> should at least have a read only role at the vCenter Server.

When executing this command, make sure that you specify the domain username in the <DOMAIN>\\<DOMAIN_USER> format. Or, the authentication will be verified against the local credentials store on the vCenter Server.

> When using the <DOMAIN>\\<DOMAIN_USER> notation to specify the username, we should be using two backward slashes. This is because on a Linux Shell, two backward slashes (\\) is an escape sequence for a single backward slash (\).

Also, if the `adauth` value is not specified by using the `authpolicy` switch, then the default `fpauth` mechanism will be used.

Adding vCenter to vMA with fastpass (fpauth) authentication

You can add vCenter Servers to vMA using the standard/default fastpass authentication (fpauth). The vMA's fastpass authentication method provides a mechanism to cache the target server's credentials, on the vMA machine, so that you don't have to authenticate every time you run a command against the target server.

 Much like the adauth policy, every connection is authenticated but not every command to the authenticated target.

Getting ready

The domain user or its AD group should be assigned at least a read-only role at the target vCenter Server.

How to do it...

The following procedure will guide you through the steps required to add the vCenter Server to the vMA by using fastpass authentication:

1. Log in to the vMA console or SSH as the `vi-admin` user.

2. Issue the following command:

   ```
   vifp addserver <vCenter> --authpolicy fpauth
   ```

   Example:

   ```
   vifp addserver vcenterhost001.vdescribed.local --authpolicy fpauth
   ```

3. Issue the command `vifp listservers` to verify that the server has been added, as shown in the following screenshot:

```
vma01
vi-admin@vma01:~> vifp addserver vcenterhost001.vdescribed.lab --authpolicy fpau
th
Enter username for vcenterhost001.vdescribed.lab: testuser001@vdescribed.lab
testuser001@vdescribed.lab@vcenterhost001.vdescribed.lab's password:
This will store username and password in credential store which is a security ri
sk. Do you want to continue?(yes/no): yes
vi-admin@vma01:~>
vi-admin@vma01:~>
vi-admin@vma01:~> vifp listservers -l
vcenterhost001.vdescribed.lab    vCenter fpauth     vCenter added
                                                    using fpauth
                                                    authentication
vi-admin@vma01:~> _
```

How it works...

Unlike AD authentication, the fastpass mechanism stores the username and password information in a local credential store.

The `vi-admin` credentials are stored in this XML file: `/home/vi-admin/vmware/credstore/vmacredentials.xml`.

By default, the added server is set as the target. You can issue the following command to verify the same:

```
vifptarget -d
```

 The <DOMAIN_USER> should at least have a read-only role at the vCenter Server.

Adding an ESXi host to vMA

Instead of adding a vCenter Server to vMA, it is possible to add just the individual ESXi hosts. This is particularly useful if a single vCenter is used to manage multiple data centers and you don't want to expose all the ESXi hosts managed by the vCenter to the vMA appliance.

How to do it...

The following procedure explains how to add an ESXi server to the vMA appliance:

1. Log in to the vMA console or SSH as the `vi-admin` user.
2. Issue the following command:

   ```
   vifp addserver <ESXi_server_name>
   ```

   Example:

   ```
   vifp addserver host001.vdescribed.lab
   ```

3. When prompted, specify the root password for the ESXi host as indicated in the following screenshot.

4. Issue the `vifp listservers` command to verify that the ESXi host was added.

```
vma01

vi-admin@vma01:~> vifp addserver host001.vdescribed.lab
root@host001.vdescribed.lab's password:
vi-admin@vma01:~>
vi-admin@vma01:~>
vi-admin@vma01:~> vifp listservers -l
vcenterhost001.vdescribed.lab     vCenter fpauth
host001.vdescribed.lab            ESXi    fpauth
vi-admin@vma01:~> _
```

Enter host's root password

How it works...

When you add an ESXi server to vMA, unlike adding a vCenter Server, vMA doesn't store the `root` password in its credstore.

Instead, it will create two users on the target ESXi server:

▶ `vi-admin` with administrator privileges

▶ `vi-user` with read-only privilege

On the ESXi server, `/etc/passwd` should show that both users have been created, as shown in the following screenshot:

```
~ # cat /etc/passwd
root:x:0:0:Administrator:/:/bin/sh
daemon:x:2:2:System daemons:/:/sbin/nologin
nfsnobody:x:65534:65534:Anonymous NFS User:/:/sbin/nologin
dcui:x:100:100:DCUI User:/:/sbin/nologin
vpxuser:x:500:100:VMware VirtualCenter administration account:/:/bin/sh
vi-admin00:x:1000:1000:ESXID=52cfc7be-6405-29a4-8b18-dcbfa2a81261;VIMAID=42284F8F-D00B-5F70
-B2DD-DFF064EDC33A;:/:/bin/sh
vi-user00:x:1001:1001:ESXID=52cfc7be-6405-29a4-8b18-dcbfa2a81261;VIMAID=42284F8F-D00B-5F70-
B2DD-DFF064EDC33A;:/:/bin/sh
~ #
```

vi-admin and vi-user entries.

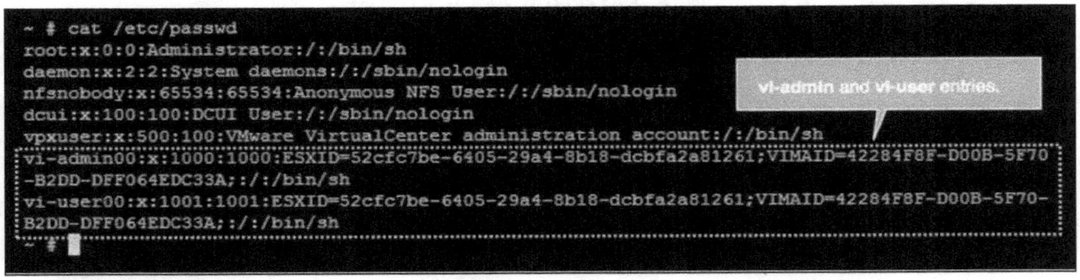

In the credstore on the vMA, you will see a `vi-admin` password entry for the ESXi host as shown in the following screenshot:

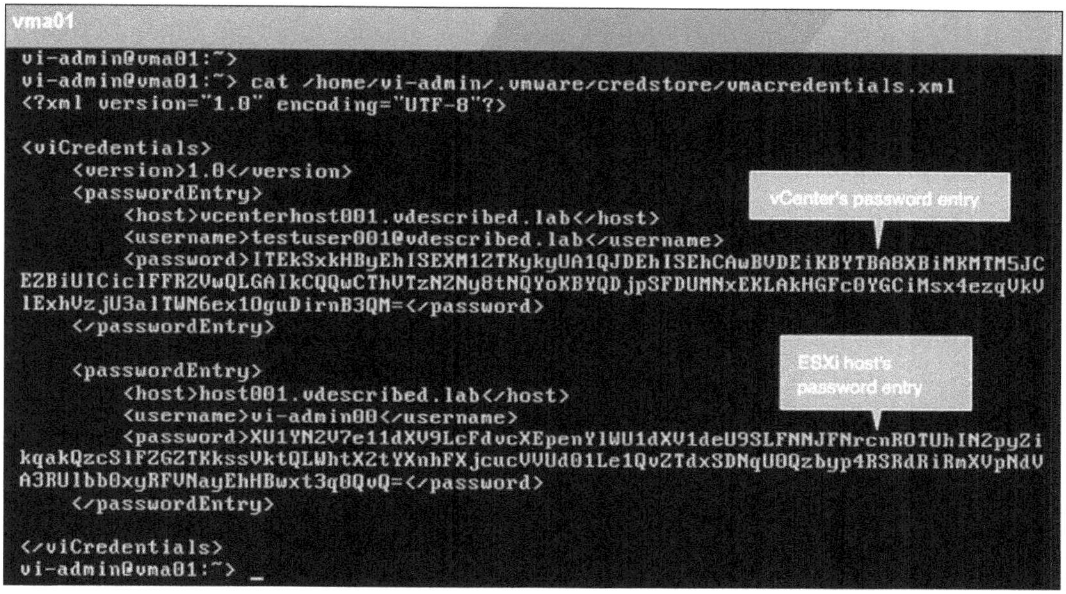

```
vma01
vi-admin@vma01:~>
vi-admin@vma01:~> cat /home/vi-admin/.vmware/credstore/vmacredentials.xml
<?xml version="1.0" encoding="UTF-8"?>

<viCredentials>
      <version>1.0</version>
      <passwordEntry>
          <host>vcenterhost001.vdescribed.lab</host>      vCenter's password entry
          <username>testuser001@vdescribed.lab</username>
          <password>ITEk3xkHByEhISEXM12TKykyUA1QJDEhISEhCAwBVDEiKBYTBA8XBiMKMTM5JC
EZBiUICiclFFRZVwQLGAIkCQQwCThVTzNZNy8tNQYoKBYQDjpSFDUMNxEKLAkHGFcOYGCiMsx4ezqVkV
lExhVzjU3alTWN6ex10guDirnB3QM=</password>
      </passwordEntry>

      <passwordEntry>
          <host>host001.vdescribed.lab</host>      ESXi host's
          <username>vi-admin00</username>          password entry
          <password>XU1YN2V7e11dXV9LcFdvcXEpenYlWU1dXV1deU9SLFNNJFNrcnROTUhINZpyZi
kqakQzcSlFZGZTKkssVktQLWhtX2tYXnhFXjcucVVUd01Le1QvZTdxSDNqU0Qzbyp4RSRdRiRmXVpNdV
A3RUlbbOxyRFVNayEhHBwxt3q0QvQ=</password>
      </passwordEntry>

</viCredentials>
vi-admin@vma01:~> _
```

To remove a server (ESXi/vCenter), issue the following command:

```
vifp removeserver <servername>
```

Examples:

```
vifp removeserver vcenterhost001.vdescribed.lab
vifp removeserver host001.vdescribed.lab
```

Reconfiguring an added target server

An added target server can be reconfigured for a change in the authentication policy, a change in the users authenticating the target, or to recover a `fastpass` user in the event of a local credstore corruption.

How to do it...

The following procedures will guide you through the steps required for the following actions:

- ▸ Changing the authentication policy
- ▸ Changing or recovering a user

Changing the authentication policy

The following procedure will help you change the authentication policy of a target that has already been added to vMA:

1. Issue the following command:

   ```
   vifp reconfigure <servername>  --authpolicy <authpolicy type>
   ```

   Example:

   ```
   vifp reconfigure vcenterhost001.vdescribed.lab  --authpolicy
   fpauth
   ```

2. When prompted, supply the credentials:

```
vma01
vi-admin@vma01:~> vifp reconfigure vcenterhost001.vdescribed.lab --authpolicy fp
auth
testuser001@vdescribed.lab@vcenterhost001.vdescribed.lab's password:
vi-admin@vma01:~> _
```

> Supply password and hit ENTER

Changing or recovering a user

The need to recover a user might arise if the login credentials corresponding to that user have changed or if vMA's credential store is corrupted. The following procedure will help you recover a target that has already been added to vMA:

1. Issue the following command:

   ```
   vifp reconfigure <servername>
   ```

   Examples:

   ```
   vifp reconfigure vcenterhost001.vdescribed.lab
   vifp reconfigure host001.vdescribed.lab
   ```

2. When prompted, supply the credentials:

```
vma01
vi-admin@vma01:~> vifp reconfigure host001.vdescribed.lab  ←—
root@host001.vdescribed.lab's password:
vi-admin@vma01:~>
vi-admin@vma01:~>
vi-admin@vma01:~> vifp reconfigure vcenterhost001.vdescribed.lab ←—
testuser001@vdescribed.lab@vcenterhost001.vdescribed.lab's password:
vi-admin@vma01:~> _
```

How it works...

When you are switching over from `adauth` to `fpauth`, or if you are reconfiguring a fastpass target, it will prompt you only for a password. Whereas, if you are reconfiguring an AD target, it will prompt you only for a username. If the intended target is not the default target, then you will have to use the `vifptarget -s` command to set the required target.

Running CLI commands on target servers

In this recipe, we will learn how to issue commands on the added target vCenter Servers or ESXi hosts.

How to do it...

The following procedures explain how to set a target server and issue direct commands to it. We will discuss all three methods.

Method 1 – issuing commands on the default target

1. Set the intended server as the default target for all commands.

   Command:

   ```
   vifptarget -s <servername>
   ```

   Example:

   ```
   vifptarget -s host001.vdescribed.lab
   vifptarget -s vcenterhost001.vdescribed.lab
   ```

2. Similar to the CLI commands, you would run at an ESXi host's console.

   Example:

   ```
   esxcli system version get
   ```

```
vma01
vi-admin@vma01:~> vifptarget -s host001.vdescribed.lab
vi-admin@vma01:~[host001.vdescribed.lab]> esxcli system version get
   Product: VMware ESXi
   Version: 5.5.0
   Build: Releasebuild-1331820
   Update: 0
vi-admin@vma01:~[host001.vdescribed.lab]> _
```

Method 2 – issuing commands by specifying a target server

1. Issue the command specifying the server name.

   Example:

   ```
   esxcli --server host001.vdescribed.lab iscsi adapter list
   vifptarget -s host001.vdescribed.lab
   ```

2. Supply the username and password when prompted:

```
vma01
vi-admin@vma01:~> esxcli --server host001.vdescribed.lab iscsi adapter list
Enter username: root
Enter password:
Adapter    Driver      State     UID               Description
--------   ---------   -------   --------------    -------------------
vmhba33    iscsi_vmk   online    iscsi.vmhba33     iSCSI Software Adapter
vi-admin@vma01:~> _
```

Method 3 – issuing commands against a vCenter added as the target

1. Issue the command specifying the vCenter Server and ESXi server:

   Command:

   ```
   esxcli --server <VC_server> --vihost <esx_host> system version get
   ```

   Example:

   ```
   esxcli --server vcenter5x.vdescribed.com --vihost esx02.
   vdescribed.com system version get
   ```

2. Supply the vCenter username and password when prompted:

```
vma01
vi-admin@vma01:~> esxcli --server vcenterhost001.vdescribed.lab --vihost host001
.vdescribed.lab system version get
Enter username: testuser001@vdescribed.lab
Enter password:
   Product: VMware ESXi
   Version: 5.5.0
   Build: Releasebuild-1331820
   Update: 0
vi-admin@vma01:~> _
```

 Note that this method will only prompt you for the vCenter's username and password. It will not prompt you for the ESXi host's root password.

Updating the vMA

VMware vMA can be updated using its management UI. The vMA appliance can look for updates and provide an option to install them if available. However, if your vMA appliance does not have access to the Internet, then you will have to decommission the existing vMA and deploy the newer version.

Getting ready

To perform the upgrade, you will need access to the vMA management UI. The URL for the same can be found at the start screen of the appliance virtual machines console. The syntax is `https://IP Address of VMA: 5480`.

How to do it...

The following procedure will guide you through the steps required in updating the vMA appliance:

1. Connect to the management Web UI of the vMA appliance that you intend to upgrade to and log in as the `vi-admin` user.

2. Navigate to the **Status** sub tab under **Update** and click on **Check Updates** as shown in the screenshot. If it finds an update that can be applied, then it will be listed as an available update. You could then click on **Install Updates** to initiate the upgrade of vMA.

3. Click on **Install Updates** and accept the EULA.

4. You will be prompted for a confirmation again. Click on **OK** to confirm.

5. You will now see an **Installing updates...** window appear on the screen. The window will stay put until the upgrade is complete.

> **Installing updates...**
>
> Installing vSphere Management Assistant (vMA) - 5.5.0.2 Build 2170308, please wait...

6. Once done, it will indicate the need for a reboot for the upgrade process to complete:

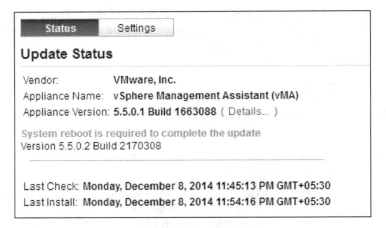

Status	Settings

Update Status

Vendor: **VMware, Inc.**
Appliance Name: **vSphere Management Assistant (vMA)**
Appliance Version: **5.5.0.1 Build 1663088** (Details...)

System reboot is required to complete the update
Version 5.5.0.2 Build 2170308

Last Check: **Monday, December 8, 2014 11:45:13 PM GMT+05:30**
Last Install: **Monday, December 8, 2014 11:54:16 PM GMT+05:30**

7. Navigate to the **System** tab and click on **Reboot** to restart the appliance's virtual machine and complete the upgrade process. You do not have to navigate away from the management UI session. Once the reboot is complete, it will automatically refresh and display the login screen.

8. Log in to the UI again as `vi-admin` and navigate to the **Update | Status** tab and verify the appliance version to make sure that the update is complete, as indicated in the previous screenshot.

How it works...

vMA fetches the update information from the default repository URL preconfigured with the appliance. To check the update URL, you can navigate to **Update | Settings** tab and look for the **Update Repository** URL:

Update Repository

⦿ Use Default Repository

RepositoryURL   https://vapp-updates.vmware.com/vai-catalog/valm/vmw/449bf27f-
                       70b9-476e-af17-fc4369637c25/5.5.0.2.latest

When you hit **Check Updates**, it will connect to the update URL to check whether there is a newer version of vMA available.

When you hit **Install Updates** it will have to download the update and upgrade the vMA, which would then need a reboot to finish the upgrade and start the newer version of the vMA appliance.

> Keep in mind that this process is only for an update to the current version of vMA, in this case 5.5. You cannot upgrade vMA 5.1 to 5.5 using this procedure. For a major version upgrade, you will need to deploy a new instance of vMA.

There's more...

The upgrade initiated from vMA's management UI requires less manual work, but it would only be possible if vMA has access to the Internet. If the vMA is behind a DMZ or has no access to the Internet, then you will have to choose between the use of a CD/DVD image mapped to the appliance VM or a custom repository, as shown in the following screenshot. The options are available at **Update | Settings**:

Update Repository

◉ Use Default Repository

    RepositoryURL   https://vapp-updates.vmware.com/vai-catalog/valm/vmw/449bf27f-70b9-476e-af17-fc4369637c25/5.5.0.2.latest

○ Use CDROM Updates

○ Use Specified Repository

    Repository URL

    Username (Optional)

    Password (Optional)

15
Monitoring the Performance of a vSphere Environment

In this chapter, we will cover the following recipes:

- ▸ Using esxtop to monitor performance
- ▸ Exporting and importing esxtop configurations
- ▸ Running esxtop in batch mode
- ▸ Gathering VM I/O statistics using vscsiStats
- ▸ Using vCenter performance graphs

Introduction

Any vSphere infrastructure, once deployed, needs to be monitored for performance during its life cycle. Continuous monitoring helps configure the infrastructure in a manner that maintains optimum performance to meet the business needs, which can bring cost savings. There are several methods and tools available, such as **vRealize Operations Manager** (**vROPS**), which aid in performance monitoring. Unlike other monitoring tools, vROPS does what VMware calls predictive analysis, which learns what is normal in an environment over time and provides recommendations, facilitates capacity planning, and allows policy-based automation. It can also monitor/manage environments. It is the tool that most infrastructures want to use to be efficient in IT operations. It can be found at `http://www.vmware.com/in/products/vrealize-operations`.

This chapter primarily concentrates on using **esxtop**, **vscsiStats**, and vCenter's performance monitor.

For anyone who is familiar with Linux operating systems, this wouldn't be something completely new. Linux uses a command-line performance monitoring tool called **top**. It is used to view real-time CPU, memory, storage, and network statistics on a Linux machine. VMware has worked on creating something similar to monitor the resources managed by VMkernel; it is known as **esxtop**. This tool runs from the **command-line interface** (**CLI**) of an ESXi host. For someone who would like a visual representation of the performance statistics, vCenter's performance tab is the place to go. It presents statistics in terms of graphs.

In this chapter, we will introduce you to the tools that can be used in a vSphere environment to collect and review performance data. This chapter does not go deep into how each of these tools work; performance monitoring and analysis are large topics to cover and cannot be confined to a single chapter or recipe. Refer to the *See also* sections of the recipes in this chapter for further reading.

Using esxtop to monitor performance

The esxtop command line can be used to monitor the CPU, memory, storage, and network performance metrics. The default output of this tool can further be customized to display the information you need. The esxtop tool has two operating modes—interactive (default) mode and batch mode. In interactive mode, the screen output of the tool can be changed based on what or how much information you would like to view and in batch mode you can collect and save the performance data onto a file.

Getting ready

To run esxtop, you will need access to the CLI of the ESXi host. The CLI can be accessed on the host's console via an IPMI interface (such as Dell's DRAC and HP's ILO), or by connecting to the server using an SSH client.

How to do it...

The following procedure will help you run esxtop and switch between different modes:

1. Connect to the console of the ESXi host using any of the methods mentioned in the *Getting ready* section of this recipe.

2. Once you are at the CLI of the host, type `esxtop` and hit *Enter* for the tool to bring up the default interactive mode output.

The following table will provide you with a basic list of keys to switch between the various statistics modes the tool can be in:

Key	Statistics mode (with a default set of columns)
c	CPU statistics
m	Memory statistics
d	Storage initiator statistics
u	Storage device (LUN) utilization statistics
n	Network utilization statistics
v	VM-specific storage statistics
V	VM-specific compute, network, and storage statistics
i	Interrupt vector information
p	CPU power utilization statistics

Although the preceding keystrokes will allow switching between different modes, each mode can be further expanded and customized to dive into a level of detail that you would need to understand the performance and also troubleshoot issues.

How it works...

Information displayed in interactive mode is refreshed at regular 5-second intervals. This can be modified by hitting the *s* key while in interactive mode, specifying the interval in seconds, and hitting *Enter* for the change to take effect, as shown in the following screenshot:

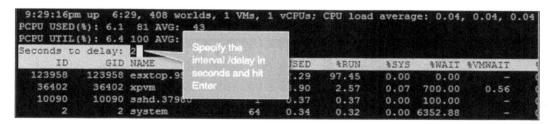

The esxtop output can further be customized in terms of the metrics and counters that are displayed on the screen. Once you have launched esxtop, while at any metric view, hit the *f* key to bring up the field customization view.

Here, you can choose to include or not include a field/column by hitting the alphabet key listed against it. The fields chosen for the display are marked with an asterisk (*). Once the needed selections are made, just hit *Enter* to exit the field customization view and return to the metrics view with the customized field view, as shown in the following screenshot:

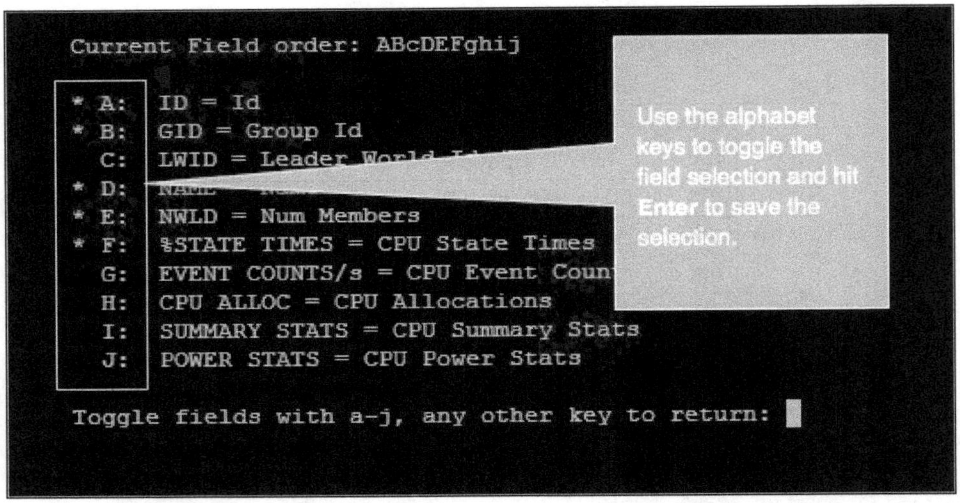

```
Current Field order: ABcDEFghij

* A:   ID = Id
* B:   GID = Group Id
  C:   LWID = Leader World
* D:   NAME
* E:   NWLD = Num Members
* F:   %STATE TIMES = CPU State Times
  G:   EVENT COUNTS/s = CPU Event Coun
  H:   CPU ALLOC = CPU Allocations
  I:   SUMMARY STATS = CPU Summary Stats
  J:   POWER STATS = CPU Power Stats

Toggle fields with a-j, any other key to return:
```

Use the alphabet keys to toggle the field selection and hit *Enter* to save the selection.

See also

▶   For more information on retrieving esxtop performance data, go to `http://www.virtuallyghetto.com/2013/01/retrieving-esxtop-performance-data.html`

Exporting and importing esxtop configurations

All the output customization that is done during interactive mode is lost the moment you exit the tool. You do have the option of exporting the output configuration to a file and reimporting the configuration to avoid spending time customizing the columnar output again.

Getting ready

To get started, we need access to the ESXi CLI via the console or SSH.

How to do it...

To export the esxtop configuration to a file, first launch esxtop, customize the output as required, hit the *W* key by shifting to uppercase, specify a directory patch to save the configuration file, and then hit *Enter*:

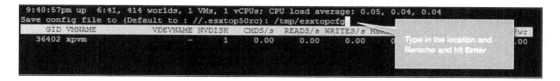

The file created can then be used to display the configuration template, without the need to go through the customization again.

In this example, we have created the `esxtopcfg` file. Now, to launch esxtop with the configuration template, issue the following command:

```
# esxtop -c <filename>
```

An example of using the preceding command is as follows:

```
# esxtop -c /tmp/esxtopcfg
```

How it works...

Keep in mind that the default location is `//.esxtop50rc`. If you hit *Enter* without specifying the location and name of the new file, the changes will be written to the `esxtop50rc` file. Thenceforth, every time you launch esxtop, it will start with the custom output.

Running esxtop in batch mode

Unlike interactive mode, this mode will let you issue a command to collect all or some of the statistics for a period of time and at the interval of your choice. It is particularly handy when you want to monitor the performance of an ESXi host for a certain time period.

Getting ready

We need access to the ESXi CLI via the console or SSH. You need to plan the number of performance snapshots that you want to gather and the interval between each snapshot.

How to do it...

To run esxtop in batch mode, connect to the ESXi host's CLI (usually done by using an SSH client) and run the following command:

```
# esxtop -a -d <delay> -n <iterations> > exportfilename
```

Here's an example:

```
# esxtop -a -d 10 -n 50 > perfstats.csv
```

Switch	Effect
-a	This will gather all the esxtop statistics
-d	This inserts a delay (in seconds) between every performance snapshot
-n	This is used to specify the number of snapshot iterations that have to be collected

How it works...

Once exported, the comma-separated values can be viewed in any MS Excel file, or can even be imported into **Windows Performance Monitor** (**PerfMon**) for analysis.

Gathering VM I/O statistics using vscsiStats

Unlike esxtop, which collects real-time data, the vscsiStats tool is used to gather the I/O statistics of a VM at a per-virtual-disk (VMDK) level. It can collect statistics such as the number of outstanding I/Os, size of the I/Os, and seek distance and latency.

Getting ready

You will need access to the ESXi CLI via the console or SSH. Also, make note of the World IDs corresponding to the VMs you would like to fetch the statistics for. The esxcli vm process list command will list all the running VMs with their World IDs.

How to do it...

To fetch the I/O statistics corresponding to a VM, you will need to find the worldGroupID corresponding to the VM. This is achieved by issuing the following command:

```
# vscsiStats -l
```

Consider the following screenshot:

```
~ # vscsiStats -l
Virtual Machine worldGroupID: 35571, Virtual Machine Display Name: vma01, Virtual
 Machine Config File: /vmfs/volumes/53122d6a-d8e245f6-af1a-000c295122de/vma01/vma
01.vmx, {
   Virtual SCSI Disk handleID: 8193 (scsi0:0)
}
Virtual Machine worldGroupID: 35874, Virtual Machine Display Name: xpvm, Virtual
Machine Config File: /vmfs/volumes/53122d6a-d8e245f6-af1a-000c295122de/xpvm/xpvm.
vmx, {
   Virtual SCSI Disk handleID: 8194 (ide0:0)
   Virtual SCSI Disk handleID: 8195 (scsi0:0)
}
~ #
```

Now, this will be a huge list if you have a lot of VMs running on the host. If that is the case, then there are several ways to filter the list. One of them would be to send the output of the command to a file and then find the VM in it using its display name.

Once you have the VM's `worldGroupID`, then the next step will be to fetch the statistics. The following command syntax can be used for this:

```
# vscsiStats -s -w <worldGroupID of the virtual machine>
```

Here's an example:

```
# vscsiStats -s -w 35874
```

This will start a collection against every disk (`vmdk` or `rdm`) associated with the VM. The collection will continue to run for 30 minutes from the time it was started, unless you choose to stop it by using the `vscsiStats -x` command:

```
~ # vscsiStats -s -w 35874
vscsiStats: Starting Vscsi stats collection for worldGroup 35874, handleID 8194 (
ide0:0)
Success.
vscsiStats: Starting Vscsi stats collection for worldGroup 35874, handleID 8195 (
scsi0:0)
Success.
~ #
```

Once the collection is complete or stopped, you can view the data gathered by the collection, based on the histogram type you need.

The following are the histogram types that are available:

Histogram type	Description
all	All statistics
ioLength	Size of the I/O
seekDistance	Logical blocks; the disk head must move before a read/write operation can be performed
outstandingIOs	Number of I/O operations queued
latency	I/O latency
Interarrrival	Time gap between the VM disk commands (in microseconds)

The following command syntax can be used for the `vscsiStats -x` command:

```
# vscsiStats -w <worldGroupID> --printhistos <histogram type> -c <output
CSV>
```

An example for the preceding command is as follows:

```
# vscsiStats -w 35874 --printhistos outstandingIOs -c OSIOS.csv
```

The CSV file can then be imported into MS Excel or other similar tools for better presentation of the data collected.

Using vCenter performance graphs

You can use vCenter performance graphs to provide a graphical insight into the performance metrics. Supported metrics include CPU, cluster service, datastore, disk, memory, network, power, storage adapter, storage path, system, virtual flash, and vSphere replication.

Getting ready

You will need access to vCenter with a role that has permission to view and modify the performance charts.

How to do it...

To be able to view the performance charts, have a look at the following steps:

1. Connect to vCenter Server and select an object/hierarchy you want to monitor performance for.

2. Navigate to **Monitor | Performance** to bring up the **Performance Overview** or **Advanced** view.

   Performance charts can be pulled against a vCenter instance, a data center, a cluster, an ESXi host, or a VM. The **Overview** pane shows the past day's performance. The **Advanced** view displays real-time data.

3. By default, the real-time CPU data is displayed. You can switch between the different metrics available by using the dropdown at the top-right-hand corner of the chart:

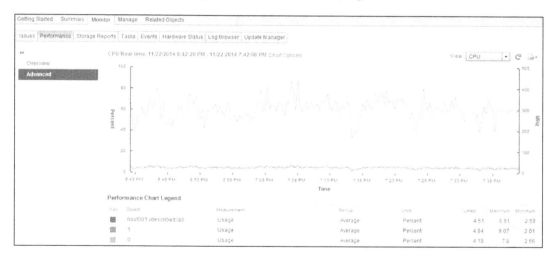

4. You can change the chart options to customize the charts in terms of the metrics, timespan, chart type, and counters to be included. From the **Advanced** view, just click on the **Chart Options** hyperlink to bring up the options:

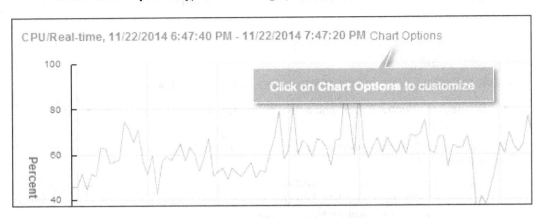

How it works...

vCenter performance graphs collect data using collection intervals. vCenter uses four default intervals, namely a day, a week, a month, and a year. A collection interval defines the amount of time the performance data has to be stored in vCenter's database. Only the data for the collection intervals is saved in the database. In other words, the real-time performance data will not be saved. Every collection interval has a corresponding collection frequency. For example, the default collection interval frequencies are 5 minutes for a day, 30 minutes for a week, 2 hours for a month, and 1 day for a year.

vCenter performance charts support the following different chart types:

- ▶ Line charts
- ▶ Bar charts
- ▶ Pie charts
- ▶ Stacked charts

See also

- ▶ For more information on vCenter performance charts, refer to the *vSphere Monitoring and Performance* whitepaper at `http://bit.ly/vSphere55_Performance`

Index

D

data
downloading, in UMDS 493, 494
database compatibility
checking 17
database connectivity
preparing, for VUM 448-459
data center
VDS, importing into 255, 256
datastore
about 273
seen by ESXi hosts, viewing 277
user-defined capability tags,
adding to 363, 364
viewing, with ESXi CLI 278
viewing, with vSphere Web Client 277
datastore cluster
creating 330-333
requisites 330
datastore heartbeating
configuring 419-421
deploy rule
activating 189, 190
creating 187, 188
DHCP server
configuring, for PXE boot 174-177
Direct Attached Storage (DAS) 272
Direct Console User Interface (DCUI) 73
disk shares, on VM
modifying 372
distributed locking 273
**Distributed Management Task
Force (DMTF) 404**
distributed port group. *See* **dvPortGroup**
Distributed Power Management (DPM) 428
download source
adding 467-469
DRAC (Dell), console access method 281
DRS automation level
fully automated 433
manual 433
partially automated 433
selecting 432, 433
working 433
DRS host groups
creating 436

DRS VM groups
creating 437
DSN, for SQL database
creating 79-83
dvPortGroup
about 201
creating 225-227
network resource pools 228
port allocation 228
port binding 227
dvUplink
about 201
physical adapter (vmnic),
mapping to 236-239
dynamic discovery 340

E

eager zeroed thick provisioning method 384
effective MAC address 245
Enterprise plus License 359
Ephemeral ports
URL 94
esxcfg-mpath command 281
esxcfg-vmknic
used, for creating VMkernel interface 213
esxcfg-vswitch
used, for adding standard vSwitch 221
used, for adding uplink 220
used, for mapping physical adapter (vmnic)
dvUplink 237-239
esxcli
used, for creating VMkernel interface 213
used, for creating vSwitch 205-207
used, for deleting vSwitch 210
used, for mounting unmounted volume 311
ESXi 5.5
about 12
features 12
installing 68-72
reference links 68
URL 68
ESXi CLI
used, for creating VMFS volume 287-290
used, for unmounting VMFS
datastore 307, 308
used, for viewing datastores 278

M

MAC address changes 245
Microsoft SQL Server 2008 SP3 Feature Pack
 URL 456
migration threshold
 setting 435, 436
Most Recently Used (MRU) 282
Multipathing Plugins (MPP) 282
multi-portal storage array 348

N

Native Multipathing Plugin (NMP) 282
NetFlow
 enabling, on VDS 265-267
 settings 267
Network Attached Storage (NAS)
 about 272
 iSCSI 272
 NFS 272
Network File System (NFS) 340
Network Resource Pools. *See* **NRP**
NFS Datastore
 about 340
 creating 355, 356
NFS Export 340
NFS fundamentals
 NFS Datastore 340
 NFS Export 340
NFS volume 274
NRP
 about 228
 creating, on VDS 256-260
 criteria 259
 system 260
 user defined 260
NRP, criteria
 limit 259
 Physical Adapter Shares 259
 Quality of Service (QoS) tag 259

O

offline bundle
 about 144
 ESXi image profile, exporting as 157, 158

Open Virtualization Archive (OVA) 404
Open Virtualization Format (OVF) 404

P

patches
 staging 488
paths
 masking, to LUN 325-327
 unmasking, to LUN 328, 329
Path Selection Plugin (PSP) 282
path selection plugins, VMware
 fixed 283
 Most Recently Used (MRU) 282
 Round Robin (RR) 283
performance
 monitoring, with esxtop 522, 523
per-host level
 power management, enabling 444
physical adapter (vmnic)
 mapping, to dvUplink 236-239
Pluggable Storage Architecture (PSA) 282
port allocation
 about 228
 elastic 228
 fixed 228
port binding
 about 227
 dynamic binding 228
 ephemeral binding 228
 static binding 228
 used, for iSCSI multipathing 345
port group
 about 201
 deleting, from standard vSwitch 214-216
 deleting, with esxcli 215
 deleting, with vSphere Web Client 214
port mirroring
 distributed port mirroring 264
 distributed port mirroring (legacy) 264
 enabling, on VDS 260-263
 encapsulated remote mirroring (L3)
  source 264
 maximum packet length (bytes) 264
 remote mirroring destination 264
 remote mirroring source 264
 Sampling Rate 264

Thank you for buying
VMware vSphere 5.5 Cookbook

About Packt Publishing

Packt, pronounced 'packed', published its first book, *Mastering phpMyAdmin for Effective MySQL Management*, in April 2004, and subsequently continued to specialize in publishing highly focused books on specific technologies and solutions.

Our books and publications share the experiences of your fellow IT professionals in adapting and customizing today's systems, applications, and frameworks. Our solution-based books give you the knowledge and power to customize the software and technologies you're using to get the job done. Packt books are more specific and less general than the IT books you have seen in the past. Our unique business model allows us to bring you more focused information, giving you more of what you need to know, and less of what you don't.

Packt is a modern yet unique publishing company that focuses on producing quality, cutting-edge books for communities of developers, administrators, and newbies alike. For more information, please visit our website at www.PacktPub.com.

About Packt Enterprise

In 2010, Packt launched two new brands, Packt Enterprise and Packt Open Source, in order to continue its focus on specialization. This book is part of the Packt Enterprise brand, home to books published on enterprise software – software created by major vendors, including (but not limited to) IBM, Microsoft, and Oracle, often for use in other corporations. Its titles will offer information relevant to a range of users of this software, including administrators, developers, architects, and end users.

Writing for Packt

We welcome all inquiries from people who are interested in authoring. Book proposals should be sent to author@packtpub.com. If your book idea is still at an early stage and you would like to discuss it first before writing a formal book proposal, then please contact us; one of our commissioning editors will get in touch with you.

We're not just looking for published authors; if you have strong technical skills but no writing experience, our experienced editors can help you develop a writing career, or simply get some additional reward for your expertise.

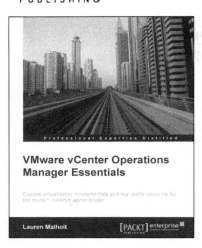

**VMware vCenter Operations
Manager Essentials**

ISBN: 978-1-78217-696-1   Paperback: 246 pages

Explore virtualization fundamentals and real-world
solutions for the modern network administrator

1. Written by VMware expert Lauren Malhoit,
   this book takes a look at vCenter Operations
   Manager from a practical point of view that every
   administrator can appreciate.

2. Understand, troubleshoot, and design your virtual
   environment in a better and more efficient way
   than you ever have before.

**VMware Horizon Workspace
Essentials**

ISBN: 978-1-78217-237-6   Paperback: 158 pages

Manage and deliver a secure, unified workspace to
embrace any time, any place, anywhere access to
corporate apps, data, and virtual desktops securely from
any device

1. Design, install, and configure a Horizon
   Workspace infrastructure.

2. Deliver a user's workspace to mobile devices such
   as Android and iOS.

3. Easy to follow, step-by-step guide on how to deploy
   and work with Horizon Workspace.

Please check **www.PacktPub.com** for information on our titles

VMware vCloud Director Essentials

ISBN: 978-1-78398-652-1   Paperback: 198 pages

Build VMware vCloud-based cloud datacenters from scratch

1. Learn about DHCP, NAT, and VPN services to successfully implement a private cloud.

2. Configure different networks such as Direct connect, Routed, or Isolated.

3. Configure and manage vCloud Director's access control.

Disaster Recovery using VMware vSphere Replication and vCenter Site Recovery Manager

ISBN: 978-1-78217-644-2   Paperback: 162 pages

Learn to deploy and use vSphere Replication 5.5 as a standalone disaster recovery solution and to orchestrate disaster recovery using vCenter Site Recovery Manager 5.5

1. Learn how to deploy and use vSphere Replication as a standalone disaster recovery solution.

2. Configure SRM to leverage array-based or vSphere replication engine.

Please check **www.PacktPub.com** for information on our titles

www.ingramcontent.com/pod-product-compliance
Lightning Source LLC
Chambersburg PA
CBHW060920060326
40690CB00041B/2758